5.46
3,3234
B847

MADISON AREA TECHNICAL COLLEGE IRC

W9-ADO-558

DISC

JUL 16 '04

DATE DUE

SEP 2 0 2004		

Demco, Inc. 38-293

DISCARD
MATC-TRUAX-LIBRARY
3550 ANDERSON STREET
MADISON, WI 53704

CONSERVANCY

The Land Trust Movement in America

O C L C Record (handwritten)

CONSERVANCY

The Land Trust Movement in America

Richard Brewer

Dartmouth College

Published by
University Press of New England • HANOVER AND LONDON

Dartmouth College
Published by University Press of New England, 37 Lafayette St.,
Lebanon, NH 03766
© 2003 by Richard Brewer
All rights reserved
Printed in the United States of America
5 4 3 2 1

Library of Congress Cataloging-in-Publication Data

Brewer, Richard.
Conservancy : the land trust movement in America / Richard Brewer.—
1st ed.
    p.   cm.
Includes bibliographical references and index.
ISBN 1-58465-350-7 (cloth : alk. paper)
1. Land use—United States. 2. Nature conservation—United States.
3. Land trusts—United States. 4. Conservation easements—United
States. 5. Natural areas—United States. I. Title.
HD205.B74 2003
333.3'234—dc21   2003012938

Disclaimer:
Nothing in this book should be construed as legal, tax, or financial advice.

For Katy

CONTENTS

PREFACE

More than a decade ago, several citizens concerned with the loss of open space, natural land, and farmland in southwestern Michigan began to talk about starting an organization to counteract that unfortunate trend. We met through the summer of 1991 and incorporated in October. All over the nation, others with similar thoughts were banding together. The Southwest Michigan Land Conservancy (SWMLC) was one of 53 land trusts that formed in 1991. In the three years between 1990 and 1992, 181 new land trusts formed.

When we began meeting to talk about saving land, I knew something of the ecological and conservation biology basis of land conservation and had some familiarity with The Nature Conservancy. I knew little about local land trusts or the other national trusts. When I tried to read about them, I found a few articles, most of which said almost exactly the same things, and a few books, all written for land trust practitioners.

More books have come along since then—good, useful, nuts-and-bolts books on such topics as conservation easements, tax law, and doing deals. Magazine and newspapers articles are now easy to find, though most follow the same repetitive pattern—how many trusts there are, descriptions of a couple of successful trusts, what a conservation easement is, tax advantages to land owners, and a few good recent deals.

What was not available to me in 1990 or later was an overview of the land trust movement. No book existed to tell where land trusts came from, exactly what they do, how they vary, how this kind of land conservation fits into the broader conservation movement, where land trusts are going, what they're doing right, and what they ought to be doing but aren't.

This is the book that I've tried to write. I've tried to make it informative and also interesting to anyone interested in land conservation. I also hope it will be helpful to people already associated with land trusts—members, volunteers, board, and staff. They get on-the-job training in certain essential operations, but the bigger picture is something they usually have to put together piecemeal and on their own. This book may speed up the process.

People interested in land conservation as one part of environmental protection will find the book of interest. Others, who own land that ought to be preserved, will find it of direct practical use. Anyone with such land ought to begin their quest—and probably end it—with a land trust. They will learn in this book the things they need to know about what land trusts do and how they do it.

My aim has been to write a book that combines accuracy and readability. In both, I've had a great deal of help from many people. Three people read virtually the whole book. These were John Eastman, Emma Bickham Pitcher, and Katy Takahashi. All are excellent writers and editors and are knowledgeable about land trusts, natural history, or both. I profited from their comments.

Several other persons gave me much-appreciated comments on one to several chapters: Frank Ballo, Phil Brewer, Steve Brewer, Kim Chapman, Kay Chase, George Cox, Becky Csia, Joe Engemann, Jennie Gerard, Maynard Kaufman, Kenneth Kirton, Robert Pleznac, Stan Rajnak, Ann Schwing, Mary Anne Sydlik, Kim Traverse, and Joan Vilms.

I have probably learned something about how land trusts work from everyone I've been associated with at SWMLC. Especially enlightening were interactions with Frank Ballo, Becky Csia, Renee Kivikko, George Lauff, Bob Pleznac, Stan Rajnak, Jim Richmond, Nancy Small, Gary Stock, and Kim Traverse.

In 1996, I conducted a mail survey of land trusts, which I have referred to occasionally in later pages and described in the notes at the end of the book.[1] I'm indebted to the land trust representatives who took time to fill out the questionnaire. Their information formed a valuable picture of what land trusts around the country were doing and not doing.

I'm grateful also to those SWMLC land and easement donors who answered a set of questions about their reasons for preserving land.

In connection with this project (and many others), members of the Resource Sharing section of Western Michigan University's Waldo Library have been diligent in providing copies of sometimes obscure publications. I'm grateful.

The list of people who provided information is long. All the readers provided information in addition to editorial comments. Sometimes, this information was extensive and otherwise unavailable. For information or access to information, I'm also indebted to Jim Aldrich, Alexander Arpa, Ralph Babcock, David H. Behm, Martha Benioff, Samuel N. Berry, Jon Binhammer, Terry Blunt, Dan Burke, Robert T. Chapel, Cheyenne Chapman, Carolyn Chipman-Evans, Crecia C. Closson, Richard D. Cochran, Robin Cole, Pamela Cooper, Ken Crater, Melissa Danskin, Doug Dietsch, Eugene Duvernoy, Jack Eitnear, Allison Elder, Brenda Engstrand, Cathy Engstrom, Dave Ewert, Tom Exton, Virginia Farley, Dulcie Flaharty, Mary V. Flynn, Diana Freshwater, Brian Gallagher, John Gerber, Annette Gibavic, Jane E. Gillies, Holger H. Harvey, Reid Haughley, Jean Hocker, A. Ryland Howard III, Huey Johnson, Margaret Kohring, Jayne R. Kronlund, Phil Lamb, George

Lauff, Andy Laurenzi, Zad Leavy, Barry Lonik, Jennifer Lorenz, Jeanie McIntyre, Moyna Monroe, Jean Morgan, Eleanor Morris, Charles Niebling, Linda Nordstrand, Jim Northup, Anita O'Gara, Lou Parrott, Brian Petrucci, Marty Pingree, Pat Pregmon, Caroline Pryor, Nina Raab, Victoria Ranney, George Ranney, Jr., Henry Raup, Ann Raup, Kieran Roe, Julie Roszkowiak, Jim Scott, Susan E. Shea, Lynne Sherrod, Mark Silberstein, Daniel Skean, Kendall Slee, Mary Anne Sohlstrom, Cindy Southern, Christy Stewart, Edmund W. Stiles, Robert Sugarman, Nancy Thompson, Bob van Blaricom, and Jack Walker. Thanks, too, to Diane Worden of WordenDex for timely help with the index.

I'm grateful to all of these for their time and trouble. And, despite good intentions, I've probably omitted someone who provided information or was otherwise helpful; my apologies as well as my thanks to anyone in this category.

Kalamazoo, MI   R.B.

INTRODUCTION: SAVING LAND THE OLD-FASHIONED WAY

Land trusts, also called conservancies, are private nonprofit organizations that protect land directly, by owning it. They are the most successful and exciting force in U.S. land conservation today and perhaps the most effective component of the whole environmental movement. The history of land conservation in the United States has been protection by government through ownership or regulation. Because the land trust model of saving land by private action has become dominant only in the past two decades, many people don't know what land trusts are, what they do, or their importance to conservation now and in coming decades.

There are international land trusts like The Nature Conservancy, national ones like the Trust for Public Lands, and state trusts, like the first one of all, the Trustees of Reservations in Massachusetts. But most land trusts are local. There are about thirteen hundred of these. Some serve an area no bigger than a New England town (a township to most of us) or a village. Others cover several counties. The Southwest Michigan Land Conservancy, with which I have some personal experience, takes as its service area the nine southwestern counties of the state, an area of about 5,300 square miles.

Collectively, the thirteen hundred local land trusts have about one million members, many of them avid, hard-working volunteers. The Nature Conservancy, the biggest land trust, also has about one million members. Doubtless there's some overlap, but clearly a sizable number of American citizens are involved in the land trust cause.

A while back, a national magazine carried an essay by the owner of a small plot of mostly natural land. The time came when she needed to move away but wanted to make sure her carefully stewarded land was preserved. "Public lands," she wrote, "can be projected as having as many recreational, aesthetic, or environmental benefits as can be devised for them, but private land, on this skinny Florida key and almost everywhere in this country, is considered too economically valuable to be conserved. . . . Land is something to be 'built out'."[1]

The owner had a deed drafted providing that the property not be subdivided and that half be left in its natural state. Real estate agents were reluctant to take on property restricted in this way, but eventually the owner was able to sell it to a buyer who supported her aims.

It's an encouraging story. A land owner wants to protect her land in perpetuity, finds buyers who are similarly conservation minded, and thereby prevails against what sometimes seems the inevitable journey of privately held open land in America, a death march that ends in strip malls, condos, or expressways.

But it's also a discouraging story. Local land trusts exist to do exactly what this owner wanted, protect privately owned land. The most effective way to ensure permanent protection while continuing to own land—and eventually sell or bequeath it—is to donate a conservation easement to a land trust.[2] Trying to protect land by deed restrictions is a weaker option, because of the eventual lack of anyone with the legal standing or the will to enforce them.

Not every part of the United States is yet covered by a local land trust, but much of it is. Conservation-minded land owners are an increasing breed. Many—but still too few—know that local land trusts are the place to turn for permanent land protection.

I grew up in southern Illinois, at that time a poor, rural region with many wild areas. The popular image of Illinois as corn and soy bean fields, flat, productive, and boring, applies to central and northern Illinois. The southern fifth of the state is unglaciated, with woods, bluffs, ravines, and swamps. In the swamps and river bottoms, the ranges of southern plants and animals, such as bald cypress and cottonmouth moccasins, reach fingers northward to diversify a mostly Midwestern biota.

Several high school friends and I spent weekends and after school snake hunting, bird watching, and keying out plants. Some of the best natural areas that we visited in those days were eventually preserved, mostly through the efforts of the Illinois Natural Areas Commission.[3] But even in southern Illinois—in the 1940s and early 50s as far from the path of progress as anyplace in the United States—natural land was being lost. Commercial strips began to bud out along the highways, open-pit coal mining spread across the land, the Corps of Engineers flooded creek beds and oak-covered slopes, and the Forest Service began speeding up logging in Shawnee National Forest.

One Saturday morning, two of us were looking for birds on Forest Service land in Cave Valley. We had left the overgrown fields with their yellow-breasted chats and white-eyed vireos and gone into the woods. Cave Creek flowed brownly between muddy banks. On the far side of the floodplain on slightly higher ground was a large, dense canebrake, the cane twelve feet tall and tangled with greenbriers. Sycamore grew along the stream, hackberry, sweet gum, ash, and oaks on the floodplain. Sloughs too wet for the cane were habitat for some rare aquatic plants of southern affinities.

We pushed and splashed our way around and through the cane and vines, listening for birds. We had heard hooded warblers here earlier, but this day my friend, who has a marvellous ear, heard something different. The song was like the hooded warbler's—bold, with a "whip-poor-will" ending, but it began with three or four clear, slow notes. It sounded something like the Louisiana waterthrush, but the waterthrushes lived along the rocky streams running down through wooded ravines.

We finally caught a few glimpses of an unspectacular small brown and buff bird with a dark line through the eye and a paler line above it. It was the Swainson's warbler, a southern bird that had been found in Illinois in the breeding season only four times before.[4] We found Swainson's warblers in Cave Valley in several succeeding summers, and then we both left the area except for rare visits. Not long afterwards, the Forest Service sold the cane and then the trees, and the Swainson's warblers were gone.

Perhaps the logging of Cave Valley wasn't a global catastrophe. Marine biologist Joel Hedgpeth, as a ten-year-old living in the Sierra foothills, witnessed the building of O'Shaughnessy Dam, which turned the Hetch Hetchy Valley of Yosemite into a reservoir.[5] The logging of Cave Valley doesn't measure up to the flooding of Hetch Hetchy on the calamity scale, but it and other losses led me to ideas like those Hedgpeth later expressed.

When spelled with a capital letter by politicians, Progress is a specious excuse for the continued rape of the natural environment in behalf of maintaining and increasing our material civilization. . . . We hold, in effect, a lease upon this earth, and the blind pursuit of material progress is a violation of that lease. We are forgetting to cultivate our gardens.[6]

These were sentiments not often uttered in the 1940s and 1950s.

In 1958, toward the end of my graduate student days at the University of Illinois, I was helping on a class field trip to the Indiana sand dunes with my major professor, Charles Kendeigh. After a spent day sampling litter invertebrates and sweeping the herbs and shrubs for insects, we were sitting around the campfire in the state park, drinking coffee from enamelware cups. Strong, boiled coffee was a staple of Kendeigh's field trips. Kendeigh was stocky with a beak of a nose and gray hair brushed straight back. Fifty-three years old, he was a distinguished scholar with interests in both physiological and ecosystem ecology.

Kendeigh's own major professor, Victor Shelford, had taken ecology classes to the dunes beginning in 1908. Some of the field study sites still existed, but many were gone, and the loss of dunelands to steel mills and harbor construction was continuing. The Save-the-Dunes movement had begun, but it would be fourteen hard years before Indiana Dunes National Lakeshore was dedicated.[7]

Talk around the campfire turned to habitat destruction and other environmental issues such as rapidly increasing pesticide usage. Rachel Carson had started her research for *Silent Spring,* but its publication was four years away.[8] Field biologists knew, of course, that birds and other animals were dying of pesticide poisoning. At Michigan State University, George W. Wallace was speaking and writing about the DDT spraying that had begun to leave the campus littered with dead robins.

For his efforts, Wallace took a great deal of abuse from the agricultural faculty, the dominant force at that land-grant school. In the late 1950s, dicky bird watchers and nature lovers in general, with a few exceptions like Wallace, had been nearly silenced. "You can't stand in the way of progress," was still the national motto. Even people who recognized "progress" as a misleading euphemism—or specious excuse—were unwilling to step in front of the progress bulldozer.

Opposing destruction of natural ecosystems, out-of-control pesticide usage, and water and air pollution, was cast as un-American, fuzzy-headed, impractical, and when technology was involved, anti-intellectual. One fairly typical review of *Silent Spring,* by a professor of biochemistry, said, "[This book will appeal to] the organic gardeners, the worshipers of 'natural foods,' those who cling to the philosophy of a vital principle, and pseudoscientists and faddists."[9]

Few of us around the campfire that night felt anything but cynicism about the situation. For one thing, we didn't see that being a conservationist would advance us professionally, but we also thought that the anti-conservation, pro-development forces of business in partnership with government were too strong to fight. To some degree, we bought the pro-development, pro-pollution arguments. We'll lose a few robins, ingest some chlorinated hydrocarbons, have fewer acres of dunes and forest to walk in, but would it make a lot of difference in the long run?

Kendeigh thought it would. Kendeigh's voice was slightly nasal and he spoke with a flat Ohio accent. He was not an eloquent man—had no wish to be eloquent, I suppose—but he knew his mind and was willing to speak it. That night he said the things that many others would be saying in a few years. The simplification of ecosystems, the accumulation of manufactured, evolutionarily novel chemicals in organisms and the environment were not just annoying and ugly but dangerous to the functioning of the biosphere and to humans as a part of that system. The destruction of nature was harmful, it was unnecessary, and it ought to be opposed. Kendeigh's remarks that night reassured me that the conservationist feelings of my youth were intellectually respectable.

We each come to conservation in our own way. Some people view a new grandchild and realize that unless they act, clean streams and wildflower-filled woods will not be around for that child to experience. Some walk through an old-growth forest and find it so sacred a place that they can no longer comprehend destroying it for something no more important than another plat or shopping mall. Others want to save biodiversity and to keep the natural systems in place for cleaning the water and air and buffering pest insect outbreaks. Some people come to be conservationists by an epiphany, some by intellectual analysis.

Whatever the route, the conservationist's journey these days increasingly leads to the land trust movement.

The land trusts of America are diverse, shaped by their missions and adapted to their local environments. Though they are diverse, we can tell one when we see it: A land trust is a private, nonprofit organization for which the acquisition and protection of land by direct action form its primary or sole mission.

This last requirement leaves out organizations, such as Audubon societies, museums, or nature centers, that sometimes own land as a part of a broader mission. A university may own a nature preserve, but we'd never mistake a university for a land trust. Its mission is too broad and its constituencies too numerous. The voices of a few nature lovers asking for the permanent protection of a preserve are easily lost, or ignored, amid the clamor from students, parents, alumni, donors, corporate partners, football fans, congresspeople, city managers, and state legislators.

"Direct action," in the land trust definition, means the time-honored method of voluntary transfer. Land trusts often portray themselves as saving land by buying it. We save land the old-fashioned American way, they say: We buy it. But an even better American way, considering that there's never enough money to buy all the land that ought to be conserved, is to acquire it as a gift. A donation of land to a land trust will often allow civic-minded conservationists to save on income, property, and estate taxes, while ensuring that the land they cherish is safeguarded in perpetuity.

Conservation easements are a newer, third way by which land trusts save land. In this method, the owner retains ownership of the land but gives up certain rights. In doing so, the owner enters into an agreement allowing the land trust to protect in perpetuity the conservation values of the land.

Land trusts are nonconfrontational and apolitical. They work with willing landowners in voluntary transactions. In these ways, the land trust model differs from the second model of private land protection: land advocacy.

Advocacy is pleading in favor of a position or action. Land advocacy groups aim to protect land by promoting government purchase or regulation. They are a subcategory of the broad environmental advocacy movement, which tries to persuade governments to enact and enforce laws over the whole range of environmental protection from pesticide use and water pollution to carbon dioxide emissions and population policy. Land advocacy groups lobby, protest, and litigate in favor of setting aside parks and wilderness areas and against cutting old-growth forest or rezoning farmland for condos.

Although the earliest land trust and the earliest land advocacy organizations were formed about the same time in the early 1890s, advocacy was the dominant private approach to land protection until the last third of the twentieth century. The distinction between the two models of private land protection hasn't always been understood. During the several decades when land trusts were rare, the distinction was of little practical significance. Later, in the heyday of the popular environmental movement, conservation organizations of any sort tended to be lumped together with the great variety of newly arisen environmental organizations. The public and the politicians often made little distinction between, say, The Nature Conservancy (land trust), the Wilderness Society (land advocacy), and advocacy groups with no specific focus on land, such as Greenpeace, the Environmental Defense Fund, and Zero Population Growth.

Even today, the difference between the two models isn't consistently understood. In mid-2001, the concluding article of a newspaper series critical of most environmental groups noted:

Change is knocking on the door of America's environmental movement. Change is remodeling it from within. . . . No longer is influencing public policy so lofty a goal. Today, some groups focus on a more tangible prize: buying, protecting and restoring land.[10]

The "groups" are land trusts, and "today" is any day between 1891 and now.

The land trust model, as a concept, doesn't include advocacy. This doesn't mean that any particular organization can't be a hybrid. A land trust that does combine the two models should do so as a conscious choice and know where its land trust activities end and its advocacy begins.

The temperament to be a successful land advocate is, I think, rare or, perhaps, just short-lived. I was once part of a large audience at a township board meeting. What had brought most people out was a reconsideration of the board's month-old action to develop a Frisbee "golf course" at one of the two township parks.

Frisbee golf has a superficial similarity to real golf, but the tees are concrete slabs, the fairways are cuts through whatever vegetation the site supports, and the cups are chain baskets hanging from a metal pole a couple of meters tall. The Frisbees used in the game are rigid, weighted, flat-edged disks.

The park land was old field, partly grown up with volunteer shrubs and trees and partly covered in conifers planted by township residents, who also volunteered. There was a bluebird trail on the proposed course.

Two of the first three speakers opposed the course, and that ratio prevailed through the ninety minutes of comment. Arguments in favor of the course came both from the audience and from three members of the parks committee who were part of the seven-member board. Their arguments included the idea that the township had always planned to use the area for recreation, not just as a nature preserve, that Frisbee golf is fun, and that the Frisbee course would hardly impact the area. The parks committee claimed that less than an acre of the park would be affected by the Frisbee course. One of the open space speakers questioned this claim, since it was clear from the map displayed that the course occupied more than 20 acres. A park committee member explained that the 1-acre figure was derived from the length of each of the nine holes times the width of two brush-hog swaths.

Open-space speakers pointed out that the rapidly growing township had only two small parks, one of which was already devoted to soccer and softball. Frisbee golf would remove one-third of the second park from quiet pursuits available to a variety of people in favor of one activity for a small special-interest group. Frisbee golf, the opponents suggested, is incompatible with other uses of the 20-odd acres because the Frisbee throwers would be unsympathetic to non-players strolling across their fairways. Also, bird-watchers, mushroom hunters, and anyone seeking a quiet walk would avoid the area for fear of being hit by one of the disks.

The most dramatic moment occurred when a young man who had worn a suit and tie for his presentation tossed a couple of ordinary Frisbees into the audience and then wound up and slammed one of the disk Frisbees into the wall with a resounding crash. "If you're in the way of that, you're getting whacked," he said.

Although the pro-Frisbee speakers claimed that the pastime was for people of every persuasion, the speakers were, in fact, all male but one, and looked to be of ages twenty to early thirties. The pro–open-space speakers looked to be between twenty-five and seventy, but mostly forty and over. They were about equally male and female. All the pro–open-space speakers were residents of the township, whereas all but one of the pro-Frisbee speakers lived elsewhere. One of them was a paid employee of a Frisbee golf association.

Through the whole discussion, the board sat with noncommittal expressions, except for one of the park committee members who occasionally smirked at comments by the open space proponents. The township attorney looked indescribably bored.

Once the parade of speakers ended, the township supervisor asked if there were comments from the board members. Two responded. Both favored the course and had little sympathy for the open space supporters. One actually used the 1950s expression, "You can't stop progress"—about a Frisbee golf course.

Since only one vote in addition to the three park committee members was needed to approve the course, the outcome was now clear. The only question was how badly the open space proponents would lose. When the vote was taken, it was six to one.

Many of the open space proponents paused briefly outside the township hall to commiserate with one another. Someone shook hands with the young man who provided the disk Frisbee demonstration. "You did a good job," he was told.

He shook his head dispiritedly. "No, I didn't. How can they do this?"

A day later, the local paper ran a short editorial, "Park Big Enough for Both." It was journalism of the maniacally even-handed variety. If the question had been breathing versus choking, the writer would have found merit in each.

A night at the township commission brings home the same points as larger battles, the fights to save Hetch Hetchy, the Tongass, the Arctic National Wildlife Reserve. One lesson is that we cannot depend on government to save land. In this important battle, some staffers may have strongly pro-conservation feelings, but the government as bureaucratic entity is no more likely to be on the side of conservation as on the side of the despoiler.

A second lesson is that land advocates are mostly amateurs, unpaid, acting out of conviction. This has been true beginning with Hetch Hetchy. Those who urged the dam did so as a part of their job or in the expectation of profits down the line. Those who opposed it were on their own time and paying their own way.[11]

A third lesson is that land advocacy—convincing government to save land—is hard, frustrating work. It is also essential work, and those who have the disposition and constitution for it deserve our gratitude and donations.

Compared with some of the fiery advocacy groups like the Sierra Club or Greenpeace, land trusts may seem colorless. However, both approaches to land protection are valid and both are necessary. Neither is more in tune with basic American values than the other. Often, the most productive situation is one in which an advocacy group is the fist and a land trust is the helping hand.

The publication in 1962 of *Silent Spring* is a convenient marker for the beginning of public awareness of the environment. Many good things followed. The Wilderness Act was passed in 1964, the Water Quality Act in 1965, the National Environmental Policy Act in 1969. By 1973, with the passage of the Endangered Species Act, most current major Federal environmental legislation had been signed into law.

By the late 1970s, the popular environmental movement was in decline. In 1980, Ronald Reagan was elected president on a profoundly anti-environmental platform.

The land trust movement had grown along with the general rise of public awareness and support for environmental protection but started from a low base. In 1950, fewer than fifty local trusts existed. The most rapid growth occurred in the 1960s and into the early 1970s. Unlike the popular environmental movement, however, rapid growth in new land trusts continues to the present time. Of the approximately thirteen hundred local land trusts, well over half have appeared since 1980.

Americans believed for a long time that federal and state governments were going to do the job of conserving land; all that was needed from us was encouragement. By the mid-1970s, this belief had faded. Opposition had surfaced to the government's acquiring land for the purpose of preservation and even to protecting land that was already government owned. Some people began to object to paying taxes for any public good. Government always has many voices competing about how to spend money, and other issues seemed to gain priority by 1980.

As a result, citizens around the country began to recognize that government was no longer up to the task of saving all the land that needed to be saved; they'd have to do it themselves. From 1986 to 1995, people were forming new land trusts at the rate of one per week.

Adding impetus to the land trust boom was the dawning awareness of how fast cherished lands and landscapes were disappearing. Ecologists and naturalists had understood the magnitude of our losses much earlier. A famous example is a set of maps compiled in 1956 by John T. Curtis, plant ecologist at the University of Wisconsin.[12]

The four maps show the vegetation of one township near the Wisconsin-Illinois border at four times in history. In 1831, just before white settlement, about 90 percent of the land was occupied by maple or oak-hickory forest and the rest by prairie. By 1882, the prairie was cropland and the formerly continuous forest had been chopped into seventy woodlots. The fragmentation continued in the 1902 map; there were now only sixty woodlots and the size had dropped from an average of 91 acres to 34 acres. By 1950, there were still fifty-five woodlots, but average size was now a diminutive 14 acres. Only about 4 percent of the originally forested land remained. The four maps provide a compelling example of the loss of our wild areas, first to agriculture and then to what we now call urban sprawl.

By the later 1970s, even individuals with only a remote connection to the natural world were likely to have experienced the loss of a wild or scenic area they had grown up with.

Most land trusts have been started by a few citizens banding together to try to slow the loss of natural areas, open space, or farmland to development and sprawl. After deciding some specifics such as name, service area, and mission, an early step is incorporation as a nonprofit in the state or states to be served and gaining 501(C)(3) status (as a publicly supported charity) with the U.S. Internal Revenue Service. With this done, donors of land or money are eligible for tax relief of various sorts.

Land trusts are run by boards of directors. In a 1996 survey that I conducted of randomly selected land trusts, the average board size was fifteen, the range five to thirty-six.[13] Some land trusts are formed with a self-perpetuating board of directors, others as membership organizations. Most nonmembership land trusts eventually want financial support beyond what they can bring in from grants, garage sales, and contributions of board members and their friends. They also want the legitimacy conferred by a community base. The land trusts then begin to solicit donations from people in the community. These donors are usually called members but since they can't vote on anything, perhaps they should be referred to as "notional" members.

Most land trusts start out as all-volunteer, with the board and a few friends negotiating land deals, keeping the books, applying for grants, sending out press releases, and the like. The few things they can't do themselves they outsource, for example, hiring an accountant to audit their accounts. Some excellent land trusts stay all-volunteer, or have up to now, but many evolve into the staffed category. This usually starts with the hiring of one staff member—often part-time to begin with—to do some of the things the board needs help with.

The percentage of all-volunteer land trusts dropped from 65 percent in 1985 to 50 percent in 2000.[14] The increase in staffed trusts is greater than this percentage change suggests because of the steady growth in numbers of land trusts. The 1985 census found about 535 trusts, while the 2000 census counted 1,263. So the number of staffed trusts went up from about 185 to about 590 in this interval. The two years between 1998 and 2000 were boom years. Full-time staff members increased from 1,939 to 2,640 (17 percent per year) and part-time staff increased from 958 to 2,638 (65 percent per year!).[15]

Probably about half of all staffed land trusts have a single staff member. Goodly numbers of trusts have two to six staff. Few have as many as ten.

In my 1996 survey of land trusts, I found that the backgrounds of executive directors were diverse; seventeen different academic fields were represented. Biology was highest (17 percent plus another 9 percent with a biology undergraduate degree). Next were planning, natural resources, architecture, and business, but law, agriculture, fine arts, history, psychology, and seven other subjects were also represented. At that time, it appeared that a new executive director (often the first employee) tended to be chosen from the local pool of people with nonprofit experience. This pattern seems to have faded in the few years since the survey. Executive directors, especially replacements, increasingly have previous land trust or, at least, conservation experience.

Someone with land to protect or just wanting to help in the effort can find out if a local land trust already serves his or her geographical area by getting in touch with the Land Trust Alliance (LTA). Its current Web address <www.lta.org> has a geographical listing of land trusts. For those more comfortable with print, the LTA publishes a *National Directory of Conservation Land Trusts;* however, only the more comprehensive libraries are likely to own a copy.

For concerned citizens who find that no local land trust yet exists in their area, LTA offers a useful book, *Starting a Land Trust.* Reading it would be a useful first step in a process that might lead to the very serious act of forming a new land trust. In the past, local groups have sometimes started new land trusts blithely without understanding that forming an organization dedicated to protecting land in perpetuity means a perpetual dedication to keeping the organization viable.

There is no necessary connection between a local land trust and the Land Trust Alliance, a national umbrella organization, but many land trusts—around 60 percent—are sponsor members of LTA. The organization also publishes a list of standards and practices that, if followed, tend to yield an ethical and efficient operation.

Many people, even those with an interest in conservation and the environment, are still unaware of local land trusts. They are more likely to have heard of The Nature Conservancy (TNC). A frequent question, especially for land trusts with "conservancy" in their name, is whether they're connected with TNC. The answer is generally no, except informally. But the question opens the door for the local land trust to describe how their mission of saving lands locally differs from the global aspirations of TNC.

The land trusts this book is about are conservation land trusts. Community land trusts (CLTs) are another type of organization. Like conservation land trusts, CLTs are private, generally nonprofit organizations that own land. Otherwise, the two are not much alike. CLTs have as a main aim providing low-cost housing. Most are urban, though a rural land trust, New Communities, Inc., in southern Georgia, incorporated in 1968, is generally credited with being the first American CLT.[16] Occasional attempts have been made to join the two approaches.[17]

In a 1996 speech to a California land trust, Michael Fischer, former executive director of the Sierra Club, the country's most influential land advocacy group, called the land trusts "the strongest arm of the conservation movement."[18]

One measure of strength is the amount of land protected. A census by the Land Trust Alliance found that local land trusts had protected a total of about 6.5 million acres as of the year 2000. More than 80 percent, 5.6 million acres, had been protected since 1990, a decade in which, federally and in most states, very little new land was being preserved by government.

Fischer listed several factors that give land trusts their power and explain their attractiveness to a growing number of people. He pointed out that land trusts use love of the land, not anger at its despoliation, as their principal motivating force. This is an important reason for the low burnout rate.

Also, land trusts work in the green sector of conservation rather than the brown. That is, they protect beauty in the form of natural areas and open space, rather than fighting ugliness in the form of pollution and other types of environmental degradation.

Land trust projects are place-based, connected to a piece of the Earth rather than being abstract or abstruse, like the destruction of the ozone layer, for example. If we set up a new preserve, we can hike it, bird it, hug the trees, and wade in the water.

The people of the land trust movement are taking direct action. They're not depending on a town council or a state fish and game department or the U.S. Congress to agree with them.

Land trust deals are nonconfrontational. They are voluntary. Land trusts work with willing owners to help them protect their land. There is no loser in the battle—there's no battle.

Most land trusts are local. They aren't trying to save the tropical rain forests. They hope the tropical forests will be saved, of course, but what they are working hard at is saving land at home, perhaps within biking distance of where their members live.

Land trust accomplishments are permanent. At the end of the cooperative process, the land is saved and stays saved in perpetuity, rather than awaiting the whims of the next batch of politicians or bureaucrats.

These are some of the reasons why, for many people, the land trust route to saving nature is a satisfying, even happy, way of life. In this age of personal isolation and civic disengagement, land trusts are communities with a shared vision of a greener, healthier landscape, now and for the future.

HISTORY

Land conservation, like jazz, is an American invention. The idea was a response to the rapid, ongoing destruction of the natural landscape in the second half of the nineteenth century. Increasing population drove the destruction. Human numbers were 17 million in 1840 and 63 million in 1890. The rate of increase was between 2 and 3 percent for every year in this interval, and, in fact, for a couple of decades more.

Population growth in already occupied rural areas and the spread of settlement into new ones worked together with the resource demands of cities. The losses of natural lands that had occurred and the certainty that more were coming led some people to a new, heightened appreciation of the American landscape. Thoreau saw wilderness on trips to the Maine woods in the 1840s and 50s, but it was being lost to lumbering at a rapid pace. The white pine tree you saw last spring on the shore of Chesuncook Lake, he suggested, should now be sought at the New England Friction Match Company. In a famous passage in *The Maine Woods,* he wrote:

Why should not we have our national preserves in which bear and panther, and some even of the hunter race, may still exist—not for idle sport or food, but for inspiration and our own true recreation? or shall we, like villains, grub them all up, poaching on our own national domains? [1]

Plenty of Americans besides Thoreau had seen nature undisturbed, and some reacted with similar thoughts of preservation. It was not so in Europe, for a good reason. Although there was pleasant and even spectacular scenery in Europe, almost no pristine sites existed, or had existed for centuries.

Out of these times of disappearing natural areas, dwindling bird and mammal populations, and overpopulating cities arose many conservation organizations, and, of course, other organizations devoted to reform in education, public health, and municipal government.

Charles Eliot and the Trustees of Reservations

The first land trust, originally called the Trustees of Public Reservations, was formed in 1891 in Massachusetts. "Public" was removed from the name in 1954 to discourage the perception that the organization was tax supported.

The idea for the organization came from Charles Eliot, at that time thirty years old. Photographs of Eliot show him as tall and thin, wearing pince-nez and with the full beard customary in those post–Civil War years. Eliot had a privileged, rational, enlightened upbringing in Cambridge, where his father, Charles William Eliot, a mathematician, became president of Harvard when Charles was ten. There were books, music, and conversation daily, the Unitarian Church on Sundays, and summers at the seashore on Mount Desert Island.

After graduating from Harvard, Eliot spent the summer of 1882 debating what he wanted to do with his life. He rejected most professions, his father noted, and also "decided that there was no form of ordinary business which had the least attraction for him."[2] He decided finally that his calling was the just-emerging profession of landscape architect. After a year studying agriculture and horticulture at the Bussey Institute at Harvard, Eliot did an apprenticeship with Frederick Law Olmsted. Olmsted, sixty-one years old in 1882, was effectively the inventor of landscape architecture as a profession, as well as the field of urban planning.

Eliot then spent a year in Europe studying natural and cultivated landscapes from England to Russia.[3] He learned plants at the botanical gardens, read the European books on landscape gardening, and visited well-known landscape gardeners such as Eduoard André. André suggested places to see around Paris and gave Eliot pointers on the business operations of his office.

Although Eliot enjoyed the Mediterranean region and the countryside of England, he was glad to get home. He had disliked London, which in the 1880s was the London of the Sherlock Holmes stories, with coal fires and bronchitis and muddy streets crowded with drunken men and women. The thick London fogs, mysterious and picturesque in fiction, we now know were actually smog, full of particulates and sulfuric acid droplets from the burning of soft coal. "The yellow darkness is particularly disheartening and oppressive," Eliot wrote.

Back in Boston, he opened an office in December 1886 and practiced landscape architecture successfully for several years. In about three dozen articles, mostly for a new landscape magazine, *Garden and Forest,* he set forth his principles of landscape design. His emphasis on the native and the natural seems thoroughly modern today. One of his first articles (written in 1887) was "Anglomania in Park Making." The English greensward with wide-spaced stately hardwoods, he suggested, was inappropriate for most of the world, including much of the United States. "On the rocky coast of Maine each summer sees money worse than wasted in endeavoring to make Newport lawns on ground which naturally bears countless lichen-covered rocks, dwarf Pines and Spruces, and thickets of Sweet Fern, Bayberry, and wild Rose."

An early commission, for land given to the town of Concord, New Hampshire, illustrates his approach. He wrote,

[Concord] proposes to . . . set aside and preserve, for the enjoyment of all orderly townspeople, a typical, strikingly beautiful and very easily accessible bit of New England landscape. Would that every American city and town might thus save for its citizens some characteristic portion of its neighboring country. We should then possess public spaces which would exhibit something more refreshing than a monotony of clipped grass and scattered flower beds.

In 1893, Eliot joined Olmsted's firm as a partner. In the meantime, at Thanksgiving 1888, he had married Mary Yale Pitkin, whom he met on the voyage to England. They eventually had a family of four daughters.

As an adolescent, Eliot was diffident, somewhat hypochondriacal, and sometimes lonely and depressed, but his adult life was happy, successful, and well-ordered. As a subject for biography, he is almost too perfect. If he ever suffered from angst, ennui, envy, snobbery, addiction, or any other sort of bootless or fruitless attitude, there is no evidence. He did not engage in picturesque behavior such as climbing to the top of pine trees to experience wind storms as John Muir did. There is little to tell about Eliot other than his abilities and accomplishments.

He wrote clear, uncluttered prose usually to provide information, facts, and figures, often with the aim of persuading other rational people to some plan of action. He was also persuasive in talks and discussions whether in small groups or before a crowd. His style was low-key, patient, commonsensical, and nonconfrontational. He was an excellent botanist and ecologist. A biographer noted "his exceptional ability to identify broad problems and develop appropriate, sophisticated, and novel solutions, and to mount impressive public education and lobbying campaigns that ensured success."[4]

As far we can know, Eliot was well content with his life and lot. He was not content, however, with what was happening to the land or to the people in the cities. The proposal for forming the Trustees of Reservations came from the merger of his profession with his feeling of duty toward society.

In 1840, 93 percent of the U.S. population was rural, and no city was as large as 400,000. By 1890, the strictly rural percentage had dropped to 65 percent, and the largest city, New York, had a population of nearly two million. Accounts by some historians and sociologists suggest a picture of the rural areas emptying as men and women sought jobs in the factories, mills, and sweat shops of the cities. Such migration occurred, though the main growth of the cities came from heavy foreign immigration. The population of the countryside declined only in certain localities, mainly those with the poorest soils for agriculture. Overall, the rural population grew and by a larger number, though a smaller percentage, than the urban population.

Thomas Jefferson's opinion that cities were bad for morals, health, and freedom was being confirmed.[5] Because of air pollution, lack of sanitation, and the promotion of infectious disease by crowding, death rates were high. In the tenement districts, five or six thousand people might live in a square block, and the yearly mortality rate of children under five years old was around 15 percent.⁶ With this mortality rate, to put it another way, fewer than half the children born would even live to their fifth birthday.

And, of course, the cities were hotbeds of crime and vice. "The lack of opportunity for innocent recreation," Charles Eliot wrote with characteristic mildness, "drives hundreds to amuse themselves in ways that are not innocent."

Many writers, such as Jacob Riis and Lincoln Steffens, described the degraded conditions of life in the cities. We can read grim and grisly accounts of murder, mayhem, thievery, drunkenness, and prostitution among the slum dwellers and of dishonesty and corruption among the landlords, businessmen, and politicians.

These are potent images. For those of us interested in the connections between people and land, life in the nineteenth-century city may be captured almost as well in a smaller, almost trivial, vignette. Riis told of seeing two children in the yard of their tenement in New York. ⁷ They were writing "Keeb of te Grass" in chalk on the fence. There was no grass in the mud, ashes, and filth in which they lived, but this was their attempt at the words they had always seen at any patch of greenery in the radius of their lives.

By 1890, it was clear to Charles Eliot that the time was not far away when the majority of the U.S. population would be urban. He believed, like Olmsted, Theodore Parker, and Edward Bellamy, among others, that with forethought and intelligent action, the lot of the city dwellers could be improved. "If the human race is destined to be more and more closely crowded into towns and suburbs," Eliot wrote in 1891, "should we not endeavor to make these as decent, as healthful, and as refreshingly beautiful as possible?"

The idea for the Trustees was broached by Eliot in a letter to *Garden and Forest* in February 1890. An association was needed, he suggested, to choose and acquire reservations—that is, land reserved from development. "Within ten miles of the State House there still remain several bits of scenery which possess uncommon beauty and more than usual refreshing power. Moreover, each of these scenes is, in its way, characteristic of the primitive wilderness of New England, of which, indeed, they are surviving fragments." The proposal: "As Boston's lovers of art united to form the Art Museum, so her lovers of Nature should now rally to preserve for themselves and all the people as many as possible of these scenes of natural beauty which, by great good fortune, still exist near their doors."

The idea was new, but its roots included Eliot's knowledge of other New England organizations, such as village improvement societies and historical and natural history societies, some of which owned land. In England, he had visited with representatives of the Commons Preservation Society and the Lakeland Defence Association.⁸

Eliot persuaded the Appalachian Mountain Club to invite interested and influential men from around the state to a meeting in Boston at noon on

Saturday, 24 May 1890. About one hundred people showed up. Henry Sprague, president of the Massachusetts Senate, presided. Letters of support from Oliver Wendell Holmes, Francis Parkman, John Greenleaf Whittier, and the governor, among others, were read and heartily applauded.

A committee was appointed "to promote the establishment of a Board of Trustees capable of acquiring and holding, for the benefit of the public, beautiful and historic places in Massachusetts." Eliot became secretary. This was the station he usually chose, out of the spotlight but situated to move the process along. The other twenty-eight members were mostly other Brahmins—affluent descendants of founding fathers of the United States, mostly Harvard graduates, Episcopalians or Unitarians, and movers and shakers on other boards around the state. Also included were three women and at least one Democrat.[9] The committee drafted an act of incorporation and sent it to the Massachusetts legislature. An example of how Eliot got things done is the seven hundred letters he sent to supporters encouraging them to attend the legislative hearing. The bill passed easily, and the governor signed it into law on 21 May 1891.

Although a few private organizations and some governmental bodies in the United States held natural lands in the late nineteenth century, this was the first private organization that included the essential feature of a land trust: a mission dedicated to acquiring, holding, and maintaining natural, scenic, and historic sites. The charter included a second, all-but-essential, feature: tax exemption. A third feature that went to the heart of the organization's reason for existence was the pledge to keep the lands they owned open to the public.

In the invitation to the original meeting Eliot wrote, "There is no need of argument to prove that opportunities for beholding the beauty of Nature are of great importance for the health and happiness of crowded populations." For several years, Eliot had been making the case for both country parks, or natural areas, and urban parks, for picnicking and games, on the grounds of physical and psychological health.

The Trustees' mission was based on this understanding of the human need for open space but was also grounded in Eliot's ecological knowledge. His interest in ecological matters can be traced back at least to 1880. That summer, after Eliot's sophomore year of college, he organized a natural history survey of Mount Desert Island. Several students calling themselves the Champlain Society camped on the east shore of Some's Sound, which runs up the middle of the island. For a month and a half, on foot and on the *Sunshine,* the Eliots' boat, they made observations of the landforms and vegetation. One of the products was a book on the island's flora and geology.[10]

Ian McHarg, probably the most famous of later twentieth century landscape architects and planners and author of *Design with Nature,* credits the work done that summer with being "the first ecological study undertaken, ever, anywhere."[11] This is hyperbole, but the observations could be thought of as the first ecological *survey,* a thorough study of a circumscribed area with an eye to understanding habitat relations.[12]

Eliot's understanding of ecological principles is best shown by his *Vegetation and Scenery on the Metropolitan Reservations.* Written in 1897, this amounts to an ecological monograph on the development, status, and management of the vegetation types found on newly acquired lands of the Boston Park Commission.

Eliot probably did not think of this work as ecology; he may not even have known the word. Ecology as a distinct field of study was developing in the United States at this time, but in the Midwest, not in the Eastern colleges and universities.[13] Eliot's insights into vegetation processes were as valid as those of contributions by the acknowledged ecological pioneers, but his aims went beyond describing vegetation and analyzing the processes that produced and maintained it. He wanted to use the knowledge to manage and restore vegetation types, thus anticipating by many years such applied ecological fields as restoration ecology.

In the concluding section of *Vegetation and Scenery,* he wrote, "The present vegetation has resulted from repeated or continuous interference with natural processes by men, fire, and browsing animals. . . . It follows that the notion that it would be wrong and even sacrilegious to suggest that this vegetation ought to be controlled and modified must be mistaken."

The first meeting of the Trustees was held 1 July 1891. They had already been offered their first reserve; Mrs. Fanny Foster Tudor wanted to donate a 20-acre parcel that included a small stream and a stand of white pine, hemlock, and oak. It would be named Virginia Wood, a memorial to Mrs. Tudor's daughter. The Trustees were agreeable but delayed acceptance until an endowment was raised.

Before 1891 was over, the Trustees had begun to put in motion another of Eliot's ideas by launching a drive for a metropolitan park commission. A private organization to acquire and hold lands was a new and important concept, but as a practical matter assembling open lands on the scale necessary for the park system of a large urban area would require government involvement.

Eliot understood that a parks commission had to be metropolitan; the dozen or so municipalities each looking out for their own interests could never achieve a unified system that preserved the large-scale landscape features such as the ocean front and nearby islands, the rivers, and the larger forested areas. Metropolitan and regional approaches to planning are still rare today; in some states they have never been tried and, by all indications, never will be.

Eliot's motivation was again two-pronged. He had calculated the ratio of parkland to population in U.S. cities and found that Boston had the worst ratio: nearly 3,500 people per acre of park. A part of the work of a park commission would be to provide the city parks that the people needed. But the commission would also locate and protect such fragments of the original vegetation as still existed.

Legislation creating the metropolitan park agency—drafted by Eliot—passed in 1892. Charles Francis Adams was appointed chairman, and Eliot was landscape architect. When Eliot became Olmsted's partner, the firm of Olmsted, Olmsted, and Eliot became the official landscape advisor. Eliot remained in charge of the park project and was now able to draw on the firm's staff and other resources.

Eliot's approach was thoroughly ecological. Studies of geology, topography, and vegetation were the foundation for siting and developing the parks. Ian McHarg commented on Eliot as a planner:

I have been described as the inventor of ecological planning, the incorporation of natural science within the planning process. Yet Charles Eliot . . . preceded me by half a century. He had associated with some of the most distinguished scientists of his day and employed environmental insights in the preparation of his "Emerald Necklace" plan [of preserved green space] for metropolitan Boston. . . . He invented a new and vastly more comprehensive planning method than any pre-existing, but it was not emulated.[14]

By 1902, about 9,250 acres of open space had been bought at a cost of about $5 million and dedicated as public parkland in the city. The people-to-park ratio was thereby reduced to well below one hundred persons per acre of park, the best of the large cities of the United States.[15]

Unfortunately, Eliot lived only six years after the founding of the Trustees, dying in the encephalitis outbreak of 1897. His father wrote a 770-page biography, *Charles Eliot, Landscape Architect,* with the elegiac subtitle: "A lover of nature and of his kind who trained himself for a new profession and practised it happily and through it wrought much good."

Eliot died when he was thirty-seven years old. We can only guess what he might have accomplished if he'd lived longer. His father lived to be ninety-two, his younger brother, Samuel, to eighty-eight, dying in 1950. If Charles had lived out a full Eliotian life span, his later contributions to conservation, urban planning, and environmental protection in general might well have produced a healthier land than that in which we currently live. Perhaps no other conservationist or environmentalist has had his combination of vision, insight, and organizing ability.

The Trustees of Reservations continues in vigorous operation today. It has a membership of 27,000 and owns about ninety properties, natural areas as well as historic sites such as the Old Manse in Concord, where Nathaniel Hawthorne lived for a few years. The first preserve, Virginia Wood, is not among them. It was conveyed to the Metropolitan Park District to become a part of the large Middlesex Fells Reservation, targeted by Eliot in his first report for the Park Commission.

Most of the things that land trusts do by way of planning, inventorying desirable natural areas, fund-raising, cooperating with government, establishing local committees to steward preserves and later adding professional stewardship staff, restoration of damaged ecosystems, and providing educational programs were anticipated by the Trustees. Conservation easements (and an easement defense fund) were added to the repertoire in 1971.[16] The Trustees currently holds about two hundred easements.

The Trustees of Reservations presses forward in the twenty-first century, a modern organization despite its nineteenth century origin and name.

Early Advocacy Organizations

The Trustees of Reservations, in 1891, was the first land trust. Various environmental advocacy groups also invented themselves in the later nineteenth century, and many more have come along since, with a notable surge in the 1960s and 1970s. Several of the early advocacy groups, such as Audubon societies and mountain clubs, had at least a secondary interest in land preservation.

The impetus behind the Audubon movement was the outright destruction of birds. A modern ecological viewpoint might put saving habitat in first place, but at this time in history, stopping the slaughter was more important. Natural land still seemed plentiful, but almost every kind of bird and mammal was being killed in now-inconceivable quantities for food, sport, or other, sometimes ridiculous, reasons, such as hat ornaments.

The lasting achievements of the bird conservation movement were new state and federal laws protecting nongame birds and narrowing the scope of what was considered game. Although protective legislation was the big achievement, the bird protection movement also led eventually to land being protected. One of the first examples was Pelican Island, Florida, a brown pelican nesting site. Audubon members raised money to buy the island from the federal government, acting in this instance like a land trust. For some bureaucratic reason the deal couldn't be concluded.[17] Persuaded by the Audubonites' advocacy, Theodore Roosevelt simply declared Pelican Island a preserve. By 1909, when he left office, Roosevelt had established fifty-two more bird sanctuaries.

There are now many sanctuaries and preserves owned by local, state, and national bird clubs. The National Audubon Society currently has eighty-odd sanctuaries totaling a quarter of a million acres.[18] Although the Land Trust Alliance includes state Audubon societies in its land trust directory, few of them are actively adding to their land holdings. Advocacy is their strong suit, today, as in the past. The Massachusetts Audubon Society is one exception, being almost as much a land trust as an advocacy, research, and education organization.

On his first Maine excursion, Thoreau reached the top of Mt. Ktaadn on a day when it was almost continuously shrouded by fast-moving clouds. He did not find it a comfortable place and commented that Indians consider mountain tops as sacred, mysterious locales and avoid them. "Only daring and insolent men, perchance, go there," he said.[19]

Perhaps such daring and insolent men formed the core of several organizations springing up a little later with the aim of enjoying and protecting various mountainous regions. Daring and insolent women need to be added in the case of the first U.S. mountain club, the Williamstown (Massachusetts) Alpine Club, begun in 1863.[20] This club seems to have been composed about equally of male faculty and students from Williams College and young women from the town. It was a light-hearted bunch whose aim was to explore the interesting places nearby and to become acquainted—"to some extent at least"—with their natural history. The club lasted only a couple of years.

The Appalachian Mountain Club (AMC), which Charles Eliot used as a springboard to launch the Trustees of Reservations, was founded in 1876. Like most of the early mountain clubs, AMC's founding membership was long on scientists, engineers, and other faculty, in this case from MIT and Harvard.

The mountain clubs were primarily advocacy groups, promoting appreciation of the mountains, leading to acquisition or dedication of land by government agencies. AMC and a few other mountain clubs also held land, generally donated as a byproduct of the mountain hikes they led. Eventually, AMC owned nearly twenty reservations in Massachusetts, New Hampshire, and Maine, but by the 1930s, it and other mountain clubs had conveyed most of their land holdings to new state and federal agencies charged with protecting natural resources.[21]

One mountain club, the Sierra Club, was at its formation in 1892 close to a pure land advocacy organization. Later, by the 1970s, it broadened its advocacy to include other environmental issues.

Compared with most of the West, California got a head start on settlement—and on the development of conservation organizations—because of the California Gold Rush. By 1890, the state's population had passed one million; San Francisco was the tenth largest city in the nation at 300,000. The University of California at Berkeley was in operation, as were no less than a dozen and a half other colleges and universities.

Best known among the founders of the Sierra Club is John Muir, as famous in conservation history as Charles Eliot is obscure. Muir arrived in California in March 1868, a month short of his thirtieth birthday, about the age at which Eliot founded the Trustees of Reservations. The dozen years starting about 1890, when Muir was in his sixties and seventies, were his most productive as a writer and as a conservationist. He was pulled into the public conservation battles by Robert Underwood Johnson, an editor of

Century Magazine, a well-respected voice of the eastern Establishment. Johnson visited San Francisco in the summer of 1889 and made a point of getting together with Muir, who had been a popular contributor to *Scribner's Magazine,* predecessor to the *Century.*[22]

In the course of a camping trip to Yosemite, the two devised a plan to promote a national park modeled after Yellowstone, which had been created in 1872. Muir agreed to produce two articles setting forth the case; Johnson would testify at Congress and lobby friends for help. At Johnson's urging, Frederick Law Olmsted wrote an open letter to the newspapers. The appropriate legislation was passed and Yosemite National Park was created 1 October 1890, not much more than a year after Johnson and Muir had hatched the idea.

The Sierra Club grew from two roots. Johnson saw the need for a group that would lobby for protection of the Yosemite area. The new park was a ring around Yosemite Valley. The valley itself had been set aside by Federal action in 1864—the Yosemite grant—but given to the state of California, which proved comprehensively incapable of taking care of it. A watchdog organization was needed to reduce or prevent human intrusions in the valley and the new national park.

The second source was a group of Berkeley faculty and students interested in forming a mountain club, like AMC and the short-lived Rocky Mountain Club, but for the Pacific coastal mountains. Muir evidently was the go-between that led to a merger of the two separate ideas into the Sierra Club.

Twenty-seven men gathered on Saturday, 28 May 1892, at the office of a San Francisco lawyer to sign articles of incorporation. The stated aims reflected the division in the framers. On the one hand, the club would "explore, enjoy, and render accessible" the Sierras. On the other, it would enlist the support of the people and the government in preserving the region's natural features.[23]

Muir disliked formal meetings but agreed to be president of the new organization. He stayed in the office for twenty-two years until he died in 1914. The other founders and many of the 130 charter members were scientists or academics, connected with the University of California, Stanford, the U.S. Geological Survey, or the California Academy of Sciences. The others were mostly professionals and businessmen. There were a few women, including Muir's older daughter, Wanda, ten years old at the time.[24]

The Sierra Club's advocacy efforts began immediately. A prominent feature of the *Sierra Club Bulletin* was Stanford professor William Dudley's column, "Forestry Notes," which focused particularly on legislative issues. One of the most important was the on-going disposal by the federal government of public domain land. From 1841 to 1909, 726 million acres—well over a million square miles and about half the nation's public land—had been given away or sold at give-away prices.[25] By the 1890s, little land was going to bona fide settlers, but the transfer to various sorts of speculators continued unabated.

The club's biggest early conservation battle was the fight over Hetch Hetchy. Hetch Hetchy, a valley on the Tuolomne, was a smaller version of Yosemite Valley—"a wonderfully exact counterpart," according to Muir—and had been included in the national park. The problem was the desire of the city of San Francisco for a water supply for future growth. The battle began in 1901 and ended in defeat in 1913, when the bill to allow construction of a dam to flood Hetch Hetchy was signed by President Woodrow Wilson. O'Shaugnessy Dam was completed in 1919. San Francisco did not begin to use Sierra water until 1934.[26]

The crux of the battle was that San Francisco wanted water and money from power generation. The Sierra Club and its supporters—in California and eventually over much of the United States—wanted Hetch Hetchy left alone, for its own sake and for the enjoyment of Yosemite visitors. They were also defending a larger proposition, that of preserving the integrity of national park lands.

The battle, then, pitted the utilitarians against the preservationists. Gifford Pinchot, first head of the U.S. Forest Service, was point man for the utilitarian viewpoint. In this view, the Earth is a basket of resources to be extracted in a manner to provide the greatest benefit to humans. About Hetch Hetchy, Pinchot wrote, "I am fully persuaded that the injury by substituting a lake for the present swampy floor of the valley is altogether unimportant compared with the benefits to be derived from its use as a reservoir."[27]

Muir can be taken as the spokesman for the preservationists. His writings contain ideas that anticipate the more thoroughly developed land ethic of Aldo Leopold (see chapter 5). It seems likely that the Sierra Club leadership didn't fully understand the subversiveness of this view of man in nature until Leopold spelled it out in *Sand County Almanac*. At least, there were utilitarian slips over the years, and not until the 1950s and 1960s did the Club begin to espouse the ecological conscience consistently and to lionize John Muir for his philosophical insights.

For the battle for Hetch Hetchy, Muir provided some fine rhetoric. "Dam Hetch Hetchy! As well dam for water-tanks the people's cathedrals and temples, for no holier temple has ever been consecrated by the heart of man."[28]

The battle was a prototype of many others that the Sierra Club would fight in later years, over an expanding geographical scale. It also foreshadowed hundreds of environmental battles that local advocacy groups would wage with exploiters of the environment.

As Stephen Fox pointed out in *John Muir and his Legacy,* the contest was between preservationists and utilitarians, but also between amateurs and paid staff. It was, in other words, "between those who urged the dam *as part of their jobs* and those who *took time from their jobs* to oppose it."[29] (The emphasis is Fox's.) This has continued to be the pattern for many such conflicts, though the last twenty years has seen a tendency for advocacy groups to grow, hire professional staff (especially lawyers), and move their headquarters to Washington, D.C.

In retrospect, it's clear that the Trustees of Reservations and the Sierra Club exemplify the two models of private land protection, the land trust and the land advocacy group. At their beginnings, however, the differences in approach grew out of the landscapes where the two organizations developed and the characters of the founders.

The Trustees and the Sierra Club, and, for that matter, most of the land conservation groups of the late nineteenth to early twentieth centuries, were alike in being started by generally well-to-do, well-connected individuals, with a heavy sprinkling of persons with a scientific or technical education. The organizations chose to save land because they feared that, without their efforts, land that ought to be protected would be lost.

The Trustees organized in a region where only remnants of natural land remained; their efforts were devoted to saving as many of these as feasible, to keep them available for the enjoyment and health of the populace, including the urban masses. Most of the land was privately held, hence had to be purchased or obtained by gift.

The Sierra Club concentrated on the Sierra Nevada. Since enormous blocks of natural land were still in the public domain, advocacy for federal protection was the obvious way to proceed. The Club wanted to save the land partly for its intrinsic value and also to provide places for people to have a wilderness experience. By and large, these people were not the urban poor.

Early Land Trusts

From one land trust in 1891, there has grown to be close to 1,300 today. The middle land trust, say, number 650, was founded around 1989. Just which land trust was number 650 is hard to say; about 70 were founded that year.[30] If it took ninety years to reach halfway up the curve and a little more than ten to climb the other half, to today, it's clear that the early growth of land trusts was slow.

By 1901, the Trustees of Reservations owned 431 acres in six preserves, all received as gifts.[31] Even though the Trustees was immediately successful, few new land trusts were started. Instead, advocacy organizations, some of which occasionally owned land, were forming throughout the East in the years prior to 1900.

Besides the Audubon societies and a couple of Ohio museums (Cincinnati and Dayton), only one organization listed in the Land Trust Alliance's directory had a pre-1900 founding date. This was the Connecticut Forest and Park Association, founded in 1895.

The Trustees' influence was felt more immediately in England, where a small group of preservationists followed the model of the Massachusetts group and incorporated as The National Trust for Places of Historic Interest and Natural Beauty in 1895. For many years their by-laws included a provision for a representative of the Trustees to sit on their governing council.[32] Later, other countries formed their own national trusts, stemming indirectly from the Trustees of Reservations. Among them were Scotland in 1934, the United States (the National Trust for Historic Preservation) in 1949, and Canada (Heritage Canada) in 1973.

Sempervirens Club. California was a few years behind New England in forming a land trust. The Sempervirens Club, started in 1900, almost qualifies. It shared the task of protecting land in the coastal redwood belt with the Save-the-Redwoods League. The League, founded in 1917, clearly follows the land trust model, but the Sempervirens Club was basically an advocacy organization.

Because of the early entrance of the railroad, exploitation of the southern groves of redwoods became a matter of concern sooner than in the north, where the Save-the-Redwoods League eventually worked. The event that triggered formation of the Sempervirens Club was an encounter between an artist, Andrew Hill, and the owner of a redwood grove southwest of San Jose, not far from Santa Cruz. The owner was operating it as a roadside attraction and refused to let Hill take photographs unless he paid for the privilege.[33]

Like many other persons, Hill saw the redwoods as a natural wonder that everyone should be able to experience. In early May of 1900, he assembled a group to tour redwood groves in the Big Basin. This region, up the coast several miles from the grove Hill had tried to photograph, was chosen on the recommendation of the Stanford University botanist and Sierra Club activist William Dudley.

As the group sat around their campfire on the banks of Sempervirens Creek the evening of May 18, Hill suggested that the time had come to start an organization to save redwoods. We can call it the Sempervirens Club, someone said. They passed the hat, raised a $32 bankroll, and began lobbying for a Big Basin Redwoods State Park. A bill authorizing the park was signed by the governor in 1901, and in 1902 the park, initially about 3,800 acres, was created.

The Sempervirens Club raised $7,000 in 1913 dollars to buy the right of way for a road into Big Basin from the east, and also members and friends donated land to the park, so there were land trust elements to its operations. However, most of the Club's efforts went into advocacy. It organized public support for saving redwoods and lobbied the California legislature and the three counties around Big Basin very effectively.[34]

The Club shared the generally held belief that an important role of government was to see that natural wonders were protected for the good of the American people. The *San Francisco Chronicle* had endorsed the idea of a redwood park early on, invoking Yosemite and Yellowstone and writing, "We know of no way in which the public money could be better invested." All the area colleges supported the concept of a Big Basin park. The President of Santa Clara College wrote that the park would be a place where

[O]ur children and workmen, factory girls and others breathing all the week impure air, might, amidst the great trees and along rippling brooks, breathe pure air and rest amidst those great forests, where their minds and hearts are lifted to higher, purer, nobler things.[35]

This idea—that natural areas promote the physical and mental health of the populace—had been an important part of Charles Eliot's rationale for the Trustees of Reservations.

Sempervirens Club's efforts continued over several decades, but its peak came early. By 1904, the club had a few hundred members in several chapters around the state. A photo, probably at the time of the club's first campout at the new park, shows a group arrayed at the base of a redwood. The men wear suits and ties; most have taken off their fedoras for the picture. The women wear long skirts and have long hair done up in Gibson girl and related styles. An unusual feature of Sempervirens was the high degree of participation by women; eleven of the twenty-eight people in the photo are women.

In the late 1960s, a small group of land preservation activists revived the Sempervirens name for an organization that would continue to add land to the various parks of the Santa Cruz mountains region and connect them with trails.[36] Called the Sempervirens Fund, it uses standard land-trust methods for acquiring land, most of which it transfers to Big Basin Redwoods State Park or other parks and preserves. By 1998, according to the LTA directory, the Sempervirens Fund had protected more than 8,500 acres and had 15,000 members.

Save-the-Redwoods League. The Save-the-Redwoods League arose from a fabled August 1917 camping trip by three conservation-minded individuals, Dr. John C. Merriam, Professor Henry Fairfield Osborn, and Madison Grant.[37] They left the Russian River area of Sonoma County and drove north on Highway 101 through Mendocino, Humboldt, and Del Norte counties, in the redwood belt in the northwest corner of California. The three men were impressed by the beauty and scientific importance of the redwood groves but also saw many cutover areas where the then-new highway had allowed access by loggers.

By the end of the trip, they had plans for an organization that would seek to preserve the best groves in the northern part of the redwood belt. Apparently, the League was an independent re-invention of the land trust concept; however, two of its founders were Easterners and could have been aware of the Trustees of Reservations.

It's worth knowing a little about Merriam, Osborn, and Grant. Merriam, an Iowan by birth, had been on the faculty of the University of California for about twenty years. He was a researcher, writer, and chairman of the paleontology department at the time of the August 1917 camping trip.

Osborn was also a paleontologist by training. Born to a wealthy family in New York, he did undergraduate work at Princeton and then studied in Europe, as had Merriam. After teaching stints at Princeton and Columbia, Osborn in 1917 was president of the American Museum of Natural History in New York City.

Grant was also a New Yorker, wealthy, a good friend of Osborn and Teddy Roosevelt, among other rich and famous people. A lawyer by education (Columbia), he occupied most of his time hunting, exploring, studying nature, and sitting on the boards of various worthy organizations, several of which he helped found. Among these were the New York Zoological Society and the Boone and Crockett Club, which was dedicated to the preservation of big game mammals, including the defense of Yellowstone National Park.

By the fall of 1918, Grant and Merriam had begun to enlist "a group of patriotic Californians" to be members of the proposed organization.[38] By early 1919, it had a president, Franklin K. Lane, who was, in fact, a Californian though he was currently in Washington, D.C., serving as Secretary of the Interior. In this role, he had been a major player in the loss of Hetch Hetchy. The League also had an executive committee of about twenty members, chaired by Merriam.

We have seen that the lands available for protection by the Trustees of Reservations were privately owned, relict fragments, while the Sierra Club targeted large blocks still in the hands of the federal government. Large stands of coastal redwoods north of San Francisco Bay, the focus of the Save-the-Redwoods League, still existed, but the government had already given the land away. The groves were falling to the lumberman's ax at an increasing rate and, realistically, most could only be protected by purchase. At the first meeting of the officers in August 1919, Merriam outlined the purposes of the Save-the-Redwoods League: It would acquire the stands of redwoods along the rapidly extending highways and others threatened by lumbering and assist in the establishment of a Redwoods National Park.

By 1920, the League had nonprofit status and was in full operation with over 4,000 members spread over the United States. The earlier executive committee was now a self-perpetuating Council of twenty-six members, including William F. Badè, one of the long-time operational leaders of the Sierra Club. An executive secretary had been hired, Newton B. Drury. Drury was an important figure in the League for close to sixty years, though he took a few years off to be Director of the National Park Service and Chief of the California Division of Beaches and Parks.[39]

The Web site of the League states that they preserve the redwood forests of California "in the simplest way possible—we buy redwood forest land."[40] This is the essence of a land trust. However, the Save-the-Redwoods League also has often engaged in advocacy, mostly privately rather than publicly, through its officers and wealthy supporters pressing governmental agencies to buy land or support favorable legislation.

The League has been highly successful. In the eighty-plus years of its existence, it has spent about $100 million to protect more than 180,000 acres of redwood forest, worth perhaps $4 billion at today's prices.[41] Most of the land has been turned over to one or another of the state redwood parks. Its money has been raised from large and small contributors, but as with most organizations that depend on philanthropy, most has come in large donations from the wealthy. One notable donation was $2 million from John D. Rockefeller, Jr., used in buying 10,000 acres that became the Rockefeller Forest.

There is a puzzling feature about the 1917 trip of Merriam, Osborn, and Grant—not the trip itself, but rather, how they happened to come together at the starting point in what was then the wilds of Sonoma County. The answer is that, along with many others, they were at Bohemian Grove, where the summer gathering of the Bohemian Club of San Francisco is held.[42]

For many decades, these 2,700 acres have been the site of a highly private gathering of conservative leaders of business, politics, and the professions.[43] In recent years, newspapers have endeavored to keep track of some of the more prominent attendees and have documented the presence of the CEOs of such corporations as Bechtel Corporation, Dow Chemical, and the Bank of America; many Republican presidential hopefuls, cabinet officers, Supreme Court justices, and generals; and heads of media corporations. Added to the powerful are other rich and famous men from around the country, as well as a good many Californians—lawyers, physicians, stockbrokers—who are merely affluent and well-connected. Perhaps a couple of thousand members of the conservative establishment visit Bohemian Grove sometime during the two-week camp.

Some people are troubled by this yearly gathering of powerful right-wing white males. They see it as a place for conspiracy or, at the very least, networking and deal-making that will have no favorable consequences for the majority of Americans. Defenders claim it's just a vacation, differing only in its exclusivity (and extreme privacy) from the week that Joe Six-Pack might spend in deer camp. The Bohemian Grove guys drink, tell stories, sing, urinate on the redwood trunks—the "grove" is a redwood grove—and, in general, just kick back and relax, away from the cares of the world.

Susan Schrepfer, a historian at Rutgers University who studied the history of the Save-the-Redwoods League, called the League an overwhelmingly conservative movement.[44] Most of the affluent founders and members of the Council believed in free enterprise, private property rights, divine will, state's rights, and industrial and technological progress. Their aim was to save the most nearly pristine redwood sites as temples, laboratories, and classrooms that would educate society about religion and science and, by their grandeur, stimulate nationalism. They were content to let the rest of the redwood belt undergo whatever development might ensue.

Early Twentieth Century Trusts in the East

Among early twentieth century land trusts that formed in the East were two New Hampshire organizations: the Society for the Protection of New Hampshire Forests (1901) and the Squam Lakes Association (begun in 1904 as the Squam Lake Improvement Association). Both remain thriving organizations today.

In Maine, on Mount Desert Island, Harvard President Charles W. Eliot followed his son's precepts and formed the Hancock County Trustees of Public Reservations. The Eliot family had been visiting the island summers since 1871 and had bought property and built there in 1880. Much of the island was still natural, with grand views of mountains and sea and virgin sites of spruce forest, white pine forest, mixed conifer-hardwoods, pitch pine areas similar to the New Jersey pine barrens, bogs, and cedar swamps.

By 1901, as the population of the island grew, many places where the Eliot family and their neighbors had once walked and picnicked had been built upon and closed to the public. "By what means," President Eliot asked, "can some public reservations of interesting scenery be secured for the perpetual use and enjoyment of all the inhabitants of Mount Desert, natives, cottagers and transient visitors alike?"[45]

The question was rhetorical, and the group of wealthy summer people he brought together in the fall of 1901 agreed to form a corporation, the Hancock County Trustees of Public Reservations, to acquire and hold lands for free public use. A special act of the Maine legislature in 1903 exempted these lands from state, county, and town taxes.

A gift of about one hundred acres of wild, scenic land energized the Trustees, particularly George Dorr. Dorr, a well-to-do dilettante with a soup-strainer mustache, found that the land trust provided a direction to his life. He began to devote most of his time and eventually almost all his money to the cause.[46] By 1913, the Trustees owned about 5,000 acres, mostly steep rocky sites and including land acquired to protect the water supply of three of the island villages.

"What needs to be forever excluded from the island is the squalor of a city," wrote Eliot. "Not even the appropriate pleasures and splendors of city life should be imitated at Mount Desert." Not all the residents agreed; unlike Charles W. Eliot and his friends, they were not necessarily there to escape the noise, dirt, and ugliness of the city. Land speculators were unhappy that about a tenth of the island (in addition to the land owned individually by the rich cottagers) was unavailable for lumbering or development. The unhappiness existed despite the fact that the Trustees specifically refrained from buying good building sites. Another sore point for residents of Bar Harbor, the largest village, and elements in the state government was that the cottagers at the town meetings of Northeast and Seal Harbors voted to continue excluding automobiles from the island.[47]

In January 1913, the representative from Bar Harbor introduced a bill in the state legislature to revoke the tax exempt status of the Trustees. George Dorr hastened to the state capitol and rallied support. The annulment effort failed, but it showed the Trustees what a shaky guarantee their state charter was. Dorr was sent to Washington charged with donating the land to the federal government as a national monument.

This turned out not to be a simple task. Not until 1916 was Sieur de Monts National Monument established. It became the core of Acadia National Park, formed in 1929 with additional lands donated by the Trustees. Acadia today occupies about 48 square miles, including land on the adjoining mainland.

John D. Rockefeller, Jr., owned property on Mount Desert Island beginning about 1910—a latecomer. He did not become involved with the Hancock County Trustees until the transition period to the National Monument, when he provided a small grant to help clear up title and boundary problems. Later on, he donated land to the National Monument and then to the Park.[48] Rockefeller's Mount Desert Island experience was the start of his contributions to land conservation, which eventually came to total about $25 million in pre–World War II dollars.[49]

Transferring their major holdings to the federal government did not mean the end of the Hancock County Trustees. They continued to acquire land, transferring most of it to the park. The organization exists yet and acts as caretaker to Woodlawn, a 185-acre estate on the mainland that includes an 1820s Georgian house.

Outside New England, the Highlands Improvement Society was started in 1905 to preserve the natural beauty and rural aspect of the Highlands region in the southwestern corner of North Carolina. Calling this organization a land trust oversimplifies it. It seems to have been a combination village improvement society, mountain club, and land advocacy group. The leaders of the society were women. One of their first projects was to buy Satulah Summit, priced at $500, which they raised in just over a month. The 32-acre park was dedicated to public use in perpetuity in 1909.

Professor Thomas G. Harbison wrote, "[The top of Satulah Mountain] is OURS, ours to keep forever. No money grubbing skinflint . . . can ever acquire this top and then put up a toll gate to charge admission to what he the same as stole from God. . . . No man has a right or can acquire a right to charge his fellow man toll to visit the tops of God's mountains."[50] Besides being a good statement of what land trusts do, the words express the very American sense of obligation to protect nature's wonders and keep them accessible to the public.

In 1987, after a complicated history, the group incorporated as the Highlands Land Trust, with fairly standard land preservation aims.

Development through the Post–World War II Period

Only a few more land trusts were formed in the early decades of the twentieth century. The Western Pennsylvania Conservancy claims a 1932 founding date, but this is misleading. What was formed in 1932 was the Greater Pittsburgh Parks Association, which accomplished nothing in the way of land protection until 1945. The name Western Pennsylvania Conservancy was adopted in March 1951, the group becoming the first local land trust to call itself a "conservancy."[51]

Some of the early trusts, notably the Trustees of Public Reservations and the Save-the-Redwoods League, continued through the 1930s and 1940s to pursue their mission with great success, but overall, the idea of private land conservation had still not caught fire.

The LTA directory claims more than thirty land trusts in existence as of 1940, but over a dozen of these are Audubon societies, museums, or other organizations that fail the land trust test of having as their sole or primary mission the acquisition and holding of land. Nineteen is probably a generous estimate of the number of trusts in active operation in 1940. The LTA figure of fifty-three land trusts in operation in 1950 is also inflated. [52]

We may wonder why the idea of land conservation by private organizations was slow to penetrate the national consciousness. Probably most people didn't encounter the idea; the organizations that, with the perspective of history, we now identify as land trusts were evidently not good proselytizers. People were much more apt to hear from land advocacy organizations, for which a strong PR effort was essential.

Also, federal and state governments were saving land at a good pace. For example, eighteen of our National Parks were established between 1910 and 1940. By 1938, there were 196 million acres of public forest lands, of which 122 million were in the national forests. The idea that providing parks and open space is a legitimate public function has always made sense to the majority of the American people. Radical and recent is the minority notion that government shouldn't buy or regulate land for the general welfare.[53] Over many decades from the 1890s to the 1970s, the state and federal governments, egged on by land advocacy organizations, accomplished much good, and the land trust model seemed of minor importance.

There were other, sociological reasons why not much private land-saving action—other than by individuals—went on during different parts of this time period. The years from 1930 to 1941 were hard times, the years of the Great Depression. Most people were focused on their own family's survival, not on forming organizations to save land. In hindsight, of course, the depressed land prices would have made this one of the best times for land trusts to be operating.

World War II ended the Depression, but also put many people who might have had conservation interests into the armed services or at work in the war effort in this country. Immediately after the war, the general public showed little interest in conservation. Progress and technology ruled the day. "We are remodeling the Alhambra with a steam-shovel, and we are proud of our yardage," Aldo Leopold wrote in 1947, providing an apt metaphor for the post-war decade.[54]

The first national land trust was The Nature Conservancy. It was founded in 1946 as the Ecologists Union and adopted The Nature Conservancy name in 1950. The other well-known national land trusts were formed much later, the Trust for Public Land in 1972, the American Farmland Trust in 1980, and the Rails-to-Trails Conservancy in 1985. More about the history of the national trusts is given in the chapters devoted to each.

Growth in the Later Twentieth Century

Strong growth in numbers of local land trusts became evident just before 1960. From 1955 to 1959, eighteen land trusts were founded, compared with seven in the preceding five years and three between 1945 and 1949.[55] From the mid-1980s to the mid-1990s, new land trusts were forming at the rate of one or more per week. The LTA's 1998 census identified 1,213 land trusts and the 2000 census, 1,263.[56]

What is striking about many of the trusts formed in the 1960s to 1980s is their lack of connection with local land trusts that had formed in the late 1800s and early to mid-1900s. Apparently, the early land trusts were rarely direct models for the later ones. Where, then, did a bunch of people in Ohio or Montana get the idea to form a local land-saving group?

Few got the idea from articles in magazines, because there was little media coverage of land trusts for the first eighty years of the twentieth century. The first sixty years are virtually blank. In 1973, Jack Gunther, president of the New Canaan (Connecticut) Land Conservation Trust, wrote "How to Preserve Small Natural Areas," published in the obscure journal *Catalyst for Environmental Quality*.[57]

Potentially more broadly influential were two articles in the late 1970s. In the *Smithsonian* for 1977, F. J. Pratson in impeccable prose and photographs by Alfred Eisenstaedt chronicled the Trustees of Reservations. A 1979 *Sierra* article, "Reserves, Preserves and Land Trusts," by Hal Rubin, was wide-ranging, describing activities of conservation, community, and farmland trusts.[58]

There seems to have been little outreach by the older trusts. Several Connecticut land trusts founded in the late 1960s and 1970s probably profited from the example and advice of the New Canaan trust, which itself was only established in 1967. An occasional new trust was started as a result of land trusters from New England or elsewhere moving to a new location and talking up the possibilities.

More influential than anything else in the 1960s and 1970s were a handful of books and the examples of two national land trusts. The earliest work of importance was probably *Securing Open Space for Urban America: Conservation Easements* by William H. Whyte, Jr., published in 1959.[59] Whyte was an establishment figure—an editor at *Fortune* magazine, best-selling author of *The Organization Man,* member of presidential task forces and commissions. He also had an abiding interest in preserving open space that had begun in his childhood home, the rolling country of Chester County, Pennsylvania.

Whyte was a writer of plain and lucid prose, rather like that of E. B. White. *Securing Open Space,* though a monograph on conservation easements, is thoroughly readable. He concentrated on easements because of the then-unrealized potential of this approach to saving open space. Stemming from Whyte's book was not just acceptance by the conservation community but also eventual widespread legislation giving an explicit legal basis for conservation easements.

Eight years later, in 1967, Russell L. Brenneman took a broader view in *Private Approaches to the Preservation of Open Land.*[60] A lawyer with a Connecticut firm, Brenneman consulted with The Nature Conservancy on land and tax issues and was also an officer of the Connecticut Forest and Park Assocation, one of the pioneer land trusts mentioned earlier. Although *Private Approaches* is a legal treatise on transfers, easements, and covenants, it has a progressive, hopeful tone that is very much an expression of the era when it was written. The foreword says, "I assume that today the main focus has shifted in our United States from quantity to quality in living; I assume that to recover the relation between man and nature we must have open land." From this book, more than most other sources, people wanting to save land learned what the legal landscape was.

A third important book, Ian McHarg's *Design with Nature,* appeared in 1969.[61] There is nothing about easements or land trusts in it, but the message that we should consult the land to learn how to live on it was said powerfully and beautifully.

The first Earth Day, in April 1970, quickened the pulse of many young conservationists. Earth Day was much more focused on pesticides, pollution, and population than on saving natural lands, but it was an energizing event in an energizing time for old and new environmentalists.

In this atmosphere of concern for the Earth, the activities of The Nature Conservancy and the Trust for Public Land were taken as models for land-saving action by groups of concerned citizens around the country. It's curious that these national groups were the impetus for many reinventions of the idea of a local land trust, but so it happened.

The Nature Conservancy (TNC) served mostly as a model. Only occasionally did it actively encourage the formation of local land trusts. One instance of such encouragement has been its Connecticut Land Trust Service Bureau, dating from around 1980. Two-thirds of Connecticut's approximately 115 trusts were already in operation by the 1970s—mostly formed in 1960s and 1970s—but the Service Bureau helped later ones get started and also provided assistance to pre-existing trusts.

But all around the country, even in states where the TNC chapter was aloof, people saw what the organization was doing and decided that they needed an organization to do locally what TNC was doing nationally.

A little later on, by 1980, TNC had shifted emphasis to large, landscape-scale projects. It was no longer available to help a local group save an oak woodlot of merely local importance. By this shift, TNC again gave impetus, in a back-handed sort of way, to the formation of local land trusts.

Like TNC, the Trust for Public Land (TPL) helped by being a model; unlike TNC, it also actively encouraged the formation of local groups. Huey Johnson, TPL's founder and first executive director and also Joel Kuperberg, its second executive director, were strong advocates of local land trusts.[62] TPL's Land Trust Program, with its circuit-riders visiting groups wishing to organize, was most important in the late 1970s and early 1980s and in the West, especially California.[63]

Why the Save-the-Redwoods League hadn't spawned California imitators isn't clear. Perhaps it was so focused on saving redwoods that it had no time for mentoring. Perhaps it seemed too rich and conservative to be recognized as a model by small, poor local groups with what they saw as a revolutionary impulse.

The materials TPL supplied to groups coalescing as new land trusts included writings from people associated with land trusts in the East, including Kingsbury Browne, Robert Lemire, Russell Brenneman, and Jack Gunther. To this degree, the disconnect between the old land trusts and the new was not as total as it may seem.[64]

The year 1981 was pivotal because of two national meetings held that fall. Perhaps as many as 400 land trusts were operating in the United States by this time, a dilute soup nationally, especially since most were either north of the Mason-Dixon line and east of the Mississippi or else within 50 miles of the Pacific Ocean.

The land trust movement is curiously egalitarian. Hundreds or thousands of persons have worked hard and accomplished much at land trusts all around the country, but the accomplishments of only a few persons have had an effect at the national level. One of the few is Kingsbury Browne, Jr.

Browne, a tax lawyer with a Boston firm and the owner of a splendid set of eyebrows, began working with conservation organizations in the early 1970s as a result of a friend's suggestion to look at how tax policy was affecting conservation. The friend was Hank Foster, that is, Charles H. W. Foster, who a few years earlier, had briefly been president of The Nature Conservancy. In the mid-1970s, Browne began a memorandum service to inform land trusts about tax developments. *Case Studies in Land Conservation*, which he edited in 1976 and 1977, included examples of such then-innovative techniques as limited development and conservation easements.[65]

In 1980, when he was in his late fifties, Browne was able to take a sabbatical leave to study land trusts. Although his sabbatical was at the Lincoln Institute for Land Studies and Harvard University, his model was John Steinbeck's *Travels with Charley*. This 1962 book describes a journey in which Steinbeck toured the United States, driving a small camper named Rocinante and accompanied by his poodle Charley. Browne proposed to do much the same thing, but to visit land trusts. Another difference was that, upon the strong representations of Browne's family, they—not Charley— went along, in relays.[66]

From July to December 1980, Browne visited several land-saving organizations, beginning with Brandywine Conservancy in the suburban Philadelphia region. In the West, Jennie Gerard of the Trust for Public Land helped to set up appointments with several trusts. Browne has said, "I was intrigued with the capabilities of the people involved, almost without exception. They were all interested in what other land trusts were doing but had few contacts with them. So they were tending to reinvent the wheel."

Browne concluded that an exchange of ideas was needed among these and similar groups. "I wrote a report for the Lincoln Institute and suggested they bring these people together, which they did for two days, paying expenses."[67] This workshop was given an odd title: the National Consultation on Local Land Conservation. Held in Cambridge in October 1981, it included representatives of about forty organizations including about two dozen land trusts. As the price of admission, the attendees had to prepare two white papers that formed the basis for their discussions.[68]

The meeting was a great success. One participant compared it to an old-fashioned revival meeting. The participants refreshed, inspired, and educated one another. Most agreed that it should not be a one-time event, and out of it came the Land Trust Alliance (see chapter 9).

The other 1981 meeting, the Private Options Conference, was sponsored by the Montana Land Reliance but, for convenience of travel in November, was held in San Francisco. Among the trusts represented at both meetings were the Peninsula Open Space Trust, Napa County Land Trust, and Sonoma Land Trust—all from California—also the Montana Land Reliance, Maine Coast Heritage Trust, and Jackson Hole (Wyoming) Land Trust. Various other successful local trusts were absent from one or both meetings. Presentations from the two conferences were merged in the 1982 book *Private Options: Tools and Concepts for Land Conservation*.

Most of the organizations invited to the two conferences are still going strong, but not all. The Savannas Wilderness Trust (Florida) seems no longer to be in business. Neither is the Ohio Conservation Foundation, which promoted conservation easement legislation and the use of easements but evidently never accepted any.[69] The Ottauqueeche Regional Land Trust became the state-wide Vermont Land Trust not long after the Cambridge meeting.[70]

The Land Trust Movement

A case can be made that, despite the nineteenth century beginning of the Trustees of Reservations and the decades of successful land protection by several dozen trusts, the real beginning of the land trust "movement" was in 1981. Not until then were many of the individual organizations aware that other people, elsewhere, were doing the same thing, and not until then did machinery exist for social learning—for one trust to profit from the trials and errors and successes of another.

"It's also important to realize," William Dunham, director of the Montana Land Reliance said, in opening the San Francisco meeting, "that all of you are breaking new ground. The Morrises, Kingsbury Browne, and a few other people were pretty much alone a few years ago when they started journeying out into this area of local land preservation."[71]

Not such new ground; it had been plowed by the Trustees of Reservations, Save-the-Redwoods League, Western Pennsylvania Conservancy, Michigan Nature Association, ACRES Inc. in northern Indiana, and a good many others. It's a measure of the truncated historical horizon that has tended to characterize the land trust community that Samuel and Eleanor Morris—founders of the French and Pickering Creeks Conservation Trust (Pennsylvania) in 1967—and Kingsbury Browne could be cited as pioneers.

Today, even 1981 seems like ancient history to many people in the land trust community. The years before then are as irrelevant as the Articles of Confederation. More than 60 percent of the land trusts listed in the 1998 LTA directory were not even in existence in 1981. To the degree that today's land trust workers are aware of the National Consultation and the Private Options meeting a month later, they must think of them as lost in the mists of time, like the discovery of magnetism or the invention of gunpowder.

But 1981 is not much more than twenty years ago; 1981 is modern. Rock and roll had displaced American popular music twenty years before. The Vietnam War and Civil Rights marches were history. Presidents Kennedy, Johnson, Nixon, Ford, and Carter had come and gone and we were at the Reagan era. James Watt was Secretary of Interior. In college students I was seeing, the mood was very different from the 1960s and 1970s. A new spirit had emerged—don't make war, don't make love, make money—and these were biology students in an ecology course for majors.

People of the land trust community tend to be interested in today—and tomorrow—but are often unaware of where today is in the flow of land trust history. Many are also unaware of where land trusts fit into the broader conservation and environmental movements. Today, as in 1981, many are creatures of the here and now. They are unburdened by history but also unenlightened by it.

The post-1980 boom in land trusts was fueled by the realization that the government had not just abdicated leadership in the conservation wars but had defected to the enemy army. It was the same force that produced the great increase in membership of the national environmental advocacy groups; the Sierra Club jumped from 150,000 in 1980 to 650,000 in 1991, a growth rate of over 14 percent per year. The Wilderness Society, somnolent through the 1970s, rose from 50,000 in 1980 to 350,000, for a growth rate of over 19 percent per year.[72]

Most of us tend to block unpleasant memories, so we may need reminding that a primary goal of the Reagan administration was, in Kirkpatrick Sale's words,

to dismantle government regulations and squelch environmental and other public influence. . . . What was not effected by judicious cabinet appointments was attacked by budget maneuvering or legal resistance or Congressional arm twisting, and when all else failed, with a simple refusal to act and a quiet policy of nonenforcement. . . . [The] Task Force on Regulatory Relief, under Vice President George Bush, spared countless corporate polluters from government action. . . .

Not necessarily the worst Reagan appointees but the most insolent were two right-wing lawyers, Anne Gorsuch, appointed head of the Environmental Protection Agency, and James Watt, Secretary of the Interior. "What's Wrong? Watt's Wrong," said the Sierra Club,[73] but Ronald Reagan stood by his man: "He has my full support because I think we have been victimized by some individuals that I refer to as environmental extremists."[74]

The Reagan anti-environmental campaign was successful, though we should not give Reagan too much credit, or blame. He was the mouthpiece for self-interested corporations, ideologues in right-wing foundations, and associations of Western ranchers and miners that make their living off U.S. government lands. The campaign didn't succeed in dismantling much of the machinery for environmental protection, but it began an erosive process that continues today.

One of the most effective shots was cutting the Land and Water Conservation Fund (LWCF) appropriation. The administration's recommendation was $45 million compared with $750 million in the last year of the Carter administration.[75] The LWCF had been established in 1964 to fund land purchases for federal wild and recreational land and also to provide pass-through money for states for similar projects. The money was originally from a variety of sources such as federal recreation area users fees, but in 1968 receipts from off-shore oil drilling were added, greatly increasing the pool.[76] The low point in funding was 1974, the Nixon-Ford transitional year.

The Carter administration was a time of abundance. The LWCF authorization was upped to $900 million and, though the annual expenditures never hit quite that level, they were higher than at any time before or since.[77] Land trusts, mostly the national, state, and larger regional trusts, regularly bought land deserving protection and counted on replenishing their bank accounts by reselling it to agencies that could draw on the LWCF.

This practice was nearly brought to a halt.[78] The disappearance of federal money was a major topic at the two national land trust meetings held in 1981, only months after Reagan's inauguration. One speaker at the Cambridge meeting pointed out that inholdings in Grand Teton National Park and the National Elk Refuge scheduled for purchase were now up for grabs but concluded that the cutbacks provided an opportunity for innovation: "If we use the time of fiscal austerity . . . to think creatively and to develop new skills and tools, we can emerge with land conservation programs at the private and local level stronger and more successful than ever. Perhaps then we may even have cause to thank the federal budget-cutters for giving us the unmistakable nudge!"[79]

No matter what the Chinese characters for "crisis" are, not every crisis includes an opportunity. Some crises are just bad news. The attacks on the environment by the Reagan administration encouraged the growth of conservation organizations, including land trusts, and there was some good in that. But the funding cutbacks were simply hurtful, to conservation and the nation. One of the effects of the resulting "creative thinking" was increased use of conservation easements. Done to take up the slack from the loss of money for fee acquisition, the practice spread in part because of the illusion that it is a cheap and easy way to save land.

Land Trust Growth Rates

The first census of local land trusts, done in connection with the National Consultation in 1981, reported 404 (later revised to 431).[80] By my criteria, this figure as well as those from later censuses by the Land Trust Alliance are inflated because they include various sorts of non-profits that may own land but do not have ongoing land acquisition and stewardship as their main mission. About 370 is a better estimate of the number of land trusts in 1981.

Using dates of formation, the number of trusts in existence at earlier dates can be approximated. Six years earlier, in 1975, only about 308 (or somewhat fewer) were in existence.[81] Ten years or so earlier, in 1964 to 1965, the number had been in the vicinity of 132.

In 1964, based on LTA data, twenty-two states lacked even a single land trust: Alabama, Arizona, Arkansas, Colorado, Hawaii, Idaho, Kansas, Kentucky, Louisiana, Minnesota, Mississippi, Montana, Nebraska, Nevada, New Mexico, North Dakota, South Carolina, South Dakota, Texas, Virginia, Washington, and Wyoming.[82]

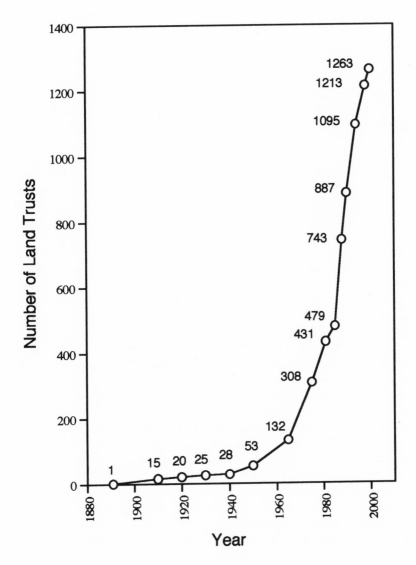

Figure 1. Growth in Numbers of Land Trusts

From this list, the geographical pattern of land trust establishment is obvious, with outposts arriving later in the South and West.

Over the years, states were added. The number of states with no land trusts dropped to fourteen in 1975, nine in 1981, and five in 1986. By 1994, the LTA claimed that land trusts were operating in all fifty states.[83] The statement is correct but misleading. Three states, Arkansas, Oklahoma, and South Dakota, had no home-grown land trusts, though multi-state land trusts did include Arkansas and South Dakota within their service areas.

By 1998, only Oklahoma had no currently operating land trust, but since then the Norman Area Land Trust has been established, so there are now legitimate pins in every state on the map.

If we glance at the curve of number of local land trusts plotted against time, starting with one (the Trustees of Reservations) in 1891, it looks at first glance like an exponential curve with a long period of slow growth and then a steeply increasing segment (figure 1).[84] On closer examination, the curve is more complicated.

In percentage terms, formation of new trusts was fastest in two periods. From 1965 to 1975, growth rate was around 9 percent per year. This corresponds with the blossoming of the public environmental movement. A briefer period of even faster growth was 1985 to 1988, when the number of trusts grew at the rate of 16 percent per year and continued above 10 percent through 1990. This was public response to the Reagan–George H. W. Bush era.

If we look at absolute numbers rather than percentages, growth was fastest from about 1985 to 1988 and continued high until 1994. In every year from 1987 to 1992, land trusts formed at the rate of one or more per week.

More recently, the growth rate has slowed, at least temporarily. A large number of new trusts are still being formed each year, but the percentage growth rate has declined since 1990. In closer view, then, the overall curve is not exponential (J-shaped), but instead S-shaped. Between 1990 and 1994, the yearly growth rate was about 5.4 percent; between 1994 and 1998, it was only 2.6 percent. The current yearly percentage growth rate, measured between 1998 and 2000, is slightly below 2 percent.

We might also like to see a curve for numbers of members, but membership figures are inherently less reliable than the tally of trusts. Membership figures change during the course of a year, and also land trusts may estimate or round numbers up or down. About the best estimates that are available are the LTA approximations of almost 350,000 members nationally in 1986, around 800,000 in 1990, nearly 900,000 in 1994, and about one million in 1998. These figures suggest a growth in members of about 20 percent per year in the late 1980s and a little more than one-tenth that, only 3 percent per year from 1990 to 1998.

SPRAWL

This ideally situated estate, comprising six acres of excellent building land, is to be developed with high class modern residences by Sutch and Martin, Limited, of New-bury, Berks. —Richard Adams, *Watership Down*

One morning two years after I came to Michigan, I set out to explore an extensive bog forest. An old logging road ran a few hundred yards to a plateau rising about 30 feet above the level of the bog. On this island of high ground grew large trees of sugar maple and American beech, as well as elm, basswood, and tulip tree. Community ecologists tend to be fond of beech-maple forest. This is the climax community in these parts; it is the more stable, less changing type of vegetation that, given enough time, will clothe many different types of the region's land, from pretty wet to fairly dry.

When I first saw it that fall, the forest was still green. On later trips, the maple leaves turned yellow and orange and then fell, first as individual pools around the bases of trees and then as a complete floor of yellow, with an admixture of browns and buffs from the beeches and elms.

Winter was a fine time too, with the smooth, pale gray trunks of the beech and the darker, furrowed maple trunks set against the snowy ground. But spring is the glorious season. The sun floods through the leafless canopy to the forest floor. On this copious energy flourish the spring ephemeral herbs; they come up early, leaf out, photosynthesize, flower, and wither by mid-May.

The names of the spring flowers of the beech-maple forest are familiar, the flowers of excursions to the woodlots of our childhoods—Dutchman's breeches, spring beauty, toothwort, trout lily, blue and yellow violets, white trillium. They grow thickly in the temporary sunlight. One early May day, some students and I set up sample plots and found an average of 159 herb stems per square meter. This means that in one May acre of this woods there were more than 600,000 flowers.

I laid out a bird census area of 15 acres and visited it several times in the early morning that summer. The forest in summer is not so much fun. Mosquitoes are a torment. Patches of thigh-high horse nettles raise itchy hives through any normal pants. Though less congenial for people, summer is the time when the forest is in high gear. The trees are making food and storing it, the insects are taking their share and tithing to the birds.

Red-eyed vireos were the most common birds breeding on this island of beech-maple forest. Based on mapping where the males were singing, I decided there were six vireo territories the summer of 1962. Also among the twenty-seven breeding species were Acadian flycatchers, singing their abrupt song like a hiccup in the early morning woods. The veery, a bird I'd never heard when I was growing up in southern Illinois, sang along the slope where the beech-maple forest merged with the bog forest of birch, pine, and ash. All thrush songs are liquid and melodious, but the downward spiraling song of the veery has a remarkable quality, as though the bird were singing in a cave.

In the second year of my censusing, I noticed painted marks on trees in the woods. I talked with the owner and mentioned what a nice woods it was. He agreed: "Yes, it's about the best one still left around." Most of the large trees were cut early that summer, and not long afterward, the bulldozers came.

Now, streets curve around the little island, and substantial houses sit each on its own lot landscaped with yews, Pfitzers, and spruces. The vireos, Acadian flycatchers, veeries, ovenbirds, cerulean warblers are gone, though there are robins, mourning doves, and grackles.

This woods was merely the first of the natural lands whose loss to development I've witnessed since I came to Michigan. Many others have disappeared, and farmland has gone too, more acres than natural lands, because there was more to start with. Robert Frost speculated on whether the world would end in fire or ice. Perhaps the more likely choice is between parking lots and lawns. Asphalt is the more destructive, but bluegrass would also suffice.

The term that has come to be used for this whole process is *sprawl*—in earlier times generally prefixed by "urban." A neutral, unemotional definition of sprawl is low density development that extends from cities into rural areas.

We all know the landscapes that result from sprawl. A housing development goes in on what was a farm a year ago. The new sprawl houses tend to be gingerbready, multi-gabled, and multi-thousand square feet. The owners return in the early evening from a job in the city and early the next morning are back on the expressway.

The expressway runs past similar housing developments on other now-disappeared cornfields, pastures, hayfields, and woodlots, then through a broad band of malls, discount stores, auto agencies, fast-food eateries, and motels. The middle of the city, where the sprawl dweller works, is a section of tall buildings that house banks, law firms, and corporate offices. At street level are a few stores and many restaurants and coffee houses. By 7 P.M., the sprawl dweller is either back home or tied up in a traffic jam. The streets and buildings of the central city are empty.

This is a pattern anyone can see in every part of the United States. There are a few sublime exceptions, where a city, a county, or even a state is resisting, but the pressure to sprawl is strong. We have created or at least acquiesced in the creation of a land full of places that exemplify Gertrude Stein's description: When you get there, there's no there there. To study it, we would have to compile a geography of nowhere, as James Howard Kunstler did in his 1993 book.[1]

Land owners who come to a land trust have positive and negative motivations. They want to save their land—the frog pond, the spring wild flowers, the big trees—for future generations. That is the positive motivation. The negative one is that they want to thwart sprawl. "Object: to keep forever from the hands of developers," wrote one widow who contacted the Southwest Michigan Land Conservancy with an offer to sell the family's lakefront property for less than half the market value.

Sprawl eats up natural and farm lands and leaves a landscape devoid of functional open space. As a consequence, sprawl is high-test fuel for the land conservancy movement. The urgency of saving land now, before it's too late, energizes the trust, its volunteers, and its donors. The urgency has produced a rough and ready atmosphere; land trust staff and board members may understandably have little interest in broader considerations that put the land trust movement in its environmental and conservation context. There's land to be saved, and the time is now.

Causes of Sprawl

Nevertheless, the land trust community needs to know more about sprawl than just that it's a major force driving land trust growth. "Sprawl" is a tag, a bumper sticker word, for the dysfunctional land use characteristic of most parts of the United States. It stems from the American character and from various federal, state, and local policies, many with a long history. The causes and the ill effects of sprawl are interconnected in complex ways; often they're mutually reinforcing.

The United States was almost predestined to sprawl by the way the country was settled. Quarter sections or bigger chunks of public land were sold cheaply or even given away, on the condition that the families live on the land. Some of us might wish that the deal had been 160 acres free and clear if the families promised to live in towns. But the government wanted unoccupied lands settled to generate a larger population and more commerce, and the method they used fitted well with Americans' predispositions concerning land.

This was probably not the origin of our liking for a cabin in the wilderness (today translated into a big house on five acres of last year's cornfield). Although we see this attitude as typically American, it derives from the settlers' European heritage: Owning your own house and land was the difference between being a free man and a slave. Homesteading allowed the pioneers to act out this belief.

Individualism. Americans are individualists. Part of our individualism may be genetic, the heritage of generations who came to this country because they were unwilling or unable to fit in where they came from. Some is cultural, starting at least as early as the Constitution's Bill of Rights, which are all individual rights. Our founding fathers had seen too much of the power of the government over individuals for them to feel any need to emphasize the countervailing rights of the community.

We don't like to be dependent on others. We take it amiss if governments, environmentalists, or neighbors have an opinion about what we should do with our land. We like to have our own car, so that we can go where we want when we want and not be dependent on the kindness of neighbors or the schedule of buses.

"It seems like I spend half my morning in the car," said one woman in Dade County (Florida), commenting on traffic congestion. Of her fellow commuters, she said, "They wouldn't use public transportation even if it was free. People like that independent feeling of driving to work themselves. . . ." A one-cent sales tax increase in Miami–Dade County that would have expanded Metrorail and bus service had just been turned down in a 1999 election.[2]

Individualism leads to sprawl. Sprawl in turn fosters a stronger, though lonely individualism, as we isolate ourselves in our cars and our houses and become even less connected to a community.

Observers of American culture from Tocqueville to today have worried about the balance between individualism and community in American life. The behavioral scientist B. F. Skinner spoke at Western Michigan University several times, invited by behaviorist protégés in WMU's Psychology Department. On his last visit, about 1980, Skinner surprised me by talking about the environment. His conclusion was gloomy. A surfeit of individualism is at the root of America's environmental problems, he had concluded, and until that is changed, hopes for improvement are slim.

The Automobile and the History of Sprawl. Sprawl rides in a car fueled by cheap gasoline.

Our nation's pattern of settlement laid the groundwork, but sprawl as now thought of first became evident around 1920. To make money from the increasing number of automobile travelers, filling stations and motor courts began to spring up at the edges of towns and along the highways beyond. Working in town and living in the country away from streetcar lines was encouraged by paved roads running out into rural areas and built with money from the 1916 and 1921 Federal–Aid Highway acts.[3]

Federal housing programs were begun in New Deal days to encourage home ownership. Federal Housing Authority (FHA) loans had low down payments, low interest, and an extended mortgage period of thirty years.

They made it possible for Depression-era families to buy a house when few otherwise could have afforded it.[4] It may be true that the major objective from the government's standpoint was to make work for the construction industry, but these programs, like the Homesteading Act, connected with the real estate part of the American dream. In the whole country, only 93,000 new houses were built in 1933. In the next eight years, over 2,600,000 were built, mostly with FHA loans.[5]

The programs were designed with biases that favored new single-family houses at the fringes of cities. Beginning with the Home Owners' Loan Corporation (1933) and continuing with the FHA (1934), rules were set and procedures followed that all but assured urban sprawl and its other face, central city blight.[6]

Each metropolitan area was mapped into four zones, first through fourth grade, indicating suitability for guaranteed loans. First-grade areas were ones that had newer, well-kept-up single family houses and plenty of vacant land. Third- and fourth-grade areas were characterized by such undesirable traits as old and unstylish buildings, "expiring restrictions or lack of them," and "infiltration of a lower grade population." In other words, these were the older sections of towns where blacks, Jews, and recent immigrants lived, often as renters in apartment buildings.[7]

World War II stopped sprawl for about four years; gasoline and tires were rationed and no new automobiles and few new houses were being built. In 1946, sprawl resumed with a vengeance. Returning veterans needed housing, and the government helped them with VA (Veterans' Administration) loans that were even sweeter deals than the FHA loans, which also continued. The old biases remained in place.

The golden age of the suburbs had arrived. The first house I bought, in 1963, had been built fifteen years before in a new plat on what at the end of the war had been farmland. It and millions of houses like it all over the country were the little boxes made of tickytacky that the folk singers sang about disapprovingly a little later on.

Other federal legislation continued to push sprawl. The biggest push of all came in 1956 when Dwight Eisenhower's interstate highway system was approved by Congress. There had been limited-access highways before, but most were toll roads paid for by the people who drove on them. The interstates were paid for by the federal government—that is, by every tax-payer.

The federal government got into the highway business for many reasons. The interstates served as yet another make-work program for the construction industry in a flat economic period. The stated reasons were improving safety and speeding travel for motorists and truckers. Most of us have now forgotten another reason; the interstates were also supposed to allow people to flee the cities in case of nuclear attacks and to facilitate troop and armament movements. The enabling legislation was, in fact, called the Interstate and Defense Highway Act.

Whatever the stated or unstated justifications, the interstates became expressways to sprawl. People from the outskirts and countryside didn't use
them to drive downtown to shop. Rather, urban workers used them to escape
the city every night and did their shopping at big new stores in the suburbs.

Cheap Gas. Cheap gasoline makes sprawl economically painless.

The price of gasoline ought to include the costs of cleaning up the environmental degradation and damages to public health caused by the oil industry as well as the costs of research and development of replacement energy sources. Just how much a gallon would be if these costs were included
has been studied and appears to be between $7 and $16, depending on how
completely the costs are internalized.[8] But adding even a couple of dollars
per gallon in taxes is politically impossible. Cheap gasoline is too important.
We have built a pipeline through the tundra, ringed our coasts with oil drilling platforms, and gone to war to protect the supply coming from the Middle East.

Energy is embedded in the cost of almost everything. Cheap, abundant
energy, consequently, means the easy life, which in turn means a happy and
tractable public. That's why the government is determined to keep the price
down. In the long run—or sooner—petroleum will grow scarce, and we'll
have to become efficient and live with limits. But that's not now. For now,
gasoline is still cheap. As recently as the spring of 1999, it was cheaper in
constant dollars than it had ever been before.

Property Taxes. Sprawl springs, or oozes, from many aspects of our way of
life. Federal programs have made sprawl almost impossible to resist, but
state and local laws have made their contribution. Property tax laws are
partly to blame.

Most states require that land be assessed for its "highest and best use,"
which, oddly enough, is not as farmland or a nature preserve but for the use
that would potentially yield the most money. For land near an urban fringe,
this would be development. Farmland in the vicinity of cities is sold daily
when the farmer's income from agriculture is insufficient to pay for his property taxes plus a middle-class life style.

This is no new phenomenon. Charles Eliot, founder of the America's first
land trust, wrote of the destructive influence of property taxes in New England in 1889: "Farm after farm, and garden after garden are invaded by
streets, sewers and waterpipes, owners being fairly compelled to sell lands
which are taxed more and more heavily."[9]

Some states have various forms of existing-use assessment, or equiva-
lents. These are attempts to tax the land based on its value considering current use rather than its value if sold for development. They help some landowners financially, but in the long run have proved unsuccessful in keeping
land out of the clutches of sprawl.[10] It's likely that the flaws in our property

tax system are too deep to be solved by this sort of tinkering and that only major restructuring could help.

Zoning. Zoning consists of dividing cities, townships, or counties into districts (zones) within which structural and use restrictions have been defined. That seems straightforward, with no particular emotional content. Why, then, did James Howard Kunstler write something like this?

The model of the human habitat dictated by zoning is a formless, soulless, centerless, demoralizing mess. It bankrupts families and townships. It causes mental illness. It disables whole classes of decent, normal citizens. It ruins the air we breathe. It corrupts and deadens our spirits.[11]

Zoning works, after a fashion. It's unlikely that your peaceful existence or the value of your house will be compromised by someone building a casino or a foundry in your residential zone. Probably zoning has been a mostly honest attempt to protect the health, morals, safety, and general welfare. However, the beginnings of zoning were not honest and were intended to protect, not the general welfare, but the welfare of the white and privileged.

In California in the 1880s, Chinese laundries came to function as social centers for the substantial number of Chinese originally brought to this country to build the Western railroads. San Francisco attempted to legislate against the laundries to get rid of the Chinese gathering places, but a federal court refused to go along.

The city of Modesto had a better idea. It crafted a statute that restricted laundries to "that part of the city which lies west of the railroad tracks and south of G street." Modesto had invented zoning, one zone that allowed laundries, hence Chinese, and one zone that didn't.[12]

The early attempts at zoning typically were on this model of restricting undesirable activities—and people—to a particular part of town. By 1916, New York City had put together a comprehensive zoning code, with residential, commercial, and industrial zones. A dozen years later the author of this code wrote a model zoning statute for the U.S. Department of Commerce.

The comprehensive approach to zoning has been perfected over the years, so that now most communities have a complicated structure with zones for various uses—single family housing only, for example—and with rigid specifications as to height, setbacks, parking spaces, and the like. As a result, life for most people today requires daily use of an automobile to get to their place of work, stores, physician's office, schools, the library, restaurants, government offices, the mall, the movie theater, all more or less segregated into different parts of the city.

Another result is that it has become nearly impossible to replicate the kind of neighborhood or small town that some of us think of as the best of America. On the street where I grew up, a couple of blocks from Main, a strip of lawn with trees growing in it lay between the street and the sidewalk. You could walk down the block at night and speak to people sitting on their porches and hear the St. Louis Cardinals game coming from nearly every house. Parking on the street was permitted, but most people put their car in the garage, accessible through the alley behind the houses.

Several blocks of Main Street were lined with stores—furniture stores, men's clothing, women's clothing, drugstores with soda fountains, a jewelry store with a large clock on a pole, banks, a tavern or two, an ice cream parlor, a movie-house. The post-office, the firehouse, and the police station were all in this stretch of a few blocks. Above most of the businesses were either law offices or apartments.

In most cities and townships today, you couldn't reproduce either street. Zoning and building codes wouldn't permit it.[13]

Current zoning practices have helped make cities unlivable and make fixing them difficult. The reformist planners who think of themselves as practicing New Urbanism are trying to reintroduce traditional methods of neighborhood design into the cities; in fact, Traditional Neighborhood Design is an approximate synonym for New Urbanism. We should wish them success. If people find life in the city or older suburbs interesting and satisfying, they will live there contentedly, even joyfully, rather than continually trying to escape.

Competition Between Units of Government. Another, though not the only other, way in which governments make sprawl almost inevitable is by their competition for development. Many villages, townships, counties, and even states fall all over themselves trying to entice a company or a developer to locate there. The politicians in power are often willing to provide tax breaks and even outright gifts of money to lure new development.

A few years ago, by some mischance I was flipping through one of the national business magazines. I was startled by a full-page ad that was an invitation to businesses and developers, paid for by a local taxpayer-supported booster group. The ad said, "You've got a pal in Kalamazoo." I wrote to the *Detroit Free Press* to issue a general disinvitation: "If you're thinking of coming to Kalamazoo County—don't. We're not your pals. Don't write, don't call. Stay away."

I wish I could claim that my disinvitation was effective, but I'm afraid the businesses that avoided Kalamazoo did so for other reasons. The ordinary companies that didn't come went someplace else because another government unit gave them a better deal.

The extraordinary companies—nonpolluting, educated work force, civic-minded—mostly decided to go someplace else because the local units of government here have spent too much of their time and money quarreling and competing instead of doing the things that will attract the employees that such companies want: things like making the central city attractive, building trails, adding parkland, and discouraging the destruction of the countryside by sprawl.

And so the corporations attracted here and to many similar places around the nation build not on restored brownfields, where a rational regional plan would put most commercial and industrial development, but on sites that were hayfields and marshes last year. The taxpayers suffer as they shoulder the burden of paying off the sweetheart deal the corporation got. Even more, the land, water, and air suffer as construction runs sand and silt into the streams, and, a little later, semi-trucks by the dozens clog the interstate.

Sprawl as Disproportionate Use of Land

In Michigan, it's projected that by the year 2020 the human population will grow by about 12 percent but, if current trends continue, the urbanized land will increase by 63 to 87 percent. Chicago and Los Angeles have increased their land area ten times faster than their population.[14]

Some people restrict the definition of sprawl to this disproportionality—the excess area urbanized per unit of population growth. In the old days, a million people lived on, let's say, an urban area of one million acres. A thousand added people would take up another thousand acres. Today a thousand added people take up, not one thousand more acres, but five or ten thousand. This, by the disproportionality definition, is sprawl. If the new residents were content with an acre apiece, it wouldn't be sprawl.

This definition makes an important point that otherwise tends to get obscured these days. Environmentalists in general and the land trust community in particular like to say that it's not population growth that's the threat to the natural and scenic landscape; it's sprawl. They find it unpolitic to talk about human population growth whether by natural increase or immigration.

But the disproportionate land use definition of sprawl makes clear that open land disappears whenever human populations grow. It's just that with sprawl, it disappears faster. In the long run, our only hope lies in controlling population growth.

Detrimental Environmental Effects of Sprawl

The virtual necessity to drive everywhere depletes petroleum reserves, putting us in the hole for future petroleum needs (for chemicals, for example). It also pumps more carbon dioxide into the air, hurrying global warming, and more nitrogen oxides, acidifying rain.

Sprawl eats up farmland. More than 1.4 million acres of Ohio farmland were lost between 1974 and 1992.[15] Coming from subsistence farming country, I tend to think in 40-acre fields. That 1.4 million acres is 35,000 40-acre fields, gone from farming, gone from open space. In terms of yield, the loss of 1.4 million acres means we've lost the ability to produce at least 140 million bushels of corn, just in Ohio and in less than twenty years.

A cornfield doesn't produce much in the way of wildlife, although it may help feed deer, pheasants, and crows. Forty acres in hay, on the other hand, may produce several fledgling meadowlarks, bobolinks, and grassland sparrows, at least if the first hay cutting is delayed until July or August. Along the way, it will readily produce 80 tons of hay.

Sprawl destroys forests, prairie remnants, and wetlands. What it doesn't destroy, it fragments. Between destruction and fragmentation, many animals and plants are lost and, as they go, biodiversity drops at every level from landscape to genes.

Fragmentation, hence isolation, of agricultural land leads to individual farms becoming untenable. Markets for anything except specialty crops are too far away. Farming equipment and supply stores go out of business. An enormous combine chugging along what was a country road a couple of years ago leads to commuter road rage.

You might be surprised that even wetlands are destroyed by sprawl. Aren't they legally protected? Small wetlands probably aren't federally protected anymore. Enforcement may be dependent on state agencies, which are often influenced by the political climate. Michigan has a strong wetlands act that requires the state to regulate even wetlands of less than five acres. The state Department of Environmental Quality (DEQ) is required to list them and notify property owners that they need a permit for any construction. So far, the DEQ has not even prepared the list. The Michigan chapter of The Nature Conservancy (TNC) took it upon itself to identify small wetlands having features meriting protection by TNC criteria—bogs, fens, sinkholes, breeding sites of rare amphibians—but the three hundred it identified is a small subset of what should be included based on the language of the Act.

"We, frankly, have not done a lot with that list since '96 because we've been short-staffed," the chief of the DEQ's Land and Water Management Division (LWM) was quoted as saying. The Michigan Department of Natural Resources was about to dredge two of the small wetlands with rare plants to make waterfowl habitat but refrained when its plans by chance came to the attention of the author of the TNC report. Many other sites probably have already been lost—filled, plowed, or paved over in a dry season or a dry year.

The LWM chief agreed that the agency should do something but didn't know when that would happen. "I don't know how much people would object to having a wetland on their property," he was quoted as saying. "If people start suing us all over the place, that could be a considerable effort."[16]

As for large wetlands, developers can often find a way around the regulations. Wetland mitigation procedures often permit a developer to fill in a wetland—to add a hole to a golf course, for example—by creating a wetland elsewhere. The new wetlands created in these mitigation projects up to now cannot be described as successful.

Sprawl destroys or uglifies other natural and historic features. In a sprawl suburb near where I live, a new park levelled a couple of drumlins for a tennis court and a parking lot. Drumlins are odd, teardrop-shaped glacial hills, a landform worth preserving, but the city officials didn't think so or, more likely, didn't know a drumlin from a drumstick.

Indirect Effects of Sprawl

Sprawl has ramifying indirect effects. By removing population and tax revenue, it pauperizes the cities. City facilities and services, schools, the arts, and museums are all hurt.

Sprawl makes us drive farther, over routes where multi-lane roads border strip malls in a landscape as hostile to the foot traveler as Death Valley. Cars run into other cars and run over pedestrians. The past few years, an insurance company has listed the ten most dangerous intersections, based on accident reports.[17] They're in sprawl, on the fringes of such places as Phoenix, Tulsa, Las Vegas, or Chicago. You may have to check the atlas to realize the connections, though. The top spot in the 2001 list was an intersection in Pembroke Pines, Florida, which not all of us would recognize as a small node in the vast urban fringe of Miami.

The average number of hours per year that drivers are delayed by road congestion has been calculated for 1999 as thirty-six, nationwide.[18] Perhaps this is a trivial number considering that many of us spend five hundred or one thousand hours a year commuting. Still, it means that we spend very close to one full work week each year just sitting in gridlock or behind an accident or crawling through yet one more construction zone.

In Los Angeles, the average delay was fifty-six hours per person. Since there are a lot of people driving in Los Angeles, this amounted to over 700 million hours of lost time. In other words, the annual lost time for Los Angeles adds up to more than 350,000 lost work-years—not in commuting but just in commuting delays.

One of the deadliest effects that sprawl has is destroying our interconnections with other people and our sense of belonging to a community. A political scientist, Robert Putnam, has made a small stir the past few years with articles such as the "The Strange Disappearance of Civic America." His studies show that America has undergone a loss of community since the 1970s. Putnam uses social science terminology, talking of the loss of social capital and civic engagement.

The data show that fewer and fewer people belong to or attend civic organizations, political organizations, labor unions, parent-teacher groups, youth clubs, veterans' organizations. Putnam uses strong words to summarize the trend: "There is striking evidence that the vibrancy of American civil society has notably declined . . . linked to a broad and continuing erosion of civic engagement that began a quarter century ago."[19]

Putnam demonstrates that the difference is mostly a difference between generations—specifically, between the generations that have grown up since World War II compared to those that grew up earlier. From a long list of possible causes of the decline in community, he originally decided television was most important.[20] Children growing up post–World War II spend hours per day watching TV, and many continue to do so as adults. Just the time removed from productive pursuits is significant, and to this has to be added the resulting loss of imagination, initiative, and connections with the real world.

More recently, as a result of a more complex analysis, Putnam has implicated several additional factors as having made a significant deduction from our community life. One of these is sprawl, which surged about the same time as television. In his new analysis, Putnam calculated that each additional ten minutes of commuting time cuts involvement in community affairs by 10 percent. After returning at night to the aggregation of strangers where we live, we often don't have the time or energy to drive back to a meeting or lecture.

Another investigator also tied a lack of social ties to sprawl. The culprit was the automobile; civic engagement was low in heavily automobile-dependent developments. Specifically, a study comparing neighborhoods showed that every 1 percent increase in the proportion of individuals driving alone to work decreased by a remarkable 73 percent the odds of a resident having even one social tie in the neighborhood.[21]

If, as Charles Eliot, Hugh Iltis, and others have suggested—as mentioned in chapter 3—the natural and the wild in our lives are essential for physical and mental health, the corollary may be that illness follows sprawl. Late in 2001, SprawlWatch Clearinghouse published a report by two investigators at the Centers for Disease Control and Prevention (CDC) drawing connections between sprawl and public health.[22] The main connections suggested were with obesity (and associated chronic illness) and respiratory disease. The pathway to respiratory disease is from sprawl to more driving to more air pollution to respiratory malfunction. Cited as evidence was a CDC study during the 1996 Olympic Games in Atlanta, when vehicular traffic was restricted. Peak weekday morning traffic counts for the period were down 22.5 percent, and number of asthma emergency medical events dropped 41.6 percent. Ozone levels, implicated in asthma flare-ups and an inverse indicator of general air quality, dropped 27.9 percent.

The pathways from sprawl to obesity are multiple: Sprawl leads to more time spent driving and also to an absence of trails, parks, and sidewalks;

these all predispose sprawl dwellers to less exercise, hence weight gain and development of such obesity-associated maladies as vascular disease and diabetes.

Free-marketeers, who see living in sprawl as a life-style choice—like homelessness—criticized the report as being Smart Growth advocacy masquerading as science.[23] Probably they would also dislike hearing that some people are connecting sprawl and mental health problems.

Rio Arriba County, north of Santa Fe, New Mexico, has perhaps the highest per capita death rate from heroin overdoses and other substance-abuse incidents in the United States. The director of the county Department of Health and Human Services blames sprawl.[24] In this case—as in most—"sprawl" is shorthand for a combination of related problems. Familiar signs of sprawl are present: strip development stretching out from the largest city, Española; population growth (20 percent in ten years); farmland converted to residential use by new arrivals; long-distance commutes, in this case to low-paying service jobs in Santa Fe and Los Alamos. But the setting is unfamiliar to many of us. This sprawl is superimposed on and displacing traditional village life of a largely mestizo (mixed Indian and Hispanic ancestry) population that was based on small-scale irrigated corn, squash, and chile cultivation and a barter economy.

The New Mexico secretary of health, disagreeing with the sprawl diagnosis, was quoted as saying that such drug problems could be found anywhere having the same problems of unemployment and poverty and that addiction also reflected a lack of personal responsibility.[25]

Opposing Views

For two hundred years beginning with Thomas Jefferson, city life has been denigrated. Why, now, is the city celebrated as a wonderful place to live? Don't cities pollute their own air and the water of whoever lives downstream from them? Doesn't high population density cause the same symptoms of stress typical of overcrowded rats? Aren't cities places of crime, corruption, drugs, drunkenness, and vice? What's all this talk about community? Cities are places of loneliness and alienation. There is only "the brutal, hurrying crowd, trying hard not to see," in Frank Lloyd Wright's words.[26]

That's all true, to some degree and in some places at some times. But from a land perspective, cities concentrate the unfavorable environmental effects in one small area rather than spreading them out over the whole continent. And many people have always recognized some good features of cities. Neighborhoods were what made cities livable; they still exist here and there in cities but, by and large, not in sprawl.

Some people like sprawl. Perhaps they lived in a part of the city where the housing was rundown and the streets were dangerous. Perhaps they're from a small town and grew tired of everyone knowing their business. They like being able to live anonymously in relatively crime-free sprawl. They like their big house with a big garage, a big lot, a big lawn, and a nice (and big) grocery store a few miles away. If where they live suffers from a loss of open space and a lack of community identity, they haven't noticed.

Another pro-sprawl position is ideological, rather than oblivious. The free market has given us sprawl, so it must be good. (Never mind all the local, state, and federal policies that have promoted abandonment of the cities.) The alternative, what has been called "Smart Growth," is actually a stealth method of advancing a left-wing anti-growth policy, according to the free-market folks. [27]

To contradict the anti-sprawl arguments, a conservative columnist cited a study by a free-market think tank to the effect that 75 percent of the U.S. population lives on just 3.5 percent of the country's land area. At that rate, just think how many people the United States could hold if we filled up the rangelands, wheat fields, pastures, orchards, woodlots, forests, deserts, swamps, marshes, parks, refuges, and sanctuaries.[28] I make it 5.7 billion.

The free market, even if it were really free, doesn't necessarily give the right answer. Sprawl is a social trap, a situation in which short-term benefits to the players, such as homeowners and local governments, don't correspond with the long-term interests of society, or even of the individuals and governments.[29] People build a house in the country for the open space, but the open space disappears under the houses of thousands more who came for the same reason.

Hopes for the Future

A gratifying amount of attention and some action has been generated to counteract sprawl. Newspapers publish articles. Cities and counties hire consultants, who recommend Smart Growth. The Land Trust Alliance (with help from the Trust for Public Land) compiles the outcomes of ballot proposals to fund open space acquisition and finds high percentages of them passing. A well-publicized example was the 1998 New Jersey vote to dedicate $98 million per year from the state sales tax for the next thirty years, to buy a million acres.[30]

The planners and landscape architects of the New Urbanism and related schools recommend redeveloping our cities to make them worth living in. We must reconstruct neighborhoods where we can walk to the grocery store, the dentist's office, and the movies. We must re-make the public realm—the streets, sidewalks, boulevards, parks, and gathering places—for the common good and a renewed civic life. We must build trails and greenways that we can use to get to school or work and, for longer trips, reinstitute mass transit as functional as most major cities had as late as the 1940s.

When we have to invade greenfield land, we must try to build communities where people can live, shop, and work or, if they must go to work elsewhere, where they can bike, use mass transit, or car-pool.

Have any of the New Urbanism communities been entirely successful? Many of them look like nice places to live, but few have shown much interest in lowering environmental impact—by emphasizing durability and energy efficiency in construction, for example.[31] Rarely has the idea of adding businesses reduced auto travel. Most of the jobs available onsite are service jobs, filled by people who drive in from the surrounding area. Most of the people who can afford to buy houses in the developments drive to higher-paying jobs offsite, in the city or the sprawl.

Of the New Urbanism developments I'm aware of, I like Prairie Crossing north of Chicago best. House lots (317) occupy only 132 acres of the 668-acre site. There are 160 acres of reconstructed prairie, 13 acres of wetlands, and a community-supported organic garden. Part of the Prairie Crossing land is protected by conservation easements held by the Conservation Fund.[32] Houses are traditional-looking but energy efficient; however, they're expensive by Midwestern standards. Within its borders are two railway stations, one on a line running to Milwaukee, the other a Chicago Metra station. Trails run though it and connect with the Liberty Prairie Reserve, an adjacent 2,500 acres.

Making the cities more livable is one of a very few ways to slow the destruction of the countryside, so we must hope for the best. But the road won't be easy; most of the forces driving sprawl also oppose walkable communities.

A Philadelphia suburb, Lower Moreland, whose residents are largely escapees from the city, had by 1999 reached the point where 80 percent of the township had been built out. A local developer became converted to the Traditional Neighborhood Design (TND) approach, after a career in which he'd built some 10,000 houses in standard plats. In March 2000, he brought to the planning commission the design for Woodmont, 107 houses on 42 acres, but on small lots around commons areas.[33] There would be porches and sidewalks, and the garages would be on alleys, rather than snout-like projections at the front. Eight acres of woods at one corner of Woodmont would be set aside as a nature preserve. It was not a radical example of TND, but even so, almost nothing in the design could be built without amending Lower Moreland's zoning ordinances.

The response by the residents and planning commission was hostile. If we wanted houses crowded together, people said, we could have stayed in Philly. The alleys would bring trash and crime. A store included in the design would attract young troublemakers. One planner, from another Philadelphia suburb, summed up the mind-set: "One acre on the cul-de-sac equals nirvana."

In an effort to educate the opponents, the developer offered a free bus trip to Kentlands, a famous TND in Maryland. He got four takers.

After several months of government inactivity, the developer filed a proposal for a standard plat. "Intentionally uninspired, unabashedly ordinary," the *Philadelphia Inquirer* called it. This plan produced some negative comments about the small amount of open space—not that it was insufficient, but that even this small amount might attract undesirables. A woman from a next-door development said, "I don't want to hear the noise of children playing basketball till 10 o'clock at night. We live in a quiet, rural neighborhood."

The Natural Lands Trust, a Philadelphia-area trust founded in 1961, had contracted with Lower Moreland in 1999 to provide advice on land use. This was through the trust's Growing Greener program, subtitled "Putting Conservation into Local Codes."[34] The full program, started in 1996, involves a community audit, a map of lands that ought to be protected, recommendations on zoning regulations, and designs of conservation subdivisions for specific sites.

Relatively few land trusts involve themselves in these issues. There is one big argument for involvement: If land use planning isn't improved, the landscape of tomorrow will be a bleak place. There are several reasons not to be involved: Planning, writing ordinances, and designing subdivisions take time and personnel that could be spent saving land directly by doing deals. When controversial issues arise, like Woodmont, the land trust may receive public attention and criticism that could detract from its main mission.

To what degree land trusts choose to become directly involved with land use issues, to what degree they support constructive land use proposals and work against destructive ones will be decided by each land trust based on its mission and circumstances.

If all the Smart Growth initiatives fall by the wayside, if the New Urbanism and Traditional Neighborhood Design hopes are subverted, land trusts will still be battling sprawl, by saving land. It may not be as much land as ought to be saved, but at least this land will not be developed, ever. And the land trust people doing the saving—the volunteers, staff, and every member—will be part of a group in which a strong sense of community lives and grows.

3 WHY SAVE LAND?

"In what way does the sooty tern serve mankind?" someone asked one of my old southern Illinois chums, later on when he was curator of birds at a museum. The sooty tern is a graceful black-and-white bird of the Dry Tortugas and surrounding waters. Some people would save the sooty tern based just on its grace and beauty without worrying about how else it serves mankind. Some who would save the tern might not be so generous to a mosquito, a skunk, or a snake.

Not just species but whole ecosystems may seem dispensable. Obviously, this was true of the bur oak openings, the mesic oak savannas of the northern Midwest, because they're gone. Their close relatives, the tall-grass prairies, are not quite gone, but only because of the hardiness or wide tolerance range of some of their component species.

The near-obliteration of the prairie was mostly a side effect of the settlers' attempts to make all the land turn a profit, but a kind of anti-nature or anti-wilderness ideology was also involved. John James Ingalls, senator from Kansas from 1879 to 1891, warned that the success of the state

cannot be indefinitely continued on prairie grass. This will nourish mustangs, antelope, Texas cattle, but not thoroughbreds. It is the product of an uncultured soil. . . . If we would have prosperity commensurate with our opportunities, we must look to Blue Grass. It will raise the temperature, increase the rainfall, improve the climate, develop a higher Fauna and Flora, and consequently a loftier attendant civilization.[1]

Well, why should humans allow a species of plant or animal or a type of biotic community to exist? If poisonous snakes might bite us, why not get rid of them? Since it's hard to tell poisonous and non-poisonous ones apart, it might be just as well to get rid of the whole suborder Serpentes. If a marsh stands in the way of building our dream house, on land we own free and clear, shouldn't we be able to fill it in and get on with our life?

Isn't it true that all other species and the ecosystems of the earth exist on our sufferance? We are the dominant species of the Earth; in fact, it has been said to us that we have dominion over every living thing. We are, in short, the boss. At our convenience, we may let some wild nature survive, but if we say it goes, it goes.

We may not hear this point of view from most of our friends. Few of them are likely to ask, "What is the sooty tern good for?" If they did, we might well respond, "What are *you* good for?" But sometimes a smart answer won't suffice. Questions that may seem misguided to us may, nevertheless, be sincere requests for information.

A land trust aiming to save cedar barrens or the habitat of the Santa Cruz long-tailed salamander should be able to give a satisfying explanation to the public—and to itself—why a piece of land or a species ought to be saved from obliteration or extinction. That's why it's well to look systematically at the philosophical and factual underpinnings of the mission of land trusts: Why save land?

We can put the reasons into three categories—aesthetic, practical, and ethical or moral—though we could, of course, use a more complicated classification. Most of what follows deals with saving natural lands. Some trusts save farmland as part or the whole of their mission. The arguments for saving farmland, mostly in the practical and aesthetic categories, are discussed in chapter 12.

Aesthetic Justifications

Who has an aesthetic sense so deficient that they don't appreciate the sight of a wood duck or the sound of a wood thrush? A sunset over a wild marsh, the cathedral look of a redwood grove or a beech-maple forest are beautiful. To many of us, this is a compelling reason to preserve them.

Although a powerful inspiration, aesthetics has too many limitations to be a complete argument for preserving species and natural areas. To begin with, beauty is in the eye of the beholder. If we showed a random sample of Americans a video tape of great egrets feeding in a coastal marsh or a bald eagle sailing above a wild lake, I'll bet a majority would vote to preserve both. The verdict might be thumbs down, though, on a good many other species. Cockroaches could go, along with wood roaches, palmetto bugs, and big beetles.

We might get similar results with plant communities and landscapes. Some, such as the temperate rainforests of the Northwest, the longleaf pine savannas of the Southeast, the Sonoran desert, and the mixed mesophytic forests of the Appalachians are obvious winners. Several others are marginal at best. Floodplain forest in the Midwest, with its mucky soil, skinny trees, and frequent windthrow doesn't suggest comparisons with sacred groves to most people. Wetlands, in general, are appreciated now for their practical services, but well into the 1960s, most people thought of them as wastelands, to be drained or filled and turned into something better.

Then, too, for many people, handsome is as handsome does. Few people would argue that steel mills along the shores of the Great Lakes are more beautiful than the sand dunes and marshes they displaced. But industry means jobs and taxes—at least for awhile—so the beauty of greenbacks needs to be added on the industrial side of the equation.

Many of the early settlers in Michigan took land on or at the edge of the prairies. In old age, they would reminisce that, as nice as their farms were now, with their white fences and neat fields of corn and hay, the land had never been as beautiful as when in a state of nature. By then, the only prairie left was a few narrow strips along the oldest railroad lines.

The settlers did appreciate the beauty of the prairies. They appreciated more what the prairie soil could do: Grow cash crops that brought prosperity to the family.

Saving land so that its beauty can be enjoyed by us, today, and also by future generations is a powerful argument for many people. Although it has limitations, the aesthetic argument is probably the one most persuasive argument a land trust can use for most of its land projects. Photographs and, better yet, field trips, are important tools to show land owners what they have that's worth saving and to help potential financial donors see what they'd be helping to preserve.

Practical Justifications

There are also many practical reasons why land should be protected. Some of these may be convincing to persons not persuaded by aesthetic arguments alone.

In 1917, a committee of the Ecological Society of America—the Committee on the Preservation of Natural Conditions—tried to list the remaining natural areas of North America. It was an enormous task, and the committee inevitably fell short of such an ambitious goal. Nevertheless, its 1926 report, a 761-page volume called the *Naturalist's Guide to the Americas,* is a useful overview of what remained and what was already gone in the early twentieth century.[2]

The book begins by listing uses of natural areas. Someone who is proud to call himself a practical man will often choose one of the narrower definitions of the term "practical." Such a person might wonder at the first use listed in the *Naturalist's Guide:* the value of natural areas to literature and art.

Literature and Art. A writer can, if necessary, find nature to write about in an abandoned landfill.[3] Most nature literature, though, has dealt with more nearly pristine areas. Poets need such areas for inspiration. The rest of us need them for reference.

How can we understand *My Ántonia* if the prairie is gone? What will we make of Marjorie Kinnan Rawlings' writings if the sand-pine scrub continues to be converted to citrus groves, theme parks, and subdivisions? James

Fenimore Cooper's novel *The Oak Openings* is already ungrounded, with descriptions of Michigan oak lands that can be encountered only in the pages of pioneer recollections.

Landscape Architecture. The second use of natural preserves listed by the *Naturalist's Guide* is for the landscape architect. Some may think this value is insignificant. Why do we need natural areas to teach us to stack railroad ties or to plant shrubby potentilla around the entrance of a McDonald's?

Landscape architecture was begun in this country by giants—Frederick Law Olmsted and Charles Eliot—and there have been occasional giants since—Jens Jensen and Ian McHarg, for example.

Olmsted designed New York City's Central Park and set forth principles for a National Park system in a report on Yosemite in 1865 while John Muir was still waiting out the Civil War in Canada.[4] Eliot, as we know, was responsible for the Trustees of Reservations and the Boston metropolitan park system.

Jens Jensen, a Danish immigrant, arrived at ideas of landscape design much like those of Eliot after exposure to the prairies and sand dunes of the Chicago area. In 1911, he was one of the founders (with the plant ecologist Henry Chandler Cowles, among others) of the Prairie Club, a kind of midwestern Appalachian Mountain Club.[5] A little later he founded the Friends of Our Native Landscape. Both organizations were involved in the establishment of Indiana Dunes State Park and the Cook County Forest Preserve system.[6]

Ian McHarg, who grew up in Scotland, founded a Department of Landscape Architecture and Regional Planning at the University of Pennsylvania. His 1969 book on ecologically based planning, *Design with Nature,* has been as widely read by ecologists and conservationists as by planners and landscape architects.[7]

Much of what these men did would now be classified as land-use planning, and we must hope that planners of today are as grounded in ecology and as appreciative of natural areas as they were.

Landscape architects in the narrow sense often do not seem to be practicing the promise of the giants; but they should. In the *Naturalist's Guide,* Stanley White, professor of landscape architecture at the University of Illinois, wrote that natural areas teach both architect and layman what beautiful landscapes look like. The architect learns what to strive for and how to achieve it. The layman learns what he should ask for. White concluded:

We must bring to the most humble cottage in all parts of the land at least a suggestion of nature's charm, power and delicacy, the inspiration for which, unless these natural preserves are secured, will disappear for all times in spirit and in fact.[8]

Although much current landscape architecture is hum-drum, the strongest movement in the field today follows the example of White, Eliot, Olmsted, and Jensen in using natural vegetation types as models for landscaping. Examples range from residential lots to industrial sites to whole developments. A national organization, Wild Ones, is devoted to natural landscaping. It began in Wisconsin in 1979 and now has around 3,000 members in about thirty-five chapters in a dozen states, mostly midwestern. Its newsletter, *Wild Ones Journal,* includes information on natural landscape projects, techniques, and practitioners.

Our Innate Need for Wildness. Another practical value of natural areas at which some practical men and women might quibble is the innate human need for open space, natural land, or even wilderness. Nearly everyone will agree that a free-flowing stream in a wooded valley or a forest full of spring wildflowers is valuable as scenery and as a place to escape from the pressures of modern life—an escape from urban closeness, in the language of conservation easements.

What I'm suggesting is something more: That despite the remarkable ecological amplitude of humans—their ability to survive under a variety of conditions including ones with no contact with wildness—they need wild nature for optimal functioning. Humans are the product of a million or more years of evolution, most of which occurred in grassland, forest, and savanna, not condos and parking lots. I suspect that Hugh Iltis, a University of Wisconsin professor of botany, was right when he wrote more than thirty years ago that "for our physical and mental well-being nature in our daily lives is an indispensable biological need."[9] We may remind ourselves that Charles Eliot said much the same thing eighty years earlier in proposing the Trustees of Reservations.

The adaptability of humans makes the existence of the need for nature a difficult proposition to test, but there are studies that support it. One example: Bavarian high school students ranked positively statements like "I have a sense of well-being in the presence of nature," and "I would really enjoy sitting at the edge of a pond watching dragonflies in flight." They reacted negatively to ones such as "I prefer if trees in a forest stand in neat rows."[10]

This was a questionnaire study about preferences and attitudes, but experimental studies showing that living with nature is good for us have also been done. One study tried to get at how various environments differ in their ability to relieve stress.[11] Undergraduate students were hooked up to a machine like a polygraph and shown two 10-minute videos. The first, shown as a stressor, was a training film for woodworking classes showing realistic simulated accidents. Immediately following it, the students viewed a video showing (with accompanying sounds) one of three basic environments: a natural scene, a commercial street with auto and truck traffic, and an outdoor shopping mall with foot traffic.

The physiological measures all showed that the gory mutilations of the woodshop video were effective stressors. While watching the second video, all three experimental groups showed reduced levels of stress, but stress dropped faster and lower for those watching natural scenes. Actually, one measure of stress, blood pressure, stayed at the same elevated level for people shown the traffic video.

In another study, students (at a different university) with dormitory rooms looking out on a woodland scored better on standard psychological tests measuring their ability to focus or pay attention than students whose views consisted of buildings and parking lots.[12]

Two other, older studies using the same design of natural versus man-made views studied health effects directly. At a Michigan penitentiary, prisoners on one side of several cell blocks could see the countryside of fields and trees. Those in the same cell blocks but on the opposite side looked into the prison yard. Prisoners in these inside cells went to sick call about 20 percent more often than those housed where they could look out at the countryside.[13]

Recovery rates of patients following gall bladder surgery were studied in a suburban hospital between 1971 and 1982. Patients with a view of the woods went home a day earlier than other patients matched as to age, sex, and other relevant characteristics whose room faced a brick wall. Those with a view of the woods were also less cranky and needed fewer doses of strong pain-killers.[14]

As with many studies of human behavior, these leave room for argument. Most persons with a vested interest, monetary or doctrinaire, in unrestricted land development will remain unconvinced. But even if a study proved incontrovertibly that our health and lives are poorer without natural areas, that would not mean the battle to protect land had been won. Almost everyone can agree that colored sugar water with caffeine is not a healthy drink for children, yet one of the big stories of 2000 and 2001 was the highly lucrative contracts public school systems were signing with soft drink companies.

Perhaps we don't need any test other than the nonscientific one each of us can perform: Ask ourselves whether we can do without nature in our own lives. Then follow botanist Iltis's advice to a botanical conference:

If you love your children as much as you love your flowers, get involved, . . . so that their descendants a thousand years hence, too, can revel in a tall grass prairie in full bloom, watch a bumblebee on a prairie clover, band hawks in an unpolluted fall and find joy and meaning in a diverse environment, the one which selected man and his evolutionary companions, the only environment to which life, and man, is, and ever will be, adapted.[15]

Ecosystem Services: Our Free Lunch. I strolled outside this morning on an unseasonably warm November day, tossed some scraps into the compost bin, and took a short walk through the woods before coming back to sit down at the computer.

On that trip, my eyes didn't cloud with cataracts, and my skin didn't crust over with cancer, because little ultraviolet radiation reached ground level. I had no trouble breathing, because the oxygen concentration was fine. I didn't test it, of course, but if the oxygen content was even slightly off from 21 percent, I'd be astonished. However, I know that atmospheric carbon dioxide content isn't constant. Forty years ago, about the time I finished graduate school, it was about 315 parts per million; now, it's pushed past 350 ppm. Rounding off, it's gone from 0.03 to 0.04 percent of the atmosphere.

The reason I had oxygen to breathe is that green plants give off oxygen in photosynthesis while tying up carbon in living and, later, dead tissue. The presence of plant-derived oxygen allows for the formation of ozone in the upper atmosphere. The screening effect of this ozone layer is why I didn't suffer the deleterious effects of UV radiation.

Not just the presence of oxygen, but the precise setting of oxygen at 21 percent is the result of biological processes. This buffering isn't yet fully understood but involves the activities of microorganisms in the oceans and other wet places of the world. Carbon dioxide content is obviously not buffered as precisely, but if all the carbon dioxide that has been dumped into the atmosphere as the result of coal and oil burning and deforestation had stayed there, the concentration would be higher than it is. Much of it has, instead, been processed biologically to end up as new plant biomass and as carbonate sediments.

So the ecosystems around us are doing work on our behalf and—to the degree that we've avoided interfering—life is good. But we are interfering. Our climate is changing through the addition of greenhouse gases to the atmosphere. Today, it felt good to be outside with no coat or hat, but it's unlikely that our heedless alteration of the carbon cycle will end up being favorable, on balance. And some of the same gases that are contributing to the greenhouse effect, notably the CFCs (chlorofluorocarbons), are reducing the ozone layer, increasing our risk of cataracts and cancer and tending to compromise our immune systems.

Looked at anthropocentrically, all these benefits supplied to us by the biosphere have been given the name "ecosystem services." I was aware of other ecosystem services as I took my walk. For example, earthworms and bacteria and a large number of other organisms in the soil were breaking down the organic matter in the compost and also the tree leaves that had fallen to the forest floor. In time, the nutrients contained in them will be returned to the soil where they will be available for a new round of cycling through forest and garden.

A partial list of ecosystem services includes three already mentioned:

• provision of a breathable atmosphere;
• protection from UV radiation;

- soil development and renewal of fertility;

and also:

- purification of air and water;
- tempering droughts and floods;
- detoxification and decomposition of wastes;
- pollination;
- dispersing and planting seeds;
- protection of soils and shores from erosion;
- maintenance of biodiversity with such effects as lowering pest damage;
- provision of scenery, beauty, and intellectual interest.[16]

In one sense, ecosystem services are free. The processes were going on before we arrived on Earth and they will go on after we're gone. Even though they are free, they do have value. Suppose, for example, that we killed off all the pollinating insects. How much would it cost to provide that service by technological means?

We could make a stab at calculating the cost, starting perhaps with information on the oil-palm plantations of Malaysia. These trees were imported from West Africa without their natural pollinator so that pollination had to be done by hand. When the oil-palm industry thought to introduce the weevil pollinator a few decades later, in the early 1980s, the switchover from human to beetle saved $150 million per year.[17] This was how much it had been costing to replace by human effort the services of an insect pollinator—in a country where wages were so low the average family income was $520 per month.

But, of course, if all pollinators disappeared, our society's first step would be to decide how little replacing we could get by with. Doubtless there are many plants that don't need to be pollinated. Why bother to pollinate goldenrods or asters or spring beauty or may-apple? Pokeweed? No need. There are probably thousands of species that we could let bloom on in purity for years or decades and eventually expire without issue.

The usual outcome when we replace natural processes with technology is an impoverishment. It's like moving to Biosphere II, rather than living on the green Earth.

In 1989, the New York City water supply failed EPA standards. Over the years, the water quality had been degraded by changes in the watershed in the Catskills, mostly from dairy farming. One solution to making the water potable again would have been a new water treatment facility at a cost of $3 to 8 billion. The facility would have cost additional hundreds of millions of dollars per year to run. These were the costs of technologically compensating for the weakened ecosystem services. It was decided that their level could be raised and a comparable improvement in water quality obtained by restoration efforts in the watershed. About $20 million is being spent on conservation easements with provisions that curb erosion, prevent contamination of streams with livestock waste, and restrict the use of fertilizers and pesticides.[18]

A few years ago, thirteen ecologists and economists pulled together a lot of data and tried to figure out the value of ecosystem services globally. What would be the cost of technologically replacing all the natural processes that benefit us? The bill came to about $33 trillion per year, for services rendered.[19] No one would claim that this first attempt is precise or accurate, but it's probably not an overestimate.

Let's just note one big conclusion: There's no way we could pay for these services. The gross national product (GNP) for the whole world is about $25 trillion.[20]

Since the value of ecosystem services is so self-evidently great, a naive reaction—from someone like me, for example—would be to say, Why not just hang on to all the natural lands and waters that are still left, to try to keep a little safety margin? But this isn't the way a practical person, like an economist, would approach the question.

He or she would say, Sure, having that big block of forest moderates climate, helps prevent floods, provides predators that damp pest insect outbreaks, et cetera, et cetera. Those things are worth a little something to a lot of people, but what about the needs of the owner? Keeping all this land in woods is costing money. The owner could cut part of it, sell the timber, and build some nice condos. Maybe some time in the future, cutting another thousand acres of forest would tip the balance and set off some global catastrophe, and we ought to try to avoid that. But let's make sure to cut all the forest up to that line. We just need to define the line.

Ecosystem services are real, they have value, many of them are irreplaceable. One reason for saving natural lands is to maintain these services, and nearly any natural land will do. Endangered orchids and grizzly bears do not contribute any more to most ecosystem services than common species of plants stabilizing a slope or blue jays planting acorns.

Making sure that the systems on which ecosystem services depend are not degraded is easy to do on preserves, lands that a land trust owns. It's harder on land protected by a conservation easement, but protecting ecosystem services ought to be a major consideration in drafting easements.

Ecosystem Goods. Natural and human-dominated ecosystems also yield goods—products—as well as services. We plant and harvest fields and eat the wheat or corn directly or as beef or chicken. We cut down the trees on managed or (up-till-then) natural forest lands and turn the wood into pulp or lumber. Food, wood, and fiber are necessary resources for human life, but lands used to produce these in quantity tend to yield diminished ecosystem services.

A cornfield, for example, adds oxygen to the atmosphere and sequesters carbon. But because corn is an annual, the carbon is fairly quickly released back into the air (as CO_2) from the metabolic activities of animals—chiefly, cows, pigs, and ourselves—and decomposers. The consumers and decomposers remove from the air about the same amount of oxygen as the corn crop released in its growth. Because of the cultivation of the soil and the absence of perennial roots, the cornfield also does a poor job of erosion control. Lands devoted to human residence, commerce, and industry also tend to show low levels of many ecosystem services.

One of the practical arguments often put forth for preserving nature is that it may harbor valuable crops and chemicals that have not yet been discovered or, at least, are not yet exploited commercially. Most often made in discussions of tropical rain forest, the argument applies to all natural ecosystems.

The argument may be as simple as the idea that there are a lot of edible plants and animals out there that might bring something tasty or healthy to the tables of the world. An interesting development, mostly in the past dozen years, has been selling, marketing (and eating) of the American matsutake growing in the forests of the Pacific Northwest. Permits to gather these mushrooms from Forest Service lands are bringing in hundreds of thousands of dollars per year. Sales of the mushrooms had reached $41 million by 1992.[21]

The ecosystems of the world are repositories of chemicals and genetic material that have been synthesized in the three billion years of evolution on Earth. Some of the chemicals are undoubtedly of medical value. About half of our current medicines are based on plant, animal, or microbe chemicals. Old examples are quinine, aspirin, and penicillin. Somewhat newer ones include anti-cancer agents from the yew tree of our Pacific Northwest and from the rosy periwinkle of Madagascar. A compound, sirolimus (rapamycin), derived from an Easter Island soil fungus, began to be used a few years ago to help prevent rejection of kidney transplants. Then, in 2001, a new use for sirolimus was found in counteracting the re-narrowing of coronary arteries after balloon angioplasty. If the stents—the metal mesh tubes inserted into coronary arteries after angioplasty—are coated with sirolimus, a study showed the rate of reclosing to be reduced from around 20 percent to close to zero.[22]

Those arguing for the preservation of nature on practical grounds also point to the storehouses of genes that our ecosystems are maintaining for us. Biotechnology draws, not on the end-product chemicals, but on the genes that tell cells to make them. Currently, such chemicals as insulin for human use and both bovine and human growth hormones are made by transgenic bacteria in chemical factories. Who knows what genes await us in the deserts, rain forests, and coral reefs of the world?

Most of the talk about "bioprospecting"—hunting for genes and biological compounds for human commerce—involves the tropics, but several useful chemicals have come from temperate regions. One example is ivermectin, isolated from a soil fungus collected in Japan. Many people know of ivermectin as the heartworm preventative they give their dogs once a month, but it's a broad-spectrum anti-parasitic drug.

An innovative collaboration for temperate zone bioprospecting was put together in 1998 by Cornell University, the Finger Lakes Land Trust, and the drug company Schering-Plough. Fungi were collected by Cornell mycologists over a period of three years at the 286-acre Lindsay-Parsons Biodiversity Preserve of the Land Trust, cultured as necessary, and sent on to Schering-Plough for screening. The land trust received a fee for collecting privileges and will get a share of the profits from any new drugs.[23]

The potential for food, medicines, and other as-yet-undiscovered products is an argument for protecting nature that appeals to some of us, but not all. We are being asked for prudential restraint. Protect the tropical forests because here may be chemicals or genes that will do us good some time in the future? No businessman likes this idea as a general proposition. As against a certain profit this year from cutting down the rain forest, a possible profit years or decades away has little allure.

Research and Education. The Committee on the Preservation of Natural Conditions listed several good and true reasons for protecting natural areas in the *Naturalist's Guide;* however, the main reason the committee members, personally, wanted lands protected was for biological research. Useful ecological research can be done in laboratories, farm fields, conifer plantations, and vacant lots, even abandoned buildings in the middle of the city. But these simplified, artificial situations need to be related to the real biological world, the unreconstructable baseline generated by the mutual evolution of plants, animals, and microbes interacting through time.[24] Natural areas are the touchstone.

The essays in nature educator May Theilgaard Watts's book *Reading the Landscape of America,* are accounts of field trips, some in her college classes, some with other groups, some she led herself. One begins

"You're walking on a history book," said the professor. "It happens, you may notice, to have a flexible cover."

"And to be extremely absorbing," said the undergraduate, using both hands to pull his other foot out of the ooze.

That was my first introduction to Mineral Springs bog—to any bog.

A member of the class broke through the flexible cover that day, up to her waist, and had to lie down on the sphagnum moss and cranberries before we could pry her out.[25]

Field trips to bogs are the way to learn about bogs, field trips to desert are the way to learn about desert, and trips to heron colonies, the way to learn about heron nesting. You learn by doing, St. Francis de Sales said in the seventeenth century, and many others have said similar things since.

My impression is that the use of field trips is declining. Probably there are many reasons: fewer natural areas still exist in or near urban areas; there is the liability issue; class periods have been shortened; the teachers who come out of today's biology departments know much about molecules and little about the biota. Whatever the reasons, the trend is unfortunate. A student can learn a great deal about forest succession from a slide show and a computer simulation. But being on the ground, seeing a canopy of oaks and an understory of maples and beeches, gives an in-the-bones kind of understanding of the process that is otherwise hard for most of us to achieve.

Others besides biologists can use preserves for teaching and research. Foresters can learn timber cruising and the value of standing dead trees for wildlife. Historians can learn the connection between human settlement patterns and plant communities. Agriculture students can learn about soil as a living system.

Land trusts can't solve all the problems of education, but they can help provide accessible areas for study. They can lead educational trips of their own. They shouldn't duplicate what the local nature center does, but they can design trips that give adults and especially children a feeling for the land and our connection with it.

Cost of Community Services. One practical reason for saving land, based on strictly economic considerations, and applicable to all types of open lands, is of special relevance for land trusts: This is the low requirements for tax-supported community services by any kind of open space.

There are about 62,000 cities, villages, and other local governmental units in the United States. Somewhere at this moment, in one or more of those, a councilman is saying either, "We've got to get more development in here to expand our tax base," or "We've got to get some of these tax-exempt properties back on the tax rolls."

Two of the myths fostered and sometimes believed by politicians are that development lowers tax rates and that tax-exempt properties raise them. Neither is true, though the truth may be more complicated than most politicians care to deal with. Development does increase "the tax base." Adding new taxable property usually means that the total amount of property tax collected by the city goes up. What is not true is the implication that this will lower the taxes paid by the taxpayers already there. In fact, it will probably raise their taxes because it's unlikely that new development will pay as much in taxes as it costs in services. What the increased tax base does is give the city council and the city manager more money to play around with. You will know if your city has a history of using its revenues wisely.

Well over eighty studies have been completed of the cost of community services (COCS) for various types of land use.[26] They've been done in twenty-odd states, from Maine to Washington and Georgia to Utah. If we look at a one-year balance sheet of cost of services versus taxes paid, the results are always the same and easily summarized. Residential development costs much more in services than it brings in in taxes. Open space such as farmland and preserves costs much less in services than the amount it pays in taxes. Commercial and industrial development have ratios similar to farmland.

Table 1. Cost of Community Services Relative to $1.00 Paid in Taxes

| Locality (year) | Land Use Category | | |
	Residential	Commercial/ industrial	Farmland & other open space
Massachusetts/Brewster (2000)	$1.30	$0.48	$0.31
Georgia/Oconee Co. (1998–1999)	$1.09	$0.80	$0.94
Michigan/Scio Twp. (1994–1995)	$1.40	$0.26	$0.62
Texas/Hays Co. (1997–1998)	$1.26	$0.30	$0.33
Washington/Skagit Co. (1994)	$1.25	$0.30	$0.51

Table 1 gives a small sampling of COCS studies.[27] The values in the table are the costs of providing services for each land use category relative to each dollar paid in taxes. For example, in Brewster, Massachusetts, residential properties require services costing $1.30 for every $1.00 in taxes they pay.

Residential development is very demanding of community services. The new plats need roads, and the higher population generates more traffic on existing roads, which need more repairs, traffic lights, et cetera. There are the costs of new water lines, sewers, and land-fills. Planning and mental health departments need more staff, and the courts and probation officers have bigger case loads. Police and fire/rescue costs go up: more personnel, more equipment, more miles traveled.

These are facts we all know, but just to get some figures on one category of services, a farming area in Michigan with rapid urban sprawl showed the apportionment of police and fire calls displayed in table 2.[28]

The biggest expense tied to residential development is usually schools. New developments require new schools, if not now, eventually. The schools need more teachers, more clerks and administrators, and more equipment and supplies. Most children get to school on buses, so new plats mean more buses are needed, and they travel farther.

In a study of three towns in Maine, a remarkable statistic emerged that puts the cost of residential development in a new perspective. Consider an average-sized family living in a median-priced home. They would have to pay property taxes for 170 years to pay for twelve years of public school education for their children.[29]

Residential development never pays for itself; rather, it has to be subsi-

Table 2. Apportionment of Service Calls in Sprawl Area

	Police (% of time)	Fire (% of number)
Residential	67	51
Commercial/Industrial	30	39
Agricultural	3	10

dized with increased tax rates to other taxpayers. Without this increase, the quality of community services to all will necessarily decline.

Although it's true that residential development doesn't pay for itself, this doesn't mean that all residential development is equal. A study in Loudon County, Virginia, illustrates the differences. High-density developments (4.4 or more households per acre, such as might be found in a section of a city with a mixture of single-family dwellings and apartments or condos) had a ratio of costs to taxes of 1.26. In other words, for every dollar paid in taxes by one of these households, it required about a dollar and a quarter in services.[30]

Medium-density developments (2.7 households per acre) had a similar ratio, 1.23. Rural cluster developments (1 household per acre) had a ratio of 1.69. Rural sprawl developments (0.2 households per acre; that is, 5-acre lots) had a ratio of 1.82. The high-priced single-family houses on these big lots required $1.82 in services for every $1.00 they paid in taxes.

Politicians who have run into COCS data and are scuffling to counter it sometimes bring up gated communities and retirement villages. Gated communities that pay for their own streets and security force will, to that extent, cost the other taxpayers less; however, I haven't heard of any gated communities that run their own school system. I know of an upscale, though not gated, community that's operating a charter school, but charter schools are tax-supported.

Areas with large concentrations of retirees tend to have fewer children and less need for schools. But retirees want amenities. Preserved land and open space are attractions for these desirable residents with their pension dollars and low requirements for schools, police, and reproductive health agencies.

On the basis of COCS studies, commercial and industrial developments seem to be good deals, costing perhaps fifty cents for every dollar they pay in taxes. But more sophisticated fiscal impact analyses cast doubt on even these types of development. Beginning around 1990, results began to come in showing that nearly any kind of development is a net fiscal loser.[31] As a result, many well-run communities began to impose "impact fees" on developers. The rationale was that growth, if it's to happen, should pay its own way.

Have things changed? Did development once pay its way, but now it doesn't? Perhaps not; during the great growth period of the 1950s to 1970s local development was heavily subsidized by government. In the Reagan presidency, public financing to support private development dried up, first at the federal level and then at the state level, leaving local communities to deal with growth pretty much on their own.

Several reasons may account for the fact that areas with commercial and industrial development are fiscally worse off than low-growth areas. One reason is that new jobs draw people. If a new factory opens, local residents may fill some of the jobs, but many industries require skills that may not be available locally. Even if some new jobs are filled by current residents, this opens up the jobs they held. The result is usually population growth from an influx of new residents. Commercial/industrial development tends to set off a cascade that brings residential development and all the costs it entails.

The extravagant tax breaks that local governments now almost routinely grant to corporations to move in may also contribute to commercial/industrial developments being net fiscal losers. Somebody has to pay those missing taxes; the somebodies are the other taxpayers.

One more reason why commercial/industrial development is not as good a deal as COCS comparisons suggest: The COCS data are a snapshot, the balance sheet for a single year. Life-cycle comparisons are what is needed. Industrial plants and malls are constructed to have a lifetime of no more than thirty or forty years. Consumer preferences may change in less than thirty years. In almost any sizable city, you can find large enclosed malls that are all but abandoned. A stroll through such a mall can be an eerie experience. The plants are dead and the fountains turned off. Empty storefronts have makeshift signs from their last incarnation—as income tax preparers or a branch office of some social service agency. The roof leaks, and there is a smell of mildew in the air. There are no shoppers. For the past few years, they've been going to strip malls and big boxes, just across the street or even in the same parking lot as the enclosed malls.

Industrial properties also show life cycles that end in senescence and death. Technological requirements change; corporations that needed high ceilings five years ago now want low ones. Processes that are done in the United States today may be shipped to Mexico next week.

During their youth, commercial or industrial properties may pay plenty of taxes. Later, the amount drops. The properties tend to be occupied by less and less lucrative businesses. Property owners may fall behind on their taxes or abandon the property altogether. At this point, it becomes a brownfield that pays no taxes but still requires city services to deal with the drug usage, vandalism, and arson that abandoned buildings attract. Vacant urban buildings account for more firefighter deaths and injuries than any other situation.[32]

All states make provisions for exempting from taxes organizations that contribute to the public good. Governmental agencies, churches, and nonprofit organizations involved in health, education, and scientific research are examples. Land trusts generally make use of such exemptions from property taxes for their preserves. In some states, the property tax exemption is not available. In states where it is, a land trust may continue to pay property taxes in particular rare situations where taking the exemption would irremediably jeopardize future community relations.

Some tax-exempt properties, such as schools and hospitals, require governmental services at a level similar to residential or commercial properties. Agricultural land, by and large, requires little in the way of services, and preserved natural areas, still less. Scenarios can be constructed where a pre-serve will need help from the police or fire department, but generally the sound of sirens on their way to a preserved natural area is a rare event.

The economic case for farmland as a desirable land use is very strong. The taxes, even when paid at farmland rather than potential development rates, far exceed the cost of services required. The case for preserves if left on the tax rolls is even stronger. For preserves removed from the tax rolls, the case is also strong, but slightly more complicated to make.

The case is this: A parcel of land can be used as a preserve or it can go to some other use. The preserve brings all the aesthetic and practical benefits that this chapter outlines in detail. The preserve adds to the quality of life of all the residents. Consider what an alternative use might bring—a commer-cial strip, perhaps, or a drugstore most of whose floor space is devoted to charcoal lighter fluid or plastic halloween costumes. The worst-case sce-nario, of course, is for the land to be used for residential development.

Preserving a parcel of land and taking it off the tax rolls will lower the tax base and, considered as an isolated act, could result in a tax increase for all the residents. In Vinalhaven, Maine, a $200,000 parcel of land removed from the tax rolls would increase the annual tax bill on a $80,000 property in the village less than a dollar. This is less than the tax increase that would result if someone built a new $80,000 house on the property.[33]

We may understand intellectually that residential property does not pay for itself, but this outcome may still come as a surprise. Building a new house will, on the average, cause a greater tax increase to every resident than taking the land off the tax rolls as a preserve.

This way of looking at development alternatives is unfamiliar enough to most of us that it may be worth restating one more time: If the choice for a piece of land is between (1) preserving it and removing it from the tax rolls, and (2) developing it as residential property, the community's tax-payers are hands-down better off with the preserve. This conclusion is strictly in terms of economics, without even considering the other advan-tages of preserved land.

"Permanent protection of land should not be looked at as precluding a more lucrative option," the authors of the Maine studies wrote; "it may be more appropriate to look at it as protection against a more expensive option."[34] To put it another way, protecting land saves us from ourselves. We already know this is true in terms of beauty, water and air quality, wildlife, and our hopes for the future. The COCS studies show it's also true economically.

Other Strictly Economic Reasons for Saving Land. In general, preserved land raises the desirability, hence, value of other property in the vicinity.[35] It was shown as early as the 1970s that residential property prices increased with proximity to a greenbelt in Boulder, Colorado, and a 1,300-acre park in

Philadelphia. Property next to the Philadelphia park was worth almost 30 percent more than similar property half a mile away.[36]

A study in the Green Mountains (Vermont) examined the price of residential property in relation to distance from wilderness areas. Property decreased in price more than one percent for every mile of distance from wilderness. Another way of stating the findings is that a parcel selling for $1,000 per acre in a town or township without wilderness would sell for $1,130 per acre in a town with wilderness, other things being equal.[37] The clear winner from the trend of increased value of land next to protected property is the city, township, or other political unit. Increased land values give rise to increased taxing capacity. Frederick Law Olmsted understood this relationship and predicted that the increase in tax revenues on surrounding property would more than pay for New York City's Central Park, which was the case.[38]

There will, of course, be a point at which increased property taxes from adjacent lands will be overshadowed by the loss of tax revenue from protected lands. Based on the COCS studies, the balance will be at a point with quite a high percentage of protected land.

Asking politicians to believe that you can increase the tax base by taking land off the tax rolls is asking for a subtlety of mind that might keep someone from going into politics in the first place. Refusing to accept this fact and pushing for keeping open space on the tax rolls or for payments in lieu of taxes will yield the political unit a double payoff, giving the politicians more tax money to spend on pet projects. Perhaps this is another way of being subtle.

The effects of enhanced value for land next to preserves or other open space differ between newcomers and people already living there. Newcomers have a choice of buying near protected land or away from it. If they choose to be close, they know they'll be paying more. People already living near land when it's protected will see a rise in the value of their property and in the quality of their life. They may not have asked for either, and it's true that only if they sell out and move away will their increased land value translate into money in their pocket.

If the increase in land value results in higher property taxes, some landowners may not see it as a pure benefit. We can sympathize with them. We may, nevertheless, feel that they've gotten a better deal than someone living next to a new expressway or pig factory.

Higher taxes might seem a logical consequence of increased property values, but this isn't necessarily what happens. Several studies have shown that political units with a large amount of open space have lower property tax rates than units with little or none.[39] There are at least two reasons why this could be true, and both might be correct. One is the saving-us-from-ourselves effect: the more protected rural land, the less need to spend money on roads, sewer lines, and bigger schools.

The other reason is that, with higher land values, a community can produce the total operating money it needs with a lower property tax rate. The tax bill of someone living next to a preserve will be higher than that of someone living farther away, but everybody's taxes will be lower than in some unfortunate community with little or no protected land.

For individual land owners, tax savings are another practical reason to preserve land. Owners can often gain tax advantages by donating land or a conservation easement to a land trust or selling it to the trust at a bargain price. More information on these matters is given in later chapters.

Moral and Ethical Reasons for Preservation

. . . the hot dog stands, the neon shill, the ticky-tacky houses, the sterile core, the mined and ravaged countryside. This is the image of anthropocentric man. He seeks not unity with nature but conquest, yet unity he finds, when his arrogance and ignorance are stilled and he lies dead under the greensward. —Ian L. McHarg, *A Quest for Life*

If aesthetics is the criterion for saving nature, we should save only what humans consider beautiful. If practicality is the criterion, we should save only what serves humankind. Reasons for saving nature that transcend these human perceptions lie in the realms of morals and ethics.

The decision to destroy a forest or a marsh ought to be looked at as an ethical or moral decision not much different from deciding whether or not to murder someone. A field with a population of endangered pocket gophers blocks our use of the land for convenience or profit in the same way that a relative might stand in the way of an inheritance. There are people who solve the latter problem by murder, but most of us do not.

There may be aesthetic reasons against murder: guns are loud, knives are bloody. There may be practical reasons: planning a murder is time consuming, and we might get caught. But probably few of us get to the point where aesthetic or practical considerations come into our reckoning. Most of us avoid murder for basically ethical reasons. It's not the right thing to do. Killing another human being is a forbidden act, by ethical or religious teaching and because we understand the remorse we'll feel and the revulsion of our friends and family.

In the end, nature will be saved only if we evolve similar ethical restraints, proscriptions, or taboos against being the agent of death of prairies and dunes and populations of plant and animal species.

The prevailing view of man's relationship with the world in our society and many others is that the world was made for man and man was made to rule the world. As far as Judeo-Christian thought goes, the controlling statute is given by Genesis 1:28

Be fruitful, and multiply, and replenish the earth, and subdue it: and have dominion over the fish of the sea, and over the fowl of the air, and over every living thing that moveth upon the earth.

Unfortunately, the dominating role that humans have assumed has led to extinctions, diminution or obliteration of many of the world's natural ecosystems, global pollution of air, water, and soil, and an assortment of other planetary and human ills. The solution, according to the prevailing paradigm, is to increase our control. The disasters are the result, not of our grip on the Earth, but of our grip not being firm enough. If we can just bring the whole planet under total human control, everything will be fine. We can clean up the oceans, make agriculture so efficient that we can dispense with most farmland, clone endangered, or even extinct species. With modern technology—computers, bioengineering—we're almost there.

The Land Ethic. The primary philosophical alternative to the anthropocentric point of view is Aldo Leopold's land ethic. Iowa-born and a graduate of the new Yale Forestry School (1909), Leopold began his career in the Southwest with the U.S. Forest Service, which was also new. After moving to Wisconsin, he worked for a sporting arms institute and wrote *Game Management*.[40] It's a long but readable treatise that attempts to ground the developing craft of game management in ecology. That same year, 1933, an academic position in game management was created for Leopold at the University of Wisconsin. He lived out the rest of his life in Wisconsin—Madison during the week, weekends at the family shack in Sauk County about 40 miles north. He was there, planting pines during the 1948 spring break, when he died of a heart attack at age sixty-one while helping neighbors fight a grass fire. It had been one week since a publisher called expressing interest in a book of his essays that became *A Sand County Almanac*.[41]

Although Leopold's background was forestry and wildlife management, the view he developed of man's place in nature is far removed from those utilitarian ways of dealing with the world. The land ethic is best expressed in two *Sand County Almanac* essays, "The Land Ethic" and "On a Monument to a Pigeon."[42] Almost no one is likely to comprehend the land ethic from a brief synopsis of it. For most of us, thinking like Leopold requires a kaleidoscopic shift in our sensibility that will only happen after several readings of those two essays.

Nevertheless, we need a brief synopsis to start with. Mine would be something like this: Humans need to live like good citizens of the Earth's ecosystems, rather than as the biospheric bully or planetary potentate. Humans are special, but the way they're special is the consciousness belonging to them alone that all life on the planet is kin. This gives them a special responsibility, not to subjugate but to nurture.

These are powerful ideas, and Leopold was the first to comprehend their ramifications; however, others had developed similar thoughts earlier. It's well known that John Muir had climbed that mountain, though not to the top. In his writings, Muir makes the point that such questions as, Why was poison ivy made? are meaningful only in showing the narrowness of the utilitarian vision. "Man and other bipeds were made for bears," he mocked, "and thanks be to God for teeth and claws so long."[43]

John Burroughs, a contemporary of Muir, had reached similar conclusions. Burrough's nature writings were even more widely read than Muir's, but his position on the role of man in nature is less well known. Muir's proto-land ethic sentiments have been widely publicized by the Sierra Club. Burroughs wasn't a joiner, but he made many of the same points. In his journal for 1866, Burroughs wrote:

Nature exists for man no more than she does for monkeys, and is as regardless of his life or pleasure or success as she is of fleas . . . Man is at the top, in his own estimation, and thinks the sun and the moon are for him; but he is no more an end than a frog is.[44]

Fifty years later, the books of James Oliver Curwood were best sellers. Though not nearly as talented a writer as Burroughs, Muir, or Leopold, Curwood was an outdoorsman and an observer of nature, and he reached a similar ethical position.[45] More explicitly than the others, Curwood made the connection between human destruction of nature and the Biblical charge to subdue and dominate.

One of the most satisfying explorations of the land ethic I'm familiar with, though he doesn't use the term, is in recent writings by Daniel Quinn. His novels *Ishmael* and *The Story of B* are required reading for anyone with an earnest desire to save the world.[46]

Stewardship. Some people have suggested that, though our culture's approach to the Earth has been one of domination, the Bible could also be construed to support a stewardship approach. In this view, the world was, in fact, made for man, but the idea was that he would tend it, like his flock or his garden.

A good statement of this viewpoint is given by a group of scientists from a small Christian college in a book called *Earthkeeping: Christian Stewardship of Natural Resources*. "We have concluded, based on Scripture," they write, "that humans have been given dominion over nature and that they are to use that dominion to serve nature and humanity."[47]

Stewardship is a prominent part of the job of most land trusts, ranging from simple monitoring to major intervention. Examples of the latter are attempts to prevent oak forest from undergoing succession to a more mesic forest type by using prescribed burns and selective cutting and attempts to construct prairie on former cropland by some combination of herbicide treatment, planting prairie seeds or seedlings, weeding, mowing, and burning.

The stewards may believe they have good reasons for these types of management. Some persons, however, find this sort of management of nature merely the more benign end of a continuum that also includes such forcible or violent treatment of the landscape as clearcutting, draining or filling wetlands, and strip mining. Comparatively, restoring prairie seems harmless to most of us. But in all these situations, the paradigm is man in control. We are saying that we know what the land should be, which species should live and die.

Accordingly, the idea of stewardship as an ethical basis for preserving nature looks weak to some. It seems to be trying to substitute, for our current ruthless exploitation of the Earth, a somewhat more compassionate exploitation.

As a practical matter, the stewardship model may be as good as can be hoped for any time soon. At its best, as suggested in the following quotation by Joseph Horne, it might be an approach that could save land and, perhaps, the world.

The goods of nature and fortune, nay, even of grace itself, are only lent. We think ourselves masters, when we are only stewards, and forget that to each of us it will one day be said, "Give an account of thy stewardship."[48]

And, again speaking practically, the stewardship model at its best and the land ethic model tend to converge. The benign stewards and the ethicists with their empathy with the Earth based on ecology and evolution may, in practice, perform much the same good deeds.

4 WHO WILL SAVE THE LAND?

Edward K. Warren made a fortune manufacturing corset stays from feathers rather than whale bone. Very likely he would have become as rich as John D. Rockefeller or Commodore Vanderbilt if corsets hadn't gone out of fashion. Around 1880, Warren bought a beech-maple forest near his home town of Three Oaks, Michigan, and preserved it for its great natural beauty. He set it aside in order "that future generations may have an example of the primitive floral and fauna conditions, that nature lovers may find here many of the animals and plants which are being exterminated elsewhere, and that students of biology may have available a place where they can study native animals and plants in their native habitats."[1]

Held for many years by the Warren Foundation and eventually transferred to Michigan as a state park, Warren Woods is probably the finest example of beech-maple forest left on the continent. If Edward Warren had not taken individual action, it would now exist only as a few lines in the Berrien County history books.

Nearly every locality has lands that were bought, protected, and cherished by individuals or families and, but for their efforts, would now be merely part of the general background sprawl. The outstanding example of individual land conservation in our time is Ted Turner who has bought, at last report, 1.8 million acres in several large parcels in ten states from Montana to Florida. The largest, at 580,000 acres, is the Vermejo Park Ranch on the Colorado-New Mexico border. Turner has set up two foundations to manage the land for biodiversity conservation.[2] Sometimes the persons who save a piece of land are wealthy, like Warren and Turner, but often they're of modest means, rich only in their ownership of a well-beloved and well-stewarded part of the Earth.

Land preservation by an individual, rich or poor, has its limits. One limit is that person's lifetime. The likelihood of preservation drops precipitously when heirs begin to make the decisions. Even within a conservationist's lifetime, changing circumstances may lead to losses of land whose preservation had seemed guaranteed. Novelist Louis Bromfield spent fifteen years, from 1939 on, at Malabar Farm in central Ohio, in a grand experiment with what we might now call sustainable agriculture. Soils were restored, creative approaches to farming were tested, 140 acres of woods were fenced off and allowed to recover from livestock grazing. At the main house, the rich and famous rubbed shoulders with agricultural experts.

Bromfield's writing income, which had subsidized Malabar Farm, began to decline in the 1950s. He developed bone cancer. Shortly before he died, needing money for the farm and medical expenses, he was reduced to selling timber rights to the forest. Fortunately, his friend Doris Duke bought the rights back and gave them to the Bromfield children. When they were unable to operate the farm profitably, they sold it to an Ohio nonprofit, Friends of the Land, which their father had helped found.[3]

The woods at Malabar Farm and eventually the farm itself were saved, but in countless other cases, lands preserved by individuals are lost. Not all landowners have an heiress to come to their rescue.

Thoughtful owners need to make provisions for the protection of their land beyond their own lifetimes. They may have no heirs, or the heirs may have no special interest in land conservation, or the owners may simply be looking beyond the next generation and wishing to ensure the long-term protection of this piece of land on which they place great value.

Natural lands and other open space are owned and protected with varying degrees of competence and permanency by many different agencies and organizations. Government entities from the National Park Service down to small villages own blocks of land that they've agreed to protect. Colleges, universities, and even public school systems sometimes see the desirability of maintaining natural areas for teaching and research and as a part of their role in their community.

Many nonprofit organizations such as museums, Audubon societies, and nature centers own areas that they maintain as habitat, for education, for research, or for public enjoyment. Land trusts are a special case in this general category. The difference between land trusts and nearly all the other organizations and agencies is that land trusts have land protection in perpetuity as their sole or central mission.

There may be special circumstances that make one organization especially appropriate for an owner seeking to preserve land. The property may be an inholding in a state park or adjacent to a nature center. It would make eminent sense in these cases to give the land to the state parks commission or the nature center—eminent sense, anyway, if these agencies will agree to enforceable provisions for treating the land as the donor desires.

This may be a sticking point. Many organizations that protect land as one of several missions in their charter place a premium on flexibility. They'll decide how any piece of land best meets their needs now and in the future. This unwillingness serves their purposes but not necessarily the purpose of the potential land donor or the cause of land protection.

Land trusts, especially local land trusts, are more apt to be amenable to guaranteeing—as far as earthly possible—that land will be preserved permanently in the manner the donor wishes. This will be true for land having conservation values that justify its protection and as long as the donor's wishes do not conflict with maintaining those values.

A land trust might be reluctant, as an example, to accept a patch of prairie if the owner wanted to attach a proviso that it couldn't be managed by burning. In the eastern half of the continent, prairie is nearly always a fire-dependent community. Also, a land trust likely will not commit itself to management requirements that are expensive or time consuming unless the land comes with a stewardship donation sufficient to endow these activities fully and permanently.

Many preserves donated to government agencies and nonprofit organizations other than land trusts have been held and managed appropriately for long periods of time. But enough examples of breakdowns in protection exist to suggest that the most important question a landowner must ask her- or himself is, Who will do the best job of permanently preserving my land?

My thesis is that local land trusts are the most trustworthy repositories of preserved land. Their mission, by-laws, and articles of incorporation, the oversight of their members, and the culture of the land trust community combine to make unlikely the dishonoring of a pledge to preserve land.

Furthermore, the record is that local land trusts are more reliable than most other organizations and government agencies. None of a long list of cases I've found of the abdication of conservation responsibilities has so far involved a bona fide local land trust; the closest approach was a nature center.

It would be rash to claim that there never will be an instance in which a land trust fails in its effort to protect land permanently and in accordance with its commitments to the previous owner. Despite the nineteenth-century origins of the land trust movement, half the currently existing trusts are less than fifteen years old, so the historical record, while good, is short compared with some other kinds of institutions.

Why Not Give Your Conservation Land to a College or University?

Some colleges and universities have been good stewards of lands entrusted to them. A few—very few—have protected lands they own with conservation easements. Examples are Kalamazoo College, which gave a conservation easement on part of its arboretum to the Southwest Michigan Land Conservancy, and The University of Vermont, which placed an easement on its Centennial Woods Natural Area with the Vermont Land Trust.

A more typical pattern is shown in a bequest to Iowa State University (ISU). A widowed owner of a 240-acre farm tried to ensure that it would remain farmland after she died. Her will leaving the property to ISU directed that it be operated as the Kiley Powers Farm, after her husband, and that the remainder of the estate amounting in value to about $600,000 be used to improve and maintain the farmland and buildings.[4]

The University accepted the bequest, but then the ISU Foundation petitioned the District Court to overturn the will, sold the land, and used some of the proceeds to help bail out construction of an ISU livestock facility.

There are many similar cases involving institutions of higher education; following are a couple in a little more detail.

The Ott Preserve. At the east edge of Battle Creek, Michigan, lies the 260-acre Harvey N. Ott Preserve. Currently owned by Calhoun County, it consists of a ridge (an esker, in glacial geology terms) and the surrounding lowlands, including three small lakes. The low ground supports swamp forests of birch, ash, and tamarack, and a type of open wetland called fen. Both fen and forest are rich in rare plants.

The esker is occupied by a diverse forest that until the winter of 1993/1994 was dominated by large oaks. That was when timber cutting occurred in about 20 acres of the best forest.

I took an ecology class to the preserve a few months later and we spent a warm September day measuring stumps and counting annual rings. Several cut trees were more than 40 inches in diameter on the stump, and a fair percentage were more than 200 years old. The oldest was a white oak 278 years old. In other words, it was a seedling in 1715, sixty-one years before the Declaration of Independence was signed.[5]

The site's unique features were recognized as early as 1911, when Ed Brigham, a highly regarded local naturalist, joined with a friend to buy 105 acres to protect and study. Later, Brigham bought more land as an agent for John Harvey Kellogg. Dr. Kellogg was one of *the* Kelloggs, but not the cereal Kellogg, who was brother W. K. John Harvey Kellogg was, among other things, the founder and superintendent of the Battle Creek sanitarium, a nationally renowned health spa in the early decades of the twentieth century.

Kellogg donated the land to a small liberal arts college that he'd founded in 1923. The Battle Creek College Biological Preserve was used for research and as an outdoor laboratory for biology and geology classes.[6] Although the college had an excellent faculty, it was unable to outlast the Great Depression and closed its doors in 1938. The preserve, still intact, was sold to Albion College, located twenty-five miles to the east. Harvey N. Ott enters the picture as an Albion College benefactor whose bequest funded the 1946 purchase.

Albion kept the land as a preserve for research and teaching for about three decades. Then they received a gift of 60 acres next to their campus.

This land, which they named the Whitehouse Nature Center, lacked the plant diversity of the Ott Preserve, but it had a major advantage in proximity.

In 1977, to raise money to buy a 40-acre addition to the Whitehouse holdings, Albion sold the Ott Preserve to Calhoun County.[7] The understanding at the college was that the Ott Preserve would remain a natural area. There was some reason to believe this because half the purchase price came as pass-through federal money from the Land and Water Conservation Fund (LWCF). Conversion to other than outdoor recreation uses of properties bought with LWCF money is prohibited.[8] Also, the County's application claimed, "The full intent of Calhoun County is to continue with the preservation."[9]

The next sixteen years were uneventful. Then, on 2 December 1993, the County Commissioners voted unanimously to sell 305 trees, mostly large oaks, from the most accessible upland area of the Preserve. A hardwood and veneer company paid the county $36,000.

Neighbors complained to township officials almost from the beginning of the logging operation. By mid-January, the concerns had reached the media. An article in the 14 January 1994, Battle Creek *Enquirer,* headlined "Kindest Cut of All for Forest," dealt with the controversy by interviewing the president of the logging company. He was quoted as saying, "This is a very, very bad woodlot. It hasn't been managed. The ground can't feed all of this."[10]

In a followup letter to the editor, a local biology teacher recalled van Helmont's classic seventeenth-century experiment in which a small willow weighing 5 pounds was planted in 200 pounds of soil and allowed to grow for five years. The tree by then weighed 169 pounds and the soil weight had declined by 2 ounces, demonstrating that most plant biomass comes from carbon dioxide and water. The letter concluded, "So those trees standing 'unattended for 100 years' were taking CO_2 (of which we have an increasing amount from automobiles and industry) out of the air and replacing it with oxygen."[11]

At its February meeting, the County Commission voted to go ahead with phase two of the timber operations, which would have continued logging on the other upland areas of the preserve. Before that could happen, the tide had turned. At the March commission meeting, Albion College botanists Ewell Stowell and Daniel Skean voiced their outrage over the logging. Said Skean, "What happened here was apparently a quick-and-dirty 'sweetheart deal' that has seriously damaged the integrity of the biological preserve, and to add insult to injury, was not based upon sound business practices."[12]

The $36,000 was a small fraction of what 300 large, veneer-quality oaks were worth.

Reacting to many complaints from citizens and township officials, the board voted to halt phase two in order to "engage the community."

As anti-logging sentiment soared, county officials defended what they had done as a limited, selective cut to "improve the woodlot" and to clear out the "culls"—dead or hollow trees—which were a liability concern (in danger of "blowing over on mothers, babies, and the like," Skean commented sarcastically). The aim was to generate funds to operate the county park system, the budget of which had been cut to zero a few years before. The general counsel for the county, who had been point man for the timber sale, pointed out that the deed from Albion College had come with no restrictions.

Eventually, the will of the citizens prevailed; no further cutting was done, the money from the sale was dedicated to upkeep of the preserve, and a friends group has provided continuing oversight.

Dan Skean characterized the procedure that led to the logging as "quick and dirty." It's hard to quarrel with this designation, remembering that "dirty" in this science jargon phrase means "sloppy." At the very least, the process was full of flaws.

The county commission, all but one member new as of the previous election, had little or no knowledge of the Ott Preserve, yet failed to ask for a briefing. The county administration had little understanding and no interest in the history or sanctuary nature of the property.

The proposal to cut was made and approved in a single commission meeting with no input solicited from the citizenry or even from the county planning commission. Anyone with any knowledge of forest management will be surprised at how the tree sale was conducted: The county took the offer of the first timber buyer who drove up.[13] Guidelines for timber owners emphasize the need to have a consulting forester mark the trees to be harvested, to get three to five bids, and to take your time.

Of course, the overriding question is not, Why did the county do such a poor job at selling timber? but rather, How could logging in a preserved natural area ever happen? Chronic financial problems in the county, pressure on staff to generate income, and commission and staff turnover all contributed, but there is one broad answer to the question.

For eighty-three years, it was the intention that this land be permanently preserved, but in the end the agencies entrusted with the task were not up to it. Battle Creek College and Albion College both kept the land undisturbed, but eventually sold it, for reasons of their own. The mission of colleges is, after all, education, not natural area preservation. Calhoun County bought the land with good intentions, but any unit of government is charged with a multitude of tasks. When pressure on preserved land comes, politicians and bureaucrats are apt to develop short memories and flexible interpretations of past commitments.

The lesson of the Ott Preserve is, It's not preserved till it's preserved. Permanent preservation comes from choosing the right organization to hold the land. Perhaps it's true that nothing lasts forever. But to the degree that perpetuity exists, it exists for land held by local land trusts.

This is a scary story but, after all, it involves two small colleges and a financially strapped county. Surely, other schools have done better. What about, say, Harvard?

Black Rock Forest. In 1949, Harvard University received Black Rock Forest by bequest from alumnus Ernest G. Stillman. This tract of 3,785 acres is located in the Hudson Highlands on the west bank of the Hudson River fifty miles north of New York City. Stillman, by profession an epidemiologist, was interested in forests and forest restoration. At the suggestion of the head of Harvard Forest, he had set up Black Rock in 1928 as a private demonstration forest for long-term research. To ensure that the site would be permanently protected and the research continued, Dr. Stillman began an endowment which, when it was also transferred to Harvard, amounted to $1.1 million.[14]

In 1989, Harvard sold the forest but kept most of the endowment, grown by then to more than $3 million.

An objection might be raised that this bald statement makes the situation sound worse than it was. The sale was to the Black Rock Forest Preserve, an education and research nonprofit whose aim is to keep the tract as a natural area in perpetuity. The site is administered and used as a field station by a consortium of twenty-two organizations running from the Newburgh Enlarged City School District to the Brooklyn Botanic Garden and American Museum of Natural History. It's quite possible that the Black Rock Preserve's approach to the land hews closer to environmental purity than Harvard's ever would have.

We can't know what Ernest Stillman's reactions would have been to all this. What is known, however, is that not all of his sons were happy. John S. Stillman told *The New York Times,* "I'm saddened at the way I consider Harvard has breached faith with my father and ignored the trust they accepted forty years ago."[15]

The $3 million endowment (minus $125,000 that Harvard chipped in to help start a new Black Rock Forest Preserve endowment) is now used to support research at Harvard Forest. Stillman had a long interest in Harvard Forest and, in fact, had been its principal benefactor. In establishing the Black Rock endowment, however, he stated that the income was to be "used to defray the cost of operating, first, the Black Rock Forest, and, then, the Harvard Forest."

George W. S. Trow, a *New Yorker* writer and Harvard graduate, wrote of the time when Harvard was planning to get rid of Black Rock Forest but had not yet done so. "In response to the *new, tough reality* in American life, Harvard University has been looking closely, ruthlessly at its assets. Where an asset *does not perform,* it is suspect. . . . Recently, Harvard University decided that the Black Rock Forest . . . *had not performed* and should be sold."[16] (The emphases are all Trow's.) Those of us who have been around universities for several decades can remember a time when it really was true that some universities knew their strengths and tried to retain and build on them rather than making yearly ad hoc decisions based on where the biggest federal or private dollars were.

Trow talked with two administrators, Harvard's general counsel, who was also a vice president, and the dean whose purview included Black Rock. They pointed out that Harvard didn't need two forests and, consequently, were considering "alternative ownership" of Black Rock Forest. The vice president/general counsel told Trow, "It is clear to us that Harvard is not a conservation organization. Dr. Stillman understood that. . . . I think it would be wrong to make an assumption that Dr. Stillman had required, or even expected, that Harvard would hold on to it. If I were interested in preserving a forest, I wouldn't give it to a university."

And there, I think, you have it.

How about Some Nonconservation Nonprofit, Such as a Church?

We might expect that a church would follow a donor's wishes to preserve land for conservation purposes. The Christian virtue of stewardship would come into play. The case of Belt Woods suggests that the path to righteousness may be a circuitous one.[17] When Seton Belt died in 1959, age eighty-nine, he left his 624-acre farm in Prince George's County, Maryland, in a trust for the benefit of the Episcopal Diocese of Washington, D.C., and his local parish. One hundred acres or so of the farm was old-growth hardwoods.

Chandler Robbins, a biologist with the U.S. Fish and Wildlife Service, had come across Belt Woods while working on a prototype breeding-bird atlas for Maryland.[18] He censused 36 acres of it in 1947 and found high populations of the forest-interior birds that would later be termed neotropical migrants. There were, for example, nine pairs of scarlet tanagers, thirty-six pairs of red-eyed vireos, nineteen pairs of ovenbirds, and fourteen pairs of wood thrushes.

Seton Belt, Robbins remembered, "was excited to learn that the wood thrushes he was hearing—they are a classic forest interior nester—had the highest breeding population density anywhere for the species. He was obviously aware of the trees' uniqueness, and treasured them. Foresters had begged him many times to timber them, he said, but he refused to allow anyone to touch them."

Robbins suggested that Belt consider protecting the woods by leaving it to the Maryland Ornithological Society. No need, Belt had replied. "The home farm absolutely would never be developed or the woods cut. He had ensured it in his will."[19]

The will provided that the beneficiaries could not sell any part of the farm and, further, that the timber should be used only for repairs and improvements to the buildings and fences and for firewood. Nevertheless, in the mid-1970s, the church and the executor, a bank in Baltimore, petitioned to have the will's restrictions overturned and, with the help of the Maryland attorney general, succeeded.

The story of the following twenty years is complicated and not pretty. The tall, forest-grown-white oaks and tulip trees on half of the old-growth area were sold and cut for veneer in 1981. The church and bank began to plan a residential development of about 650 units that would remove or fragment the remaining woods. Between 1991 and 1995, the church spent $764,000 on development-related fees, as the development progressed through the planning and permitting stages.

Salvation arrived in the person of the Western Shore Conservancy, specifically formed to save what remained of the Belt farm—515 acres including about half the old-growth forest. Pamela Cooper, founder and still president of the Conservancy, called the Trust for Public Land. With its help, other groups and various government agencies were brought into the effort. Many individuals also provided support. Some were relatively well known, such as New Age musician Paul Winter and a children's author, Lynne Cherry, who wrote a book about the wood thrushes of Belt Woods. Most of the individuals, though, were the anonymous altruists who are at the heart of most good things that get done.

In the end, in 1997, the church sold the property to the Trust for Public Land for something more than $4.5 million. TPL transferred it to the state of Maryland, where it is now protected as part of the state's Wildland Protection system. Language similar to the Wildland Protection program is included in deed restrictions, and there is a reverter clause to The Nature Conservancy, presumably giving them legal standing to enforce the restrictions.

Pamela Cooper believes that so far state ownership has proved to be the best choice. At the time the woods was slated for development, Prince George's County made plans to expand an existing two-lane road next to the woods to four lanes. One lane was to come out of the Belt property and one from the opposite side. Development on the opposite side of the road proceeded under the specifications for a four-lane road. "I think that if the Western Shore Conservancy owned it right now," Pamela Cooper said, "the County would have condemned part of the property for [the] road."[20]

Considering the history of the property, it seems inconceivable that Prince George's County would show such poor judgment as to try to add to the damage; but the situation remains unresolved.

Government Ownership of Natural Lands

Federal, state, and local governments own large amounts of land and are sometimes good stewards of it. Anyone who has paid attention to the management of government lands, however, will know of cases in which the natural features have been diminished or destroyed. Governments react to many pressures, and their treatment of land they own or regulate is often a compromise between competing views, even when some of these lack validity.

Whatever the record of an agency in general, a landowner thinking to preserve land needs to get answers to a more specific question: What is the record for land given, bequeathed, or sold to it with the expectation that the land be preserved?

To begin with, the potential donor should be aware that many governmental units and agencies will be unwilling to accept land with enforceable protections, such as a conservation easement held by an organization with the will and the means to require compliance. As a consequence, landowners intending protection sometimes end up transferring land with only vague and unenforceable restrictions, or none. Occasionally, as after Belt Woods was saved, a government agency will accept stronger restrictions in cases where public scrutiny has been intense. But even when land is accepted with absolutely straightforward language stipulating protection, the restrictions may later be ignored, interpreted mendaciously, or lost through inefficiency or incompetence.

Robert Frost spent summers at Middlebury College's Bread Loaf writers' school for thirty-nine of forty-two years, beginning in 1921. The Bread Loaf site and the mountains and forests around it were willed to the college by Joseph Battell. A member of a wealthy Vermont family, Battell went to Middlebury but left school without graduating because of ill health. Later on, he bought property a few miles east, within sight of Bread Loaf Mountain and resided there until he died at an advanced age in 1915. The Web page of the Bread Loaf School of English refers to Battell as a "breeder of Morgan horses, proprietor of the local newspaper, and spirited lover of nature."

After Battell's death, his home compound became the site of the writers' school, but over the years, he had accumulated additional land in the Green Mountains. A parcel of 1,200 acres farther north that included Camel's Hump was deeded by him in 1911 to Vermont for a state park. The deed included the restriction that "trees growing on the land herein conveyed are not to be cut except those which it is necessary to remove in building paths or roads, and the whole forest is to be preserved in a primeval state."[21]

This has been done; this story is not about actions of the state of Vermont.

When Battell died, he left about 25,000 acres of forested mountain land around Bread Loaf to Middlebury College. Another 5,000 acres to the north was left to the federal government for a national park, but it was declined and also came to Middlebury as part of the residue of the estate. The clauses dealing with the Middlebury land and the proposed national park land both directed in language as plain as anyone could make it that the forests should be preserved.

Here is some of the language from Battell's will for the land left to Middlebury:

Being impressed with the evils attending the extensive destruction of the original forests of our country and being mindful of the benefits that will accrue to, and the pleasures that will be enjoyed by the citizens of the State of Vermont and the visitor within her borders, from the preservation of a considerable tract of mountain forest in its virgin and primeval state, [I] give and devise to the president and fellows of Middlebury College in trust forever, all those portions of wildlands in [the description follows]. And it shall be the duty of said trustees to preserve as far as reasonably may be the forests . . . and neither to cut nor permit to be cut thereon any trees whatsoever except such as are dead or down and such as it may be necessary to cut in making and repairing needful roads; it being a principal object of this devise to preserve intact said wild lands . . . as a specimen of the original Vermont forest.

It's worth looking at how the lands were treated if only to see the tortured interpretations that a donor's language may receive once he's no longer around to defend himself. Jim Northup, executive director of the Vermont Forest Watch, who brought the Battell land situation to recent attention, referred to "Battell's bequest and its deconstruction."

A college committee appointed to study the matter, wrote in 1925, "This cutting limitation in its most literal sense would be well calculated to defeat the object which Battell had in mind. . . . On the other hand, it could not be said that Battell did not mean anything by the cutting restriction."

Also, the committee said, "It is to be noted that the cutting restriction . . . is not expressed as a condition or command and . . . is expressly limited by the words *as far as reasonably may be*."

Northup noted that the will's interpreters assumed that if forests were left untouched, insects, disease, and fire would destroy them. "They believed," he summarized, "that preservation of forests and scenery *required* logging."

A twenty-first century ecologist wishing to be as generous as possible might assign a small amount of truth to this idea. The forests that Battell protected—mostly northern hardwood forest at lower elevations and red spruce-balsam fir higher up—had developed under a regime that included fires (rare in undisturbed forests of this region) and deer populations kept low by large predators. With a change in those factors, the forests would be likely to change, hence some sort of management might be called for.

A less generous ecologist might conclude that the comments of the committee were simply pious justifications for cutting and selling timber, which had begun soon after the bequest was made and long before the 1925 committee report.

Middlebury sold 20,000 acres of the Battell land to the federal government in the 1930s. This was in the depths of the Great Depression, but the college then sold another 10,000 in the 1950s. It still owns a few hundred acres of undeveloped Battell land that the trustees protected through a resolution in 1999, when petitioned by a group of Environmental Studies students.

But this is not just another cautionary tale about colleges. The parcels sold in the 1930s and 1950s became part of the Green Mountain National Forest. Northup wrote:

The land was sold to the USFS conditioned by the public charitable trust created by Battell's will, but without any restrictions imposed in the deeds transferring title. Over the years, the agency lost sight of its duties as trustee and developed and heavily logged much of the land once owned by Battell. The Sugarbush Ski Area, under lease from the Forest Service, covers most of the east side and portions of the summit of the ridge Battell wished to be preserved in its "original and primeval condition" as a national park.

Questioned by a *Boston Globe* reporter, the Forest Service agreed that it had logged the tract, claimed no knowledge of Battell's restrictions, and indicated that whatever the restrictions had been, they disappeared when title was transferred to them.[22] The question of future management of the Battell lands is unresolved. The advocacy organization Forest Watch is committed to opposing any actions by the USFS that would violate Battell's stated wishes.[23]

Conservation Organizations other than Land Trusts

The California Academy of Sciences (CAS) is "committed to fostering a spirit of scientific discovery and stewardship of the natural world;" nevertheless, in 1997, it put up for sale its Pepperwood Ranch Preserve, 3,100 acres donated for education and research in 1979 by Kenneth and Nancy Bechtel. In a message to CAS members—sent after the news broke—the chairman of the board of trustees wrote that they were "exploring a creative plan to generate much needed funds . . . while . . . preserving the original mission of this important bequest." What they were hoping to do was sell the land—redwood and Douglas fir forest, oak woodland, grassland, chaparral, vernal pools—and persuade the Sonoma Agricultural Preservation and Open Space District to buy a conservation easement on it.[24]

As it turned out, public outrage was too great, and by 2002, a CAS spokesman stated, "There is no intention to sell Pepperwood. If anything, we hope to make even more use of the property for research and education."[25]

National Wildlife Federation. The National Wildlife Federation (NWF) is, by its calculation, the nation's largest private, nonprofit conservation education and advocacy organization. Waterfowl populations had reached such a low ebb in the mid-1930s that sportsmen began to pressure government for conservation measures. The Duck Stamp Act and taxes on guns and ammunition that would be used to purchase wildlife refuges were two federal responses. The NWF, founded in 1936 by the political cartoonist J. N. "Ding" Darling, one of the most effective wildlife advocates of the time, was a private initiative from the same period.[26]

The NWF's emphasis through most of its existence was on education, such as provided by its magazines *Ranger Rick* and *National Wildlife*. State affiliates also engaged in local advocacy aimed at conserving habitats.

In the 1970s, largely through the efforts of a retired biologist, Ray Nesbitt, NWF began to acquire preserves. In what came to be called its Land Heritage Program, NWF eventually owned five major sanctuaries and several lesser ones.[27] About the same time, it began to hire lawyers to enforce environmental legislation in state and federal courts.[28]

Within a decade, NWF started divesting itself of its sanctuaries. One of these was the Moore Conservation Education Center, near Washington, D.C., in Loudon County, Virginia. The land had been donated to NWF in 1975 by Dr. Claude Moore, a radiologist and philanthropist—and NWF's honorary president—with the understanding that it would be kept in perpetuity as a nature education sanctuary. At Moore's request, each member of the NWF board had signed a letter explicitly restricting the land's use. The 357 acres included forest, ponds, marsh, and meadows. The rapidly declining Henslow's sparrow had nested in the wet grasslands, though not in the years immediately preceding the sale.

Most of the land was sold to developers for $8.5 million. Fifty-three acres were retained as open space, as required by local law. Moore, ninety-six at the time, opposed the sale in a suit charging "fraud and deceit" on the part of NWF.[29]

In unusually plain language, a representative of NWF told the *Washington Post,* "We're interested in getting the money out of it because the land is not terrifically useful. . . . It is not a beautiful piece of land."[30] Alston Chase, who wrote of the matter, concluded "this sale is not an isolated incident. The group's entire sanctuary policy, known as the Land Heritage Program, has been quietly scuttled." A 1987 book on the *Story of the National Wildlife Federation* mentioned the Land Heritage Program only to say that it had "evolved into the Planned Giving program of today."[31]

"We discontinued the Land Heritage Program because we found it was a poor way to raise money," Chase quoted NWF's director of media relations as saying. NWF had already sold the 2,700-acre Lava Lake sanctuary, a Pacific Flyway stopover point near Mount Shasta in California. It had also successfully petitioned an Indiana court to remove deed restrictions from a property in Ann Arundel County, Maryland, that had been bequeathed to NWF on the condition that it be preserved.

Ray Nesbit, who had started the preserve program, was incensed. "The important thing to keep in mind is that we raised money to buy sanctuaries. We didn't use sanctuaries as a way to raise money."

Points can be advanced in NWF's defense. Any land trust knows that owning a preserve costs money. If a preserve can pay for itself, that's good. If it generates enough good will on the part of donors to help support other programs, that's even better. In hindsight, one might question NWF's decision, knowing that when Claude Moore died four years later, his $25 million estate went to education. Had circumstances been different, some of that money might have supported NWF's education efforts at the Moore Conservation Education Center and elsewhere.

It could also be argued that NWF needed money to support lobbying and litigation, along with broad public education. Selling its sanctuaries could be considered as much a return to its roots as a new direction. It had tried what amounted to a land trust approach, found it not appropriate to its aims, and returned to advocacy.

Even if the sale of the Moore Center can be rationalized in these ways, the fact is that a nonprofit conservation organization accepted the responsibility of protecting conservation land and defaulted on that responsibility. Moore and other donors to the Land Heritage Program had been given reason to believe that certain lands would be protected in perpetuity, and they were not.

Pass-throughs to Government by Land Trusts

Many conservation organizations, including land trusts, sell or donate conservation land to state or federal agencies rather than managing it themselves. This is frequently true for The Nature Conservancy and almost invariably true for the Trust for Public Land and the Rails-to-Trails Conservancy. More than 150 local land trusts have passed through land to government agencies; several have this mode of operation as their stated mission. As examples, the Anza-Borrego Foundation in San Diego County, California, acquires private lands to transfer to Anza-Borrego Desert State Park, and the Wilderness Land Trust headquartered in Colorado aims to acquire private inholdings in federally designated wilderness areas and transfer them to public ownership.

Most land trusts that regularly practice pass-throughs don't attempt to protect the land with conservation easements, reverter clauses, or other protective covenants. This is because of the general unwillingness of governmental agencies or bodies to accept such restraints. Nevertheless, many such land trusts express reasonable satisfaction or only moderate dissatisfaction with the treatment their lands have received. Their acceptance of the agencies' handling of the pass-through lands seems to result from some combination of the following circumstances:

• professional and ethical conduct on the part of the agency;
• participation by the land trust in the management plan or in the management itself;
• limited or no expectations on the part of the land trust as to stewardship by the government agency;
• lack of monitoring by the land trust;
• insufficient time for problems to develop.

Of course, abuse of passed-through conservation land does occur. Towns in several New England states hold conservation lands acquired by land trusts and passed through. Conservation lands in Massachusetts can be converted from conservation use only by two-thirds votes of the municipal council and state legislature; nevertheless, a study found many requests for conversion reaching the legislature and a high rate of success once they got there. Between 1989 and 1998, 150 of 176 requests for conversion forwarded from the municipal councils were approved by the legislature.[32] Almost every conceivable public and private use was involved from residential construction to cemeteries. School construction proposals in Massachusetts and elsewhere in New England often seem to target conservation lands.

Lamb Brook. A 3,956-acre tract of forested land on Lamb Brook in southern Vermont was given in the 1970s to The Nature Conservancy by Henry F. Harris for conservation purposes.[33] As part of a complicated deal involving other conservation lands, TNC sold the land to the Forest Service for about $1 million in 1979 and 1980. The land was conveyed with no restrictions. The current director of land protection for the Vermont chapter of TNC stated, "I know from more recent projects . . . that the federal government will not accept restrictions or any other title defects on properties they acquire." Federal agencies may, in fact, be reluctant to accept land with conservation easements, or restrictions, but this reluctance is rarely, if ever, a matter of law.

In 1987, the Forest Service proposed to build a road in the Green Mountain National Forest compartment into which the TNC land had been incorporated, and log about 4,000 acres. Local conservationists believed that the road building and logging would decrease the suitability of the area for resident black bears and for neotropical migrant birds.

Several conservation organizations, not including TNC, challenged the operation in federal court and prevailed. The judge agreed with the plaintiffs that the Forest Service had to do a site-specific Environmental Impact Statement and enjoined it from any further timber harvesting or road building until the EIS was completed.

The Forest Service appealed and the Circuit Court of Appeals upheld the district court's decision just before Christmas 1997.[34] Only slightly daunted, the Forest Service requested that the district court allow them to widen and improve a snowmobile/ATV trail into the Lamb Brook area, cutting timber on about 300 acres including a 28-acre clearcut. They argued that they were improving a trail, not building a road and that, since they would leave the cut trees on the ground, it was not timber harvesting.

The conservation groups characterized it as a back-door attempt to begin the logging process, and the court refused the request on 9 November 1998.[35]

Mount Kearsarge. Mount Kearsarge is a little south and west of the middle of New Hampshire. It's largely encompassed by Winslow State Park, of which more than 4,000 acres consist of lands purchased by the Society for the Protection of New Hampshire Forests (SPNHF) and donated to the state. The 520 acres that include the summit were donated in 1949 as a memorial to Frank West Rollins, New Hampshire's governor from 1899 to 1901 and SPNHF's first president.

Most of New Hampshire's nineteenth-century political leaders saw forested land as little more than an impediment to agriculture. The legislature decided in 1831 to sell all the state's public lands to encourage deforestation and did so in a hurry, at fire sale prices. By 1840, less than half the state was forested, and the percentage declined rapidly in later decades as logging railroads and portable sawmills penetrated the mountains.[36]

In the 1890s, many of the farms carved out of the forests were abandoned as people fled to the cities or to better land in the West, but logging continued. "The Great White Mountains are being denuded and burned over, and the summer visitor turns away in sadness and disgust," Rollins said. He recommended parks, scenic roads with bicycle paths, and clean, well-kept taverns with healthy food.[37]

In 1901, Rollins's successor as governor suggested that the state begin to buy back the cutover forest land it had sold in the past, but the legislature rejected the idea as foolish.[38] To counteract the short-sightedness of the state, SPNHF was formed that same year by Rollins, seven other men, and one woman, Ellen McRoberts Mason, "writer, suffragist, and lecturer."[39] SPNHF became one of the earliest conservation organizations and one of the earliest land trusts, though, of course, ten years after the Trustees of Reservations was founded.

The deed from SPNHF for the summit of Kearsarge stipulated that it be used "as a forestry and recreational reservation for public use and benefit." My 1979 edition of the Appalachian Mountain Club's *White Mountain Guide* mentions that the "bare summit with fine views in all directions" has a fire tower and an airways beacon. That description is obsolete. Over the years, the state added several public safety telecommunications structures. The 2,937-foot summit now bristles with towers, of which residents and visitors have fine views from all directions. Structures around the fire tower wear antennae that look like enormous metal bustiers.

In 1997, the New Hampshire Department of Resources and Economic Development permitted a cellular phone company to build a 180-foot tower for state use in exchange for the right to rent space for commercial purposes. SPNHF, which had not objected to the earlier additions to the property, now argued that the commercial use was a violation of the deed restriction. After unsuccessful negotiations with the state, SPNHF sued in county superior court.

After sixteen months, in May 2000, the court ruled against SPNHF. The group decided not to appeal but vowed to be more diligent in monitoring deed restrictions, if any, on the other 12,000 acres they have passed through to government.[40]

Can a Land Trust Help Preserve Your Land if You Give It to Another Organization?

In most states, donors to charities have no legal standing to force nonprofit organizations to use the donated assets (land or anything else) the way the donor intended.[41] If you donate a few million to a university to fund scholarships in nutrition and the school drops its holistic health program and uses your money to pay the meat and liquor bills for the president's parties, there's little you can do about it.

The rule is, once they've got it, they've got it. Legal language that retained control for the donor would cause trouble with the deductibility of the gift. Reverter clauses designed to return the asset to the donor or family have the same flaw and, in any case, expire after a few tens of years.

If a landowner is set on giving his land to his alma mater or other charity, one solution might be first to give a conservation easement to the local land trust. The easement would spell out how the land could be used and would need to be accompanied by a defense endowment for the trust's legal expenses when the university sought to sell the land or build a new engineering building on it. The amount would have to be quite large; if it were only $50,000 or so, one court challenge could exhaust it and the university or some other charity with deep pockets could then proceed unimpeded to do what it wanted with the land.

Another possible solution would be language in the gift contract that provided that if the land were not used for the intended conservation purposes, it would go to the land trust. This would also require a substantial endowment to the land trust for legal fees to compel the school to live up to the contract.

Of course, many charities would refuse a gift with these strings attached, depending on how badly they want or need the gift and how interested they are in ingratiating themselves with the once and future donor.

All in all, for land whose main value is for conservation purposes, giving it directly to a land trust is the cleanest course.

Tradelands

Every once in a while one hears about one of the national trusts that was given land for a preserve and then turned around and sold it. When I give talks about the Southwest Michigan Land Conservancy, a frequently asked question, though not in the top ten, is a somewhat hostile, "Are you like The Nature Conservancy?" When I seek clarification, the questioner usually has in mind some incident involving sale of land thought to have been accepted for protection in perpetuity.

I haven't managed to unearth a definite instance of this happening with a local land trust. As for The Nature Conservancy, it's hard to tell, partly because it rarely answers such charges directly, instead speaking in generalities about policies. Usually, I believe, such cases are a matter of land being given to the organization as an asset, like stocks or a piece of art, with the expectation that it would be sold to support the organization's programs.

The land trust community has a term, tradelands—coined by TNC, as it happens—to designate this kind of land as distinct from land intended for preservation. Ideal tradelands are ones that have no conservation value and can be readily converted to cash. A lot in an upscale subdivision would be perfect.

If any land trust accepts and then sells a piece of land donated as tradeland, outsiders may misinterpret the deal. They may see it as selling a preserve. It's desirable to avoid this appearance. The donors should thoroughly understand the trust's intentions, and the donors and trust should sign a letter of understanding that spells out simply and explicitly—in language that will be clear when people read it in the local paper—that the land is being donated with the expectation that the trust will sell it.

Conservation Buyers and Sellers

Land trusts occasionally find themselves in a situation where they can protect a property only by buying it but can't afford not to recoup some or all of their purchase price. An approach that has sometimes been used is the Conservation Buyer technique. The land trust buys the land, negotiates a sale that includes a conservation easement that it will hold, and sells the easement-protected land for enough money to recover some or all its investment, or preferably more. As a matter of prudence, the land trust may wish to acquire an option and locate a conservation-minded buyer before it buys the property.

Often, a building envelope is specified in the easement, and the buyers acquire the property with the intention of living on it. Many permutations are possible, including dividing a large property and carving out building envelopes on most or all the parcels.

This approach differs only slightly from various pass-through and pre-acquisition deals in which the ultimate owner is a government agency. The differences are that the conservation buyer is a private party and that, with the land under easement to a land trust, it may well be better protected against mismanagement than in the pass-through deals.

The first time a land trust contemplates employing either the conservation buyer or the tradelands approach, it would do well to use its newsletter and press releases to inform its membership and the public about why it's in the real estate business.

Would a Local Land Trust Ever Divest Itself of Preserved Land?

Despite my belief that local land trusts represent a landowner's best bet for permanent protection, circumstances could arise when a trust would part with a preserve.

There is, of course, the matter of eminent domain.[42] A land trust ought to resist condemnation by talking with the government agency, elected representatives, and the press. It may go to court and make its case for retention on whatever grounds are available. In many cases, the potential for achieving some conservation purpose, such as replacement land or modification of the project, exists. But usually the government will get the land it has set its sights on.

Once in a while, a preserved site might lose the features that make it worth the time, money, and effort needed to retain it. Land trusts should minimize the possibility that this will happen. To begin with, they should accept only excellent conservation lands. They should make sure that they maintain the financial ability to manage their preserves. One aspect of this is to be sure to obtain stewardship endowments for any land gifts and, for purchase projects, to build into the fund-raising additional endowment money above the purchase price.

Suppose, though, that in its early days a land trust accepts 20 acres of pleasant though undistinguished woods. Initially, the woods are in a rural setting but over the years come to be surrounded by development. After thirty years, the woods are criss-crossed with bike trails, the ground-nesting birds are gone, the spring wildflowers are decimated, trash is dumped weekly, and the land trust receives regular complaints of late-night parties.

There are remedies for some of these problems, especially if applied when first detected. However, a land trust's resources are finite; time and money it spends on this now-mediocre preserve is time and money unavailable for stewardship of more important ones. In these circumstances, a local land trust might consider getting rid of this preserve.

Perhaps it would make a good city or county park; parks are places for people to ride bikes and walk dogs. Possibly a local government can obtain a grant and buy it. Possibly a trade could be arranged for better land farther out. If this were done, the land trust ought to work on acquiring a big enough tract to prevent similar problems from developing there in the future.

If getting rid of a preserve becomes necessary, whatever actions the land trust takes should be done in the full light of day, with members, the public, appropriate local officials, and the original donor or heirs kept fully informed.

5 CHOOSING LAND TO SAVE

Most land trusts consider themselves conservation organizations, but often the conservation is almost accidental. They save real estate and in doing so they save ecosystems and organisms, but many acquire land almost without a plan, and their stewardship often is either nonexistent or aimed mostly at improving public access.

Saving land of modest ecological importance is better than saving no land at all, but every land trust has practical limitations. Time, energy, and money spent putting together a deal on land of little value except as open space are time, energy, and money unavailable to invest in finding and protecting land of ecological significance. Giving priority to land of high conservation value makes more sense.

For localities having no remaining sites with intact, functioning communities of native species, a land trust will be still be doing good by saving open space, even alien-dominated conifer plantations and fields. Such sites provide ecosystem services, such as producing oxygen and sequestering carbon. They give the residents of the region something to look at besides condos and concrete and provide opportunities for restoration of areas that may in time approach natural vegetation.

Any given land trust may see farmland or trails or historic sites or scenery as important aspects of its mission. Well and good; but the cause of conservation will be better served—for the Earth and for the people—if, within those parameters, conservation in the ecological sense is kept in mind. Farmland trusts, for example, should endeavor to write their conservation easements so that the woods, streams, and marshes are given definite, permanent protection. They may want to reconsider the policy of "Keep it farmland at any price," if the price is more damage to the Earth by chemicals or overstocking or a variety of other practices condoned by agricultural agencies.

Conservation used to be defined as the wise use of resources. Sometimes "for human benefit" was added, sometimes not, but it was always implied. We weren't conserving forests, birds, and seashores. We were conserving "resources"; that is to say, the supplies of what humans need to live and do business.

Few conservationists today would be satisfied with that definition. Aldo Leopold changed the way we look at the world.[1] Leopold's insight was that humans are one element in the vast functioning, evolving biological-geological system that forms the Earth—the biosphere, as ecologists refer to it. It's in our biological nature to think that the human species is the most important component of the system. Probably any other species, if we could read their minds, would believe the same thing. Great auks perhaps would have said, "Great auks rule!" But we killed them and have thoroughly subdued other creatures, so bragging rights belong to us alone.

The best conservation is stewardship of the biosphere and its component interacting systems: the air and water, the woods and fields, the mountains, dunes, and swales. If we take care to maintain the natural systems in good order, then we are doing our best for people—in the long run, possibly not for this quarter's balance sheet. At the same time, we're doing our best for the other species with which we share the planet.

The old-time view of redwoods and ruffed grouse as commodities had noticeably run out of gas by the 1960s. By the 1980s it had been widely displaced by conservation biology, an approach that makes use of Leopold's insights and modern ecology and that focuses on ecological systems. I say, "displaced," but, of course, the old ideas of "wise use" and commodification still hold sway among some old-timers in forestry and natural resources agencies and in a considerable fraction of the lay public.[2]

Biological Diversity

Conservation biology looks to provide the principles and tools for preserving biological diversity. Preserving biological diversity, or biodiversity, means trying to keep species from going extinct, but more than just species may be endangered. Diversity can be lost at every level of the ecological hierarchy. Ecosystems and landscapes can be endangered at levels above the species. Genes can be endangered at a level below the species.[3]

When the last site occupied by a prairie plant community is lost from a county in Ohio, that's a loss of diversity, even if every species still exists somewhere in the county. I have friends with prairie gardens that may include three dozen prairie species. The gardens are beautiful, but they aren't prairie. Away from life in the competitive trenches, many of the species grow bushy or grotesquely large—prairie dropseed up to your thigh, rattlesnake master plants as big around as agaves in a maguey plantation. The prairie garden is not a natural community, where the interacting contingencies of dispersal, rainfall, mutualism, herbivory, and competition yield an integrated system.

When the last prairie or cedar swamp is gone from a region, the mammal, insect, and microbial species that lived with the plants may disappear. Or they may still live at a few sites that are as unlike their real homes as grizzly bears at a garbage dump. But, as communities and species disappear, the landscape itself is pauperized. It becomes one habitat: people places. The forests, bogs, and grassland are gone or reduced to triviality. The landscape is like granola in which most spoonfuls contain nothing but oats.

As the geographical range of a species shrinks, the genotypes that adapted each lost population to its place are also lost. Genetic variability is reduced, putting the long-term persistence of the species in jeopardy. For a species to continue to exist, changed conditions need to be met by evolutionary changes, and these depend mainly on existing genetic variation.

But the loss of populations of a species, the restriction of the species to a few localities, is a loss today, not just for the future. The red-shouldered hawk of Florida, hardly larger than a broad-winged, is a different bird from the red-shouldered hawk of New York. Unlike the song sparrows over most of North America, the ones resident in the Aleutian Islands are gray and large; the subspecies name is *grandis*. None of these populations is better than the others—except under the particular conditions in the place where each lives.

The seaside sparrow lives in salt marshes along the Atlantic and Gulf Coasts. One form lived halfway down the east shore of Florida. Unlike the drabber birds elsewhere, the birds there, called the dusky seaside sparrow, were nearly black above and boldly streaked below. They, like other populations of the species, were squeezed by development of the coastal marshlands. For years, they hung on at St. Johns National Wildlife Refuge. The bird-finding guide's directions read, "Exactly 2.8 miles west of State 50's intersection with I 95, turn north on Hacienda Drive, park, and continue on foot."

But the dusky seaside sparrow doesn't live there any more. It's extinct, done in by a combination of turning some marshes into ponds, draining others, and the fires that followed. By 1980, the population had declined to six individuals, all male, and now that unique gene pool and those dark, different birds are gone.[4]

The Endangered Species Act was passed and signed in 1973 in a grand period when the forces of environmental exploitation had temporarily lost their stranglehold on American government. The Act is an optimistic, forward-looking approach to saving diversity but has its limitations. Although the Act mentions ecosystems and habitats, its focus has usually been on species.

In general, the key to retaining species is keeping the ecosystems to which they belong in good working order. If we save the endangered red-cockaded woodpecker by restoring and maintaining the longleaf pine landscapes of the South, that's good. We are, at the same time, saving the plants and animals of the forests, savannas, and bogs—the hydrology, the seasons, the colors, and the smells. If we somehow save it by methods that keep a few populations of the woodpecker in a few highly managed and altered stands, while allowing the destruction or degradation of the rest of the landscape, we still have the woodpecker, but it has become just another commodity.

Let's back up one step and define "biodiversity." One conservation biology team defines it this way:

Biodiversity is the variety of life and its processes. It includes the variety of living organisms, the genetic differences among them, the communities and ecosystems in which they occur, and the ecological and evolutionary processes that keep them functioning, yet ever changing and adapting.[5]

Most other definitions are equally voluminous. They seem to mix variety, which is the common sense meaning of diversity, and ecological functioning. The fixation of solar energy by green plants, transfer of energy along food chains, biogeochemical cycling, the influence of organisms on their environments by way of soil formation, shading, water purification, are among the ecological functions that conservationists hope to maintain at healthy levels.

Only a quite gaseous definition of biodiversity, it seems to me, can include both variety and functioning. Many of these definitions could serve as high-flown definitions of the whole of biology or of life itself. But as long as we understand how big the balloon is, saying that our aim is to preserve biodiversity may be satisfactory as short-hand.

How Land Trusts Can Be Conservation Organizations: Conservation Rules for Acquiring Land

The key to conservation is protecting local ecosystems and, where possible, the landscapes into which those ecosystems are integrated. Ecology and conservation biology have yielded some generalizations that will help land trusts make the biggest impact in conserving biodiversity. Not all conservation theory is useful for local land trusts, but we can use it plus experience to formulate rules that could increase success in protecting land of high conservation value.

Rule 1. Preserve Landscapes or Representative Natural Ecosystems. Not many local land trusts will be working at the landscape level, but some are, and others could. With appropriate targeting, it might well be possible for a trust to preserve, for example, a whole small watershed. By some combination of gift, purchase, and easement, the trust might be able to ensure that the whole drainage basin is protected from pollutants (except for the now-inevitable sifting down from the atmosphere), thus keeping the stream system safe for the caddis-flies, crawfish, and creek chubs. In saving the watershed, the land trust would be protecting the woods with a great blue heron colony as well as the stream and pond where the herons fish. It would be protecting habitats where the salamanders live and making sure there are no obstacles to their reaching the water and wetlands where they breed.

Equally valid for most land trusts would be to take as their aim protecting one or more examples of each major ecosystem in their service area. In southwest Michigan, this might be a dozen and half, ranging from beech-maple, oak, and pine forest to the various kinds of wetlands to prairie and oak barrens. Several of these major community types could reasonably be subdivided, and the sand dunes and wetlands along the Lake Michigan shore add subtypes that ought to be separately represented. In any vegetationally diverse region, saving even a single representative of each type will be a formidable task. Probably most land trusts will fail in the endeavor because they will be in a race with the forces of sprawl, and the latter have the money and a powerful incentive, the hunger for more. But the attempt is worthy and the result, however short it falls of completeness, valuable.

Why "one or more" examples of an ecosystem? In fact, why should a land trust save even one beech-maple forest or cedar glade or coastal redwood forest when there is a perfectly good one already preserved not far away, in another county, another state, or another ecoregion? It's a good question, and there are several good answers.

First, not all the species and not all the interspecific interactions of, let's say, beech-maple forest are included in one stand, even a large one. A stand or a preserve is a sample that catches some of the traits and not others, as a dipperful of water fails to catch everything living in a pond. By adding more preserves, we save more of the variability, that is, the diversity, of the community type.

Some differences from one beech-maple forest to another are related to minor habitat differences; a forest on flat, clayey land has vernal pools, for example, but one on well-drained slopes doesn't. Still other differences are related to geography and climate. The rich woods in southwest Michigan often have a large white trillium that stands more than a foot tall. Similar woods in southern Indiana also have a large white trillium, but it's another species that differs by having the large white flower nodding, below the level of the leaves.[6] An animal example is the summer tanager of the forests of the South and the scarlet tanager of the North.

These are examples of geographical trends in the way these communities are put together and that can only be known, shown, and studied by having many representative preserves scattered over the range of the community type.

Some differences between stands are pretty much chance events, based on which species have dispersed there recently and which have gone extinct. I witnessed an extinction in a beech-maple forest where I lived. Yellow touch-me-nots, an annual plant with tender, succulent stems, occurred there in small patches. Early in the fall, they produce fruits that, if you touch them when they're ripe, explode and shoot the seeds out.

In one year of severe summer drought, few touch-me-nots came up and none of the wilted, struggling plants produced any fruits. Most annual plants have a seed bank—seeds that lie dormant in the soil and germinate when conditions are right—but if the touch-me-nots had one, it never showed itself. No touch-me-nots appeared the next summer, or in the decade and half since.

This example suggests another reason for having a multiplicity of preserves of a particular biotic community: The likelihood of regional extinction of the species composing it is lowered. Small populations of a species tend to go extinct from random causes: An unusually hot, dry summer comes along, a particularly efficient predator moves in, all four of the resident chickadees die one winter, each bird for its own reason. If other preserves of similar vegetation exist nearby, the species that are lost may be re-established by immigration from one of them.

Creatures that can move about fairly readily, like larger animals and plants with seeds spread by larger animals—cherries, nuts, and beggars-ticks, for example—can get from one woods or one marsh to another without human help. For highly motile species like birds, the process can be entirely silent; when none of the chickadees makes it through the winter, dispersing individuals from elsewhere may take up residence, and we never know the difference.

Touch-me-nots are very good at dispersal over a short distance—a meter or two—but poor for longer distances. For species such as these, especially if they're rare, a land trust might wish to intervene if a local disappearance is detected. I'm sure I could have yellow touch-me-nots back in my woods if I gathered some seeds from another forest this fall and sowed them in the moister spots.

One more reason for a multiplicity of preserves, spread as widely as possible: Conditions on the Earth are changeable. Most of the changes are temporary or more or less cyclic. But others go on over a much longer time span, and that is true of several of the human-produced changes. Since the Industrial Age began, we have poured carbon dioxide into the air in quantities above the input from such natural sources as volcanoes. As atmospheric carbon dioxide has increased and as other greenhouse gases have been released, the worldwide climate has begun to warm.

Just how this global climate change will play out has been described in various large-scale computer models. The different models don't agree in all particulars, but few ecologists doubt that the Earth will experience long-term, directional changes in summer and winter temperatures, seasonal and geographical rainfall patterns, sea level, and disturbance regimes, among other things. As these features change, some plants and animals will eventually find parts of their current ranges uninhabitable. In some cases, new suitable habitat will develop elsewhere.[7]

Some species may fare well under the new conditions. In one model, sweetbay, an evergreen magnolia of the Coastal Plain swamps, holds onto its current geographical range and also finds suitable conditions west to Oklahoma and north almost to southern Illinois.[8] Its expansion might, to some degree, make up for the loss of honey locust from wet habitats. In the same model, honey locust vacates most of Oklahoma, Arkansas, and Tennessee, while adding territory to the north and west of its current range. Some species, however, seem to lose range with little if any counterbalancing additions. American beech, for example, currently an important tree in the mesic forests of most of eastern North America, is modeled as becoming largely restricted to a much-shrunken range in the southern Appalachians.

With climatic change, some preserves will no longer provide satisfactory habitat for some of the plants and animals for which they were established. The cause may be changed physical factors such as temperature or the disappearance of essential biological interactions. For example, both bigtooth and trembling aspens are modeled as disappearing from the eastern United States except for the northernmost fringes of Minnesota, Wisconsin, and Michigan. Ruffed grouse depend on aspen buds and catkins for winter food, and the bark of aspen is the primary food of beaver in all seasons except summer. Both animals are likely to decline in or disappear from those preserves where the aspen have dwindled and died.

To occupy newly suitable sites, species must be able to get to them. This won't be a problem for the organisms able to live in subdivisions and roadsides. But a high percentage of our species today live mostly in remnants and scraps of natural vegetation. Some of these scraps are preserved and some not, but either way, they are isolated pockets in the matrix of agriculture and sprawl.[9] When isolation is combined with low dispersal ability, colonization becomes unlikely within any reasonable time span. Sweetbay's heavy seeds don't move very fast. Global warming may eliminate killing frosts as a limiting factor in the lowlands of Tennessee and Kentucky, but the quick establishment of sweetbay may require magnolia-planting parties.

Conservation biologists and organizations have expended a great deal of effort in recent years devising methods to figure out where biodiversity is and designing plans to capture it. Gap analysis is an example.[10] Data on diversity (usually actual or inferred species occurrence) are plotted on maps and interpreted to decide what elements of biodiversity are un- or underrepresented in existing preserves (wilderness areas, national parks, etc). These are the gaps. Selected as new preserves would be geographic sites that filled these conceptual diversity gaps: that is, the places on the ground that contain the underrepresented diversity elements, such as species or perhaps plant community types that are scarce in or absent from already protected areas. A few land trusts have made formal use of such approaches.

The schemes, however useful they may be for today, suffer by assuming a static world.[11] Much more complicated approaches would be necessary to add global climatic change to methods designed to tell us what land to preserve. The task of protecting the amounts of land that such efforts might yield might well be impossible, as a practical matter.

Few local land trusts would care to become involved in the massive coordinated effort that would be required to add this dimension, and perhaps they don't need to be. Fighting the anti-biodiversity effects of global climatic change is a contribution to worldwide conservation for which local land trusts are uniquely suited. Each trust working in its own area can provide preserves in which it tries to capture the whole variety of local habitats available. If increasing summer drought makes some preserves unsuitable for species A, perhaps the wettest of their preserves will still retain it. If species B is eliminated from preserves south of their service area, perhaps it will be retained in their preserves. When species are eventually lost from its region, the land trust will have provided an array of habitats available for immigration by other native species that now find the climate to their liking. If necessary, the land trust can hurry the immigration and establishment along. After all, many land trusts are experienced in the needed stewardship tasks.

Rule 2. Have a Vision and a Plan and Protect the High-Quality Sites that Realize Them. High-quality sites are those with intact, functioning ecosystems with a good representation of characteristic species. Recognizing high-quality sites implies knowledge of the region: What are the local ecosystems, what species and interspecific interactions characterize each, and where are the best remaining examples? Some of this knowledge ought to reside in the board and staff of a land trust, but much will need to be sought in publications, in the databases of the state Heritage Program or Natural Features Inventory, and in the brains and files of local ecologists and naturalists. Land trusts should systematically compile this information for their service area. Some necessary information will have to be freshly generated.

Choosing high-quality sites also implies knowledge of individual properties being considered for preservation. Not every property will have a history of observations good enough to be used for making decisions. Most will need to be inspected to determine what biotic communities are there, the degree of disturbance, presence of threatened or endangered species, hydrology, geology, and any special features such as bat colonies, springs, or monarch butterfly overwintering sites.

Despite their quest for high-quality sites, land trusts should be willing to accept degraded land in order to restore it—to turn abused woods, wetlands, or river-banks back into healthy ones. Restoration can be a hard job, but it's one that more land trusts are going to have to take on. Joint ventures with native plant groups, locally enlightened government agencies, and a great variety of other local groups, such as Sierra Club chapters, may be easy to set up or fit into.

Saving representatives of all the natural ecosystems of a region is one vision, but not every local land trust has to do the same thing. Both more general and more specialized visions are also defensible. Several land trusts focus on karst topography and the biota that lives in the caves, sinkholes, and underground streams. Joshua's Tract Conservation and Historic Trust (Connecticut) is an example of a land trust that specifically includes historic sites—an 1835 mill is one—in its mission.

Most land trusts may wish to leave preservation of historic structures—a rules-bound and usually expensive undertaking—to specialized historic trusts. Adding history to the criteria for *land* selection, on the other hand, may add a useful dimension without much increasing the stewardship burden. The French explorer LaSalle was the first European to cross Michigan, in 1680.[12] His route ran through the service area of the Southwest Michigan Land Conservancy. Protecting land where he walked—especially sites of natural vegetation that may approximate what he saw—provides a connection to the pre-settlement landscape that will do any citizen good.

Rule 3. Preserve the Largest Areas Possible. The conservation rule regarding size is simple: Bigger is better. There are at least three interacting reasons. We've alluded to the first reason: Small fragments have small populations, and small populations are more prone to extinction from random, or (as the conservation biologists call them) stochastic causes.

Second, many animals choose the place where they're going to settle through some sort of habitat selection behavior. For some, such as forest-interior birds—the species that like the deep forest—the size of the block of habitat available is important in their choice. You may have a very nice five-acre woodlot, with big trees and the right shrubs and herbs, but no ovenbird or black-throated blue warbler will give you the time of day.

Third, small fragments have too much edge. Bigger is better, partly because edge is bad. Of course, edge isn't bad for every kind of organism. Birds such as song sparrows, indigo buntings, and gray catbirds are forest-edge species, to use the terminology of V. E. Shelford and S. C. Kendeigh. The habitat selection behavior of these animals leads them to the border between field and forest or to fields growing up to shrubs and trees.

When the eastern United States was settled, the song sparrow might have been an uncommon bird in many locales, restricted to a few not-very-extensive habitats such as borders between forest and marsh and the willows along river shorelines. But today, there's no shortage of song sparrows or most other forest-edge birds, mammals, or plants. They're everywhere, in power-line cuts, along roadsides, in every field pulled out of cultivation to await development, and in subdivisions with their cultivated trees, shrubs, and lawns. The shortages are of plants and animals that do best in large blocks of forest, grassland, desert, or marsh.

Why edge is unfavorable and how unfavorable it is varies by species, type of edge, and geographical location.[13] Several prominent predators on birds, including raccoons, opossums, grackles, jays, and crows, are forest-edge species. Predation by these species tends to be higher near the edge of forest than farther in. If we say that 50 meters (164 feet) is roughly the distance where penetration by these species drops off, then a forest one-eighth of a mile wide (about 200 meters, or 660 feet) has only a narrow central strip where predation by these species might be low. In this case, half the woods is edge.

Brown-headed cowbirds, brood parasites of many small passerine birds, feed in open country and enter forests at the edges. Their parasitic activities, in which they lay eggs in nests of other species—especially warblers, vireos, sparrows, and flycatchers—tend to be heavier along the edge.

Forest plants suffer from another forest-edge species, the white-tailed deer. Damage from deer drops from edge to interior, but few forests today are large enough to have any portions that are wholly immune. Deer damage plants in two ways. Bucks debark and wound saplings by rubbing against them to remove velvet from their antlers. The second, more obvious way deer damage plants is by eating them, foraging on twigs and leaves. Deer browse on many plants, but they have their favorites, and many of these are plants that preserve managers would like to keep.

The list of species that are hard hit by deer foraging includes many highly desirable herbs, such as trilliums, and shrubs, such as Canada yew, both of which tend to decline or disappear in forestland with high deer densities. Deer also have their preferences among trees. They like balsam fir, white cedar, and hemlock, for example, and may deform larger individuals of these species with a browse line. The seedlings and tender young saplings of preferred species may be clipped off at a rate that makes it impossible for these species to regenerate themselves in the canopy.

Conflicts may arise between saving a small, pristine property and a large, but rough and ragged one. Bypassing the small but choice will be difficult, but the land trust needs to realize that present quality is not the only consideration. Can the future quality of the postage-stamp site be assured? If the site can be degraded by activities on surrounding properties—runoff, erosion, local pollution—then acquisition of a buffer zone would be necessary. If the buffer is unavailable or too expensive, the choice is between a small preserve whose quality is apt to worsen and a large preserve that will improve under stewardship.

Almost any land saved is apt to make a bigger contribution to the biosphere in the way of ecosystem services than land left to become parking lots, subdivisions, or intensive agriculture. Although few land trusts will want to pass up a chance to save an old-growth forest, other, much less pristine lands can have their own values. For example, if we give high priority to sequestering carbon in living plants to counteract the greenhouse effect, saving an old field growing up with young trees will do a better job than saving an old-growth forest, whose carbon stores have already reached a steady state.

Rule 4. Add Land around Preserves. One of the best ways to get a big preserve is by adding land to a small one.

Bigger is still better for any preserve, even one not composed entirely of one type of vegetation. Some of the same lessons about fragmentation apply. The bigger the preserve, the larger the population of many of the organisms, hence the less vulnerable they are to random extinctions. It's more likely that a given species will be engaged in the full range of interactions with its community associates: pollinators and other mutualists, dispersal agents, and also, of course, parasites and predators. Also, it is more likely that the organisms will find a high percentage of their routine requirements within the boundaries of the preserve: nest or den sites, food, escape cover, hibernacula, and the like.

Beyond the boundary of a preserve lies danger. When large carnivores wander out of a national park into the surrounding countryside, they are apt to get hurt or killed. This applies to bears and wolves in this country and to large cats, hyenas, and wild dogs in Asia or Africa.[14] Depending on the species and situation, they're shot legally or illegally, hit by cars, or tranquilized and removed to some remote site where they're less likely to offend human sensibilities.

On the smaller preserves of most land trusts, some individual songbirds, foxes, and snakes will have part of their home range extending onto neighboring properties. There, they may get run over, be killed by neighbors' dogs or cats, ingest pesticides, or suffer any of a number of other assaults and insults. The biggest preserves, then, are the best, because a higher percentage of the animals do not have to venture into the dangers beyond the preserve borders.

Like raccoons and cowbirds, people come in from the edge, and they may bring their dogs, cats, bikes, and off-road vehicles with them. On some preserves, land trusts will want to encourage visitors for educational purposes, but preserves are likely to get visitors whether they're wanted or not. The longer the perimeter of the preserve relative to the area of the interior, the more likely visitors will impact the whole preserve. Of course, other factors also influence the frequency and type of intrusions. A residential neighborhood next door will probably bring the most visitors.

It's desirable to extend the effective area of any preserve, if possible. One way to do this is by enlisting neighbors. For example, if a land trust owns one side of a stream, and the other side is part of a plat, perhaps the lot owners can be persuaded to quit mowing down to the water's edge and let a strip of natural wetland vegetation develop, along with the insects, frogs, and turtles that go with it. Perhaps they can be convinced that fertilizing their lawns is unnecessary, harmful to water quality, and just bad form generally.

Adding more acreage of the vegetation already well represented in a current preserve is most valuable, for all the size and edge reasons listed under rule 3. However, almost any additions will help. If the preserve is forest and the land added is old field, it will turn into more forest eventually. In the meantime, it buffers the preserve and helps regulate access. Any vegetation that tempers the abrupt boundary between preserve and farmland, lawn, or asphalt is beneficial.

Even if the land added doesn't directly abut a preserve, it can still be important. Projecting forward current land-use trends for much of the United States yields a bleak vision in which protected lands form islands of twenty, forty, or at best a few hundred acres in polluted seas of asphalt or lawn. An archipelago of preserves will likely preserve biodiversity better than individual isolated islands because the dispersal that counteracts extinctions will be easier within the archipelago than between the isolated habitat islands.

The cause of conservation may also be served by acquiring land next to one owned by an Audubon society or similar organization. This will be true—the cause will be served and the time and money well spent—if the other organization's commitment to protection in perpetuity matches the land trust's own.

Rule 5. Some Small Preserves Are Worth Saving. A land trust is offered a 10-acre preserve. If bigger is better, isn't a miniature like this just a waste of time?

The most defensible small properties are those with strong ecological credentials. Depending on the ecosystem involved, 10 acres may be the best that can be hoped for. Fens, the alkaline bogs that in this country are mainly distributed in the Upper Midwest, rarely come in large patches. One might wish for surrounding acreage as a buffer zone, but an intact and invasive-free 10-acre fen would be a prize. Also, the kinds of organisms retained in a preserve is related to scale. A small patch of forest may be a sink for forest-interior birds, or have none at all, but it may save forest herbs, mushrooms, butterflies, snails, and a rich complement of soil invertebrates.

Another consideration is that some animals look at the landscape differently from us. Forest-interior bird species characteristic of swamp forest in the Northeast, such as northern waterthrush and Canada warbler, will nest in very small red maple swamps, down to a couple of acres.[15] Their occurrence in a swamp is less related to the size of the swamp than to the overall amount of forest of any kind within the surrounding six-tenths of a mile. A 10-acre red maple swamp set in a largely forested region that's likely to stay forested might be a desirable acquisition.

Small preserves will rarely protect species from random extinction as well as bigger ones can, but could small preserves actually act counter to the regional survival of the species? An isolated woodlot of 10 or 20 acres may attract an occasional wood thrush, scarlet tanager, or great crested flycatcher, but this small woodlot often turns out to be a demographic "sink." This term is use to describe sites in which the populations of a particular species are not self-sustaining. For a population to be self-sustaining, a pair has to produce enough young in its lifetime to yield two adults that enter the future breeding population. "Sources" are habitats where the species in question is able to produce surplus offspring that can potentially disperse and repopulate other areas.

Perhaps a male bird moves into a small patch of habitat and sets up a territory but no female finds the place attractive enough to join him. If he does attract a mate, they build a nest and produce eggs, but the raccoons or grackles may kill most or all the young. In a sense, then, many of the birds that set up homes in this small woodlot are simply flushed down the drain. Perhaps we shouldn't try to protect such small patches of habitat at all. Let them slide into whatever fate the developers have in mind for them.

There is still much to be learned about how small patches of habitat, or sinks, interact with large blocks, or sources. So far, though, it seems that sink populations are helpful, not harmful, to the survival of the species. Among other things, they allow a larger overall population size that preserves more genetic variability.[16] Also, sink populations in the aggregate can act as a storehouse that helps tide the species over a bad year in one or more of the source populations. Some young animals that end up in marginal habitat are able to move to better ones in a later year when there are openings. Labeling a site as a sink is misleading to a degree; in some years, young may survive to disperse to other patches, including source habitats.

Yet another reason to protect small preserves is education. Families can be invited on nature hikes to see nature at this scale. Some of the visitors, young or old, may come to love the natural world and become the donors and voters that someday tip the balance between conservation and exploitation.

A strong argument can also be made for a small tract that has a high probability of being the basis for later acquisitions.

Some small preserves make good sense. Others don't. Saving 10 acres of Scotch pine plantation in Michigan, 10 acres of loblolly pine in Florida, or 10 acres of mesquite rangeland in south Texas would generally be ecologically pointless; there's plenty of each of these around.

Rule 6. Construct Corridors if It's Easy. "Corridors," in conservation terminology, are linear connections meant to facilitate interchange of organisms between larger patches of habitat. Visualize two 40-acre woodlots connected by a corridor of wooded bottomland along a stream.

The hope is that corridors will have at least two favorable effects. The first is obvious: The movement of organisms (or seeds or fruits) along the corridor may maintain species diversity by preventing the loss of a species from one patch by replenishment from others.

Second, the movements from one patch to another may maintain genetic diversity within a species. Small populations tend to lose genetic diversity, or variability, through a process called genetic drift. As a rough rule of thumb, a single population with an effective size of one thousand or more breeding individuals doesn't lose genetic variability with time. Smaller and smaller populations lose variability faster and faster.

Eventually, small populations (if they don't go extinct first) could come, in the extreme case, to have no genetic variability. That is, all the individuals would have the same gene for a given trait. In a human population, every person would have, say, only red hair genes, only pale skin genes; they'd all have the same genetic predispositions to have particular diseases or to be shy or bold. They would be like identical twins.[17]

Some red-haired, pale-skinned people might think that this situation would be ideal. Evolutionarily, though, loss of variability is unfortunate. Genetic variability is what evolution has to work with in meeting changed environmental conditions. We wouldn't want the prairie chickens in our grassland preserve to lose all their genetic variability, or the Swainson's warblers in our swamp preserve to lose theirs.

There is surprisingly good news about maintaining genetic variability, though. Quite a small amount of interchange between relatively isolated populations is sufficient to retain genetic variability around the level it began. In fact, theory suggests that about one successful interchange per generation is enough. Maybe, just to have a little cushion, we'd like to try for two or three interchanges.[18]

By "successful," we mean that the interchanged individual becomes a breeder in its new home. Also, bear in mind that for many small animals, a generation is a fairly short period—for small birds, perhaps a couple of years.

Corridors sound like a good idea. Many people are intrigued with them, I think because they fit so well with visions of greenways and trails. But there is still little evidence on whether they do what we hope they'll do. Also, certain spoilsports have thought of reasons why corridors might even be actively bad. Most corridors will be mostly edge, so some of the forest (or marsh or grassland) interior species might not be willing to use them. Also, the corridor might attract all the forest-edge predators we talked about, so for some species, using the corridor might be as dangerous as you or me taking a midnight stroll in the worst section of a big city.

Furthermore, diseases and parasites might spread along our corridors, and so might some alien species. We may be struggling to remove garlic mustard from one of our preserves at the same time that deer pick up mud with seeds in their hooves and trot along a corridor to another, previously garlic mustard–free preserve. If there is wheeled traffic along the corridor, the garlic mustard seeds are almost certain to be spread in mud carried by tires.

It's unclear whether corridors are good, bad or—most likely—fairly complicated in their effects. For the time being, land trusts might want to help with corridors if doing so is easy and cheap. If a local greenways group is becoming established, it might be a good idea to partner with it and encourage an ecologically sound design.[19]

Buying land to make a corridor across several parcels of privately owned land is likely to be a difficult, expensive proposition. The time and money could probably be better spent another way. It might be possible to add adjacent similar habitat to one or more of the preserves, thereby ensuring larger populations and lowering extinction and genetic drift. Alternatively, a land trust could try to add a preserve somewhere along the route between two large preserves; possibly a stepping stone would work as well as a corridor.

If a corridor seemed important enough, the use of conservation easements might produce the route with less immediate expenditure of money than buying the land.

Rule 7. Save Land with Rare. Threatened, and Endangered Species, and Take Care of Them. If land trusts get the chance, most will be interested in preserving land holding a population of an endangered species: a species in danger of going extinct either regionally or range-wide. Equally important will be saving lands containing threatened species—ones near the threshold of endangerment—and species that are rare and declining but not yet listed by the state or federal government.

If the opportunity does arise to acquire land to protect these populations, it's well to remember a couple of things: First, even if the endangered species is restricted to 1, 5, or 20 acres, the land trust should obtain as much of the habitat in question as possible, to allow the species to spread or to shift around. It should also try to acquire a surrounding buffer strip.

Second, to retain the species, some sort of habitat management will probably be necessary. Stewardship is the subject of the next chapter.

Where I live, several people within a 20-mile radius are pretty good at identifying birds and plants of the flashier types. People who can identify grasses, sedges, and rushes, or snails or crawfish or even reptiles and amphibians are scarcer. Consequently, threatened and endangered species of these groups are under-represented in preserves.

Land trusts should cultivate experts in these more obscure taxonomic groups or send one of their volunteers to take a course or two. Perhaps a marsh that looks to the unskilled like a dozen others will become a high-priority site because of previously undetected rare species.

Rule 8. Opportunism in the Protection of Land is Not Necessarily a Vice. It's a fact that acquisition of land by the majority of local land trusts is opportunistic, rather than based on a plan.[20] For established organizations with a sizable service area, enough potential land deals show up unsolicited in a week or a month that land protection volunteers and staff sometimes feel they have little time to go out and look for more.

Saving the 32,000-acre Pascagoula (Mississippi) bottomlands began with a young man walking into The Nature Conservancy office and saying he was part-owner of some land that ought to be preserved.[21] If a land trust were to ignore these land deals in favor of a strict planned approach based on biodiversity—or anything else—it would, first, save less land than it could, and, second, fail in other aspects of its land-saving mission.

Having agreed that a land trust shouldn't ignore a great deal that walks in the door, we should reiterate that a land trust needs to know what it wants to do, to have a plan, and to follow it. Otherwise, it may save land but will end up carrying water for every organization and individual that does have an agenda. The land it saves will be a hodgepodge that's unlikely to fulfill its vision.

Rule 9. Prioritize. Any land trust needs to prioritize potential land acquisitions so as to spend its limited time and money on the most promising ones and avoid the weakest ones. A scoring system should formalize considerations in three categories: quality of the land, quality of the deal, and assurance of adequate stewardship. The most attractive transactions, of course, are those with willing, conservation-minded owners who pay transaction and start-up costs and provide a generous endowment for land having high conservation value and few stewardship problems.

A scoring sheet based on the organization's priorities will inject some objectivity into the process. It's to be expected that a great deal of pragmatism will still be involved in most decisions.

Quality of the land has top priority. It's what most of the preceding rules are about, but there may be some additional considerations. For example, even high-quality natural land may have a corner with a farm dump, or something worse, that will need evaluating.

As for deal quality, the best ones are those that are so clearly problem-free that they can be completed quickly. Problems can arise in many sectors: title, boundaries, and access are common ones. A few examples of situations that would lose points on the scoring sheet are absence of mineral rights, a dozen owners and some not recently heard from, a neighbor disputing a boundary (or claiming an easement of necessity), and no road frontage.

The kind of deal—land gift, easement gift, bargain sale, fair-market sale, purchased easement, or something else—is a major consideration. Land trusts will differ as to which type they rate as most worth pursuing.

In considering the deal, a careful land trust will also want to know something of the donor's temperament, especially for donors of easements. It's a free country, so any of us can choose to be cantankerous, erratic, obtuse, or irrational; or we may be stuck with these traits by nature. But the land trust should factor into deal quality the potential for time, worry, and money for legal fees resulting from donor disposition. For a property of overwhelming conservation value, it might be worth tolerating a donor who would occupy several hours per month of a staff member's time. Since staff time is usually a limiting resource, it may not be worth it for land of lesser quality.

Trouble is more likely from second and later owners of easement property. Usually, no data will be available at the time of the deal on how troublesome future owners may be. It will be prudent to anticipate, if not a worst-case scenario, at least a hard-case scenario.

Even fee donors have been known to be troublesome if they are disputatious by nature and if their perceptions of how the land was going to be treated differ from their perceptions of how it is being treated. To a considerable degree, it doesn't matter whether the land trust's management is flawed or flawless. The problem comes from the discrepancy between expectation and reality and how the individual deals with change.

The best way to head off such problems is to make sure that the donors of land or easements are well educated in what to expect. This will lessen but not eliminate conflicts.

Although quick deals are best, a land trust should never hurry. In accepting any land, it needs to follow a carefully defined path designed to minimize later trouble.

On the other side of the table, the donors should take care to get well acquainted with the land trust. They will wish to be able to answer yes to all these questions: Are staff and other contacts friendly and easy to deal with? Does the organization show in its people and its literature a commitment to conservation that corresponds to that of the landowners? Is the organization financially sound? Are its financial and membership systems organized to keep it that way? Can it give reasonably detailed and satisfactory plans for managing the land? Has it given serious thought to what will happen to protected land if the land trust should go out of existence?

The third consideration in evaluating a potential transaction is ensuring adequate stewardship. Some land trusts are full-service operations; they acquire land and take care of it. They may also protect land with conservation easements. Other land trusts acquire land but pass the care of it on to another organization, usually some government agency. Still other land trusts take only conservation easements; the care of the land remains with the owners, original and subsequent.

All three types of land trusts need to ask themselves the question: If we do this deal, will the land be well stewarded? For preserves of full-service land trusts, the bat is in their hands. They need to assure themselves that they have the money, time, personnel, and expertise (which are all more or less fungible) to do the job.

Some lands will take a lot of stewardship effort, either because of ecosystem type or housekeeping requirements. Few general land trusts will wish to take ownership of a working farm if they're going to be expected to keep it in operation. A trust may very well accept a natural area with invasive plants, such as Scotch broom on the West Coast or buckthorn in the East. Controlling these aliens will be a continuing stewardship battle, but few or no examples of certain vegetation types without the invaders may remain.

Few land trusts will be interested in accepting land with buildings, unless it comes with a donation to pay demolition costs. There are exceptions, such as a building that can be used as a headquarters with modest conversion expenses and maintenance costs no higher than the trust's current rent.

Land trusts need to assess the level of problems likely to be associated with each parcel. For example, if a property has already been invaded by dumpers or mountain bikers, the picture may be bleak. What would be the level of effort needed to stop the intrusions and restore the site? The price might be so high that no more time need be spent considering the deal.

For conservation easements, the stewardship role of the land trust is indirect. Its voice in care of the land consists of designing restrictions in the easement deed and monitoring the owner's performance. Nevertheless, the costs of ongoing stewardship on the part of the owner and of oversight on the part of the trust need to be considered. Suppose a land trust is offered an easement over vacant land where trespass by off-road vehicles is already a problem. Will the owner have the resources, including the will, to stop it? How much time over the years may the land trust have to spend checking up and jaw-boning? Perhaps this is another situation where the land trust should cut its losses.

For land trusts that are mainly conduits to government agencies, stewardship is not a term in the equation. Whatever the agency does is the stewardship the land is going to get—good, ill-conceived, destructive, or simply absent.

6
STEWARDSHIP

Conservation organizations today like to call what they do with their land stewardship rather than management. The difference, perhaps, is that "management" carries the connotation of arbitrary control; it is man as dominator. "Stewardship," on the other hand, implies taking care of the land in accordance with some greater scheme. For some people, this may be religious: We were put on Earth to take care of God's frogs and beetles. For others, it is ethical but ecological and evolutionary: Their decisions are guided by what is best for biospheric health and diversity.

Good stewardship by a land trust includes conservation and ecology. It may also include spiritual or religious elements. It definitely includes housekeeping, such as installing and taking care of signs and trails.

Owning and Easing and Passing Through

Lands that are saved from development, where the biota are protected from destructive disturbance, and that are available for study and appreciation have been called reserves, preserves, sanctuaries, and refuges, depending on what aspect of the process is emphasized. The term "preserve" is probably the most general.

In the last several years, there has been a trend in the land trust movement toward de-emphasis of preserve ownership. A 1989 article in *Exchange* entitled "Protecting Land through Ownership" asked, "How does a land trust responsibly decide when to acquire a property and when to pursue other means of land protection?"[1] The crux of the article was this paragraph:

Is ownership by the trust the best or only protection method? Relatively few properties contain such significant and endangered conservation resources that only outright ownership can assure the necessary sophistication of protection and management. The trust may be able to protect the property using another method, such as a conservation easement. Many alternative methods leave the trust with fewer long-term management responsibilities and costs than permanent ownership of the land. Or, there may be another group or individual willing and able to protect the property.

The article's message, as I would summarize it, is When should a land trust own land? *Never.* What's the best way to protect land? *Any other way.*

I attended the board meeting of a new land trust during which the members discussed a parcel offered to them. It was 2.5 acres of an unusual vegetation type disappearing from the region under the pressure of suburban development. The vegetation was, among other things, an important stopover habitat for migrating land birds.

The new board was troubled by the small size and also the location of the property in a low-rent rural residential district. The decisive factor in turning the offer down, though, was that established land trusts had warned them against acquiring a bunch of small properties that would take a lot of time to steward.

This new land trust, which had neither lands nor easements, had learned the virtue of caution too thoroughly, too soon. My opinion, which I kept to myself, was that, even with the problems of size and location, a good example of this vegetation type was worth taking at any stage of a trust's development. As the *first* preserve of a new organization, it would draw press coverage that would attract new members and perhaps other landowners with preservation in mind. It would also reassure current supporters that they were involved with a living, breathing organization.

Is it possible that this dread of owning land is excessive? What are the advantages of a preserve of one's own?

The first obvious advantage is that the land trust can control the care of the land in a way impossible with other protection methods. The statement that "relatively few properties contain such significant . . . conservation resources that only outright ownership can assure the necessary sophistication of protection and management" is faulty. It's a sad situation if a land trust can't match the "sophistication of protection and management" of the functionaries and politicians who will be making stewardship decisions in the average public agency. "If you want something done right, let somebody else do it" is not a motto for success in the permanent protection of land.

A second, related advantage is that land owned by the land trust can be readily opened to the public. As conservation easements have developed in land trust practice, little if any public access is permitted. Certainly, the land protected by easement has public value; it better have, since significant public benefit is the legal justification for conservation easements. But the benefits to the public are mostly indirect: the land provides ecosystem services, it may be part of a nice view, it may provide habitat for wildlife, it may protect farmland—which may or may not produce anything that ends up as food on local citizens' tables. By contrast, preserves are generally land that the public can connect with directly—hiking, birding, berry-picking, or sitting and soaking up the sun on an autumn morning. In connecting with the land, the visitors also connect with the land trust and the idea of land conservation.

It may be that some semi-savvy land trusts shy away from having preserves because they fear liability; a visitor slips on the bog boardwalk, breaks his coccyx, and sues.

Most states have recreational use statutes that provide considerable protection against such claims to land trusts and other private landowners that open their property to the public, free of charge, for recreational purposes.[2] The fear of liability is not completely irrational, however. What the recreational use laws do is lower the duty of care required. In effect, as long as the landowner doesn't cause harm to the visitor by willful or malicious conduct, a law suit is unlikely to succeed. But we're a litigious society, and some supposedly injured party may find a lawyer willing to file suit against a land trust. That's what insurance is for. Every land trust should have a policy that will pay the cost of defending such a suit and any damages that may result. State recreational use laws vary; the land trust will want to have information on its state's statute and case law and follow the standards.

A third advantage is that owning and stewarding preserves is something that the public, donors, and members understand and approve of. To be sure, they can be educated to appreciate conservation easements. But owning the land itself, rather than a couple of switches out of the bundle of property rights, is something that is appealing to anyone with a heartfelt interest in conserving plants, animals, and habitats.

Buying a preserve focuses the membership and attracts new members like nothing else a land trust can do. A land purchase is always the easiest way for a land trust to raise money. At the end of a hard-fought fund drive, passing on the newly acquired preserve to a government agency is anti-climax at best.

Preserves offer fund-raising opportunities of several kinds. The trust can give supporters a chance to sponsor benches, trails, descriptive pamphlets, wildlife viewing platforms, or other items or activities limited only by the organization's imagination. It might be thought that if the land trust didn't need money for the preserve, supporters would still give the money for other operations. This presumption is only partly true. People need a reason to donate; setting up and taking care of preserves gives them a reason.

I suspect the last sentence of the paragraph from *Exchange* that I quoted earlier was hastily written: "There may be another group or individual willing and able to protect the property." No land trust should fool itself that just because another group with land conservation as one of its aims owns a piece of property, the property is thereby permanently protected. If the land trust arranges to hold a well-drafted conservation easement, it may be so, but not otherwise.

As for protection by individuals, ownership of significant land by people who love it has often been the foundation upon which land conservation has been constructed. But, as we know, it's nearly impossible for individuals to ensure permanent protection of land on their own. This fact has been one of the engines of the land trust movement. Stephen Small has made the case convincingly and repeatedly in his writings.[3] Arranging for an individual to buy conservation property will provide permanent protection only if the deal includes a conservation easement or a commitment to an eventual transfer of ownership to the land trust.

Some organizations that consider themselves land trusts have specialized in doing deals, either easements or actual acquisitions, that are then passed through to government. Some have gotten so good at raising money for deals that local citizens, when you talk with them, think the organization's function is fund-raising, not conservation.

Doing deals is heady stuff. A suggestion to the board of such land trusts that they now ought to take care of the land may be greeted with the same alarm they would show if told they ought to use their BMWs to haul manure to the community gardens.

Doing deals and even finding land suitable to acquire engages a highly important, but narrow segment of potential members of a land conservation organization. One of the best arguments for stewardship is the power it has to bring in new members and energize current members so far uninvolved in the organization.

Usually stewardship volunteers finish a work day with a sense of fulfillment and of community with the land and their fellow workers. Taking care of preserves is fun; a day in the open air with birds singing or frogs croaking. But more than that, it is tangibly worthwhile: the preserve, the organization, the environment, and society benefit. Giving people something useful to do is a more powerful way of forging bonds than inviting them to meetings at which their role is as the faces of an audience.

One California volunteer, an ivy-puller at Golden Gate National Recreation Area, wrote, "In the struggle against wildland weeds—or more broadly, in natural areas stewardship—I found a way of life. . . ." He went on:

A volunteer-based stewardship program can help build a dedicated constituency for exotic pest plant control efforts, the sponsoring organization, and conservation of natural areas in general. . . . Volunteers will rise to the challenge if managers are willing to strive for nothing less than personal, social, and ecological transformation. That may be too much to ask from an afternoon of pulling weeds. But then I wonder. Sisyphus might have enjoyed more job satisfaction if he had company.[4]

Doing things to the land where one lives is probably a basic human impulse. It's no accident that clearing trees, putting in ditches, and stringing fence are referred to in the English language as "improvements." If this impulse is an ingrained human trait, we'd do well to make use of it, but redirect it, as much as possible, from destruction to caretaking, away from fertilizing turf and landscaping with exotics to the stewardship of natural areas.

Well-advertised workdays to help cut brush, lay out trails, pull alien invaders, gather native seeds, and pick up trash are among the best ways to get new people involved with a land trust. Not only will the land trust get valuable labor and attract new members, it will be helping restore the American sense of community that in the last forty years has gotten as thin as the Antarctic ozone layer.

Goals and Targets

A good overall stewardship goal is maintaining regional biodiversity. The aim is not to maximize biodiversity on any single preserve. If the land trust has an old-growth forest with Acadian flycatchers and cerulean warblers, it does not—unlike the state DNR—clearcut holes in it to add forest-edge species. The trust will be maximizing regional biodiversity by keeping as many forest interior species possible on this particular site and letting the song sparrows and towhees stay at the pipeline corridors and county parks.

For each preserve, a target is needed. If you don't know what you're aiming for, you can't tell if you hit it. A frequent target, or model, is the structure and composition of the particular ecosystem just before European settlement began to change things.

Matching this benchmark may be difficult. For one thing, we'll never know the complete biota of presettlement habitats. Another reason is that conditions have changed. Even if we had a complete species list for, say, the bottomland forests of the South, some species are obviously extinct, like the Carolina parakeet. It may well be that other, non-obvious species are also gone, such as insects or herbs that disappeared before they were even given scientific descriptions.

Hydrology may have changed, and fires are generally less frequent. The regional climate may be different as the result of natural fluctuation and human disturbance. Alien species have been introduced. Pollution may make the growth or reproduction of some originally occurring species impossible. The balance between plants, herbivores, and predators may have been shifted, in some well-understood ways and others not so well understood.

The cascade from elimination of predators to high populations of herbivores to damage to the vegetation has been known at least as far back as the early twentieth century. An early study (1932) was done on the Kaibab plateau in northern Arizona by one of V. E. Shelford's students, Daniel Rasmussen.[5] Government predator control of cougars, wolves, and coyotes, coupled with restricted hunting led to an enormous increase in black-tailed deer between 1905 and 1925. The deer population crashed, but not before the vegetation was substantially changed. Cliff rose, a favorite winter food, was decimated, and pinyon and juniper had browse lines as high as the deer could reach. The same cascade is now observable over much of the eastern half of the United States in the effects of white-tailed deer on vegetation.

Most of us know of the decline of salmon populations but may not have thought of the effects of these losses on other parts of the landscape. Large populations of several species of fish used to leave the oceans and spawn in the headwaters of streams all along the East and West coasts. Several species of salmon were involved, but also other fish such as chars, smelt, shad, and eels. The runs of most have been reduced or eliminated by human actions, including commercial fishing, pollution, and dams.

Considering the amount of fish biomass involved, this sea-to-land transfer must have had many effects, on stream ecosystems, of course, but also on terrestrial ecosystems extending out some distance from the streams. It's difficult to know all the ways in which the structure and potential development of the plant-animal communities of these regions have been altered, but the sea-to-land movement of fish brought nutrients back from the ocean, fertilizing the marshes and forests. It also formed an enormous seasonal energy base for a great variety of predators and scavengers, residents and migrants, ranging from grizzly bears, gulls, eagles, and ravens to insects and bacteria.[6]

Exact re-creation of a presettlement ecosystem is impossible. We'll have to accept that we're unlikely ever to hit the bull's-eye and just be content with landing somewhere on the target. But the effort is worthwhile. In a landscape dominated by Eurasian species on every roadside, powerline swath, farm, and housing development, we should be grateful for the diversity—and beauty—added by a few sites devoted to something approaching what should be there based on the regional soil and climate interacting with the native biota.

Presettlement conditions need not be the target for every site. There may be good reasons for trying to keep it something else. In a region that was mostly forested at the time of settlement, grassland birds may have been rare, occurring in temporary grassy areas that resulted from fire or the abandonment of a beaver pond. The animal species associated with grassland remained in the primeval landscape by shifting around from site to site as grasslands disappeared and reappeared.[7] In large parts of the United States, there's no longer room for that natural pattern to play out. We may wish to try to provide permanent grassland by planting grasses, even alien ones if necessary, and mowing or burning these fields to keep the woody plants out. A conservation easement on a large pasture might retain nesting upland sandpipers. The target is simply grassland in a big enough packet to support grassland birds and small mammals.

How Much Management?

Dwarf or Robbins' cinquefoil is a perennial alpine plant that grows only in a small area of the White Mountain National Forest in New Hampshire. Its habitat is barren, stony flats blown free of snow in the winter and fully exposed to harsh climatic conditions generally. The species was listed as endangered in 1980. Research suggested that the probable causes for the decline of this very rare plant were overcollecting by botanists and disturbance by hikers on two trails running through the site.[8]

Transplants into other seemingly suitable habitat nearly all failed. What succeeded was rerouting the trails, building a low rock wall around the critical habitat, and putting up "No Admittance" signs. A census of older plants (stems greater than 14 millimeters in diameter) found 1,801 in 1973, a drop to 1,547 in 1983 (when the measures mentioned above were taken), and then increases to 3,368 in 1992 and 4,575 in 1999.

In this case of a harsh habitat where few other species are able to survive, just removing the agents that led to the decline seems to be enough. Plant species that in a more benign habitat might be able to shade out the cinquefoil or otherwise outcompete it aren't able to do so under these conditions. So, one way to manage a preserve, or a vegetational subunit within a preserve, is to leave it alone.

For another example, suppose the trust acquires a new preserve that consists of young forest growing up on formerly tilled land. All management takes time or its equivalent, money. What could the land trust do that would be better than simply letting nature take its course: letting succession proceed to develop a mature forest with the passage of several decades?

This is one end of a management continuum—let it be what it will be. Set it and forget it.

Probably a more frequent situation is one in which letting nature take its course leads to unfavorable alteration of the protected community or the decline or disappearance of a species worth keeping. Running buffalo clover once occurred in a band from Nebraska and Arkansas to West Virginia. It grew in several habitats, but savanna or open forest, especially along stream banks, was a favorite. Running buffalo clover looks superficially like the Eurasian white clover of American lawns; however, its flowers are larger and borne at the top of a stem that also bears a pair of leaves.[9]

By the middle of the twentieth century, running buffalo clover was absent from many of its former stations and thought to be extinct. Passage of the Endangered Species Act and formation of The Nature Conservancy's Natural Heritage Program sent botanists into the field looking for rare and declining species. Running buffalo clover was rediscovered, first in West Virginia in 1983 and later in four other states, and was added to the endangered species list.

Some of the sites where it was relocated were being grazed, or overgrazed, by cattle. Stopping the grazing with the aim of protecting the endangered clover led in some cases in Indiana and Kentucky not to the plant's increase and spread but rather to its decline or even disappearance.[10]

It appears that the plant originally grew on sites of appropriate soil and shade that were subjected to grazing and trampling by American bison. In some circumstances, cattle grazing can evidently mimic these effects. Few conservationists like the idea of using woodlands as pasture and still fewer approve of leaving cattle free to wade across the creeks; nevertheless, these actions may be what kept the clover thriving in a landscape from which it had otherwise disappeared as a result of soil given over to row crops, herbicide use, and the growth of brush through lack of fire. Whether light grazing by cattle is the best management technique or whether the objective could be attained by mowing, burning, or some other treatment is still uncertain.[11]

In the case of running buffalo clover, certain natural processes tend to eliminate, not perpetuate, a species that the land trust would wish to preserve. These natural processes are those that tend to move vegetation toward an equilibrium based on local climate, soil, and other environmental factors.[12] Species other than those included in the equilibrium pool were retained in presettlement communities by a different set of natural processes, mostly natural disturbances that humans have altered or eliminated, among them fires, grazing by large herbivores, predation, and hydrological fluctuations including floods. Restoring these natural processes is the best management option, where possible. Otherwise, retaining such species as running buffalo clover will require spending human time and energy to oppose the processes tending to move the vegetation toward an equilibrium. If the preserve manager does nothing, the ecosystem will come to be increasingly dominated by shade-tolerant and long-lived species.

If the land trust has a preserve of a vegetation type considered to be the climax community of the area—consisting mostly of the most shade-tolerant and long-lived species—it may believe it can relax and let the community continue to do what it does. This may be a mistake. At least, the trust will need to monitor its climax community. Old-growth mesophytic forest will stay old-growth mesophytic forest for a long time with little long-term change in many ecological characters. It will continue to look generally the same and have roughly the same production of organic matter per growing season.

But the mature mesophytic forests our forefathers found were products of a history of occasional disturbances, such as surface fires, passenger pigeon nestings (with attendant overfertilization and other damage), and tornadoes. With long-continued protection, some species of herbs that characterized the forest when the preserve was established may begin to dwindle because of the absence of disturbance favorable to them.[13]

It's also true for many of our mature forests of today that some plants are likely to decline or disappear because of white-tailed deer browsing. Deer are extravagantly common in much of the eastern United States because homeowners, businesses, and government agencies, all earnestly working in their own best interests, have created a landscape to which deer are perfectly adapted, provided them with an incredible abundance of food, and gotten rid of almost all of their natural predators.

Increasingly, I've heard preserve managers complain about depredations by wild turkeys. In several regions, turkeys have increased greatly, perhaps to above presettlement levels, following restocking and highly successful reproduction. The turkeys are accused of eating tops of orchids and other rare plants and seeds of sugar maple, as well as their obvious foods of acorns, beech nuts, and insects. Turkeys may become part two of a double whammy for beech-maple forests, eating maple seeds, while deer eat any maple reproduction that reaches the seedling stage.

Even in a basically steady-state community like beech-maple forest, some management is likely to be necessary. Perhaps the deer herd or the turkey flock needs to be thinned. Possibly a small experimental fire would bring back some of the herbs that seem to be disappearing. If few or no trees have been lost from the canopy in several years, so that the shade is dense and continuous, a preserve manager might want to take out a few trees—using great care and avoiding any vehicles with tires that could transport mud with seeds of noxious invaders such as garlic mustard.

What about a community a little below the climax stage, such as oak forest in much of the eastern United States? Most oaks live to be a few hundred years old. An oak forest preserve is likely to stay oak forest for a long time, but not forever. The land trust may choose to do no management and have an oak preserve now and a forest dominated by more mesic trees later. It's a respectable choice: Let the land decide. If the choice is to keep it as oak forest, time and energy will have to be expended, swimming against the natural flow of succession.

Management procedures should be incorporated into a written plan for each preserve that is reviewed and updated as needed. The plans should be based on the best science and experience available. For any particular vegetation type, there are often recent books that summarize this sort of information. A periodical that provides excellent information along with sometimes dubious philosophy is what was formerly *Restoration and Management Notes* and is now *Ecological Restoration*.

Although management should be science-based, practical considerations must weigh heavily in any management scheme. If time and money don't stretch to every preserve, the land trust should prioritize and let some be the best that they can be on their own. In the abstract, there's nothing wrong with that, and doing nothing will be better than poorly thought out, destructive management.

Invasives

[The hawkweed, *Hieracium aurantiacum,*] has now ruined thousands and thousands of acres of fallow field and clearing from the tip of Gaspé to Michigan and southward to Pennsylvania; and whereas it first came to America as Venus's paint-brush, it is now known to all farmers as Devil's paint-brush.[14]

Knowledge can bring a loss of innocence. Those of us who have learned something about botany and ecology are no longer able to see the ice plants of the sand slopes of the Pacific coast just as handsome succulents with showy yellow blossoms. Our enjoyment of the pretty flowers of purple loosestrife is tempered by the knowledge that the plant is an invader that has monotonized wetlands in half the United States. We wince at the sight of garlic mustard, saltcedar, Tartarian honeysuckle, and Scotch broom.

There are something over 2,000 alien, or exotic, plant species living on their own in the United States, more than 3,500 exotic insects and other arthropods, and close to 150 exotic birds and other vertebrates.[15] Their effects on the native biota and the functioning of natural ecosystems vary from almost nil to highly damaging. Some non-native plants can't make it beyond the garden fence; others, the invasives, spread widely into established natural vegetation.

Unfortunately, the early history of an introduced plant or animal is not always an accurate predictor of how invasive it may become. Brazilian peppertree, garlic mustard, and purple loosestrife are a few of many species that had long lag periods during which little of their biodiversity bomb potential was evident. In the northern Midwest, dame's rocket, a handsome blue-flowered mustard, formed patches on our roadsides for a few decades, but by the beginning of the twenty-first century had begun to move into adjoining forests.

Non-native plants can be tolerated or even enjoyed in some places. Who could object to the strip along our roads of chicory, sweet clover, Queen Anne's lace, and sulphur cinquefoil? In this extreme habitat with full sunlight, a soil that consists of gravel hauled in by the road commission, and salt spray in the snow season, what native species could we use to replace these Eurasian immigrants?

On sites of continuing severe disturbance, we should hail the presence of any plant or animal as encouraging testimony to the tenacity and adaptability of life. A land trust need not concern itself about the weeds in the cornfield, in the factory yard, or in the cracks in the parking lot. Its concerns are plants and animals able to invade the less disturbed or even near-pristine sites of the land trust's preserves.

There are two reasons to eliminate non-native plants or animals from a preserve. The first is simple proscription based on the management target. If we're aiming at a pre-Columbian or pre-European-settlement condition, then we'll want to get rid of the lilacs and the lilies of the valley.

The second reason is the effects that some species can have on the composition, structure, and functioning of the natural ecosystems. In some cases, detrimental effects have been proved in a scientific sense. Water hyacinth eliminates native aquatic plants by shading and causes a decline in native fish diversity by providing cover for small fish low in the food chain, among many other effects.[16] Experimental removal of garlic mustard in a Maryland forest resulted in "immediate release and proliferation of annuals, herbaceous and woody vines, and tree seedlings."[17] In the springs and streams of the Southwest, exotic fish have caused the extirpation or extinction of several species or subspecies of native chubs, shiners, dace, and other fish.[18]

In many other cases, persons dealing with invasives haven't felt that the work necessary to produce data for a peer-reviewed scientific investigation would be time well spent. Actress Gina Lollobrigida asked a reporter, "Why do you need numbers to tell what the eye can see?" A team of botanists writing of purple loosestrife invasions said the same thing: "[T]he replacement of a native wetland plant community by a monospecific stand of an exotic weed does not need a refined assessment to demonstrate that a local ecological disaster has occurred."[19]

Herbicides. If a particular management objective can be obtained by mimicking natural processes, such as by prescribed burning or periodic flooding, or by direct mechanical removal, these are probably the best approaches. Early infestations of garlic mustard, for example, can be pulled by hand, bagged, and stored to rot. If any plants have gone to seed, the process will have to be continued until the seed bank is exhausted, and the process has to catch every plant before it disperses more seeds.

Herbicides were originally for strictly utilitarian purposes such as weed control in cropfields. One of the first discussions of herbicides in managing natural vegetation was the 1966 book *The Wild Gardener in the Wild Landscape: The Art of Naturalistic Landscaping* by Warren G. Kenfield.[20]

Kenfield advocated "the herbicide-sculptured landscape." You have a brush problem? "Herbicides to the rescue!" wrote Kenfield. They'll "allow you to carve out, carefully to excise what you do not want. The view-hiding thicket, the poisonous ivy, the rank weeds will vanish. In their places will emerge the landscape that you yourself choose to sculpture. . . . Herbicides need not be the 'poisons' that some uninformed people think them. . . . Applied discriminately, they only rootkill the plants they touch. Then the chemical is utilized as food by soil bacteria, and vanishes."[21]

Unfortunately, the herbicides available at the time Kenfield wrote actually were pretty dangerous to humans, at least as applied commercially and militarily (as Agent Orange, in Vietnam). One problem was the presence of dioxin, a remarkably toxic compound, as an impurity.[22] Some of today's herbicides seem less malign. Most vegetation managers of today regularly use a few herbicides, especially glyphosate, in certain situations. For example, you can cut down buckthorn thickets repeatedly at a great expenditure of man and woman power, only to have them resprout profusely. Cutting the stems and applying glyphosate usually kills a high percentage.

Some results, such as getting rid of buckthorn or Oriental bittersweet, are hard to obtain, or perhaps impossible, without the use of herbicides. When this is true, it's up to the land trust to decide whether the exotic species or the exotic chemical is more to be avoided.

Why Get Rid of Alien Invasives, Anyway? The argument has been made that species have always migrated and invaded new communities. Why not just let it happen? Let English ivy take over the redwood forests and Australian melaleuca turn the Everglades from sawgrass marsh to forest. Let feral pigs root up the spring ephemerals in the forests of the Great Smoky Mountains.

Most invasion of native communities is human-generated in one way or another. At the very least, import of alien species to this country and their spread within it has been at a much faster rate than they could manage by their own devices. Also, most of our vegetation receives continuing disturbance, such as air pollution that reduces the vigor of the vegetational cover and soil disturbance that provides sites for alien species to establish themselves.

One could make the same it's-only-natural argument for not trying to correct water pollution or soil erosion. Humans have always polluted the water and caused erosion; it's just worse now that there are more of us and we use fossil fuels. And why worry about endangered species? Species have always gone extinct; they're just doing it faster now.

Some invasives may seem to serve useful functions. Anyone who's watched purple loosestrife in the summer has seen the flowers buzzing with wasps and bees gathering pollen. Surely, it's playing a favorable role here, providing food for the worthy pollinators. But, depending on the circumstances, perhaps not. Where purple loosestrife occurs with the native winged loosestrife, it steals pollinators from the less showy native. A study showed that where the two species co-occurred, pollinator visits to winged loosestrife dropped, as did number of seeds produced.[23]

The alien bush honeysuckles can form a continuous shrub layer in forests on almost any sort of soil, even dry areas where the natural forests are quite open underneath. The honeysuckles produce abundant fruits that birds eat and spread the seeds to other disturbed areas. They also leaf before most native trees and shrubs, hence providing attractive sites for early nesting birds. What a great plant! State conservation departments and branches of the Soil Conservation Service thought so; they gave away large numbers of them in "conservation packets."

But studies have shown that native herbs and shrubs are reduced under the honeysuckle layer, lowering diversity and perhaps foreshadowing poor regeneration of canopy trees.[24] And the birds that nest in them may be making a bad choice. A study of American robin and wood thrush nests in honeysuckles and buckthorns showed low success compared with nests in native trees. The main reason was higher predation in the alien plants, mostly from raccoons.[25]

Restoration

One more type of management needs mentioning: restoration. Ecological restoration is defined by the Society for Ecological Restoration as "the process of repairing damage caused by humans to the diversity and dynamics of indigenous ecosystems."

The definition as stated seems to imply that the native ecosystem occupying a site has become degraded, such as by overgrazing, and needs help recuperating. We may have to get rid of exotic plants, re-introduce some native species that have disappeared, restore original hydrology (by plugging a drain, for example). All of this fits readily into the sort of management already discussed.

Another aspect of restoration goes beyond that. A site may formerly have been prairie but has been been planted in corn or soy beans for decades. On this bare soil, we can produce prairie, or at least something very akin to prairie, by now well-established procedures for planting, seeding, weeding, and burning. Within two or three years, we can have a good cover of big bluestem, switchgrass, black-eyed Susan, prairie dock, coneflower, hoary vervain, wild bergamot, and many others, with several species in bloom.

This process can be called prairie restoration, though it could just as well be called prairie reconstruction.[26] It may be that this type of process, in which almost no biological elements of the original ecosystems remain as a starting point, needs to be increasingly practiced. Many successful prairie restorations have been accomplished over much the United States and many, mostly unsuccessful, attempts have been made at wetland restoration. Reconstruction of plant communities that will clearly require a much longer period of commitment have mostly not been attempted, but if Wisconsin, Michigan, Indiana, or Ohio are ever again to have a beech-maple forest of 640 contiguous acres, or even 320 or 160, someone will have to construct it.

It'll be a long process requiring the same faith in and hope for future generations that a father shows in planting a walnut grove for his children. But there's no other way in which we'll ever experience what the Midwestern pioneers saw and heard when they came to the deep woods.

Monitoring, Evaluation, Research

As soon as a land trust acquires a preserve, a couple of knowledgeable and outgoing stewardship volunteers should visit owners of adjoining properties to tell them about the organization and ask for their help in protecting the preserve. This will enlist eyes to keep track of what goes on and also educate and disarm some people who might otherwise be potential problems. Some neighbors will become members and, in the long run, may donate land. If the land trust is lucky, among the neighbors may be found a local steward who's willing to visit the site regularly and report to the land trust office.

Monitoring to discover developing problems is a continuing process. Almost no stewardship duties are one-time events. On the conservation side, brush grows back, new exotics invade, the rejuvenating effect of the last fire wanes. On the housekeeping side, signs weather or are vandalized, parking lots develop potholes, trees fall across trails. Some of these can be readily fixed by the local steward or a stewardship employee, perhaps with a little help. Others may require scheduling a work day and turning out the troops.

A few preserves may have larger housekeeping problems such as household dumpers, off-road vehicles or mountain bikes, or rogue timber operations. Involved neighbors will minimize the frequency of problems, but an occasional preserve may still cause headaches. It's important to detect infringements early and act on them, so that a tradition doesn't develop.

The Southwest Michigan Land Conservancy started pulling spotted knapweed on one of its preserves a few years ago. This Eurasian relative of the asters arrived in southwest Michigan in the 1920s. It has spread widely in the state, blanketing sandy old fields, old gravel pits, and other sites on light soils of neutral or alkaline pH, and has also become a major pest in similar habitats throughout most of the United States and Canada. The plants are scraggly, but thousands of them can produce a pink-purple haze over the landscape. The effect can be attractive, but not on a site where you want to encourage native species.

On this preserve, which was never plowed but was pastured for a time, the knapweed grew only on the higher, drier spots. Interspersed with the knapweed were other weeds, such as hoary alyssum and deptford-pink, native and introduced grasses, and also native mosses, lichens, and herbs such as wild bergamot. Although a number of species were involved, the vegetation was sparse, with considerable bare ground showing.

One concern in removing alien plants is that you produce disturbed patches of soil which potentially can be invaded by other weeds. For this reason, close attention was paid to changes in the vegetation of the sites where knapweed was pulled. In the second, third, and fourth years, there was no flood of ragweed or other annual weeds; however, the look of the vegetation changed. It became a grassland with not lush, but thriving plants of timothy, smooth brome grass, and bergamot.

Is this the outcome that was hoped for? Possibly not; timothy and brome are non-native and perhaps no more to be encouraged than knapweed. They may be able to outcompete the young knapweeds coming along from an eight-year supply in the soil seed bank. If so, they may also be able to outcompete some of the currently occurring native species.

A knapweed research team in Montana wrote, "Components of any integrated weed management program are sustained effort, constant evaluation, and the adoption of improved strategies."[27] This is as true for land trust preserve managers and stewardship committees as for range managers. The point where preserve management often breaks down is the evaluation process.

The knapweed story is an interesting anecdote but nothing more. What is needed is information with numbers attached. It would have been better to set up quadrats—sample plots—in which were recorded numbers of knapweed plants removed, stems and sizes of the other plant species, and the percent of ground that was bare or covered with moss or lichens. In the second and third and subsequent years, changes in composition would be clearer. The declining adult knapweed population could be graphed. Were new species coming in? Did the increase in grasses come from new clumps or from sparse clumps filling out? Was the number of baby knapweed plants declining?

Probably even straightforward, uncomplicated research like this is beyond the reach of most local land trusts. There is, of course, always much to do. Some seemingly respectable land trusts have no one on their staff or board with the ecological knowledge to design the research.

At a minimum, though, the land trust can keep records that ask and try to answer these questions:

• What management procedure was employed and when?
• What was the aim?
• At an appropriate later time, what happened?

The answer to the last question may tell the stewards whether they need to do something else. If two controlled burns in an oak savanna have produced, not better savanna, but a sassafras thicket, then fire as employed was the wrong technique. On the other hand, keeping careful track of what happened may yield some happy surprises. If you apply a herbicide that targets cool-season grasses to an abused former oak barren area, and prairie asters, goldenrods, and grasses that hadn't been seen for years began to pop out, you may be on to something.

The land trust can also encourage research by other people. It has sites where research can be conducted, and it has the need for information. Faculty at nearby colleges and universities may be able to help using senior or graduate theses and class studies. For example, successive classes over a period of years could repeat observations on the effects of pulling knapweed or garlic mustard.

Evaluation of the results of management techniques is only one sort of research that land trusts could use help with. Inventories of all the different groups of plants and animals are valuable to have for each preserve. Perhaps a plant taxonomist will be willing to set a student to compiling a flora of a preserve or an invertebrate zoologist would direct a senior thesis on snails and slugs. Admittedly, the current emphasis on molecular biology in many biology departments has made it harder to find faculty interested in whole organisms and field projects. There are still some, and as the pendulum swings back, there will be more.

Not just biological information is valuable. Geology students or faculty can help with hydrology, agriculture students with soils. History majors can reconstruct the history of a preserve from written records and tape reminiscences of the older neighbors.

Probably the best approach to setting up cooperative research efforts is to go to faculty members with questions that the conservancy needs answered. Let the faculty and students design the studies. It's what they do, and it saves land trust staff time. The land trust, if it's able, should help the research financially. Often small amounts of money—for plastic flagging, photocopying, buying a needed book or two, paying mileage for auto travel—will be a big help with student research.

College students in many programs are looking for internships. For some interns, various sorts of mundane clerical and quasi-adminstrative tasks may meet the mutual needs of intern and land trust. Other interns may have the background and desire to conduct research directly connected with the land.

For some interns, a stipend is immaterial; for others it may be a necessity. An ongoing paid internship program is desirable for a land trust, but even without one, most land trusts can probably scare up the money to pay a well-qualified intern or two for a given summer or semester. Education is something that many donors like to support; if the land trust goes to them with a project and a figure, the chances of a contribution are good.

"Stewardship" on Easement Property

Generally, it's appropriate to talk about a land trust's stewardship duties only for lands it owns. In drafting a conservation easement, a land trust tries to include the best feasible management practices for protecting conservation values. Afterwards, the land trust's stewardship responsibility is a police function. Stewardship is by the owners of the property.

A practice has developed in some parts of the land trust community of referring to the land trust's relationship to land protected by conservation easements as "stewardship." In fact, what land trusts do with such properties is baseline documentation, monitoring to check for violations, and defense, when some infringements have occurred or are known to be contemplated.

Why has the word stewardship come to be used to refer to these functions? Why is it that most "stewardship" sessions at Land Trust Alliance national and regional meetings tend to be about managing easements, not land?

One possible explanation is that trusts that hold land, in the classic land trust model, have a continuing relationship with the property, which is stewardship. Land trusts that hold easements have a continuing relationship with the property, which is monitoring and defense. It may be that as a kind of crude parallelism for the sake of convenience, land trusts choose to call this latter relationship stewardship.

Another reason may be that "stewardship" implies a caring relationship with the land. The caring relationship with the land under easement occurs in the thoughtful drafting of the easement document; the relationship thereafter is one of enforcement. However, the phrase "monitoring and enforcement" doesn't have the warm feeling that a land trust may wish to project.

There may be a slight recent tendency on the part of some land trusts actually to do some vegetation management on easement-protected properties—pull exotics or do a controlled burn, for example. If avoiding the burden of long-term management responsibilities is an argument in favor of easements versus fee ownership, this seems an odd, counterproductive development.

Such a practice may also open the land trust to several sorts of liability based on its management activities. For example, recreational use statutes would not apply to easement-protected land not open to the public. The land trust might be named along with the owner in a suit brought by an injured visitor. Also, if the land trust gives some owners assistance with management but doesn't extend it to others, the legal problem of private benefit may arise. Another undesired possibility, if a property were found to be contaminated, is that the land trust could be deemed an "operator," hence liable under the Comprehensive Response, Compensation, and Liability Act (CERCLA) or a related state law.[28]

It does make sense that staff or volunteers involved in the annual easement monitoring should be knowledgeable enough in vegetation science and ecology that they could note problems and suggest solutions. If a slope with oak barren plants is growing up with brush, they might float the idea that the owner could brush-hog it or perhaps do a controlled burn. Most owners will be pleased at the land trust's continuing interest, even if the suggestions go beyond the stated requirements of the easement.

The Costs of Gift Lands and Conservation Easements

The board [of the Trustees of Reservations] has been obliged to decline the gift of not a few beautiful spots for the reason that it had no funds to meet the cost of management.
—Sylvester Baxter, 1901

Protection and stewardship of land cost money—immediately, next year, and if the promise of protection in perpetuity is to be met, every year thereafter.

The Trustees of Reservations, the first land trust, delayed accepting the first property offered to them until a stewardship endowment of $1,859 was raised.[29] This amount is the equivalent of more than $33,000 in today's dollars. The blood of the pioneers is running thin in land trusts of today if they are bashful about asking for a $10,000 or $20,000 endowment.

Early on, a land trust should share with potential donors a general summary of the costs of accepting and taking care of land (or accepting, monitoring, and defending easements). Owners should be made aware that they will be asked for a cash donation. Usually, land given to a land trust for preservation is land highly prized by the donors. They've come to the land trust because they realize they can't ensure protection in perpetuity by themselves. The trust's ability to provide this protection depends first of all on its financial viability, which the donors can help ensure by a financial contribution.

The initial response of many land donors to such a request may well be unfavorable. Not only are they giving the land trust this valuable land that's meant so much to them, but now the damned organization wants money too.

It's an understandable reaction.

What the land trust must remind itself and, in doing so, help the donor understand is that protected land is only a nominal asset. The property, if worth accepting, has value to the community, for all the reasons that preserved land is good. It also has value to the land trust as affirmation of its success in fulfilling its mission. When the trust receives a fine piece of property, it will rightly celebrate.

But the land trust will never see the million dollars that a new piece of property is appraised at; it will never be able to borrow on it or get a return on it. Instead, the land brings with it a set of administrative and stewardship obligations that will require time, energy, and money . . . forever. The magnitude of the commitment is sobering and should help the land trust get over any lingering reticence on the subject of stewardship endowments.

Of course, some donors simply won't have the means to make a cash contribution toward protecting their land. This doesn't mean that the costs disappear. In such cases, for land deserving protection, the land trust will wish to accept it and begin the process of raising the money to provide actual protection from other donors, members, and friends.

In 1899, another early land donor gave the Trustees of Reservations 260 acres on Monument Mountain in western Massachusetts along with an endowment of $2,000 for its maintenance and protection. The Trustees invested the $2,000 at 4 percent in railroad bonds. "Time was to prove," Gordon Abbott, long-time executive director of the Trustees, wrote, "that endowments which accompanied gifts of land were, indeed, the best way to fund their future."[30]

Preserves

The costs of free land are in three categories: transaction costs, initial capital expenses, and costs of continuing stewardship. (Donated easements have roughly similar transaction costs, small initial capital expenses, and no stewardship costs, since the stewardship is done by the landowners. They do bring monitoring and defense costs, discussed at the end of this chapter.)

The simple acceptance of land entails transaction costs—a title search, title insurance, perhaps a survey, deed preparation, environmental due diligence, possible consulting fees, supplies for baseline documentation, etc. Donors may pay for some of these things directly (and can ordinarily claim them as deductions in the same way as accountant's fees, for example). For the first several months of 2002, Southwest Michigan Land Conservancy figures for five preserve donations (one purchase) showed transactions costs averaging just under $250 ($175 to $413).[31] If donated items, such as property surveys, were added, the average would have been $2,000 or $3,000 higher. Staff time and overhead—the fractional cost of such things as phones, lights, and paper—are also real costs, whether or not a land trust includes them in an expected donation.

Initial capital expenses will be determined by what the preserve will be like. Does it need a parking lot to encourage public use? Does it need fences to restrict visitors because of the fragile nature of the features being protected? Decisions on the use of the preserve, hence the initial capital costs, need to be made during the acquisition process, based on discussions between the owners, the land acquisition component of the land trust, and the stewardship component.

Nearly every preserve will need boundary signs, announcing that it is a preserve and who owns it. Putting up ten or fifty of these will be an immediate cost; replacing them as required will be part of the ongoing stewardship to be paid for out of an endowment. A large entrance sign giving the preserve name, the organization, and the donors associated with the project may be needed soon after acquisition.

For preserves intended for public use, a parking lot and even restrooms may be needed. Trail construction costs money, small amounts for simple trails where no special surface is needed, large amounts if boardwalks and viewing platforms are needed. In some cases, special signs and trail guides will be desirable. Costs will include materials and labor, though some of each may be donated.

Not every preserve will need all this infrastructure. What is needed should be decided by the land trust based on the wishes of the donors (and their willingness to support their wishes) and the best use of the preserve. Some preserves may need nothing other than boundary signs, or no markings at all. At a preserve that's an excellent site for public education and enjoyment, the land trust may decide to install signs, parking, trails, and the like, even if the donor is unable to provide funding.

The ongoing costs of stewardship include monitoring visits and general maintenance such as repairing washed-out trails and picking up trash. The pro rata share of the organization's liability insurance premium should be built in. More money is required for preserves that are large, have structures such as benches and boardwalks, have a large number of visitors (or are visited by slovens or vandals), need specialized management such as prescribed burns, or are far from the headquarters or other preserves.

In general, land trusts shouldn't pay property taxes on preserves; the public good supplied by a preserve is certainly equal to that provided by churches, hospitals, colleges, and other tax-exempt facilities. If, for some reason, taxes are paid, that amount will have to be added to the costs to be covered by endowment.

Volunteers may be available for many management tasks; if not, someone will be getting paid to do them. An estimated yearly cost of stewardship will include some expenses that recur almost every year but must also include the amortized cost of replacing large items such as the high-priced entrance sign.

Some provision should be made for rare events such as paying special assessments, or fighting them. Road commissions may want to condemn part of a preserve, a neighbor may dispute a boundary, drain commissions may want to assess a preserve's stream frontage, planning commissions may hold hearings on siting a pig factory next door. A preserve defense fund parallel to the conservation easement defense fund described later on in this chapter would be a good idea. A difference is that easement violations are the expectable outcome of holding easements; frequency and costs are statistically predictable, in principle. Although many, perhaps most, preserves will be menaced in some way at some time, they don't come with the same built-in problems as easement property.

In the absence of any compilation of the types and frequencies of threats to preserves and the expenses of dealing with them, it may suffice to factor preserve defense into the same contingency and liability planning as the rest of a land trust's activities. An argument in favor of a separate preserve defense fund is that the general contingency planning may fail to take preserve defense thoroughly into account, leading to inability or unwillingness to commit necessary funds.

Calculating a Preserve Stewardship Endowment

Since the need for stewardship is ongoing and, in fact, perpetual, it should be paid for out of an endowment. How large an endowment is needed can be determined by (1) estimating the expected yearly expenditure (2) calculating what size of principal would yield that amount at an annual return of 4 percent, and (3) then doubling the principal amount to yield the necessary endowment fund. The doubling is to assure that the principal continues to grow at a rate sufficient to offset inflation. We're making the assumption that a yearly return of 4 percent will keep pace with inflation, on the average. In fact, the median inflation rate between 1970 and 2000 was 4 percent, though it varied from 1.6 percent in 1998 to 13.5 percent in 1980.[32]

Put into equation form:

Necessary endowment = 2(yearly amount needed/0.04).

So, if a yearly stewardship amount of $750 in current dollars is needed, the endowment needed is 2($750/.04) or $37,500.

The Center for Natural Lands Management (CNLM) based in Fallbrook, California, has developed software (Property Analysis Record, or PAR) that can help land trusts calculate stewardship costs and the necessary endowment for a parcel. CNLM was established to provide stewardship for lands set aside in government-required mitigation of the effects of development on wetlands and rare species. Since continuing governmental oversight can be involved, it seemed desirable to CNLM to use realistic assumptions and costs. Whether or not a land trust chooses to make use of the PAR software, the documentation in the user's manual is helpful as a starting point.

Easements

Early writings about conservation easements often contained statements such as "Conservation easements are an effective, flexible, and relatively inexpensive approach to private land conservation." Whatever the merits of "effective" and "flexible," the "relatively inexpensive" part seems less true today. Of course, the upfront costs of accepting the gift of a conservation easement will be less than actually buying the land, even in a bargain sale. The upfront costs may or may not be less than the transaction and initial capital costs when accepting the land as a gift.

But the early thinking about easements was naive. Easements seemed relatively inexpensive because superficial negotiations were captured in simple boilerplate, and baseline documentation tended to be cursory or nonexistent. Today, negotiating an easement that unambiguously protects conservation values while doing justice to the donors' hopes for management can be time consuming. The research and writing that produces the baseline document takes time and money. The Bay Area Open Space Council of California suggests an average baseline cost of about $1,700, but the cost can vary greatly depending on the size and features of the parcel, the experience of the personnel, the care with which it's done, and the detail it provides.[33]

The main costs of conservation easements, though, come after they're on the books. In the early days, many land trusts must have thought that even here easements were a bargain, because the day-to-day care is the responsibility of the landowner. It's true that mending fences, picking up trash, and chasing trespassers are the landowner's jobs, but the tasks of the land trust, monitoring and defense, are not as simple and easy as they once seemed.

Monitoring is an ongoing expense. The obvious annual costs are staff time at the site and in the office, travel to and from the site, a certain amount of onsite photography, purchase of aerial photographs, and a pro-rated cost for any equipment and supplies used. Time spent includes preparation of a written report, with a copy for the owners, and conversations with them about the report and other matters of concern. When the land changes hands, educating the new owners and laying the groundwork for cordial relations are monitoring costs, though not annual.

How much all this amounts to for a particular property will depend on how big the property is, how complex it is, and how far away and how cooperative the landowners are, to name the most obvious factors. A California organization suggests a cost of $250 to $300 for a good job of yearly monitoring; another in Vermont suggests $166 to $365.[34] A large, complex, remote site with a new landowner who has many ideas about improvements he or she wants to make might cost quite a bit more. Costs also go up when more rights are reserved, especially if these involve construction or working lands requiring management plans. A land trust may wish to develop its own formula based on local costs and taking into account the aforementioned factors plus others pertinent to its specific operations.

Since the need for easement monitoring is ongoing, it should be paid for out of an endowment. If $300 per year is needed, the endowment should be around $15,000, using the calculations shown earlier (that is, Necessary endowment = 2[$300/0.4] = $15,000).

Ordinarily, the source of the endowment will be the donors of the easement. Easement donors are usually receptive to the idea of an endowment donation. They have plans for the land that they want to be carried forward beyond their lifetimes. They understand that monitoring and enforcement of those plans will take money. It has to come from somewhere and they're the logical source. In many cases, they can factor in the fact that they'll be the recipient of substantial tax savings.

Easement Defense Funds

When an easement violation occurs or is about to occur, the focus for the land trust shifts from monitoring to enforcement. Violations will occur, but which easements, when, and how much it will cost to get them corrected are questions that can't be answered ahead of time. (There's more about violations and defending easements in chapter 8.)

There is still too little research on the frequency of violations even to express average probabilities with confidence. As a starting point, we might use figures from the Bay Area Open Space Council, realizing that they weren't collected for this specific purpose.

They suggest that about a quarter of 315 easements studied have had a violation (reported frequency = 14 percent, but only about half the easements were being monitored). The median time the 315 easements had been held was about seven years.[35] If we say that 25 percent of all easements will have a violation over a seven-year period, this gives us an expectation that any one easement will suffer a violation every twenty-eight years.

Crude as these calculations are, they let us draw some preliminary conclusions. We can conclude, for example, that if a land trust holds twenty-five or thirty easements, it will have about one violation per year, on the average.

If easement donors are to endow defense of their property, how much should they expect to contribute? It's probably unrealistic to expect every easement donor to contribute money sufficient to defend the easement against any possible future violation. It might happen that a year after the gift of the easement, the property is sold and a major violation occurs requiring the land trust to spend tens of thousands of dollars. A pooled fund that, in sum, enables the land trust to defend all its easements adequately makes more sense. Any donors who wish to endow their property more amply shouldn't be discouraged.

We can, perhaps, establish a few base values that may help us decide what amounts might be reasonable contributions from an easement donor to a defense fund:

1. Violation rate, as calculated above, about once per twenty-eight years per property.
2. About one major violation for every three minor violations (LTA figures of 115 major vs 383 minor).[36]
3. Minor violation cost approximately $1,000, major violation cost approximately $75,000. (The latter is for a litigated case involving a real estate lawyer, a litigator, and expert witnesses, but also assuming some pro bono work.)

These figures are not wildly wrong, but for any given land trust and locality, they may be unrepresentative. Costs and possibly violation rates will rise in the future. Accepting the figures as is, a land trust with ten easements will expect a violation every three to four years; every twelve years (or a little more), this will be a major violation. This land trust would want to have a defense fund from which it could withdraw $78,000 in any given twelve-year period. An endowment that would generate this amount, chopped into yearly expenditures, would be about $325,000. If the land trust had twenty easements, it would need an endowment of $650,000.

Another approach, weaker but not unreasonable at least for a start, would be to build a revolving defense fund sufficient to battle at least a couple of major (and a few minor) challenges at once and depend on new fund-raising to replenish it, as necessary. $200,000 might be a realistic goal for land trusts with up to twenty or so easements.

The first approach (endowment) would suggest a contribution of $30,000 to $35,000 per land donor; the second approach (revolving fund), a contribution of $10,000 to $15,000. Some land trusts will wish to customize their requests for a defense endowment rather than use a one-size-fits-all approach. Specific features of the property (such as location in a rapidly developing area) and the easement (such as several reserved home sites) may make higher defense expenses probable.

7 HOW TO SAVE LAND

The most important person in conservation by private organizations is the willing landowner. In *Private Approaches to the Preservation of Open Land,* Russell Brenneman followed "a long, unhealthy tradition in the law" and called his landowner Mr. Black.[1] Let's break slightly with that tradition and refer to our willing landowner as the Bieber family.

The Biebers' land includes a handsome pond surrounded by marshes, with aspen forest on the uplands. They love their land and believe it's too valuable to be developed. It should be saved for the future, not sacrificed to urban sprawl. They contact their local land trust, the Muskrat Valley Land Conservancy (MVLC).

One of the important jobs of a land trust is education of the public. People need to know that natural and open lands are valuable, that they're disappearing, and that forces operating in our society make it likely that their land will meet this same fate unless they take positive steps to prevent it. Finally, they need information on how land trusts can help them save their land.

The Biebers are farther along this road than most people, but need information from MVLC about the specific ways by which their land can be saved. There are three major ways that they can work with the land trust to protect their land. They can give the land to the land trust, they can perhaps sell it to the land trust, or they can give the land trust a conservation easement over the land.

The Biebers own the property in fee simple. This is the usual way in which we own real estate in the United States today, but it is the highest type of ownership historically, in the sense that it indicates a large bundle of rights pertaining to the land, including, as usually interpreted in the United States, the rights to occupy, enjoy, use, abuse, conserve, exploit, mortgage, subdivide, lease, sell, give away, and bequeath.

If the Biebers give or sell the land to the land trust, the land trust will, in turn, own the property in fee simple. If they give the MVLC a conservation easement, they will be giving up some of the bundle of rights that we will refer to in shorthand as "development rights," but they will continue to be the fee simple owners.

The literal-minded, even though they understand the sense of ownership *in fee simple,* may want to know what the phrase actually means. The answer is, not much. In feudal England, all land belonged to the King and, by grants from him, to the lords. "Fees" were grants to a man and his heirs in return for services. "Feudal," "fee," and "fief" perhaps all have the same Latin root.

Property granted and held in fee was property that the owner could hold, or dispose of, during his lifetime and that, if he still owned it at his death, passed to his heirs rather than reverting to the original grantor (the King or in the United States, the federal government). The original grant would have read "To Castor Bieber and his heirs and assigns forever."

The "simple" in "fee simple" meant that the property descended to the heirs generally rather than in some other way that needed to be defined, such as to the sons in order of birth.[2] The "simple" has no current meaning in the United States since any other mode of inheritance would have to be accomplished by will.

Gifts and Sales

Giving land to a land trust as a preserve is probably the most straightforward way to make sure that it will be protected. The features the donors love—the riverbank with its cottonwoods and sycamores, the trilliums and the marsh marigolds in April, the herons wading among the lily-pads—will be around to be enjoyed, not just today, but in the days of their grandchildren, and your and my grandchildren, too.

These are fine sentiments, you may say, but the owners could make sure that their own children and grandchildren, at least, could enjoy the land by simply leaving it to them in their will.

That's not necessarily so. Apples sometimes do drop far from the tree. Their children may have little interest in protecting the land and may quickly sell it. They'll enjoy the proceeds, but not the land. Their grandchildren don't get the chance to spend summer hours catching frogs in the pond. Neither do mine or yours.

Another possible problem if there are several heirs is that the land will have to be sold to settle the estate. Suppose that the will leaves everything equally to four children. The value of the property—carried upward by rising land prices—is $900,000 and the rest of the estate is $500,000. To give each heir his or her $350,000, the executor may well have to sell the land.

The idea of giving away land, or anything else, is foreign to some people's way of thinking. It's true that Americans are uniquely philanthropic. No other nation has such an array of privately supported health, social, religious, artistic, or environmental nonprofit organizations. Charity is an important part of most American's makeup. Even more fundamental in the thinking of most of us, however, is economic analysis. What's the cost and what's the benefit?

In economic terms, wouldn't it make sense for the Biebers to sell their land to the highest bidder? If the Biebers aren't as enlightened as we're giving them credit for—if they have little feeling for the land and little interest in their legacy to the community—selling might seem to be the logical decision. Even considering just the balance sheet, though, a decision on whether to sell or to donate may in some circumstances be surprisingly close.

In either case, sale or gift, the Biebers get out from under the yearly drain of property taxes and also get the land out of their estate. Estate tax considerations may be important, depending on the owners' ages, the size of the estate, and the erratic course of federal tax legislation. The cash they receive from a sale will become part of their estate, of course, but may be easier to deal with in later financial planning than the land.

If the Biebers sell, they pay capital gains taxes on the profit they've made as a result of the land appreciating in value. If they give the land to a nonprofit, on the other hand, they pay no income tax but instead have a charitable donation equal to the appraised valued of the property.

What the donation translates to in tax savings depends. The general rule currently is that the donor can take a charitable donation of up to 30 percent of gross income in any one year. Suppose the Biebers' income is $60,000 and the land they donate to their local land trust is appraised at $100,000. This gift could generate a deduction in the year of the gift of $18,000. By IRS rules, similar deductions can be taken in the next five years. If income stayed the same each year, the Biebers could take $18,000 in deductions in each of the next four years. In the sixth year after the gift they would take a $10,000 deduction, thereby using up the $100,000 donation.

If the Biebers' income is lower or the value of the land higher, they may not be able to realize the full benefit of their donation in tax deductions. For example, if their yearly income were $30,000, they could deduct $9,000 per year for six years, adding up only to $54,000, so nearly half of their donation would generate no income tax benefit for them.

If landowners are able to sell their property at the appraised value—not always easy—they'll probably come out at least somewhat ahead by selling it instead of giving it to a land trust. An accountant could run those figures for the Biebers, knowing how much they paid for the land, how much it's worth now, their income tax bracket, and similar pertinent information.

In purely economic terms, they may come out ahead by selling it. But few of us make our life decisions strictly on economic considerations. Most people also include at least ethical or religious considerations, for example. For many people, saving land may simply be the right thing to do, ethically and in terms of the image they have of themselves.

Occasionally, a land trust may be in a position to buy land. Ordinarily, purchases will involve land having outstanding conservation value and from which the owner must have a cash return. In such cases, a bargain sale might be negotiated. This is a sale at below fair-market value. A land trust might, for example, pay $40,000 for land appraised at $100,000. In this case, the owner would be making a charitable donation of the difference, $60,000.

Often a bargain sale is a good deal for both landowner and trust. A well-structured deal may net the owner close to what a market value sale would. Although the land trust is put into the position of having to raise funds to pay the purchase price, money for land is the easiest money to raise.

Buying Land to Convey to a Land Trust. Suppose that the Biebers become aware of a piece of land that ought to be preserved. Perhaps a For Sale sign goes up on the last undeveloped bay of a nearby lake. When they bring it to the attention of MVLC, the land trust agrees the land meets its criteria.

The Biebers could do either of two things. They could negotiate with the owner themselves, or they could sign a pledge with the land trust to make a gift in the amount of the purchase price (up to some limit) and let the trust do the negotiating. If time isn't crucial, the second is probably the best course. If the owner has conservationist feelings, he may be more willing to talk with a land trust than with an individual buyer. The Biebers' intention, of course, is to preserve the land, but the owner has only their word for that.

If the land trust conducts the negotiation, the Biebers' donation (purchase price plus transaction and initial capital costs and a stewardship endowment) will be a charitable contribution like any other.

If the Biebers push ahead and buy the land themselves, they could immediately give the land to the land trust. In this case, they could deduct the donation (that is, the cost of property) up to 50 percent of their income in the first year and do the same thing for each of the next five years. Suppose they bought the land for $50,000 and gave it immediately to the land trust in a year when their income is $60,000. They can deduct $30,000 of the gift the first year and $20,000 the next, thus using up the $50,000 donation.

Or they could keep the land a while and then transfer it. With the immediate transfer, the cost basis of the property is the amount of the charitable contribution. If the land is kept for a year, the contribution would be the appraised market value. In a rapidly appreciating real estate market, this might make economic sense, but perhaps not conservation sense. Who knows what a year will bring? Both Biebers might die without having incorporated the gift in their wills. Even if that didn't happen, many other things could—bankruptcy, law suits—that might result in the land that they bought specifically for preservation being lost.

Gift by Will. The Biebers could leave land to the land trust in their will, rather than donating it outright. Donation of land by bequest removes it from the owners' estate after death, so heirs may benefit from lower estate taxes; however, the landowners continue to pay property taxes during their lifetime and gain no income tax benefit. The main advantage of gift by will from the donors' standpoint is retaining flexibility to do what they wish with their land.

From the standpoint of land preservation, bequests simply represent good intentions. Less politely, they are pie in the sky. Family situations may change in ways that make it desirable to leave the property to a new wife or husband, to realize money by selling it to developers, or to do any one of a hundred other things. These alternatives may make good sense for the landowner, but the upshot is that the land is not saved, but lost.

If landowners wish to name a land trust to receive land in their will, they should talk with the trust before having it drawn up. Someone from the trust will need to walk the land as with any potential preserve to determine its conservation values. They'll need to know the owners' intentions for the land. If the will designates the land as a preserve, but its conservation values are slight to none, the land trust would have to refuse the bequest. If the will places no restrictions on the use, they probably would accept such land and sell it, but the donor should be aware that this is likely to be the outcome.

If the land is to be a preserve, the land trust will ask for a donation of initial capital costs and a stewardship endowment, in the will or earlier, to help them take care of the land once it comes to them.

If the owners would like some current tax relief even though they want to retain the land until death, the land trust might be able to make some suggestions. For example, the owner could give the land trust an undivided partial interest in the land; in other words, make it co-owners. This would constitute a charitable donation equal to a part of the value of the property. The land trust would want a signed pledge that the remaining interest would come to it eventually and would expect the donors to continue to pay property taxes and maintenance costs; however, it might be interested in scheduling stewardship work days to help with certain types of maintenance.

The owners could, instead, divide the land, give the land trust title to one part, and keep the rest—perhaps the part with the spring where they like to go and sit and listen to the wind in the pines. This gift would be a charitable donation and perhaps would be appraised at higher than the undivided partial interest.

Maybe the owners just want to leave the land trust their land and don't want to get into anything fancy like giving part of the land or an interest in the land ahead of time. That's fine, but the owners should still get in touch with the trust to discuss conservation values, their hopes for the land, and, of course, a stewardship endowment.

Gift of Remainder Interest. Another way to give land to a land trust for con-servation purposes while retaining current control of it is by the gift of a re-mainder interest. You give the title to the land trust but keep a life estate, the right to live on the land and use it for the rest of your life. If you wish, you can include your spouse in the life estate. Tax advantages are that you're credited with a charitable donation based on the present value of the re-mainder interest, and the property is no longer in your estate. "Present value" is calculated from the value of the property now, reduced by an amount based on the interest rate and how long the youngest person with a life interest would be expected to live.

The property will come to the land trust upon the death of the last person holding a life estate, without passing through probate. The property is gone from your estate if only you and your spouse are involved in the life estate; however, if you name children or others as holders of life estates, these may be gifts that will trigger taxes.

The donor of the remainder interest should expect to continue to pay property taxes, insurance, and maintenance expenses. The land trust will al-most certainly be willing to help with stewardship, if that's the donor's wish.

Because the value of the remainder interest depends on the life expec-tancy of the donor and any others involved in the life estate, the charitable donation is small for younger persons, or if a young person is included. For a single person thirty-five years old, the value of the charitable donation would be less than 10 percent of the appraised value of the property. The reason, of course, is that the donor will have the use of the property for an-other forty or fifty years, on average.

For a single donor aged eighty, the value of the charitable donation would be around 60 percent of the appraised value of the property. One could wish that the federal government were more generous; nevertheless, the advan-tages of being able to live on the family property as long as one wishes but having a smooth transition from home to preserve may make the arrange-ment an attractive option for some.

One way of potentially increasing tax savings when donating a remainder interest is first to donate a conservation easement. If the land has develop-ment value, the conservation easement will probably generate a charitable donation. When you then donate the remainder interest, its value will be less, because the restricted property is worth less. The combined donation for both, however, will probably be larger than that of the remainder inter-est by itself, and, in addition, the conservation easement may result in lower property taxes.

The donor should be aware that when the property comes into the hands of the land trust, a conservation easement held by the same land trust will no longer have any force (in most states).[3] The landowner could give the ease-ment to one land trust and the remainder interest to another. The easement holder would then watchdog what the land trust owning the fee interest did with the land. Both organizations will, of course, expect stewardship endowments.

More Esoteric Ways to Save Land. There are yet more complicated ways to protect land. Most of the complications come from efforts to maximize the financial potential, immediately or for heirs. These approaches will particularly interest people of considerable net worth whose land is valued at least in the seven-figure range.

Stephen J. Small, a Boston attorney, is well known for writing, speaking, and consulting on financial and legal aspects of land conservation. While an attorney-advisor in the Office of Chief Counsel of the Internal Revenue Service, Small wrote the federal income tax regulations on conservation easements. *Preserving Family Lands,* first published in 1988, is a useful small book on basic land protection, mostly through easements. The more recent *Book II* and *Book III* deal with some of the more esoteric approaches, as do some of Small's frequent talks at Land Trust Alliance annual meetings (called rallies) and elsewhere.[4]

As an example, here's a slightly altered, condensed version of a scenario described by Small at the 1998 LTA rally (and included in the rally workbook).[5] Suppose a land trust wants to protect a magnificent property worth more than $2.5 million. The elderly owner likes the idea of preserving it but wants to provide an inheritance for the children. Because of the remarkable conservation value of the land, the land trust talks with its best supporters and gets pledges of $1.5 million. It estimates it can raise another $300,000 from smaller donors within a year's time.

It puts together a deal involving the following: (1) borrowing the remaining $300,000 from a bank and buying the property for $1.8 million (2) purchase by the former landowner of a single premium immediate annuity with the after-tax proceeds, and (3) establishment of an irrevocable trust funded with the cash flow from the annuity. The last step on the former landowner's side is (4) the purchase by the irrevocable trust of a $2.5+ million insurance policy on the former landowner's life using funds from the irrevocable trust to pay the premiums. Upon the landowner's death, the policy pays off to the children as beneficiaries.

A single premium immediate annuity is just what the name says: You give an insurance company—a good, stable one—a lump sum, and immediately (usually within thirty days) begin collecting payments. Because you do not defer payments while the amount contributed sits earning income, the percentage of taxable income in the payments received is low.

On the land trust's side, it still has to pay off its $300,000 bank loan.

If you found all this exciting and would like to know more details, this sort of approach to land protection may be for you. Putting together a clever, complicated deal can have its fascination. But for many local land trusts, such a deal, even if it works out, can take more time than several mundane transactions that may in sum have greater conservation impact.

Conservation Easements for Landowners

Mr. and Mrs. Castor Bieber could give or sell the land they want to protect to a conservation organization, in one of the ways we've talked about, but maybe they want to keep it. They see an article about conservation easements in a magazine or newspaper—anything from *Forbes* to *High Country News*. The article may have a title like "Protect Your View and Get a Tax Break, Too." The Biebers are intrigued.

They call the Muskrat Valley Land Conservancy and learn that a conservation easement is a way to protect family land for conservation purposes while retaining ownership. It's an agreement between a conservation organization (or a government agency) and a landowner by which the owner gives up certain rights to the land, particularly development rights.[6] Exactly what happens to these rights is somewhat mysterious. Although the owner gives them up, the land trust doesn't get them. One of the best-known commentators on conservation easements says this:

The development rights are gone, eliminated, extinguished. What you "give" the donee organization is the right to *enforce the recorded restrictions* on the use of your property, *against you*, and *against any future owner of the property, forever* [Emphasis in the original].[7]

There are potential tax advantages in donating a conservation easement, but the big win for the owner is that now an organization or agency has permanently taken on the responsibility of defending the conservation values of the land.

A conservation easement runs with the land; it's recorded with the deed, and all future owners are bound by the agreement. Sold with development rights restricted, the property won't bring as high a price as without the easement, but this will often be an acceptable trade-off for conservation-minded landowners. Future owners have the same rights and are under the same restrictions as the owner who placed the conservation easement on the property.

Easements are flexible in what's prohibited and what's permitted. Provision can probably be made for such things as adding on to the old house or retaining another building site. If the owners want to harvest timber under a sustainable forest plan, that can be included, if the idea or the specific plan does not violate the land trust's principles.

Stewardship of easement-protected property is by the landowners within the framework agreed to in the easement. The land trust visits the property at least once a year to be sure that the provisions aren't being violated.

For many people, easements let them eat their cake and have it too. They can keep the land from ever being developed while still owning it. Current tax benefits (which may change at any time depending on interpretations of the IRS and the whims of Congress) are these: The difference in appraised value of the property before the easement and after it's in place represents a charitable donation. IRS regulations require that the easement be made in perpetuity, exclusively for conservation purposes, and to a qualified conservation organization or government agency. The difference between the before value and the after value is pretty much the value of the development rights that have been withdrawn.

Also, the value of the property is reduced in the estate of the donor. And in most cases, the after-easement value of the property is the valuation for property tax purposes. What a deal!

The actual monetary value of these tax breaks can vary from enormous to almost nil, depending on specifics. Property having high development potential is likely to yield a large charitable donation and be the recipient of a big drop in property taxes. Remote land with slight development potential may yield little tax benefit.

Property tax relief varies markedly among states. At least two states (Alabama and Idaho) explicitly deny property tax relief to owners of easement-protected land. At the opposite end of the spectrum, Maryland provides a fifteen-year property tax exemption for vacant land on which a conservation easement has been donated to the Maryland Environmental Trust (MET), or jointly to a local land trust and MET.[8] Illinois law reduces the assessed value of easement-protected property by 75 percent.[9] In some states, some local taxing authorities may balk at accepting the reduced, easement-restricted value for property tax, even when state laws require them to consider the effect of a conservation easement on taxable value.[10] Such a case in Michigan was appealed to the state Tax Tribunal, which issued a precedential decision establishing that after-easement appraised value is the true cash value for property tax purposes.[11]

To get a federal income tax deduction, the easement donor will need an appraisal by a qualified appraiser. An appraisal for a conservation easement donation is more complicated, hence more expensive, than an ordinary appraisal, because it's a "before and after" appraisal that determines both the value of the property as it sits and the value once the restrictions are in place.[12]

Conservation Values

Conservation easements are promoted as saving land from development or containing sprawl. This they do, but these are almost side effects. A conservation easement has one purpose: to protect the conservation values of a specific piece of land. The easement does this by switching the responsibility, and burden, of defending the conservation values from the successive owners of the land to an outside organization devoted to land conservation.

Conservation values are the natural, scenic, open space, biological, and ecological features of the property that provide the public benefit on which the tax relief for conservation easements is justified. Examples are high-quality terrestrial or aquatic ecosystems; habitats for rare, threatened, or endangered species; prime farmland; and scenic vistas visible to the public. However, a broader array of values can be identified. For example, a landowner worried about the effects of light pollution might wish to include darkness as a conservation value.

The point of the easement is not just that the land possesses conservation values, but that the conservation easement protects them. If darkness is identified as a conservation value, the easement document needs to give limits on nighttime lighting. A conservation easement on a farm that identifies a high-quality stream and the floodplain forest along it as conservation values must impose restrictions that keep the livestock out and limit runoff of animal waste and chemicals.

Where Did Conservation Easements Come From?

Certain types of easements, such as rights of way, are ancient, but easements for conservation purposes were rarely seen until the 1930s and didn't become widespread as a way for private conservation groups to protect land until the 1980s. The term "conservation easement" was coined by William H. Whyte, Jr., whose 1959 monograph *Securing Open Space for Urban America: Conservation Easements* lit the easement fuse.[13]

Between 1988 and 1998, the land protected by local land trusts in fee increased 176 percent, but the land protected by conservation easements increased 378 percent. As of 2000, approximately 11,700 conservation easements totaling something like 2.6 million acres were held by local land trusts.[14]

Conservation easements are related to earlier devices that grew up in Roman and later English common law to enable one person to control the use of property owned by another person. Included are easements as they have long been known, real covenants, and equitable servitudes.[15] Historical rules still occasionally cast shadows over conservation easements, but, in most states, conservation easements have been given a statutory basis removing or at least lessening common law impediments.

In common law, there are appurtenant easements and easements in gross. An appurtenant easement burdens one piece of land for the benefit of another, usually adjacent, piece of land. For example, an appurtenant easement may allow one landowner to reach his land by cutting across a second landowner's property. Here the easement holder is granted an affirmative right, to cross his neighbor's land. Very few common law easements are negative, restricting an owner's right to use his land.

An entitlement for you to fish in the Biebers' pond would be an easement in gross. Easements in gross exist for the benefit of a person rather than for the benefit of another piece of property. The common law rule is that appurtenant easements transfer to subsequent owners of the dominant (benefited) estate, but easements in gross tended to be regarded as personal rights, unassignable and uninheritable.[16] In common law terms, the sort of arrangement that has come to be known as a conservation easement is an easement in gross. It extracts certain rights from the landowner's bundle but not for the benefit of an adjacent piece of property.

To achieve their land protection objectives and to qualify for a federal tax deduction, conservation easements must be in perpetuity. Common law has disapproved both of easements in gross and perpetual restrictions on real property. Both were considered by English and, later, American judges to interfere with the free transfer and development of land.[17]

The American title system of recording easements, liens, and the like, which began in the nineteenth century, has made obsolete one traditional concern: that an easement in gross would be forgotten and then come back decades later to haunt the current property owner. However, the American recording system does not remove the philosophical objection, that land is to be used to yield the greatest economic benefit and that whatever slows down economic progress, such as restrictions on the use of land, should be disfavored.[18]

In nineteenth-century America, there was plenty of land and development was what the nation needed, or so our forefathers thought. By the 1960s, a majority of the citizenry realized the importance of conserving land, and the idea had spread to some politicians. Here are some sentences Stewart Udall included in the foreword to his 1963 book, *The Quiet Crisis:*

America today stands poised on a pinnacle of wealth and power, yet we live in a land of vanishing beauty, of shrinking open space, and of an over-all environment that is diminished daily by pollution and noise and blight. . . . Each generation has its own rendezvous with the land, for despite our fee titles and claims of ownership, we are all brief tenants on this planet. By choice, or by default, we will carve out a land legacy for our heirs.[19]

By the 1970s, more and more people interested in the land realized that revised legal tools were needed, based on a new policy: "one that places in parity the needs for land development and for the conservation of the resources of our natural and man-made environment."[20]

Some saw such a policy as a turning away from the verities of the past. Here were people saying that drawing the most dollars from the land was not the only consideration; preservation was being favored over development. Others thought that the times, not the idea, had changed. A legal commentator wrote

In one sense, the emphasis on productive land use is not different from the policy favoring environmental protection. The underlying commitment of both policies is that land be put to its "best" use. The best use of a river may not be to dam it up and then distribute the water to irrigate farmland, but rather, allow it to run unfettered to the sea. The best use of forestland may not be timber supply but rather support, in an undisturbed state, of the ecosystems that depend on it. In short, best use should not always be determined by the highest market price.[21]

Whether we believe that conservation easements are a repudiation of the values of the past or an evolutionary development of them, the size of the shift shouldn't be underestimated. In one swoop, conservation easements changed the ancient rules that land is purely an article of commerce, hence anything that hampers its marketability is unacceptable, and overturned the limitation on "dead hand control," that is, the doctrine that the land is to be put to the uses chosen by the living, not controlled by choices made by earlier owners. Conservation is full of subversive ideas.

Just before Whyte's *Securing Open Space for Urban America* appeared in 1959, California produced a law doing what he was recommending. It stated that acquiring rights, including less-than-fee interests, in land for the preservation of open space is a public purpose for which public funds may be expended. As with many of the other early statutes, there was no provision for private nonprofits to hold easements.[22]

By 1967, Russell Brenneman, noting that several states had passed conservation easement laws, wrote, "The legislatures have acted with the diversity and ingenuity which are a hallmark of the federal system."[23] Perhaps, though, it was time to develop a standardized model with special attention to clearing away common law impediments. Not all of the state statutes to this time had done so.

The Uniform Conservation Easement Act (UCEA) was approved by the National Conference of Commissioners on Uniform State Laws in 1981. It said that conservation easements under the act are valid no matter what the common law rules were and also provided that charitable organizations as well as government agencies could own conservation easements.

Most states have either adopted the UCEA or written their own statutes authorizing conservation easements that follow some or most of the UCEA's provisions.[24] Only Wyoming currently lacks a statute. Pennsylvania was a holdout until June 2001. Although Pennsylvania was considered to have a strong common law favoring the validity of conservation easements,[25] the lack of a UCEA-style statute caused problems, including a hesitancy in enforcing restrictions that would be pressed immediately in most states.[26]

The Jackson Hole Land Trust protects land in Wyoming by the use of easements, but they must be appurtenant since only common law rules are available. Easements in gross might not be upheld by the state courts, so the land trust asks for the gift of one acre of the property. The easement is then written on the rest of the property.[27]

The statutes in the group of non-UCEA states vary.[28] A few require government approval at some level. In Delaware, the easement can't prohibit the landowner from allowing hunting and fishing. And there are variations in the allowable term of the easement, among other things. Even if less-than-perpetual easements are permissible by state law, they don't qualify for federal tax purposes.

Because conservation easements are a new animal that behaves according to a new set of rules, not all attorneys or judges are as yet knowledgeable about them or able to separate conservation easements from their law school lectures about earlier ways of putting restrictions on real estate.[29] Many new land trusts end up searching out a local attorney with some rudimentary knowledge of conservation easements and helping him or her develop expertise by providing pertinent literature from the Land Trust Alliance, law review articles, and commentary from some of the expert conservation easement attorneys around the country.

Potential easement donors will want to get their own lawyer, of course, but are as likely to be led astray as to get sound advice from the lawyer that did their routine legal work of the past. Land trusts may wish to provide some literature on conservation easements to the attorney, and also to the landowners so that they can work through it on their own, for self protection.

The Process

After talking with the Muskrat Valley Land Conservancy, the Biebers have decided they'll put a conservation easement on Aspen Acres. They negotiate the terms, retaining rights for themselves and future generations to do such things as maintain the dam, clearcut aspen patches to prevent succession to more shade-tolerant trees, and build a second lodge in a 2-acre building envelope on the other side of the pond.

The Conservancy has visited the property several times to familiarize itself with the conservation values of the site, to earmark certain habitats that should be permanently preserved, and to look for signs of potentially hazardous waste storage or other environmental problems. It has checked the title to be sure it's clear. Various technicalities have to be observed. If the Biebers have a mortgage, for example, the bank will have to agree to subordinate it—in effect to say, that if foreclosure should occur, the conservation easement remains intact. Without the subordination, the Biebers can't receive an income tax deduction.

The Biebers are congenial, conservation-minded folks, whose property has outstanding conservation values. It's easy to come to a satisfactory agreement with them. With some other properties or people, this may not be true. The owners may be unwilling to include the restrictions necessary to protect the conservation values adequately. Or they may want restrictions or affirmative obligations that are impossible to monitor or enforce. They may, for example, have unusual, time-consuming, and sylviculturally dubious approaches to managing their pine plantation that they want in the easement. In some of these cases, a good faith effort will fail to produce an easement that the land trust can monitor and defend satisfactorily through all the coming decades. It should break off negotiations as amicably as possible and move on.

Once the deal has been agreed on, but before the easement document has been signed, the Conservancy will do a baseline survey and put together a document that describes the property as it now exists. By word, map, and photograph, it should tell what natural ecosystems are present, where various sorts of disturbances exist, where the buildings and roads are, and any other relevant details. A series of photographs illustrating the main features of the property should be taken from selected points that are easily relocatable (for example, by GPS, or Geographic Positioning System). If a violation of one of the provisions of the easement occurs later, the descriptions and photographs will almost certainly become evidence.

Not long after the deed is signed, a couple of things should be done. The donors and the land trust will be feeling good about themselves, so some sort of small celebration would be in order. One possibility might be a potluck to which the neighbors and the land-trust board and staff are invited. The land trust can spring for the barbecued ribs, buffalo burgers, or baba ghanoush, depending on the preferences of the region.

Whether it's at this open house or by individual visits, the owners of adjacent land ought to be told about the easement. The donors will probably be glad to help spread the word. By this time, they know as well as the land trust the reasons for protecting land and how the conservation importance is multiplied when adjacent land is also preserved. Even if it doesn't turn out that the neighbors donate land or an easement, they need to know about the easement and about the land trust, so that they can help keep watch.

The other thing that ought to be done around this time is to walk the easement donors through the document, or over the land, and videotape them talking about the easement provisions and why they wanted them. This sort of testimonial connected to the provisions of the easement can be useful for many purposes—incorporation into a video about the land trust, for example. Another, very specific use would be in a legal situation in which an heir or later owner claimed that the donors never really meant to prevent a house from being built on the crest of the hill overlooking the pond or that, if they did mean it, they were gaga by that time in their life. An authenticated video of the donors talking about their love of the land and why and how they want to ensure the protection of the features they value is powerful evidence in upholding the protection they want.

The conservation easement document, which may be called various things including "agreement," "grant," and "deed," doesn't take exactly the same form everywhere. However, certain sections must be present to achieve the conservation easement objectives. The appendix at the end of this chapter has a brief overview that generally follows the Michigan model easement.[30]

Conservation Easements from the Standpoint of the Land Trust

A few reasons why a land trust might wish to own land to keep as a preserve are discussed in chapter 6. First is control. Management plans can be written into the conservation easement, but they will always be a compromise between what the land trust sees as most desirable based on the best science and experience and what the landowner wants, the whole thing tempered by what the land trust can reasonably expect a landowner to agree to. To the degree the land trust is able to direct stewardship of the land by management plans and later advice, it will always be management once removed, rather like talking somebody through replacing a kitchen faucet by e-mail.

A second reason why a land trust might rather own the land is a probable lower likelihood of trouble. With a conservation easement, the potential is high for the land trust to become embroiled in a variety of disputes, especially involving future owners. Such disputes will take time and money, and, in the worst case, may lead to termination of the easement and the loss of the land from protection. Land owned in fee is not necessarily trouble-free, but the long-term prospect for trouble from easements, though not yet fully known, is potentially high.

And there are some other reasons a land trust might, other things being equal, prefer to own a piece of property rather than hold an easement on it. Among them are being able to open the land to the public for many purposes, an important one being education. Here is where the land trust demonstrates the good things that come from preserved land.

From the standpoint of the land trust, what are the good features of conservation easements? The main advantage is that many landowners will donate a conservation easement on a property for which they would never donate the title. Fortunately for land preservation, many owners will donate land outright, but not every owner feels this way about every piece of property. It's an understandable position, especially for owners with families, and not necessarily just a matter of wanting the cash. Often it's rooted in heartfelt, though not necessarily well-analyzed, feelings about their land.

Also, landowners tend to be willing to donate easements on larger pieces of property than they will usually donate outright. As an illustration, the Southwest Michigan Land Conservancy (as of 2001) had about equal numbers of donated preserves and donated easements. The average acreage of the preserves was 40 acres and of the easements, 125 acres.

An excellent use of conservation easements is as buffers for a land trust's owned preserves. Forty acres of outstanding forest is not a lot in the opinion of certain forest-interior birds, such as the pileated woodpecker or worm-eating warbler. But if the land trust can protect by easement 100 acres of fair to good forest on adjacent lands, the conservation value of its 40 acres may be greatly enhanced. A stewardship benefit of such buffer zones is that some of the preserve's borders are fairly well protected from intrusion, at least from the public.

Another situation in which easements make sense is the protection of farm or ranchland, since few land trusts are in a position to own and operate a farm. If the owner's hope is that the land remain in agriculture, an easement is a good approach. For property tax purposes, the assessment is ordinarily frozen at its agricultural value. An easement on farmland can keep it from turning into urban sprawl but, in general, can't ensure that it'll stay farmland. The easement can tell a new owner that he can't turn the farm into a plastics factory, but one that tells him that he has to go out and plow and plant 120 acres every spring is unlikely to be upheld. Farmland protection is a specialized topic and there's more about it in chapter 12.

Conservation Easements from the Standpoint of the Public

A classic early application of conservation easements was along the Blackfoot River in western Montana. Though the land along the river was privately owned, the water and its banks had long been used by the public for fishing, swimming, picnicking, and camping. In the 1960s and 1970s, increasing population and changing recreation patterns made it doubtful that the free and easy practices of the past could continue. From 1975 to 1977, representatives from government agencies, the University of Montana, The Nature Conservancy (TNC), and landowners (ranchers and timber companies) hammered out a management plan that included conservation easements as a centerpiece. Landowners would agree to restrictions protecting the natural and scenic qualities of the Blackfoot and its banks, giving up rights to subdivide, establish feedlots, clearcut, and dredge.

These easements did not deny public access; in fact, the process began as a way to regularize and control access in a way that would make its continuation possible.[31] As of 2001, about 14,000 acres along the Blackfoot were protected by easements, mostly held by TNC.[32]

Another example of a conservation easement that provides for public access is the biggest easement negotiated as of 2002. The work of the New England Forestry Foundation, this easement, which was bought in 2001 at a cost of nearly $30 million,[33] covers more than 750,000 acres of Maine forest land. Traditional public access for hiking, picnicking, camping, boating, hunting and fishing is retained on most of the land.

One of the four IRS categories under which the gift of a conservation easement may qualify for a charitable deduction is "the preservation of land areas for outdoor recreation by, or the education of, the general public." But as one commentator noted, "This section is rarely used since few landowners are willing to grant the public perpetual access for recreational activities."[34] In a survey of 315 San Francisco Bay area easements by the Bay Area Open Space Council, fewer than one-third allowed any public access.[35] Usually, conservation easements are justified under one or more of the other three categories: ecological (protection of relatively natural habitats), open space (including scenic land and farmland), or historic.

The general lack of public access to easement-protected land has not passed unnoticed. A *Wall Street Journal* editorial critical of conservation easements observed that the donor, despite receiving a considerable tax benefit, may suffer only a slight abridgement of property rights. "He need not necessarily, for example, grant the hoi polloi access to his cove or hilltop."[36]

Tax benefits for the donation of conservation easements are justified on the basis of "significant public benefit." The public is paying for this benefit by foregoing certain tax payments, current and also future. Local governments, for example, are giving up some immediate tax payments and also the opportunity for tax revenue that would come from eventual development on the land, were it not protected. It's true that easement-protected land usually continues to pay some property taxes, which pleases local authorities.

When the full picture is considered, public support may amount to fewer dollars than it might seem. The presence of easement-protected land in a neighborhood may raise the value of nearby land, so the loss of tax revenue is small, or even balanced out entirely. And, as we know from cost of community service studies (chapter 3), most kinds of development don't pay for themselves in the long run. In blocking development, we're often saving local government from fiscal irresponsibility.

Nevertheless, the legal justification for conservation easements is public benefit. Without public access, this is reduced to a subset of the items talked about in chapter 3. Examples from the long list of good things that saved lands give us are scenery that we enjoy looking at and that provides relief from the monotony of housing developments and strip malls; ecosystem services ranging from water purification to sequestering carbon; places where birds, snakes, fish, and rare plants can live; and in the case of farmland, the possibility of buying locally produced fruits and vegetables.

These are real and important benefits. But looking at public benefit in this way emphasizes a couple of things:

First, conservation easements without public access ought to be written only on property that provides a good helping of these other benefits and should be written in such a way that the benefits are, in fact, protected. The bigger the easement and the more natural land it protects, the more likely it is to provide substantial public benefit. However, even small parcels may provide important public benefits in some circumstances.[37] In an area of unstable slopes where disturbance might lead to land or mud slides, it seems possible that easements prohibiting construction, excavation, and vegetation removal might be justified even on vacant lots and backyards. Less evident are the benefits provided by small parcels in heavily built up resort areas, where open space or wildlife habitat easements have been granted on small lots or parts of lots—with reserved rights for a swing set.

Secondly, land trusts might consider the desirability of negotiating at least limited public access to as many of their easements as feasible. The right to lead an annual nature hike would be a good start. Giving the public a chance to stride across the land, sniff a flower, and stroke a lichen-covered tree trunk is a benefit a little less abstract than a nice view from the turnpike or oxygen production by the green plants.

Why Do Land Owners Protect Their Land?

What makes landowners decide to donate a piece of property or an easement? The books from the Land Trust Alliance have information about appraisals, surveys, doing deals with government agencies, and running the office, but most say little about this central question other than noting what tax breaks the donor gets.

There are logical reasons why land ought to be protected—aesthetic, practical, ethical—which we covered in chapter 3. But the question of why owners actually do protect their land is much more complex because people's thoughts and feelings, their hopes and fears about the future are involved.

Answers are available in pithy but repetitive land trust folk wisdom and two academic studies done as graduate theses at the University of Michigan and the State University of New York at Syracuse. Both studies used mail surveys done in standard sociology style. Statements such as "I would still donate my land or easement even if a tax deduction was not possible" sought responses on the familiar five-point scale, ranging from "strongly disagree" (1) to "strongly agree" (5), the mid-point (3) being neutral. Both studies had sample sizes large enough to inspire confidence in the general accuracy of the tabulations.

The Michigan study concluded that the primary motivating factors were, first, a personal commitment to the future of the land; second, ecological stewardship; and third, economic concern.[38] The first two had average scores of 3.5 or above, the third, an average score of about 2.5.

Pertinent to the most important factor, personal commitment to the future of the land, were such statements as *Desire to leave behind a significant legacy* and *Concern about the actions of future inheritors or owners.*

Pertinent to the second factor, ecological stewardship, were such statements as *High ecological value of the property* and *Rare species or habitats existing on the property should be protected.*

Pertinent to the economic concern factor were *Ability to claim a tax deduction* and *Ability to reduce property taxes.*

The New York study, which surveyed donors throughout the Northeast, differed in that it considered only easement properties and included both donors and sellers of easements.[39] The questions and presentation of results were different enough that precise comparison with the Michigan study is impossible, but the general conclusions are similar.

For the original grantors of easements, a high level of agreement was found with such statements as *I am responsible for the future health of my land* and *I wanted to protect the land from development.* These probably correspond with the "personal commitment to the future of the land," motivating factor of the Michigan study.

Relatively low levels of agreement were found for such "economic concern statements" as *A tax break was the most important reason for granting the easement* and *The money I received was the primary reason for granting* [that is, selling] *the easement.*

Statements that might be construed as "ecological stewardship" questions were in the middle range of agreement, with more positive than negative ratings. Examples are *My land contains important ecological resources which need to be protected* and *What I do on my land can affect the community's environmental quality.*

The representations of donors' motives are similar enough in the two studies to suggest they have some general validity. Nevertheless, all such machine-scored, multiple-choice exercises have limitations. The questions embody the authors' assumptions and preconceptions. And, possibly, no question was asked that would catch certain important aspects of a donor's path to the decision.

Also, it is hard to know how to answer some of the questions. Suppose, for example, you are confronted with "I wanted to guarantee natural places for future generations" from the New York study. And suppose that you have the Muir-Leopold viewpoint that you want to guarantee natural places mainly for the sake of natural places. Do you "strongly agree" because of the first half of the statement, or do you just "agree" or feel "neutral"?

I did a small, impressionistic survey of Southwest Michigan Land Trust donors of preserves or easements, asking them to write in their own words what they were trying to accomplish by permanent protection of their land.[40] It is encouraging that, in many ways, what they wrote supported the findings of the two statistical studies.

The plainest message was one that could be included under "personal commitment to the future of the land." Sometimes it was phrased positively, such as "*[My wife] would walk through the area, marvel at the beauty, and I think probably started thinking about what steps could be taken to continue the land as it was.*"

Nearly every donor, including those who stated their positive expectations of protecting the land, gave an explicit statement of what they were trying to prevent. One example: "*I am anxious to prevent exploitation of the land through dividing up into small parcels for building purposes, without regard for the best use of the land or the plants and wildlife that thrive on it.*"

The features that caused the land to merit protection were usually stated. Some statements dealt just with the land, biota, and scenery. "*We bought the land because we fell in love with the woods. The buildable lot contains a heron nest, a better use than another cottage to pollute the lovely shallow lake.*"

Often, the values of the land were connected with the owners' uses of them. "*I guess I would say that we were trying to protect wildlife habitat, scenic values and also preserve a place which had been very important to us as a home for nearly fifty years.*"

More often, the use and enjoyment by future generations or by the larger human community were mentioned. "*It's a practical way to make sure our grandkids and theirs can see one little piece of Michigan that's still wild and rural.*"

Stewardship, ranked as the second important motivating factor in the Michigan study, tended to differ between preserve donors and easement donors. Preserve donors saw undisturbed land as their legacy. Protecting the land's conservation values was the whole point of the gift. In contrast, most easement donors wanted the property to include at least some working lands that would continue to be managed—and as much as possible in the same way they were managing them. "*We envision further use by owners with the same objectives and concerns as ours . . . limited agricultural use, selective timber cutting, hunting and fishing, preservation and improvement of habitat.*"

One easement donor addressed stewardship from a religious rather than an ecological viewpoint: "*I take the [biblical] mandate to stewardship seriously. God has given me this land to manage and I want to do it well. SWMLC is helping me to do that by working with me to identify and preserve for the future this land, the three streams that run through it, its wetlands, flowers, plants, birds and animals.*"

In the SWMLC survey, two reasons for donating land came up that were not anticipated in the large Michigan and New York studies. One was that preserve donors were freed from dealing with other people who wanted to use the land. They no longer had to defend the property from developers, timber buyers, or people wanting permission to hunt. The simple posting of signs indicating preserve status clearly deflects many requests and some other problems. To the importuners that still phone or show up on the donors' doorstep, the donors can simply tell them to talk to the Conservancy. If an actual problem developed, such as a new adjoining landowner claiming a few feet along one edge of the preserve, it was up to the Conservancy to deal with the matter, which it did.

This particular motive surprised me but shouldn't have. It is simply a special case of a basic motivation for donating land, to put it into the hands of an organization whose job it now is to defend it and keep it whole for the future.

The second reason was from a long-time Nature Conservancy member. *"I have . . . always embraced the concept of buying land for protection. . . . [I believed that buying the property and putting an easement on it] was a way to make a significant contribution in my lifetime and pass these values to my children."*

Several owners had protection in mind when they first acquired their property. If any others thought that donating the land or an easement would help instill conservation values in their children, they didn't mention it. But it is a good idea. Studies seeking to determine what produces environmentalists have shown that the two most important roots of their environmental commitment were experiences of natural areas and family influences.[41]

On the factor of economic concern, I asked donors to rank the importance of tax considerations on a four-point scale from "crucial" to "not important at all." I had not actually expected anyone to circle "crucial," but one family did. *"It's only fair that the government cuts you some slack,"* they said. The breakdown of "crucial–fairly important" versus "not very–not at all" was 46 to 54 percent.

For several who ranked tax considerations as "fairly important," it appeared that getting out from under the property tax burden was the most important financial consideration. In the "not very–not at all important" category, the donors of a large easement wrote, *"We had no knowledge of a tax break when we began. We just wanted to keep the land in one piece."* And from a preserve donor: *"There was an elegant side effect of an appraisal that gave us a great tax advantage but I must admit I never considered it very much in the gift."* And, *"Tax considerations were of little importance as motivation although [later events] did bring home to me the very important estate tax benefits of the donation."*

For a given landowner at a given time, the tax advantages of a donation can be the critical factor in the decision to donate. Most land trusts have experienced the phenomenon of owners being seized in November with preservationist and philanthropic ardor that they pray can be consummated by December 31. All in all, though, it seems that William H. Whyte had it right when he wrote as follows about economic considerations:

They are not themselves sufficient motivation. They are important because they enable a landowner to do what he wants to do and feel that he is being sensible and prudent in the bargain. [Potential easement donors] don't talk about the tax angles because they are looking for favors. There are much easier ways open to them if it's more money they want. They explore these angles because they are eager to justify economically what their instincts impel them to.[42]

All the lines of evidence seem to converge on the land trust folk principle: As a general rule, people donate property for preservation out of a love for the land; financial considerations are not unimportant but are secondary.[43]

That's the topic sentence, but the rest of the paragraph gives additional useful information. First, many donors do have a general love of the land, but that is nearly irrelevant. The important point is that they love *their* land. As one of the SWMLC donors said, "*I suppose peace of mind that what we had always known would continue was important.*"

This statement adds a second important dimension: The donors—of preserves or easements—are looking toward the future. They realize that, without land-saving action such as they are contemplating, the American landscape will become increasingly unlivable. They talk about "our grandkids and theirs," about "protection beyond one lifetime," about "the future enjoyment of others." "*I have a good feeling,*" one preserve donor wrote, "*that this land will remain as it is for perpetuity.*"

Perpetuity, permanent protection for *their* land, is what donors are after, and that is what the wise land trust will promise and do its best to deliver.

APPENDIX: THE CONSERVATION EASEMENT DOCUMENT

Conveyance. Early sections state that the donor (or grantor) conveys and warrants a perpetual conservation easement over a certain property to the land trust.

Conservation Values. A series of sections state, first, that the property possesses natural, scenic, historic, scientific, biological, and open-space values that are important to the donor, land trust, and public, and identifies these as the "conservation values."

The purpose is stated as assuring that the property will be perpetually preserved in its predominantly natural (or scenic, historic, agricultural, forested, or open space, or a combination) condition, and, further, that any use of the property that might impair or interfere with the conservation values is prohibited. The land trust is identified as a tax-exempt, nonprofit corporation engaged in protecting habitats, open spaces, etc.

Another section describes the property's specific conservation values and indicates that they have been documented in a natural resource inventory (baseline document) signed by donor and land trust in acknowledgment that it is an accurate representation of the property.

Prohibited Actions. Anything inconsistent with the purposes of the conservation easement or detrimental to the conservation values is prohibited. Examples of frequently prohibited actions are splitting off part of the property (division), commercial use, billboards, construction, cutting vegetation, land surface alteration, dumping, keeping livestock, and using or allowing use of motorized off-road vehicles.

Permitted Uses. These are anything not prohibited; however, prudent donors may wish to head off later misinterpretations by specifically listing as reserved rights activities of special importance to them. If structures—houses, barns, bridges, fences, dams—are present, the owner retains the right to maintain them. Replacement in substantially the same location and size is usually also permitted, but a thirty- or forty-five-day notice to the land trust must be given. Additions to existing buildings and the right to construct new buildings may be included as a reserved right, again with appropriate notice to the land trust. Additions and new buildings, if any, should be restricted to one or more specified building envelopes. Where and how agriculture and forestry will be practiced would be included here, and so also may anything else as long as it doesn't impair the conservation values that are the justification for the easement. The statements as to what is permitted need to be consistent throughout the deed and clear and unambiguous. How wide? How tall? Exactly where?

Rights of the Land Trust. The land trust is given several rights that allow it to maintain perpetually the conservation values. Included are the right to enter for monitoring and enforcement purposes, to prevent any activity or use that's inconsistent with the purposes of the easement, and to require restoration of any features that are damaged.

Land Trust Remedies. Here are included all the powers the land trust has to head off violations, to stop them, and to compel restoration if they occur. Unless disallowed by state law, there should be an asymmetry in the payment of litigation costs and attorneys' fees; specifically, the landowner should pay the land trust's costs if he loses, but the land trust, if it loses, should have to pay the owner's costs only if a court determines that the land trust acted without reasonable cause or in bad faith. The reason is that an owner wishing to violate a provision of the easement is likely to have a strong, usually monetary reason for doing so. By prolonging litigation or repeatedly putting the land trust in a position where it has no recourse but to sue, such an owner might be able to exhaust the land trust's financial reserves. This can happen more readily if each party in the suit has to pay its own legal expenses.

Litigation is, of course, to be avoided, if possible. A sincere attempt should be made to resolve a dispute by negotiation, though this in itself will probably be time consuming and may be expensive.

Ownership Costs and Liabilities. The owner, not the land trust, is liable for all costs, accidents, insurance, taxes or anything else about the property, except claims resulting from the land trust's monitoring (and annual field trip).

Cessation of Existence. Most organizations have proved to be mortal, but land trusts need immortality to carry out their mission of land protection in perpetuity. If a land trust does cease to exist or loses various of its statutory protections, the easement will be transferred to another qualified organization—another organization that can hold conservation easements. This will generally be another nonprofit conservation organization or conceivably a government agency.

A donor may reasonably want a specific backup organization named. The donor should be aware that most suitable organizations will expect their own monitoring-defense endowment.

Termination. Two conditions might lead to extinguishment of the easement. If conditions change such that the purposes of the easement can't in any way be fulfilled, the easement can be terminated by a court. The claim of changed conditions, if it came, would probably be from the owner and in most cases would be resisted by the land trust. If the owner prevailed, the land trust would be entitled to compensation based on the value of the development rights that were now being restored to the property.

The other way an easement might be extinguished is through eminent domain. Not every state extinguishes conservation easements when property is taken through condemnation proceedings, but if a taking occurs, the land trust is again entitled to compensation.

Successors. It needs to be said prominently and clearly that the terms of the conservation easement are binding upon all the subsequent owners of the property. The terms also apply to any other organization, another land trust, for example, if the easement were to be transferred to it.

Other Articles. There follows a string of routine articles such as how notice is to be delivered.

8 DEFENDING CONSERVATION EASEMENTS

Monitoring

Every year, or oftener in some circumstances, a land trust needs to revisit every easement property. A major reason is to detect and document any violation since the last visit. It's also important just to keep track of ongoing changes. Change is constant in the natural world. Hydrology changes, succession occurs, plant and animal ranges expand and contract. A land trust can't know whether it's protecting the kinds of lands it ought to unless it knows what it's got.

Buying new aerial photographs as they appear will help with monitoring and may help document violations. Remote sensing can't replace on-site visits, however. Even if nothing is seen that isn't visible on the photo, the monitoring visit should be an occasion for land trust and land donor to have a conversation about the land and to re-enforce one another's conviction that this conservation easement was a good thing.

Monitoring is one of the weak spots in the conservation easement balloon. In a study of 315 easements by the Bay Area Open Space Council, 49 percent were not being monitored.[1] For land trusts, the situation wasn't as bad as this figure suggests. Only 25 percent of conservation easements held by nonprofits (mostly land trusts) were not being monitored. The overall figure is pulled down by public agencies that hold easements; for them, a full 70 percent were unmonitored. Public bodies sometimes don't even have a list of the properties on which they hold conservation easements.[2]

A similar study for Maine, Vermont, and New Hampshire reported that one-third of the organizations (fifteen land trusts and three public agencies) "performed no documented monitoring."[3] Statistics for the rest of the United States are not readily available, but it's unlikely they're substantially better.

Baseline documentation is a thin spot right next to the monitoring thin spot. A substantial percentage of land trusts have inadequate or no baseline documents for some or all of their conservation easements. In the Bay area study, 40 percent of the easements lacked baseline documents. Again, the public agencies were the weak siblings. Land trusts lacked documents for 28 percent of their easements, which is nothing to be proud of, but 42 percent of the easements held by local government agencies had no baseline documents. For state and federal agencies, 91 percent had none.

For an easement donation to be eligible for a tax deduction, U.S. Treasury regulations require a baseline document. Easement deeds contain language echoing the regulation and saying something of this sort: "The conservation values have been set forth in a baseline document that the parties acknowledge to be an accurate representation of the property at the time of donation." The deed doesn't say: "We'll get around to finding out what the property is like within the next several years, and the baseline document will be a more or less accurate representation of the property at some time in the indefinite future."

Aside from tax deductions, the baseline document is important for the successful defense of a conservation easement in the event of a serious challenge.

What could be called the Liberty ship mentality explains why some land trusts do such a poor job of baseline documentation and monitoring. During World War II, the United States built ships in a hurry to carry cargo to the war zones. Using assembly-line techniques, shipyards were building Liberty ships in a month and a half and launching them at the rate of one per day. What happened after they were launched was of minor interest to the shipyards. Welded rather than bolted together, the ships sometimes cracked along the welds; one broke in two the day after it was launched.[4]

Land trusts tend to see themselves in a war against urban sprawl. For some, the priority is saving land, in the narrowest sense. The message to the staff is to go out and do deals. There'll be time for niceties later, when peace has been declared.

Misplaced priorities—the failure to recognize that protecting land really means protecting it, not just getting a document signed—is one reason why some land trusts do a poor job with monitoring and baseline surveys. Another explanation may be simple ignorance. They don't realize the pit of vulnerability they're digging by their lack of documentation on land they have pledged to protect.

Violations

Easement violations are an inevitable and expectable effect of the protection of land by the use of conservation easements. They will occur.

Conservation easements of the Door County Land Trust in Wisconsin prohibit billboards, as do most. In 1992, the trust was donated a conservation easement on 60 acres along the highway running down the middle of the Door Peninsula. An advertising company had a billboard on the property with a lease ending in 1994. The easement required removal of the billboard after expiration of the lease.[5] When the billboard was still standing well past the expiration date, the land trust wrote to the advertising company noting that the billboard was now in violation of the easement. The company replied that it doubted the validity of conservation easements and wouldn't remove the billboard.

The trust explained conservation easements and the specific situation in a series of letters, but these elicited no further response. Consequently, the land trust filed suit in circuit court in July 1997.

The day the court hearing was scheduled, the lawyer for the advertising company agreed to the land trust's terms. In October, the court ordered the advertising company to remove the billboard, restore the site within thirty days, and pay the land trust $2,000. Although the land trust invested board and staff time and psychic energy over a couple of years as well as about $2,000 in legal fees (much of the legal work had been pro bono), the problem was settled fairly quickly and easily.

Not all violations are so readily resolved.

French and Pickering Creeks Conservation Trust (FPCCT) protects land in northern Chester County, Pennsylvania, west of Philadelphia. In 1967, as its first major land deal, it bought 42 acres lying between French Creek and a county road.[6] The land as purchased was protected by a covenant restricting uses to farming, a wildlife sanctuary, a nature conservation area, or for the study of natural history. No buildings were permitted "other than small buildings accessory to such uses." Wishing to leverage its money, FPCCT resold the property to a farmer in March 1980, with a deed continuing the restrictions. Nine years later, in April 1989, the farmer resold the parcel. The new owners had been informed verbally of the restriction, and the restrictive language was in the new deed.

Nevertheless, FPCCT learned in late 1989 that the new owners were applying for a building permit for a house of 4,800 square feet. FPCCT informed the new owners that building a house would violate the restriction. When the owners were not dissuaded, FPCCT sued in the County Court of Common Pleas for an injunction to prevent construction.

The Common Pleas judge denied the preliminary injunction sought by FPCCT, and the owners proceeded with their construction plans. By 1993, the Court of Common Pleas had rejected FPCCT's requests for injunctive relief three times, and the house had been built. The owners had managed to obtain a $260,000 mortage, despite the existence of the restriction prohibiting anything except small buildings accessory to farming or nature study.

FPCCT appealed to the Superior Court. "As fate would have it," a U.S. Bankruptcy Judge wrote, the Common Pleas decision was reversed by the Superior Court, which ruled that the covenant should be enforced as written. The owners appealed to the Pennsylvania Supreme Court; after a preliminary hearing, the Supreme Court decided that the appeal had been improvidently granted and dismissed it.

By now it was 1995. FPCCT returned to Court of Common Pleas, which on 5 July 1996, permanently enjoined the owners from using the property for residential purposes, prohibited construction of residential structures on the property, and required that the 4,800-square-foot house be removed within six months. The owners were made liable for costs.

The owners failed to remove the house. Eventually they were found in contempt by the Common Pleas Court, which granted authority to FPCCT to demolish the house and awarded $100,000 in damages. By now it was January 1998.

At various times, FPCCT had made offers to buy the land and allow the owners, or the bank, to move the house, or for FPCCT to buy the owners a lot in a nearby subdivision and move the house if the owners returned the restricted property. These offers of settlement were not accepted.

The owners filed for bankruptcy on 5 November 1998, just before FPCCT was scheduled to demolish the house. The Bankruptcy Court permitted the demolition to go forward. The demolition was done at FPCCT's expense. By that time the land trust had incurred about $100,000 in court, legal, demolition, and other costs.

In early 2002, FPCCT was still seeking payment of attorneys' fees.[7]

This summary, complicated though it seems, leaves out much of the legal maneuvering, including claims and suits filed at various times by the owners, accusing FPCCT of civil rights violations and racketeering, for example. Also omitted are the fluctuating feelings of the FPCCT board. There must have been times during the ten-year ordeal when things looked bleak enough that throwing in the towel seemed like an acceptable, even alluring, option.

It's possible that the lack of a Pennsylvania statute authorizing conservation easements contributed to FPCCT's problems, but one of the less satisfactory outcomes of a violated easement occurred in Washington, said to have strong easement legislation.[8] The Whidbey Camano Land Trust (WCLT) came to hold conservation easements on some 10-acre lots in a scenic and historic area. WCLT operates in Island County, a group of large and small islands in the Strait of San Juan de Fuca northwest of Seattle and southeast of Vancouver Island.

Each lot had a 100-by-100-foot building envelope. The easement required the owner to provide thirty-day notice before applying for construction permits. The rest of the lot was to be kept as a natural area; cutting of living vegetation was prohibited. Shortly before Christmas 1995, WCLT discovered that the purchaser of one of the lots had cleared a substantial swath in the natural area and installed a drain field for a septic system. He had, without giving notice, applied for and received a building permit for a house and had put in a foundation nearly half of which protruded beyond the building envelope.[9]

WCLT objected. After three months of negotiation, the owner surprised WCLT by suing for equitable relief. "Equitable relief" is a term going back to early English law. It refers to situations in which the king's minister would dispense creative justice in cases where applying the strict terms of law would fail to yield a fair result.[10] The court considered the two positions and rendered a verdict that did not invalidate the easement but that effectively changed the provisions. The landowner kept his septic system where he'd put it and finished off his house where he wanted it, but he had to paint it a dark color to lessen its scenic impact and also had to give back some land in the original building envelope.

The court found several weaknesses in WCLT's position. Credence was given to the landowner's claim that he didn't understand the easement because it hadn't been thoroughly explained to him at purchase. Although the building envelope was shown on a map included in the easement document, the court concluded that WCLT should have required a survey. WCLT, in the judge's opinion, "seemed to enforce its easements in a casual manner on some occasions."[11]

WCLT, in 1995 a small organization with limited resources, had spent $35,000 on the case and did not appeal.

These three cases illustrate several of the things that the land trust community has learned about easement violations.

Most violations are not by original owners who, after all, are the ones wanting the land protected. A 1998 to 1999 survey of violations by the Land Trust Alliance found that of fifteen litigated cases, thirteen were by subsequent owners and two by third parties.[12] Nevertheless, violations by easement donors do occur; for example, a survey of violations in Michigan found that two of eight were by the donor.[13] These two were illegal dumping and failure to provide prior notification of (permitted) construction.

The LTA survey found that of some 7,400 conservation easements held by local land trusts, violations had occurred on about 500, in percentage terms about 7 percent. This low rate probably understates actual occurrence. First, most easements are new; over 70 percent of the acres currently under easement nationally have been added since 1990. Many parcels are so newly under easement that there has been little time for violations to occur; also, much of the land is still owned by the easement donor.

Second, many conservation easements are not well monitored, so that some violations are undetected. In the San Francisco Bay Area study, more intensive than the nationwide LTA survey, 14 percent of easements were reported as having suffered some violation. As context, the same study found that only about half of the easements were being monitored. Simply doubling the violation rate may exaggerate it—violations are sometimes detected on poorly monitored land—but 28 percent may well be closer to the correct figure than 14 percent.

Missing a violation by failing to monitor regularly could be a serious matter. Suppose that immediately after the land trust's monitoring visit on a property far from the home base, ground is broken for a large project. Through some circumstance, the land trust misses the next scheduled visit and returns after two years have elapsed to find a retirement village with an 18-hole golf course and banners saying "Now Leasing." Some states have short statutes of limitations for property or contractual claims.[14] The owner could argue that the land trust should have objected when the construction began, or at least when the next monitoring visit should have occurred, and that the statute of limitations bars any enforcement action. Even if the statute of limitations hasn't expired, the owner can ask that an injunction to halt construction and restore the site be denied on the basis of undue delay. In legal terminology, the owner would be claiming that the land trust, by not making a timely objection, is guilty of laches.[15]

Most of the violations in the LTA survey (77 percent) were considered minor. An example might be an adjacent landowner dumping yard waste over the fence and agreeing to clean it up and not do it again. However, what might seem to be major violations to some, such as nonpermitted construction, sometimes seemed to be included as minor in the survey if the situation was successfully resolved.

The most frequent major violations were as follows:
• Prohibited surface alteration (such as drainage ditches or new roads);
• Prohibited cutting of vegetation;
• Construction of prohibited or unauthorized structures;
• Construction outside the building envelope;
• Prohibited timber harvest.

Lawsuits were filed in twenty-one cases of violations, but most were settled prior to trial. Of six cases for which a decision was rendered, all upheld the conservation easement, and most granted full relief, as in the first two examples described above.

Any land trust has to be alert for violations and deal with them, for many good reasons. Enforcing the terms of the easement is part of its job as a nonprofit conservation organization. A judge might consider lax enforcement or non-enforcement as a waiver by the land trust of its right to enforce. Potential donors who are serious about the permanent protection of their land might become disenchanted with a land trust that lets someone get away with serious infringement.

Also, credibility is involved. Like the old Indiana farmer who did nothing when his chickens disappeared and had his horses stolen a month later, a land trust that ignores or acts ineffectually against a violation invites future infringements.

The aim of the land trust faced with a violation is to get it corrected in a way that minimizes damage to conservation values. Some violations are deliberate; a landowner builds a house where he knows it's prohibited because that's where he wants it. But most are in a broad sense inadvertent; the owner, even the easement donor, behaves the way landowners do. He cuts up some wind-thrown trees in the natural area to burn in his fireplace, for-getting that logs are supposed to remain where they fall for salamander hab-itat and mineral cycling.

Ending and restoring damage to conservation values ought to be done in the simplest and least confrontational way possible. Most owners of pro-tected property want to make things right when they understand what the problem is. Occasionally, the language of the easement is vague or at least open to misinterpretation. A new landowner may think that a permitted "additional dwelling unit," means that he can build a second house, whereas the land trust thought it was allowing an apartment over the existing garage. A judge may opine that a 4,800-square-foot house falls within the definition of "a small accessory building."

Avoiding vagueness to begin with is the best solution, but owners and judges may find vagueness in the most unlikely places. Sometimes amending the easement may be the best solution to a problem, but keeping amend-ments rare events is good for everybody—except the occasional owner who stands to make money by forcing his reinterpretation on the easement holder.

Amending an easement opens a surprisingly large can of worms, involv-ing, at a minimum, tax deductions, private benefit, conservation values, in-tent of the original donor, and public perception.[16] What has developed as the rule of thumb, or perhaps the rule of two thumbs, is as follows: An amendment should be considered only if the conservation values are not harmed and preferably enhanced by the changes, and, also, if the value of the property is increased by the easement change, the land trust must receive assets in at least equal amount.

As an example, suppose an owner wants to cut a few trees in one acre of a swath of land he had agreed to leave as natural. Perhaps his view of the lake is being obscured as the trees grow up. The land trust may conclude that adding a 40-acre woodlot elsewhere on the property to the natural area category would balance the loss of the single acre between the house and the lake. It would compensate, the trust may decide, both for the loss in conser-vation value and for any monetary increment to the value of the property by maintaining the lake view.

The conservation-minded donor and the land trust will want to cooperate in trying to make the easement language protect the conservation values un-ambiguously and to omit restrictions that have little bearing on conserva-tion but that might generate monitoring and enforcement problems later on.

The Future of Conservation Easements

I will focus my attention on one specific type of transaction which, I believe, embodies more than any other the movement's happy present and potentially troubled future: acquisition and maintenance of conservation easements by private land trusts
—Federico Cheever, "Public Goods and Private Magic"

Owning land in fee simple is the historical heart of the land trust movement. Conservation easements are new, but land trusts adopted them with enthusiasm. In 1988, local land trusts still had slightly more land under protection by fee ownership than by easement. The ratio was 1.03 acre fee to 1.00 conservation easement. But a decade later, in 1998, the ratio had reversed, to 0.6 fee to 1.0 easement. By 2000, the disparity had grown to 0.5 to 1, twice as much land protected by easement as by ownership.[17]

There have always been those troubled by the notion that conservation easements are a fast, cheap, and easy way to protect land. In 1981, Jon Roush, at that time on the board of the Montana Land Reliance and The Nature Conservancy, wrote, "Because their problems are easy to overlook, conservation easements are rapidly becoming the most misused and overused tool for land protection in the United States."[18]

The problems continued to be largely overlooked for a long time. Discouraging words were few in *Exchange,* the Land Trust Alliance magazine, though it very properly urged land trusts to monitor their easements and to raise money to help them do it. Many land trusts failed to heed even those admonitions. My 1996 survey of randomly selected land trusts found that only 11 percent of those responding said they always asked for an endowment for monitoring and defense; 42 percent said they rarely or never did. A 1997 article in *Exchange* catches the same snapshot. Of fifteen land trusts in the Pacific Northwest with properties or easements (mostly easements), over half reported a total stewardship fund (including monitoring and defense as well as preserve stewardship) of less than $10,000. More than one-third had no money set aside.[19]

But concern over the free and easy approach to easements had begun to spread. *Exchange* for 1997 brought the article just mentioned plus one on dealing with violations.[20] Later years have regularly included information on difficulties with easements.

The potential for future problems comes at three levels: the land trusts themselves, the courts, and legislative bodies.

Self-inflicted Wounds

Land trusts that don't draft easements tightly and are otherwise operationally lax are putting at risk the properties they're supposedly protecting. They are, in fact, putting their own continued existence at risk. Conceivably, failures to monitor or enforce easements might imperil a land trust's nonprofit or tax-exempt status. The extinguishment of an easement as a result of organizational sloppiness might cost enough in public respect to curtail future donations of land, easements, and money. For a land trust that is financially marginal, an expensive legal case might put it in a hole that it can't crawl out of.

Land trusts that are unprepared financially, psychologically, and in their professional practices for a serious easement challenge are good candidates to cave in to a landowner's demand for some dubious or detrimental activity. Even if such a land trust hangs tough, it may not be able to put on as good a defense as a sound trust whose board and staff are aware that challenges to easements are inevitable.

Conservation Easements and the Courts

The next few decades will bring rising land prices, sales of many eased properties, and many more court tests of conservation easements. It wouldn't be surprising if half of the 11,700 properties on which local land trusts hold easements were to be sold in the next ten years. Some of the new owners will be environmentalists, just as interested in protecting the property's conservation values as the original owners. Of the others, some will be ignorant of easements, some disdainful, and some hostile. Some will buy easement-protected land in the full expectation of breaking the easement so that they can do what they want with the land. Properties in the path of development that are worth a couple of hundred thousand dollars as restricted but millions without the easement will attract such speculators.

Over the next few decades, the land trust community will find out in court what their conservation easement statutes mean.

It's not possible to forecast whether courts will uphold the optimistic land-trust view of easements as staunch and stable instruments of land preservation. Although an LTA article on violations notes that, "No conservation easement has been overturned in a final court ruling," it would be a mistake to conclude that courts have always upheld the land trust's idea of what the easement said.[21]

What may be in store for conservation easements as more come under the scrutiny of judges? Any of us with a stake in conservation easements would do well to be—if not alarmed or pessimistic—at least heedful of the possibility that court decisions may shrink rather than bolster easement usefulness. One of the first warnings about possible dangers of the conservation easement approach to land protection was sounded by Denver law professor, Federico Cheever, in a 1996 article.[22]

Changed Conditions. One dimension of possible shrinkage mentioned by Cheever involves claims of changed conditions such that the conservation purposes of the easement are obsolete.[23] An example would be an easement granted to protect habitat for an endangered species. If the species went globally extinct, the easement might be extinguished because it no longer fulfilled its purpose. But this isn't a serious example, because no land trust today would write such an easement. They would also cite other conservation values that would remain even if their endangered species went to join the great auk and the passenger pigeon.

A more pertinent example is agricultural easements, which may be written with agriculture as the only conservation purpose. An owner—definitely including the original grantor of the easement—might seek to overturn it when he considers farming or ranching no longer practical or profitable. The land trust might disagree. A judge will decide.

Suppose that conditions really have changed so that the purposes of the easement, in truth, cannot be fulfilled. In this situation, the land trust should receive a monetary payoff that could be substantial. Its share of the property's value is supposed to be the fraction accounted for by the easement.[24] For example, if the original before-and-after appraisal reduced the market value of the property from $1,000,000 to $600,000, then the land trust's share is 40 percent.[25] If changed conditions were demonstrated and the land sold, without restrictions, for $10,000,000, the land trust's share ought to be $4,000,000.

If the land trust does get a bunch of money, it's required to use it to further its land protection agenda—perhaps even buying land in fee next time. The owner will get his payoff from building the golf course and condos.

Interpreting Conservation Easements According to Common Law Rules. Another problem is that some courts, if they find the language of a conservation easement unclear, will turn to the common law rules with which they are familiar. In describing such a case, two Colorado attorneys commented:

In cases involving conservation easements . . . the intent of the parties is expressed as preservation or conservation. Why, then, do courts . . . apply rules of [contract] construction that contradict the goals of the parties and the entire justification for the grantor's tax break? Arguably, the well-recognized rule . . . that "restrictions on land use should be construed in favor of the free use of land and against the party seeking enforcement" has no business being recognized at all by courts . . . [in] disputes concerning conservation easements.[26]

At least two states, California and Pennsylvania, have provisions in their statutes that conservation easements should be construed in favor of the restrictions.

Cost/Benefit Analysis. Another problem for the enforcement of conservation easements lies in the "relative hardship" doctrine, or applying what passes in law for cost/benefit analysis.[27] Certainly some cases in which the owner has spent a lot of money in his violation of an easement may pull a court toward considering whether the benefit to the public of putting things back the way they were is greater than the hardship on the violator.

In one case, a federal appeals court explicitly excluded a cost-benefit analysis in reaching its decision. It overturned a lower court ruling that had upheld a National Park Service decision allowing a hotel chain to expand a golf course across 240 acres subject to a conservation easement. The easement, held by the state of New York, had been bought with money from the Land and Water Conservation Fund. The Conservation Fund Act prohibits converting such land to anything other than public outdoor education without the approval of the Secretary of Interior.

The appeals court concluded that this was a conversion under the Act and that the approval was inappropriate. The court acknowledged time and money spent by the hotel chain, but said, nevertheless, "the court's duty remains to follow the law as written and intended."

At least one state, Maine, includes language in its conservation easement statute saying that economic circumstances can't be considered in determining whether an easement is in the public interest.[28]

Lack of Financial Resources. Another problem is the disparity in resources between a small land trust and a new landowner who happens to be in the development business and could make millions by developing the easement-protected land. The Land Trust Alliance, awakened to this issue, has been studying collective or communal defense strategies.[29] Most obvious approaches, such as some form of easement defense insurance, seem to be technically difficult. A general problem will be the reluctance of careful land trusts to be pooled with lax ones. How useful a communal defense will be, if one is introduced, will depend on its affordability, acceptability, and effectiveness.

In the meantime, a prudent land trust will wish to make sure that it's well prepared to defend the easements it holds. Communal defense may be fine, but as Billie Holiday said, "God bless the child that's got his own."

At the very least, a land trust faced with a case likely to go to court can probably count on advice from the LTA as well as other land trusts that have been through the mill. The land trust needn't and shouldn't allow itself to be isolated.

Each court case has importance for the specific property violated, of course, and as a demonstration to the local community that the land trust will defend the integrity of all its easements. Beyond those concerns, for at least the next couple of decades, any land trust that becomes involved in easement litigation should know that what happens in its case could become a precedent helping or hurting conservation easements in general. Each land trust owes the cause of land conservation its best legal and scientific efforts.

Conservation Easements as Charitable Trusts. Another legal complication of conservation easements is whether they can be considered charitable trusts. A charitable trust is a trust set up with the public as beneficiary. Enforcement of the terms of charitable trusts is usually the job of the state attorney general. The conservation easement statutes of some states give enforcement power to the attorney general, but if conservation easements are also charitable trusts, the attorney general would have standing to enforce the easements even in states without that provision.[30]

The question has come up a couple of times, most notably in the Myrtle Grove case. The National Trust for Historic Places (NTHP) agreed in concept to amend a historic and conservation easement it holds on a historic Maryland farm, to allow an eight-lot subdivision. When several conservation groups including the Maryland Environmental Trust and the LTA protested, NTHP recognized its error and recanted. The landowners sued the NTHP, but the crux here is that the Maryland Attorney General also filed suit to block modification of the easement on grounds that the amendments would violate a charitable trust for the citizens of Maryland.[31]

Both cases were settled in December 1998 without this point being addressed. The conservation easement was preserved as written. NTHP agreed to pay the owners $235,000, and subdivision of Myrtle Grove was prohibited.[32]

Almost any land trust, in battle with a rich developer and his battery of high-priced lawyers, would feel better with the power of the attorney general behind it. Still, the conservation easement as charitable trust concept might also bring some awkwardness. If two entities, a land trust and the attorney general, both have the power to enforce an easement, they will sometimes differ on what needs enforcing. The conflict could involve a more equivocal point than in the Myrtle Grove case. Also, amending charitable trusts usually takes court action. Amendments to conservation easements ought to be rare, but rare events still take time and money when the courts are involved.

Legislation

What will township, county, and state legislative bodies do in situations where enough land is tied up one way or another that the developers, real estate agents, and economic booster organizations are complaining? What happens when a township is built out except for preserves and properties protected by conservation easements? What will be the legislative response to the plaint, "People need a place to live"?

What the legislature gave, the legislature can take away. If easements become an obstacle to commerce, the language for terminating them can be loosened and the opportunity for new ones can be eliminated.

Some specific possibilities might be to require courts to apply an economic test in deciding conflicts over easement restrictions. Does the easement provision for no tree cutting for conservation purposes take precedence over the community's need for firewood, pulp, and lumber? Or the legislature might direct that easement restrictions be ignored for the purposes of property tax assessments. Or the state legislature could outlaw perpetual easements, making it difficult for easement grantors to receive federal income or estate tax benefits.

The list of possibilities is long. Between the judiciary and the legislature, the potential exists for a weakening of conservation easement protection parallel to the gutting of environmental regulatory law that occurred in the 1980s and 1990s.

On the other hand, environmentalists, conservationists, and just plain good guys can be making the case for conservation easements at the same time the business-of-America-is-business types are making the negative. Perhaps the legislatures will go the other way and add statutory language correcting all the weaknesses. As another law professor, commenting on the Cheever article, noted, security of property rights is in the public interest, and this includes the rights conveyed in conservation easements.[33]

Conclusion

The only fair conclusion concerning conservation easements is that the future is unclear. We have seen some good court decisions but also some bad trends. Where the charitable trust idea will lead, if anywhere, is uncertain. On the plus side, most land trusts are now more aware of what they need to be doing in drafting and defending easements. The Cheever article comments that the problems are not insurmountable and ends by saying that lawyers owe land trusts "our best thinking and best efforts in preserving the balance and the magic."[34]

Nevertheless, a prudent observer is drawn to the position that many land trusts have begun to rely too much on a single land-protection device whose durability has yet to be established. Easements are becoming the monoculture of the land trust community. Renewed attention to protecting land in fee would, at least, add some diversity and may turn out to be essential to the cause of private land protection.

9 THE LAND TRUST ALLIANCE

Early Days

On the last day of the 1981 National Consultation on Local Land Conservation in Cambridge, Massachusetts (see chapter 1), the participants visited some preserves of the Trustees of Reservations, had a clam and lobster bake, and talked about what the next step should be. Replete in the afterglow of the successful meeting, they decided that a permanent organization was needed to continue the process begun that October weekend. Wanted was some sort of service bureau to act as an information clearinghouse, organize joint action on public policy matters, and perhaps design a national public awareness program.

Allan Spader, a regional planner at the Lincoln Institute of Land Policy, had been heavily involved in organizing the Consultation. He agreed to work on the concept of "inter-organizational communication and alliance." Other participants in the Consultation "accepted responsibility for exploring sources of funding for the support of a continuing program."[1]

The concept became the Land Trust Exchange and Spader became the first executive director. Four land trusts, the Brandywine (Pennsylvania) Conservancy, Iowa Heritage Foundation, Maine Coast Heritage Trust, and Napa County (California) Land Trust were the sponsors of the organization. About two dozen other land trusts and charitable foundations also were contributors. After incorporation in Boston in February 1982, the Land Trust Exchange (LTE) began almost immediately to publish a magazine, called *Exchange*. It is still called *Exchange,* although the organization changed its name to Land Trust Alliance in 1990.

Exchange was one of three initial programs. The other two were a data base/information service and a series of task forces.[2] The first task force, on appraising conservation easements, led to a seminar attended by about eighty people in February 1983 (at Airlie House in Virginia) and later to a book.[3]

For the small staff, two to four during the first year and a half, LTE was an exciting place to work. The land trusts that hadn't been invited to the 1981 meetings, something on the order of four hundred, were pleased to find out about others trying to do the same things they were. They were glad to hear that there was now a national umbrella organization under which they could fit.

The LTE had good ideas, enthusiasm, and a hard-working staff, but grants were slow in coming.[4] A financial meltdown occurred after only about a year and a half. The office at 3 Joy Street in Boston was closed, and the board asked Benjamin Emory to step in as executive director and try to turn LTE into a going concern.

Emory, an M.B.A. and a founding board member of the LTE, had formerly been executive director of the Maine Coast Heritage Trust. To save money, the LTE office was moved to Emory's house at Bar Harbor, Maine. The only employee to survive the transition, Program Services Director Caroline Pryor, went to Maine as the institutional memory. Later, when the LTE moved to the Washington area, she stayed on with the Maine Coast Heritage Trust.

The combination of lower expenses in the rural location and increased income from contributions from land trusts, foundation grants, and revenue from conferences, publications, and subscriptions, made it possible to pay off LTE's debt by early 1984. By 1985, things were again moving ahead. The staff was back to four, one a part-time Washington representative. The organization had conducted a census of local land trusts (published in 1986), finding 536.[5] The first national meeting was held in the fall of 1985, in Washington, D.C. Eighty land trusts from thirty states were represented.[6]

With the organization functioning smoothly, Emory announced his intention to retire as of June 1987. One element of the land trust community had believed from the beginning that the organization should put major emphasis on influencing public policy. To improve visibility and access to federal offices, it was decided to move the office to the Washington area (specifically to Arlington, Virginia; it moved to Washington in 1990). Jean Hocker was hired as the new president and executive director.

Hocker, an LTE board member since 1984, was executive director of the Jackson Hole (Wyoming) Land Trust from 1982 to 1987.[7] A graduate of Boston University, she had been director of housing for the Syracuse, New York, community development agency in the early 1970s. After moving to Wyoming in 1976, she headed the Jackson Hole Project of the Isaak Walton League. Part of that job was building community support for a land trust to save rangelands around Grand Teton National Park. Hocker spent fourteen years as head of the LTA, retiring in December 2001.

Hired as her replacement in March 2002 was Rand Wentworth, vice president for the southeastern region of the Trust for Public Land (TPL). Wentworth, a Cornell M.B.A., sometimes introduced himself to Georgia audiences as a former Gwinnett County commercial real estate developer who had a "road to Damascus" conversion on conservation.[8] Gwinnett County is part of the hypertrophic metropolitan sprawl from Atlanta. Among TPL projects Wentworth worked on were the Martin Luther King, Jr., National Historic Site in Atlanta and a river cleanup and greenway project on the Chatahoochee River that included a capital campaign in which more than $130 million was raised.

The LTA National Rallies

Attendance at the first national meeting in 1985 of the Land Trust Exchange in Washington, D.C. was 257. A measure of the growth of the land trust movement is that by the 2002 meeting in Austin, attendance was 1,800. This is an annual growth rate of more than 35 percent.

The LTA calls its national meeting a "rally," a name picked by Jean Hocker. It's a good name. What it lacks in scholarly or intellectual connotations is more than made up for by the sense of assembling for a common purpose and the implication of inspiring enthusiasm.

Fifteen rallies have been held as of 2002. The rallies were at eighteen-month intervals through 1993 and yearly thereafter. The first that I attended was the 1996 meeting in Vermont with about 1,200 attendees. Vermont is one of the most environmentally enlightened states, perhaps *the* most enlightened, so it was a good choice. But the specific location chosen was curious. Vermont has fought urban sprawl pretty successfully, but the meeting was held at one of the few places where the battle has been lost, a big motel-conference center in a commercial strip near Interstate 89 on the border between Burlington and South Burlington. Perhaps the choice was meant as an object lesson, to bring home to the attendees what they were fighting against.

But some other Rally locations also seem dubious: several ski resorts and a convention center that, though designed by a famous architect, seems to violate 90 percent of William H. Whyte's or James Howard Kunstler's rules for public buildings and public spaces.

I doubt that the object lesson explanation could apply to all these selections. Perhaps no place exists that's still environmentally healthy and will hold a meeting of twelve to seventeen hundred people—or at least no place with private bathrooms, a health club, and good restaurants. Certainly, I've attended meetings of other conservation and ecological organizations at places that were even more environmentally debased and dispiriting.

What the LTA Does

By publishing *Exchange* and organizing the annual Rally, the LTA performs much of its assigned clearinghouse role. It also puts out a brief newsletter, *Landscape*, alternately with *Exchange*. Other useful services include representing the land conservation cause in Washington, D.C., and publication of a valuable series of books. LTA also encourages land trusts to adopt standards and practices that set forth ethical and practical principles for land trust conduct. All of these services are highly conducive to the successful operation of land trusts, exactly in line with the reason for establishing the organization.

The first book published by LTA was *Appraising Easements,* in 1984 (now in its third edition) in cooperation with the National Trust for Historic Preservation. Two years later, LTA published the technical *Federal Tax Law of Conservation Easements* (updated by periodic supplements). A sampling of other LTA books are the clear and instructive *Conservation Easement Handbook* in cooperation with the Trust for Public Land (1988, revised 1997), *The Conservation Easement Stewardship Guide* (1992), and *Conservation Options: A Landowner's Guide* (1993), a 55-page pamphlet of value to people who are seriously considering protecting their land.

The standards and practices were put together by a committee of land trust representatives in 1988, published the next year, and developed more fully in *The Standards and Practices Guidebook* in 1993. The *Guidebook* expounds on the fifteen standards and accompanying practices and also provides samples of documents, such as policy statements and application forms developed and used by local land trusts. As of 2000, 560 land trusts had formally adopted the standards and practices.

The introduction to the *Guidebook* says, "The guidebook is not a theoretical essay on ethics. It is a practical guide that shares the experience of land trusts nationwide. It addresses the real issues and dilemmas that land trusts face in their day-to-day work."[9] This statement, echoing sentiments expressed in the first issue of *Exchange,* captures what has been the LTA mode of operation. In many ways, it has proved a powerful approach.

About 700, or about 60 percent, of the nation's land trusts are members of LTA. In recent years, the organization has also been pushing individual memberships. These contribute to the cause of conservation just as do memberships in The Nature Conservancy, Sierra Club, or many other environmental organizations. Many readers with a general conservation interest may find *Exchange* more specialized—for the land trust insider, especially staff—and hence less interesting than such magazines as *Nature Conservancy, Land & People, Sierra,* or *OnEarth* (formerly *Amicus Journal*).

Exchange

Exchange was designed "to provide a regular medium of communication and interchange among volunteers and professionals in the land trust community as well as facilitate dialogue with others who are seeking alternative means of preserving and conserving land resources. . . ."[10] The first issue, March 1982, was newsletter-like, but the second looked not unlike the magazine today. It began with an article by Stephen Small on "the new tax regulations." There was a piece on how to get publicity, a section of short articles on land management, and news snippets from local land trusts.

In fact, individual articles from the early years of *Exchange* dealt with pretty much the same topics as might be seen in a current issue. Here are a few titles from 1982 through 1983: Phases in the Development of a Land Trust, Liability Insurance: Protecting against Negligence, and Limitations on Lobbying. There were also groups of short articles on trails and on conservation easements. The titles and, to a considerable degree, the information in early volumes could fit in any recent issue.

Perhaps this shouldn't be surprising. Going back to the origin of the Land Trust Alliance isn't like going back to the beginning of the Royal Society of London. The year 1982 is not very long ago. Perhaps if there had been a land trust magazine in 1917 or 1955—founding dates of the Save-the-Redwoods League and the Michigan Nature Association—the articles would have been different. But the continued relevance of articles in the early issues of *Exchange* suggests that the land trust movement was pretty mature by 1982. Most of the important ideas had already been brought forth by the Trustees of Reservations and other successful local land trusts and by The Nature Conservancy and Trust for Public Land.

Nevertheless, there have been differences in emphasis through the twenty-odd years that *Exchange* has been in operation. It's worth looking at just what the magazine has included, under the theory that we can learn something about a creator by examining his or her works.

Attention to some topics hasn't fluctuated much. Virtually every issue of the magazine has informative news or articles about legal issues affecting land trusts: tax laws and regulations, liability, nonprofit law. Public policy as related to land protection (conservation easements, mostly) has been generally well represented, as have fund raising and sources of financial support. The magazine has always included plenty of news about LTA and about the land trust movement. Articles about partnerships and cooperative ventures regularly make up more than 10 percent of the yearly total, which seems high. But, of course, the LTA itself is a cooperative venture, so it's logical that it would appreciate the virtues of such arrangements.

Conservation easements have always been well represented. Three and a half of the first issue's sixteen pages dealt with proposed IRS regulations concerning easements. Using *Exchange*'s biennial indexes, the number of conservation easement entries were as follows (*Exchange* did not publish indexes prior to 1990):

1990–1991: 6
1992–1993: 10
1994–1995: 7
1996–1997: 10
1998–1999: 23
2000–2001: 30

An article in the first issue of 1999 was titled, "Conservation Easements Emerge as the Decade's Top Land Protection Tool."[11] We can't know with certainty whether the steady flow of conservation easement articles through the years reflected the enthusiasm of land trusts for this approach to land protection or caused it. It's possible a positive feedback loop was involved.

Articles dealing with potential problems of the conservation easement approach were scarce until 1997. It's a healthy sign that by 1999 they were occurring regularly.

The early years of *Exchange* included occasional articles on preserve acquisition and stewardship, but these dwindled to almost none in the second decade. The spring 1987 issue, for example, had a section on stewardship and fall 1989 had a section on land management. The articles in both dealt mostly with preserve stewardship. From 1992 on, the stewardship entries in the biennial indexes overwhelmingly pertain to easement monitoring and defense.

Another indication of LTA's priorities in land protection is representation on the program at its yearly rallies. The same disproportion between coverage of conservation easements and preserves exists but is not quite as severe: At the 2001 Rally, thirty-four presentations dealt with easements, ten with issues of protected land owned by a land trust (or government), and seven with issues that could apply to either. This third category mostly had to do with methodology such as geographic information systems (GIS) and real estate technicalities. The programs at other recent Rallies show a similar distribution.

The overrepresentation of conservation easement coverage in *Exchange* and rallies may be related to a preference by LTA for this method of land protection. Another factor may be that easements are complicated, needing copious and continuing explanation, in contrast to the straightforward issues of acquisition and stewardship of preserves.

Two other topics that some might think relevant to land trust operations are sparsely represented through the whole span of *Exchange*. These are nonfinancial motives for saving land and education. The tax advantages of protecting land are, of course, important, but other reasons exist, both the good that preserved land does and the feelings of donors for their land (as we've seen in chapters 3 and 7).

People are not necessarily born knowing all the values of intact ecosystems any more than they're born knowing IRS regulations; both may need to be learned. Education that reaches beyond a land trust's own members is needed on the values of open space and natural areas and why and how to preserve them. But *Exchange* gives scant evidence that the LTA considers either education about the land or non-tax reasons for land protection as priority issues.

An editor of *Exchange* wrote, "We try to keep *Exchange* content very oriented to the practical."[12] One of the great strengths of the LTA has been its focus on the nuts and bolts of private land protection. Focus, if it's narrow enough, sometimes becomes hard to distinguish from tunnel vision.

Recent Directions

In past years, LTA publications always spoke with satisfaction of growth in numbers of land trusts. "The fastest growing segment of the conservation movement," noted the 1994 survey.[13] Even the 1998 survey spoke of "a vibrant land conservation movement that has experienced exponential growth and achievement during the past 50 years and especially during the 1990s, a decade of destiny for the land trust movement."[14]

By early 1999, LTA had begun to de-emphasize the idea that more land trusts are always a good thing. An article in the winter 1999 *Exchange* mentioned bank, airline, and oil company mergers as a prelude to speaking favorably of three cases in which local land trusts merged.[15] The President's Column in the Spring 2000 *Exchange* was a fine example of the on-the-one-hand-but-on-the-other maneuver:

In addition, some local land trusts are finding that they are simply too local or too small to succeed and are merging to form one larger, more sustainable regional organization. . . . Don't misunderstand. The local, place-based nature of land trusts is still one of our greatest strengths.[16]

The corresponding issue of *Landscape,* the LTA newsletter for staff and board of sponsor organizations, was devoted to the idea that the land trust movement needs to grow smarter, not bigger. "Success," wrote President Hocker, "is not about sheer numbers of land trusts; it's about their reach, their on-the-ground achievements, and their staying power."[17]

These indications of a new LTA position hit the right note. Marginally effective land trusts probably ought to merge, but many areas needing land trusts still exist. The impulse to start land trusts will not be easily quelled, so probably it's appropriate that the pressure should be a little heavier on the merger side.

The switch from encouraging founding new land trusts to merging old ones was just one of several things that happened rather quickly in the 1997 to 1998 period. The first half of the 1990s, or a little more, was a period of rather slow development for the LTA, not marked by strong innovation. LTA had successful programs and continued them. It first opened its Web site in early 1997, tardily perhaps for an organization of national importance. Revenue grew from about $0.9 million in fiscal 1993 to $1.7 million in 1997. It's a respectable increase, almost 20 percent per year.

Something happened around the beginning of 1998. A strategic planning process that began about this time accounts for part of the change. Revenue rose a near-phenomenal 134 percent during fiscal 1998 to 1999 (54 percent per year). And several other important changes occurred between 1998 and 2000:

- *Exchange* was revamped and enlarged beginning with the last issue of 1999.
- LTA demonstrated greater success in obtaining funding from large foundations that provided money to pass through as grants to individual local trusts. Many large foundations for reasons of convenience won't deal with grant applications from individual local land trusts, so this role of LTA as an intermediary is significant.
- In June 1998, LTA announced plans for four new regional offices to add to those in New York State (1993) and the Northwest (1995).[18] By early 2000, it had raised its sights to six new ones, the eight regions "encompassing the entire country."[19] Regional offices bring information closer to individual land trusts and may relieve state consortiums of the need to hold their own meetings. Regional offices can encourage formation of new trusts where they're needed and they'll undoubtedly also be pushing mergers. The danger is a switch to a top-down system, with the result that approaches and practices become increasingly homogenized. A great strength of the land trust movement has been the innovation coming from individual local organizations.

Such changes are part of the first of four goals stated in the strategic plan, that of "increasing quality, professionalism, and effectiveness of land trusts."[20] An April 1998 LTA document spoke truthfully: "Land trusts assume responsibilities rarely thrust on small organizations. . . . Regardless of size and resources, a land trust, whether staffed or all-volunteer, must be an enduring organization capable of carrying out these obligations over time."[21]

Another aspect of the first goal is increased training opportunities for land trust staff and board. Beginning in 1998, a partnership (the Land Conservation Leadership Program) with The Conservation Fund has helped LTA strengthen the coursework aspect of educating land trusts. Similar to daylong seminars that open the annual rallies, the courses, offered here and there within the LTA regions, cover such topics as conservation easements, fund raising, and things executive directors ought to know.

The second goal in the strategic plan is to beef up conservation easement procedures. The first two goals are related in that much of the vulnerability of land trusts is caused by the heavy dependence of many on conservation easements. Studies of how well baseline documentation and monitoring are being done and the feasibility of collective defense against violations are part of the second goal.

The third goal is to "identify new opportunities for conservation and expand the tools and incentives available for voluntary land conservation." This is mostly about public policy, convincing legislators and agencies to do a better job of helping the private side of land protection.

The fourth goal is to "increase the public's understanding of land trusts and the importance of voluntary land conservation." As of 2002, this seemed the least fleshed-out of the goals.

Anyone interested in land conservation will have to applaud the LTA's new directions. The lesson on quality and professionalism was timely and the one calling on land trusts to recognize the gravity of conservation easement responsibilities was overdue. Some might wish that the strategic plan had recommended diversification of land protection methods, such as a renewed attention to acquiring (and keeping) preserves. But in most ways LTA seems ready to confront the twenty-first century.

10 THE NATURE CONSERVANCY

"The Nature Conservancy is turning into another God-damned Audubon Society," Victor E. Shelford told me one August day in 1958. We were driving back to Champaign-Urbana from Indiana University. The Nature Conservancy (TNC) had met in Bloomington in conjunction with many other biology societies that were members of the American Institute of Biological Sciences.

I'd attended mainly for the Ecological Society of America (ESA), where I gave a paper summarizing my thesis research. I was a callow twenty-five-year-old graduate student at the University of Illinois. Shelford was eighty years old, almost eighty-one. In a long life, he had accomplished many things. It would be fair to call him the father of animal ecology in America and, for that matter, the father of The Nature Conservancy, as we shall see. He had been retired for ten years but still kept an office at the University, where he was working on trimming his book *The Ecology of North America* down to publishable size.

Of average height, Shelford was wiry and erect, with white hair parted on the left, and thick wire-rimmed glasses. He always wore a suit and tie, and the collar points of his white broadcloth shirts tended to curl up.

I was driving his car, a red Buick coupé from some year in the late 1940s. Shelford had driven himself to Bloomington. Another graduate student and I had ridden down with our major professor, Charles Kendeigh, who had been a student of Shelford in the late 1920s and who had succeeded him at Illinois.

Though he was a skilled—and fast—driver, Shelford was tired after several days of the conference and had asked if I'd drive him back to Champaign-Urbana. We'd leave, he'd said, the next day right after the annual meeting of The Nature Conservancy.

Shelford was already in the classroom where the meeting was to be held when I arrived. There was a moderate crowd, thirty-five or so in a room that could have held a few more. Early in the meeting, Shelford rose to make a motion he'd prepared. It wasn't on the agenda, and the chairman was somewhat buffaloed. Shelford was still highly respected, but TNC was moving in directions that he was known to be unsympathetic with. The chairman was reluctant to allow Shelford to open up these issues, but was uncertain how to handle the situation.

The solution was handed to him by one of the attendees, who suggested that he rule Shelford's request out of order. Relieved, the chairman did so. Shelford crooked a finger at me, I jumped up and followed him out of the room, and we were soon on the road.

Shelford wasn't angry. He hadn't expected to prevail but had felt duty bound to make the attempt.

If I ever knew exactly what Shelford's motion was, I've forgotten it, but his comment—condemning in one sentence two of our premier environmental organizations—will help us reconstruct the general nature of his unhappiness.

Nature Preservation in the Ecological Society of America

John Sawhill, president from 1990 to 2000, described The Nature Conservancy as "an international nonprofit environmental organization dedicated to protecting biodiversity. Put simply, it protects the rare plants, animals, and natural communities that represent the diversity of life on Earth by safeguarding the lands and waters they need to survive."[1]

A 2001 fact sheet stated that TNC had protected over 12 million acres of ecologically significant habitat in the United States and helped protect over 60 million acres elsewhere in the world. Membership is well over one million. It has a staff of nearly 3,000. TNC has been successful financially; it is in fact the nation's tenth largest nonprofit.[2] Its financial summary for 2001 showed total income of more than half a billion dollars. Its endowment stood at $637 million. Sawhill attributed TNC's success to its being science-based and nonconfrontational and to its partnerships involving both private and public sectors.

Such is The Nature Conservancy today.

It began as a committee of the Ecological Society of America. The ESA was founded in 1915 with Shelford as the first president.[3] In 1917, at his suggestion, a Committee on the Preservation of Natural Conditions for Ecological Research was formed. The aims of the committee show the size of Shelford's vision: (1) to list all the areas in the United States and Canada suitable for ecological study that were already preserved and also the ones that weren't preserved but ought to be; (2) to work for the preservation of this latter group; and (3) to urge proper care of preserves.[4]

Over the years, the ESA leadership blew hot and cold, or rather, warm and cold, over the idea of actively pushing land preservation, but Shelford pressed the cause aggressively. At ESA annual meetings, the Preservation Committee regularly presented numerous resolutions urging ecologically responsible positions on such topics as draining swamps, importation of alien species, predator control, damming rivers, overgrazing in national forests, and support of proposed national parks and monuments.[5]

The Preservation Committee was heavily involved in the 1925 campaign to set aside Glacier Bay as a national monument. In 1926, *A Naturalist's Guide to the Americas* was published, fulfilling—as far as possible by a few people in a few years—the committee's first charge to list preserved areas and ones that deserved preservation.[6] A nature sanctuary plan developed by the committee in 1933 was adopted by the National Park Service. Among other things, the Park Service set areas aside for ecological research and, in theory, reversed their long-time practice of killing predators.

The original Preservation Committee had been split early on into a Study Committee, headed for a good many years by my advisor Kendeigh, and a more action-oriented committee retaining the Preservation Committee name. This committee was to "urge governmental agencies to act in certain ways."[7] As a long-time professor, I feel the urge to underline this sentence a couple of times on the overhead transparency. The Preservation Committee was a land advocacy group. It was, certainly, an esoteric one, composed of some dozens of ecologists proselytizing government bureaucracies to save lands for ecological research.

In 1945, the Executive Committee of the ESA recommended that the Preservation Committee be limited to fact finding, with no authority to take direct action. The ESA leadership was evidently unaware that this was exactly the charge of the Study Committee.[8] Probably the ESA leaders were irked by an article by Shelford in *Science* stating that, contrary to the wishes of the majority of ESA members, the organization had never put the Preservation Committee on a permanent, adequately financed basis.[9]

If that was an immediate reason, there were other issues, old and new. Some ESA members had never wanted the organization to take positions on societal issues; they wanted it to be a proper scientific society that published journals and held an annual meeting and did little more. Some feared that the organization's nonprofit status could be jeopardized if what the Preservation Committee did could be construed as lobbying. Also the field of ecology was broadening; a diminishing percentage of ecologists was interested in natural communities and an increasing percentage in such topics as population ecology studied on grain beetles in laboratory culture and the representation of ecological interactions by mathematical models.

Despite assurances by the Executive Committee that they weren't diminishing the Preservation Committee's importance but merely redirecting its efforts, the Preservation Committee chair, marine biologist Curtis Newcombe, was unpersuaded.[10] Believing the Committee could no longer function effectively, he recommended that it be discontinued. When the ESA leadership obliged, Kendeigh resigned as chair of the Study Committee.[11]

The Ecologists Union

Shelford was not one to abandon ideas just because other people didn't like them. Although he lived on a professor's salary all his life—his highest salary was $6,300—he contributed $300 to bankroll a campaign to set up a new, independent organization with the same mission as the Preservation Committee.[12] In January 1946, a letter of invitation, endorsed by Shelford and three other past-presidents of the the the ESA, was sent to about four hundred supporters of the old Preservation Committee.[13]

By March 2, based on an enthusiastic response to the invitation, the temporary secretary of the incipient group wrote, "I declare the Ecologists' Union in existence." The name came from Shelford and Kendeigh, probably as a parallel formation to American Ornithologists' Union. Kendeigh and several others always wrote the name as Ecologists' Union, but the organizational letterhead didn't use the apostrophe.

The Ecologists Union (EU) held its first meeting four weeks later, 28 March 1946, in connection with the ESA meeting in St. Louis, Missouri. EU's objectives were given as the maintenance of original conditions in natural areas, the preservation of additional scientifically valuable original plant and animal communities, and the encouragement of scientific researches in preserved areas.[14]

One of the EU's first actions was to set up Preservation and Study Committees with exactly the roles they had had in the ESA. Newcombe and Kendeigh resumed their chairmanships.

By December 1949, the EU was holding what it called its fifth annual meeting, at Columbia University.[15] For the first couple of years, ecology Ph.D.s had dominated the six-member board of governors, but the addition of Richard Pough in 1948 and George Fell in 1949 broke that pattern.

Fell was an Illinois product, though he had a master's degree in wildlife management from the University of Michigan. He had taken courses from Shelford, Kendeigh, and plant ecologist A. G. Vestal while majoring in botany at the University of Illinois. After a few years teaching high school, he was working at the Rockford, Illinois, Public Health Department at the time he became involved with the Ecologists Union.[16] Pough was an older man; in 1949, he was forty-five and Fell was thirty-three.

Like Fell, Pough had held various jobs following college (he studied management at MIT). He had at this time just joined the American Museum of Natural History as Curator of Conservation and General Ecology after twelve years on the staff of the National Audubon Society. He was author of an excellent field guide to birds with paintings by one of America's best bird artists, Don Eckelberry. Among Pough's conservation accomplishments had been assisting Rosalie Edge with her purchase in the 1930s of Hawk Mountain, Pennsylvania, which led to the Hawk Mountain Sanctuary.[17]

Besides their true and deeply felt concern for land conservation, Fell was interested in creating a job in conservation for himself and Pough was interested in getting conservation work started at the American Museum. Both believed that the EU needed to increase and broaden its membership base, which stood at 294 members, mostly university and government ecologists.[18]

Pough was quoted in 1984 as saying, "Presumably, the members were out to preserve interesting ecological areas. I learned they had been talking about such activities since World War I, but professors usually aren't good at that sort of thing. So, when I protested that they hadn't actually preserved anything, they appointed me chairman of a 'committee on the preservation of natural conditions.' I found another member of the union, George Fell, who shared my interest in preservation, and I persuaded him to open an office in Washington."[19]

Shelford and the other old-timers of the Preservation Committee wouldn't have agreed that they hadn't preserved anything. They had repeatedly guided federal, state, and local agencies, and their own universities toward land that deserved preservation. Brownfield and Trelease Woods and parts of Allerton Park were among the natural areas administered by the University of Illinois as the result of Shelford's diligent advocacy at home.

The difference between this viewpoint and Pough's points out a crucial juncture in the line from ESA committee to The Nature Conservancy. The Protection Committee was a land advocacy organization, though an unusual one. It was a group of professional biologists and conservationists that tried to guide public and private agencies toward the protection of appropriate land.

Pough's view of preservation, on the other hand, was that of a land trust. "I don't protest anything," Pough said. "If someone comes to me and complains that a majestic forest is about to be cut down, I [tell them,] 'Don't cry about the forest. Go out and buy it!'"[20] Embedded in this admonition is another, unspoken one: "Go out and raise the money for it!"

Pough was a New Yorker but had spent five years in Massachusetts, including one at Harvard. If he had heard of the work of the Trustees of Reservations or other New England land trusts, he seems not to have mentioned it. It's possible that he thought he invented the idea.

A short history of TNC published in 1981 stated that George Fell and his wife Barbara left the 1949 Columbia meeting and drove directly to Washington to look for an office, "without returning to Illinois for either clothing or furniture."[21] It's a fact that Fell moved to Washington, where the American Nature Study Association gave him a desk to pursue the EU cause with legislators and other conservation organizations.

Creation of The Nature Conservancy

At its 11 September 1950 meeting, the EU voted to change its name. Some members liked the old name, others didn't. Not enough people knew what "ecologists" were, and, according to the *EU Circular* number 6, "Some object to the name 'union' because of its unpopular connotation."

Among possible names mulled over were Nature Protection Foundation, Nature Conservation Society, and Nature Preservation Society.[22] In the end, of course, the Ecologists Union became The Nature Conservancy.

I suspect the name was Fell's choice. *EU Circular* number 6 (April 1950) noted that "our vice-president [Fell] has been developing tentative plans of organization and a program for developing such a Nature Conservancy." It's known that he had persuaded a Florida congressman to introduce a bill in May 1950 to set up a Nature Conservancy that would have duplicated for the United States the Nature Conservancy established a year earlier in England.[23] The English version was a governmental body with a royal charter to provide scientific advice on the conservation of the natural flora and fauna and to establish and manage nature reserves.[24]

The bill pushed by Fell went nowhere, and four months later the EU adopted the Nature Conservancy name for itself.[25] The new organization was granted federal nonprofit status in 1950 and in 1951 incorporated as a District of Columbia nonprofit corporation. The first Board of Governors consisted of Shelford and two other academics and three non-academics including Fell and Pough. A little later, Fell became executive secretary and then executive director, though for a long time there was no money for a salary.[26]

At first, the new organization continued in the Preservation Committee/ Ecologists Union mold. The national office, consisting of Fell and his wife, was a clearinghouse; identification of natural areas was to be done on the state or regional level through local representatives, as had been true of the Study and Preservation Committees.[27] A logical outgrowth was the chapter structure, which Fell began.

George and Barbara Fell devoted this decade of their lives to TNC, working long days and nights on correspondence and publications. Barbara supported the family as well as the Conservancy office by working as a medical technician from 1950 to 1954. Their efforts paid off: membership passed 500 in 1951 and 1,000 in 1953.[28]

The first major publication coming out of TNC was a 45-page inventory by Kendeigh and the Study Committee of nature sanctuaries in the United States and Canada.[29] An updating of one aspect—already protected areas—of the *Naturalist's Guide,* it was begun under ESA auspices, completed under the EU, and the name change to TNC was given in a footnote.

In a January 1951 letter to the board, Fell talked about a pamphlet he'd prepared: "Living Museums in Primitive America: A Need and an Opportunity."[30] The pamphlet's title and terminology were Shelfordian. Fell included a copy of his letter that had accompanied the most recent mailing of the pamphlet, to the Wilderness Society: "You will note (perhaps with disapproval) that the emotional side of the picture is stressed and the scientific side is bypassed. I think the scientific side of the Nature Conservancy should be dominant over the other. Perhaps, though, even the scientist requires the emotional approach to get him interested."

Later in the letter, he commented, "Sooner or later, we may have to consider the possibility of adding provisions to our constitution to assure that leadership of the Conservancy remains in the hands of scientists."

In 1952, the board was expanded to twenty-six members. About twenty of these were scientists, including all four of the officers (giving Pough the benefit of the doubt), but the dilution would begin soon.[31] By 1962, the board had expanded again, to about thirty-five; none of the officers and only eight overall had scientific credentials

In 1951, there were still no plans for TNC to buy and own land, but this changed too. The change came partly through events and partly because of the growing dominance of Pough's point of view over that of Fell. Rutgers University asked for help in buying what became the Hutcheson Memorial Forest. Shortly thereafter, Pough brought TNC into a deal in which they raised the money to buy the Sunken Forest, 60 acres of beach, dune, and barrier forest on Fire Island, to be managed by a New York–based preservation group.[32]

The first real TNC preserve, memorialized in prose, poetry, and song, came a little later, the result of a process that began in 1953 when development and a proposed reservoir threatened the Mianus River gorge in southeast New York next to Connecticut. Much of the potential damage from the reservoir was deflected by regulatory means, a limitation on the height of the dam.

Then, the owner of a prime 60 acres of the gorge, including a cathedral-like stand of ancient hemlocks, received an offer for her land. She notified the Mianus River Gorge Conservation Committee on Christmas Eve 1954 that they had until New Year's Day to match it. The committee managed an offer, a down payment, and in the next several months all but $7,500 of the purchase price.

With this last payment looming, a new member of TNC's board visited the gorge. He was connected with the Old Dominion Foundation (precursor to the Andrew W. Mellon Foundation), which had helped TNC on the Rutgers and Fire Island deals. He proposed that the foundation grant TNC $7,500 to be loaned to and repaid by the Mianus Gorge Committee. This was the beginning of the TNC revolving fund, now called the Land Preservation Fund, through which TNC lends money so that worthy land can be bought by local groups (now primarily its own chapters), which then fundraise to repay the loan. The revolving fund kicked TNC's efforts into a higher gear. It was another of George Fell's ideas.[33]

TNC received the deed to Mianus Gorge in June 1955. By 1958, the year of the Bloomington, Indiana, TNC meeting, another 100 acres had been added, and ten other preserves had been acquired, half by purchase and half as gifts.[34] Four more were in the offing, including two in Illinois, where Kendeigh and others had started a chapter in 1951. There were by this time seven chapters. A western office had been opened in Berkeley.

What Did Shelford Mean?

Shelford's unhappiness with TNC in 1958 was connected with differences of policy and opinion within the organization that led to George Fell being forced from his position of executive director shortly thereafter. Fell and his wife packed up and went home to Illinois, where they immersed themselves in land conservation at the state level. Fell drafted and the Illinois legislature passed in 1963 a bill establishing the Illinois Nature Preserves Commission along lines similar to the British Nature Conservancy. Working in collaboration with the Illinois Department of Conservation, it quickly compiled an enviable record of success. Within ten years, the Illinois Nature Preserves system contained fifty preserves; the three-hundredth was dedicated in 2001.

Many contemporary readers of *Audubon,* the National Audubon Society's glossy magazine, might find Shelford's unfavorable view of that organization surprising. His assessment, forged especially in the first four decades of the twentieth century, was of an organization that had become more interested in empire building and image polishing than saving birds. Its highly successful fund raising often seemed to have no clear conservation purpose. Wary of offending potential donors, business interests, and advertisers, it seemed to take timid stands on certain conservation issues. The organization was undemocratic, dominated by a small group of cronies from a few Eastern organizations.[35]

Shelford was not alone in these opinions. Rosalie Edge, whose Eleanor Roosevelt–like voice and refined manner made her fiery conservationist rhetoric that much more effective, wrote in 1942:

How does the National Audubon Society differ today from what it was ten or twenty years ago? It is richer, it is more extravagant, and it supports a more luxurious overhead.
   Actually, it differs very little.[36]

Whether any of these criticisms were still valid for the National Audubon Society of 1958 or later periods is of no consequence for understanding Shelford's remark. Whether it was a correct characterization of The Nature

Conservancy's direction is of historical interest. The Nature Conservancy of today is genetically related to the organization of the late 1950s and early 1960s, but it has been remade several times in the past forty years.

The Katharine Ordway Years

The Nature Conservancy of the 1950s and 1960s was close to a pure land trust. *The Nature Conservancy News* of the time reads like a newsletter from one of the better land trusts of today. TNC was buying land or receiving it as gifts from private landowners. Land was being snatched from the jaws of developers through the swift action of a chapter or local group. An occasional foundation grant was reported. Russell Brenneman, young, slim, horn-rimmed, and crewcut, spoke on private methods of land protection at the 1963 meeting. A little later, an ad for conservation easements ran— "Protect the land you love with an easement"—but easements played only a small role in land protection at most TNC chapters for a long while.

Beginning in 1966, TNC's corporate structure shifted to the business model with a "professional" president instead of an executive director; the old president position became chairman of the board. The first president in the new sense was Charles H. W. Foster, hired with money from the Ford Foundation. Foster had spent several years as Director of Natural Resources for Massachusetts. Among other things, he'd been on the board of the Trustees of Reservations; later he'd be Dean of the School of Forestry and Environmental Studies at Yale.

Foster moved on after only about a year, and thereafter, no TNC president (as of 2002) has had a biology, ecology, or natural history background. Naturalists and biologists have been involved with the organization, but the business of the Conservancy came to be done by lawyers and M.B.A.s.

Richard Pough left the board in the late 1960s, but he continued to be influential via his connection with Katharine Ordway and her Goodhill Foundation. Pough had also left the American Museum, but while there he had started a series of conservation luncheons for garden club women. One of the wealthy women who attended was Katharine Ordway, daughter of one of the founders of Minnesota Mining and Manufacturing (3M).[37]

Ordway had studied botany and art at the University of Minnesota, nearly finished an M.D. at Yale, and took graduate courses in biology and land use planning at Columbia in the 1950s. Born in 1899, she was in her fifties at the time. Ordway was small, thin, and stooped at an early age from the first stages of osteoporosis. In the field, she carried a large umbrella to keep off the sun. The Nature Conservancy has published a charming book about her: *Katharine Ordway: The Lady Who Saved the Prairies*.

Her first substantial help to TNC came in the mid-1960s when she made it possible to buy Devil's Den, 1,500 acres of rugged forestland in south-western Connecticut. The largest part had originally, in 1918, been given to the Yale University School of Forestry to preserve, but in the early 1930s, a water company had acquired it by eminent domain, uncontested by Yale. It was fortunate that the land had not been despoiled and that TNC was able to buy it. But the fact that Katharine Ordway had to spend $750,000 to save land that had supposedly been preserved half a century earlier offended Pough for years. It re-enforced his view that the way to protect land was to own it. "Don't trust anybody—not even the Boy Scouts," he wrote.[38]

Katharine Ordway was seventy-one when the Devil's Den purchases were completed. In the following ten years, she helped save a great deal more land, mostly through TNC and concentrated on the fast-disappearing large tracts of prairie. She died in 1979, and the bulk of her estate went to her Goodhill Foundation. Its share turned out to be something over $40 million, roughly $100 million in 2002 dollars.

Ordway's directions to the foundation board—Pough and two others—were that the money should be spent to buy land for conservation and, further, that Goodhill should wind up its business within a reasonable time after her death. Showing admirable respect for the wishes of the donor, the board decided that the sun would set in five years. By 1984, when the Good-hill Foundation dissolved, it had distributed $53 million, 80 percent to TNC, on such projects as 54,000 acres along the Niobrara River in Nebraska, the 24,000-acre Katharine Ordway Sycan Marsh Preserve in Oregon, and a National Critical Areas Conservation Program.

In all, Katharine Ordway personally and through her foundation gave at least $64 million for land conservation. During the Ordway years, TNC had changed from an organization that preserved good, but small pieces of land to one that preserved chunks big enough to capture many of the essential features of the ecosystem or landscape targeted.

Doing so has a sound ecological basis, but much of the change was driven by the ideas of Katharine Ordway. TNC's largest donor had known the vast Minnesota prairies of the early part of the twentieth century. To President Patrick Noonan, she'd say, "Can't you get me a prairie that we can go out on and not see *anything* else—no houses, no powerlines, *anything*?"[39] In 1966, at the time of the first Devil's Den purchase, the average TNC preserve was 190 acres. In 1984, the new preserves averaged nearly 1,000 acres.

Preacquisitions and Other Deals

A private inholding in a New York state park in the Catskills was put up for auction early in the 1960s. Although it was land that the parks commission had long wanted, the commission was restricted from bidding at auction and in any case didn't have the money. The commission asked TNC to bid on the land and hold it while the commission sought an appropriation.[40]

Not long before, TNC had begun discussing how to work with government in saving land. A 1950s surge in land prices along with the increasing loss of natural lands had made the board believe that they couldn't raise money and save land fast enough on their own. Consequently, they saw the proposal as an opportunity. They did buy the Catskills land, not without some jitters about tying up so much of their capital. The state allocated the necessary money and cashed them out in a short time, and TNC had done its first preacquisition deal.

A slightly later project was on a much larger scale. TNC bought and then resold to the California Parks Department 10,000 acres of second-growth redwoods not far from Santa Cruz.[41] In 1963, this became the Forest of Nicene Marks. By 1967, TNC had been involved in thirty-nine such deals, including several with the U.S. Forest Service. Impressed, the Ford Foundation the next year gave TNC a $6 million guaranteed line of credit to purchase land to be held for federal acquisition programs.

Patrick Noonan as Director of Operations and later President, and Huey Johnson, TNC's western regional director, liked these leveraged land purchases. They amplified TNC's ability to save land, especially when bought at a bargain price and sold for full-market value. By 1993, a book on public-private partnerships in land conservation was able to report that of the 6.3 million acres protected by The Nature Conservancy in its then forty years of existence, almost half—more than 3,000 individual transactions—had been preserved in cooperation with government agencies.[42]

The process continues today, although a few years beginning in 1981 when Ronald Reagan brought in James Watt as Secretary of Interior, marked a low point. Watt put the kibosh on Interior buying more land and even canceled several deals approved by the previous Interior Secretary, Cecil Andrus, temporarily leaving TNC with $20 million worth of "pre-acquired" land.[43]

This role of TNC is one that generates periodic unfavorable media attention. News reporters or columnists find property rights activists who criticize TNC and occasionally other organizations as "unaccountable arms of government land agencies."[44] A frequent charge is that TNC makes a profit off the deals. "Profit" usually means that it sells the land for more than it paid, with the addition being charged to interest or overhead. The critics particularly dislike the interest since TNC is usually borrowing the money from itself. They worry also about the deals in which TNC buys land at a bargain price and then sells it to a government agency at fair market value.[45] TNC and other land trusts are often able to buy land at a bargain because the seller can claim a charitable donation for the difference between fair market value and the sale price.

The second charge is lack of accountability. If the public agency were negotiating a deal on its own, several other players, such as the media and property rights organizations, would potentially be involved and the usual bureaucratic procedures, perhaps including public notice and hearings, would be followed. The private deal followed by the turnaround sale to the government can be fast and nearly silent.

The land trust community and conservationists in general see the ability by private organizations to save land that would be otherwise be lost because of the slow response time of government as an unqualified blessing. The possibility for abuse perhaps exists. It's unclear how many instances there have been in which the sellers didn't understand that their land would end up in the hands of the government.

TNC has been involved in several highly creative land deals, some involving later transfer to the government and some not. Hans Suter, a Texas conservationist and admirer of TNC, described one such deal in the establishment of the Virginia Coast Reserve. "In Virginia, where the Nature Conservancy acquired a string of barrier islands, one owner of one island refused to sell it to the Nature Conservancy. In this case, they set up a bogus development corporation, bought the island at market price and turned it over to the Conservancy."[46]

A somewhat fuller account of the deal appears in "A Light in Someone's Eye" in *The Nature Conservancy News*.[47] The owners who had refused to sell to TNC sold to a private individual. He, in turn, sold to "Offshore Islands, Inc., which appeared to be just another land speculation company. It was, instead, owned and controlled by the Conservancy. In December, 1975, Offshore Islands, Inc., donated its only asset, Metomkin Island, to the Conservancy."

Suter described another deal, which did involve transfer to government. "The state of Mississippi wanted to purchase 32,000 acres near Pascagoula as a preserve for the endangered sawback turtle. It had the money, but the company that owned the land refused to sell. The Nature Conservancy simply bought a controlling interest in the company, voted a dissolution, and sold the land to the state."[48]

Either deal, done as described by a for-profit corporation, would be considered good solid business practice, but some would argue that nonprofits, especially large, powerful ones, need to meet higher standards than those typical of American commerce.

A different version of the 1973 to 1976 Pascagoula deal was given by The Nature Conservancy vice president who was responsible for it. The Pascagoula Hardwood Company owned 42,000 acres of virgin swamp forest. Four families owned the corporation and were interested in selling. Some liked the conservation aspect; the land was to become the Pascagoula Wildlife Management Area. Some liked the money; the state was willing to pay $15 million. However, the largest block of stock, 25 percent, was controlled by one of the older members of the clan who preferred to let the land sit and appreciate. He hated the idea of paying taxes.[49]

To satisfy the diverse requirements, TNC devised a complex plan. "The Conservancy would make a tender offer for 75 percent of the company's stock, implement a tax-free dissolution of the corporation, trade the patriarch 25 percent of the land for his family's stock, and sell the remaining 75 percent of the land to the state." TNC used the state appropriation to pay back the money they had borrowed to buy the stock.[50] The bare outline of the deal is similar to the original story, but in this version, the deal was wholly above-board and all the participants were happy with the outcome.

Over the decades, TNC has transferred many properties to governmental agencies, some as preacquisitions, some as gifts. A question that should always arise about such arrangements, whatever land trust is involved, is how faithfully the government agency will protect the conservation values of the land now in its charge. As part of its Conservation by Design initiative, TNC has added explicit measures to see if its projects are actually achieving their conservation goal.[51] Perhaps it's time to do the same for land transferred to government agencies: Have these projects been managed in such a way that they've contributed what they should to saving biodiversity?

A Golden Age

David E. Morine, vice president of land acquisition for much of the 1970s and 1980s, reminisced about the TNC of the early 1970s: "When I started with the Conservancy, saving land was a relatively simple business. We'd look around, find some land that we liked, and buy it. . . ."[52]

It was a heady time. There were only forty-eight full-time employees, but things were happening. Deals such as those involving the Pascagoula River and the Virginia Coastal Preserve had begun. Patrick Noonan, with a master's in planning (and working on an M.B.A. at American University), was director of operations and would become vice-president in 1970 and president—at age twenty-nine—in 1973.

Morine recalled those days of the early 1970s:

Every Friday afternoon, Pat hosted an informal "Happy Hour" in our conference room. He'd personally buy a couple of cases of beer, and while attendance wasn't mandatory, everyone who was in town always showed up. These get-togethers would often last far into the evening. Pat would set the tone by highlighting what we'd accomplished that week.

"Miriam wrote the check that saved 1,500 acres of environmentally sensitive tidal marsh in Georgia," he'd announce. "Thank you, Miriam." There was enthusiastic applause. Miriam would flush, overcome with the significance of her deed.[53]

And in such pleasant wise, in that golden age, they celebrated their land deals, their new members, their big donors.

The Jenkins Era

The Nature Conservancy was born in science but by 1970, most of the scientists had gone.[54] The organization decided to open a science office and hire an ecology adviser. Robert E. Jenkins was chosen, a brand-new Harvard Ph.D. who had worked on the life history of a fish, the sicklefin redhorse, for his doctoral research. He came into an organization whose direction was largely determined by Patrick Noonan. Noonan's combination of energy, imaginative approaches to deals, ability to connect with donors, and business-like approach to operations made him a highly effective leader.

In 1973, the year Noonan became president, strategic planning, stemming from a grant requirement, led to a fateful decision. Discussion focused on what should be TNC's place, its niche, in the land conservation ecosystem. Scenic beauty? Open space? It was decided that land protection based on science had been its strength and should continue to be.

With a new science advisor on staff and a renewed emphasis on science, selecting land for protection became a more complicated business. It was no longer enough to find a piece of land they liked and buy it. Cost being equal, should TNC acquire a lot of little preserves or one big one? Should it protect a site that was ordinary but had one endangered species or a site that held a high diversity of common to rare species? If there were a choice between a great example of shrub-steppe and a degraded stand of riparian forest, which should be preserved? To the early 1970s question, which do we like the most? had to be added the context. Wrote Jenkins:

[Inadequate evaluation systems] often lead to the gully and hemlock syndrome, in which habitat types are preserved redundantly while others are not preserved at all. . . . Types which remain as only a few damaged remnants are passed over. It might seem absurd that the last, best example of ecosystems close to extinction could be rejected as "not good enough" for preservation but this is exactly what can happen.[55]

The answers to the questions posed above are not strictly scientific, but no sensible answers to them are possible without science. A theoretical framework for such science was developing in the 1970s and began to be strong enough to support a few conclusions in the 1980s. Most of the new developments were in the fields of population ecology and population genetics. Community/ecosystem ecology was also important because—as ecologists knew then and everyone knows now—the way to protect endangered species is to save the ecosystems to which they belong. Community/ecosystem thinking also gave rise to the ideas of landscape ecology, emphasizing the interactions on a broad scale among, say, forest, river, and marsh. The field that began to combine all these ideas became known in the 1980s as conservation biology.[56]

As useful ideas in conservation biology emerged from the universities, the scientists at TNC began to put them into practice. The organization's stated mission changed from protecting land to protecting natural diversity and then biological diversity.[57] By the mid-1970s, as data on effects of habitat fragmentation became more widely understood, TNC's protection efforts began to concentrate on larger tracts and eventually landscapes. According to Vice President for Land Acquisition, David Morine, Jenkins announced, "Henceforth, the Conservancy will no longer haphazardly acquire little lifeboats of biotic diversity. We will protect entire ecological systems."[58] Katharine Ordway and her Goodhill Foundation helped make this new approach feasible.

These changes in TNC's approach are justifiable on scientific grounds, and the nation is lucky that a conservation organization has existed with the resources to undertake projects of this magnitude. At the same time, such changes meant that TNC was no longer interested in the parcels of local or even statewide importance that had dotted the pages of *The Nature Conservancy News* in past years. No more hemlock gullies or small patches of prairie.

People still call state TNC offices about their 40-acre maple forest with a spectacular spring wildflower display and are surprised at TNC's lack of interest. Most *local* land trusts *are* interested in the 40-acre wildflower woods; in fact, it is exactly the sort of property they organized to protect. Increasingly, the state TNC office will pass the name of the appropriate local land trust on to the owner, and everybody comes out okay. TNC continues on its higher course, the owner finds a group enthusiastic about his 40 acres, and a site of great local importance is saved.

Natural Heritage Programs

A year after Bob Jenkins arrived, he began a long-running series in the TNC magazine called "Ecology Forum" that informed the members about scientific issues in land preservation. He also began one of his and TNC's most influential projects, the Natural Heritage Programs. These are inventories of the natural features of each state. Inventories of natural areas and biota have a long history in taxonomy and ecology. The 1926 *Naturalist's Guide to the Americas* by the ESA's Preservation Committee was an inventory with much the same aim as the Heritage Programs. Breeding-bird atlases and even state floras are similar inventories.

The time was propitious. The federal Endangered Species Act in 1973, followed by similar legislation in many states, provided a focus for a modern inventory. Once endangered, threatened, and rare species were listed by state committees, searching out their sites of occurrence was a logical next step in providing for their protection and hoped-for eventual recovery.

Not just species had become rare; ecosystems—the union of plant-animal community and abiotic habitat—could also be rare, or extinct. They needed to be classified and inventoried, also. The Eurasian meadow ecosystem that occurs in parks, golf courses, and highway medians is widespread and unlikely to be endangered until there is a drastic change in our values and lifestyle. Eastern tall-grass prairie, to the botanically ignorant a somewhat similar ecosystem, is rare, threatened, endangered, or gone wherever it once occurred.

Certain other natural features linked to plants, animals, or the abiotic environment lend themselves to the Heritage process of locating, evaluating quality, and assessing likelihood of obliteration from ongoing development. Examples are nesting colonies of social animals such as terns or prairie dogs and features of the land and water such as cliffs and vernal pools.

The information leads to rankings of species and communities that TNC uses to set priorities for land acquisition. There are separate state and global rankings.

The first Heritage program, in 1974, was in South Carolina. A 1975 grant from the Andrew W. Mellon Foundation helped hire the staff to spread the project nationally. By 1989, all fifty states were represented, and today similar programs are in effect in Canada and several Latin American countries.

The Heritage program was begun at the right time for another reason besides the newly available endangered species focus. File cards and even punch cards couldn't have done the job, but computer databases had begun to reach a level that would make it feasible to accumulate and handle the needed masses of data. Geographic information systems (GIS) are still undergoing development that will make them easier to use, but they are increasingly being used to deal with this kind of information.

The state Heritage programs put a lot of biologists and naturalists to work, permanently as part of the full-time staff or temporarily for field surveys. Something of the process and also the excitement is conveyed by the following comments on the early days of the program in Indiana. After developing a plant community classification and coming up with preliminary lists of rare plants and animals, the crew got leads from published papers and books—such as Alton Lindsey's *Natural Areas of Indiana and their Preservation*—visits to herbaria, and interviews with professors, naturalists, wildlife biologists, and foresters.[59]

Finally, we took to the field. . . . We wandered Indiana, fortunate to see some of the most beautiful remaining natural areas, finding plants not seen for a hundred years, and talking to landowners who remembered talking to Charlie Deam when he stopped by in his "weed wagon" [Deam was a druggist turned plant taxonomist who collected specimens all through the state from 1915 into the 1930s, using a succession of automobiles modified for botanical exploration.] . . . Our biggest limitations seem to be our imaginations. We will begin to track new groups of organisms: amphipods and spiders; mosses and lichens.[60]

TNC's inspired approach was to begin the Natural Heritage Program with grant money and then persuade the states, or most of them, that it was in their interest to take over the program. The databases now form a uniquely valuable guide to what sites are worth preserving in terms of saving rare species, first-rate examples of natural communities, and certain other natural features. None is complete, and completeness will be approached slowly and asymptotically; there are always some places and some groups of organisms that have not been checked thoroughly or at all. Not every site where rare plants grow gets saved, so that at the same time that more field work adds new sites, sprawl takes other sites away.

Some politicians don't like the idea of the Natural Heritage Program. To the degree that it has done its job completely, it knows where the threatened and endangered species live. Property rights advocates are horrified that an organization knows where protected species are to be found on private property. Even worse, if possible, is the thought that the organization with this knowledge is connected with a government agency.

In 1995, Bob Jenkins left TNC. He'd been there for twenty-five years, arriving when Thomas W. Richards was president, departing halfway through John Sawhill's term, and in between steering a steady course through the presidencies of Warren M. Lemmon (interim), Everett M. Woodman, Patrick Noonan, William D. Blair, and Frank D. Boren.

With Jenkins gone, the Natural Heritage component of TNC was spun off on a convoluted trajectory. A separate nonprofit, the Association for Biodiversity Information (ABI), was formed in 1999 to work with the data and with the eighty-five Natural Heritage programs and Conservation Data Centers (as the programs in Canada and Latin America were called). Around the end of 2001, ABI changed its name to NatureServe. Shortly before that, ABI and TNC produced an attractive volume, *Precious Heritage,* using the Natural Heritage data to talk about the status of biodiversity in the United States.[61]

TNC Chapters

The local representatives of the Preservation Committee and, later the Ecologists Union, were the forerunners of TNC's chapters. Several chapters were formed in the early days, in the 1950s, on George Fell's initiative, but not until the mid-1970s, when Patrick Noonan was president, did the push begin that produced the current state programs. The 1974 long-range plan called on the chapters to raise money to hire regional and state executive directors, a challenge they accepted enthusiastically.[62] William Blair is credited with further encouragement of the chapter system. The number of field offices increased from fewer than thirty to more than forty while he was president (1980–1987). As of the year 2000, there were chapters in all fifty states and in at least twenty other countries.

Most members know TNC through the magazine *Nature Conservancy* and their own state chapter, which they see as the in-state presence of a large, high-butterfat cow with a half-billion dollar cash flow and capital assets of more than a billion (omitting land). In fact, the individual chapters have a degree of autonomy that makes this view misleading, especially as related to the ability of the state chapter to draw on the financial resources of the national organization. One could almost think of the chapters as franchisees. On TNC's form 990, the federal form for reporting income by non-profits, many of the chapters are listed as wholly owned subsidiaries.

Most of what TNC does on the ground is done by the chapter staffs. Such activities include land deals, stewardship, recruiting a board, cooperative arrangements with other organizations, the chapter newsletter if there is one, and most fund raising. Decentralization accounts for much of TNC's effectiveness. The chapters get to know the places and the people and have enough independence to think of new initiatives and take them—as long as they fit within the current overall model coming from Arlington.

The home office sets the overall course. It (or regional offices) also performs such functions as producing the magazine, handling most of the planned-giving aspect of fund raising, helping set up partnerships with federal agencies, attending to membership and some administrative functions, running the benefit plans for the chapter employees, and providing some types of technical assistance too specialized for chapters to include on their payroll. These things cost money and chapters pay for them through an assessment on membership donations. For land purchases, the chapters can borrow from the Land Protection Fund at a fairly reasonable rate.

Cooperative Stewardship Arrangements

TNC has become involved in stewardship on both federal and state lands. In many states, land owned by agencies of federal and state governments holds much of the remaining biodiversity. When that diversity exists in the form of fens, old growth, butterflies, or songbirds, there may be little agency interest in making sure it's protected. Often the agency has few or no professional staff members with the knowledge or inclination to manage for anything other than commodities: deer, grouse, quail, saw timber, and pulp.

In such situations, help with identification and inventory of organisms, management plans, techniques, and related stewardship items are badly needed by the government agencies. Providing a modern conservation direction in a cooperative effort can be more effective than providing the same direction in confrontations where the backwardness and short-sightedness of the agency is laid bare. It's possible that a situation in which one private organization provides the pro-environmental confrontation and TNC provides the gentle helping hand is more effective than either one alone.

As a sample of cooperative efforts involving stewardship, the Allegan State Game Area in southwest Michigan is attempting, with TNC guidance, to manage some of its land for the endangered Karner blue butterfly. Previously, under the standard DNR regime of clearcutting blocks of woodland for forest-edge game species and plowing open areas to plant wildlife food plots, the oak barrens habitat on which the Karner blue depends was disappearing.

In the southeastern United States, TNC is involved with the U.S. Forest Service and Fish and Wildlife Service in fire ecology projects aimed at maintaining or restoring the longleaf pine ecosystem. At Eglin Air Force base in the panhandle of Florida, TNC is cooperating with the Department of Defense in managing one of the largest stands of longleaf still in existence.[63] Many species of plants and animals have been imperiled by the near-obliteration of the longleaf ecosystem. Possibly the premier endangered animal is the red-cockaded woodpecker, a ladder-backed social woodpecker that makes its living scaling off longleaf bark for the insects underneath. The controlled burns that return the longleaf areas to favorability for the woodpeckers will also benefit many of the other species of the longleaf ecosystem.

Under the same 1988 contract (updated in 1995) bringing a management partnership with Eglin, TNC agreed to help at more than 150 other military bases, including Fort Hood in the Texas Hill Country southwest of Waco. In its 340 square miles, oak-juniper woodland is the main object of attention.[64] Two endangered species of restricted range live here: the little black-capped vireo with its white spectacles and large, pale red eyes, and the golden-cheeked warbler, yellow faced like its relative the black-throated green warbler but with a black back. Both suffer from parasitism by brown-headed cowbirds coming from leased grazing land on the Fort. One of the prime management tactics so far has been cowbird trapping, though reduction of grazing to make the habitat less attractive to the cowbirds should also be brought into play.

Helping federal and state agencies manage their lands well can be one of the most powerful ways that TNC has of protecting biodiversity. TNC need not spend time and money to find, buy, and steward property for species or biotic communities already protected on government land. But there are potential drawbacks. The agency follow-through may be inadequate. Supposedly secure land held by government agencies may become vulnerable with changes in missions, agency managers, and political administrations. Also, the partnership process is likely to be expensive in scientific staff time. And most TNC members and donors are more excited by a new scenic, biodiverse preserve than by a new management partnership.

Because TNC's focus is on species and natural communities that are globally imperiled, there is a large potential for local trusts to partner with state agencies to help retain local and statewide diversity. Unfortunately, not every local land trust will have the biological expertise to design effective management strategies. Also, even well-qualified local land trusts—lacking TNC's clout—may be rebuffed by state agencies protective of their time and authority.

TNC's Own Land

It's an often-told fact that TNC owns and manages the largest private system of nature preserves in the world. Many of these are marvels: hummingbird-rich Ramsey Canyon in the Huachuca Mountains of southeastern Arizona; the bluffs, cliffs, and meanders of the Kentucky River Palisades; Florida's Appalachicola bluffs—hot, tick- and chigger-ridden but a spectacular center of biodiversity; the sweep of the prairie preserves such as Konza and Oklahoma.

A 2001 issue of *Nature Conservancy* gave the current number of TNC preserves: 1,397. It's an impressive number. But wait—in 1996, according to TNC president Sawhill, the Conservancy had more than 1,500 preserves.[65] In five years, the number of preserves shrank by more than one hundred. The reason TNC preserves are contracting instead of expanding lies in the way it handles both new and old land.

The newsletters of TNC chapters often highlight land acquisitions. "Natural Wonders Protected at Fisheating Creek," trumpets the spring 2000 Florida newsletter. But if you read past the headlines, the acquisitions often don't end up as new TNC preserves. In this case, what TNC did was arrange a deal whereby the state bought from a third party title to 18,000 acres and a conservation easement on another 40,000. In other cases, TNC does, in fact, buy land, but its ownership is a way-station; the destination is resale to government agencies or to private individuals in conservation buyer programs.

Chapter newsletters include lists of workdays on which volunteers put into practice management plans the stewardship staff has worked out. Generally the plans are based on more or less adequate findings from research or, at least, experience. The research is sometimes done by cooperating university scientists, occasionally by TNC (or Heritage) staff, sometimes by biology students paid stipends of one sort or another. Workdays are attractive to many TNC supporters. They enjoy getting out on the weekend for good works: helping build a boardwalk, cutting buckthorn in a Michigan fen, planting seedlings of the native grass sacaton in an Arizona ciéniga.

A 1981 "Ecology Forum" by the national Director of Stewardship mentioned that TNC had made great strides in identifying and selecting preserves by using data from the Natural Heritage inventories. The stewardship program, though, was struggling.[66] The reasons were several: finding and acquiring a piece of land takes weeks, months, or years, but stewardship is forever. Most of the new preserves were hundreds or thousands of acres; the 5-acre wetland and the 30-acre woodlot were relics of TNC past. Often, the new parcels came with strings, such as existing timber-harvest leases that had to be taken into account and monitored. For example, the sellers of the 23,605-acre Katharine Ordway Sycan Marsh Preserve in southern Oregon reserved a forty-year grazing lease when they sold to TNC in 1980; the needs of the sandhill cranes, upland sandpipers, and long-billed curlews had to be balanced against the needs of the cattle.[67]

Also, many of the new preserves were remote. Turning out a bunch of TNC members for stewardship duties in the Great Plains or the southwestern deserts isn't as easy as for a Saturday morning stint a few miles from Ann Arbor or Madison.

An argument against even owning land on which stewardship might occur is that TNC pays property taxes on many of its preserves, mostly in the West. Although this is rarely a legal requirement, the organization has deemed it prudent in places where environmental organizations are hated.

Although TNC has a good stewardship endowment policy for land gifts, expecting a donation equal to about 25 to 30 percent of the appraised value of the land, endowments for purchased lands are harder to come by. Funding for older preserves, acquired before the costs of stewardship were fully understood, are a particular problem. TNC understands the need now, of course. "The ultimate error," wrote the vice president of their Midwest office in 1989, "is raising enough money to buy a piece of land but not enough to take care of it."[68] But even Katharine Ordway wanted her money to be spent for acquisitions, not management.[69]

TNC's Stewardship Department was started in 1973; before that stewardship was catch as catch can based pretty much on local volunteers. During the next several years, TNC added stewardship staff to chapters and also hired stewards for important, high-maintenance preserves. In 1979, twenty-four preserves were professionally staffed; by 1981 the number was thirty-five. But sometime in the 1980s, the stewardship tide began to ebb. By 2002, the Michigan chapter, for example, with its 121 preserves, had a stewardship staff of two.

Even in 1981, TNC was taking stock of its "current holdings, reevaluating each preserve's ecological values and weighing the significance (rarity, viability) of the protected natural elements." The aim was "to design the wisest, least costly programs to ensure their safety."[70]

Left unsaid was the idea that the least costly program might be to get rid of preserves that no longer met TNC's changing agenda. The drop from more than 1,500 in 1996 to fewer than 1,400 in 2001 resulted from adding a few new preserves that fit today's criteria and getting rid of a good many older ones that don't.

Some are shuffled off to federal or state agencies. One example is Lanphere Dunes Preserve (California), transferred to the U.S. Fish and Wildlife

Service in 1999. The preserve, notable for an endangered mustard, the Humboldt Bay wallflower, had begun with a gift of about 130 acres from two local biologists. "When a project like the Lanphere Dunes matures," according to the California newsletter, "the Conservancy often transfers it to a public or private organization qualified to carry on long-term conservation management."[71]

"Matured" projects are sometimes transferred to local land trusts that have stewardship programs. To ensure its own long-term viability, a local land trust will expect a stewardship endowment from TNC just as it would if the land gift came from an individual. An acceptable alternative is for TNC to join with the local land trust in a small, successful fund drive targeting TNC's supporters in the counties around the preserve.

If an adequate endowment is provided, a local land trust will probably steward these preserves at least as well as TNC. Stewardship by government agencies may be more problematic.

Money and Business

As far back as Patrick Noonan, TNC presidents have proclaimed, "We are science driven." But the organization also prides itself on being run as a business.[72] No president since Hank Foster has been a scientist; around the nation, only four or so of the field office vice presidents have a science or natural history background. At times there must be conflicts between what science says and what business practice dictates. The tension may often be creative, but there are probably occasions when decisions driven by the bottom line are destructive. The ongoing divestment of preserves may be one.

Are there times when TNC takes a position or fails to take one, based on the wishes of its financial supporters? If TNC ever falls into this trap, it must be a rare event. One reason is its well-defined, science-driven mission. Another reason is simply that the land trust model is apolitical and nonconfrontational. Staff, board, and volunteers of a land trust may be appalled at what's going on in Washington, Albany, or Baton Rouge, but, as organizations, they rarely take positions except on the need for protecting more land.

The simple fact that TNC didn't accept advertisements in its magazine for a long time allowed it an independence that may be compromised in some organizations. The no-advertising era came to an end with the spring 2002 issue. Most of the environmental organizations reaping advertising revenue are advocacy organizations (though some advocacy groups don't do it). The day when advocates were amateurs has passed, at the national level. They must raise money to carry on their lobbying and litigation.

Land trusts have to raise money too, to buy land and take care of it. There are land trusts that depend on memberships and modest, wholly voluntary donations from members and friends to fund their operations, but these land trusts are nearly always small. Nearly always, too, they could probably save more land if they worked harder on fund raising.

We observe in politics that he who pays the piper calls the tune. It would be contrary to the conventions of human society if TNC's major donors aren't, at least, listened to with unusual respect. William Weeks, Director of TNC's Center for Compatible Economic Development, wrote as follows concerning corporate support:

[TNC] will accept those gifts without reservation, and will provide wholehearted recognition. The Conservancy neither condemns nor even much assesses the broader environmental record of its donors. . . . Instances in which a donor has tried, even by subtle means, to constrain the Conservancy from pursuing its mission are vanishingly rare—as well, it goes without saying, as unsuccessful.[73]

We can catch a glimpse, not necessarily of major donors' influence, but of the care, and flair, with which TNC handles them in David Morine's always informative memoir.

Whenever possible, the Conservancy likes to take potential donors to see preserves during a full moon. Nocturnal animals are visible; waterfowl are active and feeding; trees shine in a fantasy of silhouettes. . . . Plus, most people don't realize that a full moon rises in the east at precisely the same moment that the sun sets in the west. . . . We rented [a house] with a screened porch where the [potential donor] could feel the cool breeze and watch the harvest moon rise over the beach. We spared no expense to provide a sampling of the local cuisine.[74]

This is offered here, not as a terrible example, but as evidence that in the care and feeding of donors, TNC wrote the book. Faced with the need to raise money, most land trust directors or presidents hope that their staff or volunteers will show equal ingenuity and attention to detail.

International Programs

The Nature Conservancy had a Latin American Desk in 1967, but not until 1980 did it establish its International Program. Soon thereafter, it exported the idea of the Natural Heritage programs to the Caribbean and Latin America. In 1990, it began its Parks in Peril program to deal with the problem that many tropical parks are "paper parks" with no government support or protection. The same year, it opened an office in the small—very small—western Pacific country of Palau, its first venture outside the western hemisphere.

These tropical programs were a logical extension of TNC's mission. Most of the world's biodiversity is in the tropics. As a quick example, six times as many bird species breed in Panama as in Pennsylvania, and many of the Pennsylvania breeders spend their winters in Panama or elsewhere in the neotropics. If we are to save the Earth's biodiversity, the saving will be done in the tropics.

John Terborgh, a tropical ecologist, calculated that the last stand of tropical rain forest would be cut in about forty-five years.[75] There were between 7 and 8 million square kilometers left in 1990, and the rate at which they were being cut was in the neighborhood of 150,000 square kilometers per year. If we assume the rate stays the same, all the forest will be gone before 2050. This calculation is oversimplified, of course. Not every country is the same, economic conditions may lead to more or less timber being cut, social and technological changes may have good or bad effects.

Tropical parks exist in which the forest is supposed to be protected. Terborgh's calculation assumed these parks will remain, oases in a heavily disturbed matrix. Unfortunately, a high percentage of the parks have no facilities, no staff, not even boundary signs. Where there are guards, they are usually poorly paid; they may have to hunt and fish in the park to feed themselves and their families. Local residents and local officials may be unaware that the park exists, and, depending on changes in the central government since the park was established, the same may be true of the relevant federal agency.

One approach of TNC and other international conservation organizations has been to hire, train, and equip park guards. *Global Currents,* TNC's International Program newsletter, often has a photo of such guards—a squad of half a dozen men wearing khaki pants and shirts. Unfortunately, the guards rarely are granted the authority to arrest violators. Such powers tend to be held closely by the federal military or police forces. Unable to do anything about squatters, hunters, loggers, and miners, the guards, wrote Terborgh, "occupy themselves with controlling tourists and scientists."[76]

In 1997, three tropical biologists published an assessment of the threats to tropical rain forest parks based on information from scientists familiar with parks in seventeen countries from Brazil to Vietnam. The picture that emerged was fairly bleak. On the average, the integrity of 80 percent of the parks was threatened by agricultural encroachment.[77] In every country but India, hunting and/or fishing occurred in nearly 100 percent of the parks. Logging or firewood cutting was a threat to 67 percent of the parks.

Most infringements on parks come from local residents, some with a long history in the area, others recently arrived because of wars or tribal conflicts elsewhere or simply because the government has put a new road into a formerly remote region. The road attracts a flood of new immigrants to practice slash-and-burn agriculture. Often, large-scale logging and mining eventually follow.

TNC's Parks in Peril project is an example of an Integrated Conservation and Development Project (ICDP).[78] The conceptual basis for these is the biosphere reserve model proposed in the UNESCO Man and the Biosphere program of the 1970s and 1980s. This model envisaged a wholly protected central core area surrounded by a buffer area where land uses are supposed to enhance or at least be compatible with the conservation values of the core. Beyond the buffer zone would be the transition zone, where more intensive human activities could occur, but even here the aim was development that would be sustainable.[79]

In the buffer areas of the ICDPs might occur such activities as hunting and fishing using traditional methods, harvesting fruit or mushrooms, and sustainable seasonal grazing. In the transition zone, the local people might learn to serve as guides for tourists, plant better crop varieties, and engage in sustainable agriculture or (in coastal areas) sustainable fishing.[80]

The conceptual bases for ICDPs are (1) that preserves are tied to the surrounding area, and (2) that protecting them depends on giving the residents ways to make a living that do not involve destroying the parks. These are valid statements. In the opinion of many, however, the ICDP projects that have sprung from them have not yet shown themselves capable of saving the preserves and associated biodiversity.

The reasons for doubt are many.[81] Few parks have the spectacular scenery or charismatic animals to attract large numbers of tourists, so ecotourism will rarely be a complete solution. In fact, the areas most successful at attracting tourists may suffer degradation like the most heavily visited national parks of the United States. Proponents point out that, at the very least, ecotourism is better than the obliterative alternatives of logging and agriculture.[82]

Some initiatives ignore economic law or market realities; for example, as more people harvest Brazil nuts and latex, the lower the prices they will receive (unless there's a corresponding increase in demand).

Some agricultural techniques taught as part of the ICDP may encourage a doubtfully sustainable dependence on developed-world seeds and chemicals.

Although prospecting for medically useful plants may bring income, later steps for pharmaceutical companies are unlikely to involve continued harvesting from the wild as a source of drugs. There has been an unfortunate side effect of the Convention on Biological Diversity, the treaty adopted to protect Third World nations' property rights in the chemical compounds of their flora and fauna. Fearing "biopiracy," many governments have adopted rules making difficult or impossible the basic ecological and taxonomic research needed to document biodiversity.[83]

To the degree that the development guided by the ICDP plan is successful, it's likely to draw new settlers, adding to the population in the vicinity of the park and the degradation that almost inevitably follows.

The list goes on, but the point is clear. Even if ICDPs achieve some or all of the hoped-for development, there's no assurance they will achieve a useful conservation goal.

Many aspects of life and culture in most tropical countries seem to lead to the same destination: land degradation and loss of biodiversity. Among them are ethnic tensions, ever-increasing human populations, political corruption, drug trafficking, an atmosphere of lawlessness, a continuing immaturity of civic institutions, government instability, and the maldistribution of wealth and land that has produced a large and growing population living in poverty but yearning for material goods. These factors have complex interconnections, and, of course, they exist in a context of interactions with the developed world.[84] Some outside influences help the local human populations or biodiversity or both, but many are obviously harmful except to the short-term balance sheets of the corporations or agencies from which they emanate.

John Terborgh wrote, "It is in this vastly different social context, contrasting in nearly every respect with the comfortable conditions we enjoy in the United States, that tropical nature must be preserved, if it is to be preserved at all."[85] Pessimism is pointless, but TNC supporters should realize that despite hard work, enthusiasm, and money, the payoff—maintaining tropical diversity—is not assured.

Changing Fashions in Saving Land

When I heard the name "Last Great Places," it sounded like a good description of what TNC had been doing for a long time, but that wasn't the case. It was the title given to the 1991 reinvention, one of several, of TNC's basic conservation mission.

First Great Places. The 1950s and 1960s were a time of saving relatively small parcels of pristine or near-pristine, usually scenic land. Land needed to qualify under one of three criteria: natural community types not adequately preserved elsewhere, habitat for rare species, or accessibility to users without other adequate areas at their disposal.[86] Most of the land saving was done by volunteers—mostly ecologists and naturalists—at the state level.

The Age of Deals. By the late 1960s and through the 1970s, preacquisition deals for government were prominent, as a matter of formal policy. The 1972 masthead of *TNC News* said TNC "works in three ways to protect threatened natural areas: by purchase of land with funds raised through public subscription, by acceptance of donations of land, and by advance acquisition of land for local, state, and federal governments." The size of parcels protected was increasing both because of the government money and Katharine Ordway's money and ideas. This was the heyday of deal-making by Noonan and Morine, by Huey Johnson, the time of the Virginia Coastal Preserve and the Pascagoula Hardwood Company deals.

Identification, Protection, and Stewardship. By the mid-1970s, not long after the arrival of Bob Jenkins, the objective switched from saving land to saving diversity. Natural Heritage data began to be used to pick sites; the catch phrase set forth in 1977 was "Identification, Protection, and Steward-ship."[87] For the protection aspect, a goal of acquiring at least 250 natural areas per year was set; to achieve that, another goal was set (and met) of increasing the revolving Land Protection Fund to $20 million in five years. Nags Head Woods, according to Jenkins, "was the initial project where the Conservancy employed every step of the biodiversity conservation planning process, from the site's identification to its preserve design."[88] Nags Head is a 1,400-acre preserve of maritime forest and associated ecosystems on the inland side of a barrier island on the northern North Carolina coast.

The aim was to save "the last of the least and the best of the rest," a catchy though slightly obscure phrase coined by Jenkins. It means that TNC would take whatever sites it could of the nearly obliterated vegetation types but look for the best examples of vegetation types still fairly well represented. In addition to natural heritage elements data (mostly presence of rare plant and animal species), various other aspects were also considered in ranking sites for protection. These included ecosystem service contributions and such benefits as recreation, aesthetic enjoyment, and historical and archaeological significance.[89]

In other words, the criteria were much the same as TNC and various other organizations had always used; however, the species occurrence data were more formally developed, and the process provided a more complete context on the rarity of species and vegetation types than had hitherto existed—except in the heads of the best ecologists and naturalists of each region.

Last Great Places. In the late 1980s, an increasing scale of projects, often involving government partnerships, was one of the threads leading to the Last Great Places initiative, announced in 1991 by a new president, John C. Sawhill. Sawhill, a New York University Ph.D. in economics, had served as an energy consultant in private industry, as energy administrator in the federal government, and in the 1970s as president of New York University. Another thread was a developing attention, more in some states than others, paid to the ideas and feelings of local residents.[90]

It isn't stretching things to think of the Last Great Places program as Integrated Conservation and Development Projects imported back to the United States from the Third World. In fact, a synonym for Last Great Places was "the bioreserve [that is, biosphere reserve] era." The Last Great Places subtitle, however, emphasized not the scale, but the human connections: "An alliance for people and the environment."

TNC wants to save, among other places, the Florida Keys and the Texas Hill Country. These were two of the first twelve Last Great Places; others have been designated since. In other words, TNC is trying to save large landscapes composed of many ecosystems and including large proportions of working land in the form of ranches, farms, and even cities. The likelihood of protecting these landscapes by buying them is nil, even for an organization as rich as TNC. What it proposed instead is to acquire key parcels; to tie up others through easements or by coaxing other nonprofits, government agencies, or businesses to buy or otherwise protect them; and by conducting outreach to the citizens of the Last Great Places.

This outreach differs in detail but not in intent from the outreach programs in the tropics. "It is entirely compatible with our conservation objectives," wrote President Sawhill, "for watermen to harvest oysters off the Virginia Coast Reserve, providing that it's done sustainably."[91] It's also entirely compatible to develop and promote local products such as gourmet sweet-potato chips.[92]

The Director of the Virginia Coast Reserve, a Last Great Place, was quoted as saying, "There can be no long-term protection of ecosystems unless those protection efforts take human needs into account. . . . We need food, habitat, and a community that provides a good quality of life for our families. Conservation measures that do not enhance the quality of life are destined in the long run to fail."[93] The statement has a Trust for Public Land ring to it. It would have been an out-of-character pronouncement for TNC before the late 1980s.

TNC staff were moved into the small towns of the Last Great Places. I'm not sure exactly what their range of duties has included. In some places, I know, they drive the country roads with their cell phones, hunting for land and deals. Judging from the trickles of information in *Nature Conservancy,* some spend a lot of their time showing up with their children at the local Dairy Mart, wearing oak leaf logos and hoping to defuse resentment against environmental organizations.

A few other fragments in the magazine, though, make me hope that by talking about and perhaps exemplifying sustainability and living in harmony with the land, they may be accomplishing more. I visualize TNC in the unlikely role of spreading the gospel of the sixties: simplicity, self-sufficiency, energy conservation, use it up and wear it out, live lightly on the land. This may be pure fantasy on my part. But it could work, in the twenty-first century and connected, as it would be, with particular, special places.

Conservation by Design. John Sawhill died unexpectedly of complications from diabetes in May 2000, as Conservation by Design was coming into being. The new president, Steven McCormick, had chaired the team that designed Conservation by Design. An attorney, he had been director of the California chapter and is the first president to have served in the TNC ranks rather than being brought in from outside.

The newest version of TNC's conservation mission is approximately a magnified Last Great Places with a couple of new wrinkles. Perhaps feeling that no matter how fast biodiversity is being saved, it's not fast enough, TNC plans to add another five hundred or so landscape-scale projects by

2010. This many new large projects will take a lot of fund raising, in a tight economy. Reorganization of chapter staffs and boards has been occurring and the assessment levels on chapters have been revised.

"Of course," as President McCormick has written, "we can't buy *all* of these precious places. . . ."[94] As a consequence, the whole bag of land and environmental protection tools will be brought into play. Within the designated landscape site, a few properties will be purchased, of which some will be kept and stewarded, most passed on. There will be continuing emphasis on management agreements and conservation easements. There will be more use of the conservation buyer approach.

As a TNC tool, conservation buyer deals began in the West but are spreading widely. The general idea is that the chapter buys a large piece of property having conservation values and then resells it, protected by a conservation easement. There are many possible permutations. In the West, part of a several thousand-acre property might be sold to the state or federal government and the rest to an individual to be used as a working ranch. In the Midwest, a 160-acre parcel next to a TNC preserve might be purchased, split into its forties, of which one might be added to the preserve. A single building envelope might be identified on each of the other three before they were resold, easement-protected, to a conservation-minded family.[95]

Increasingly, TNC is involving itself in deals that retain working landscapes as such. For example, in 2001, it bought a 9,200-acre farm in the Sacramento–San Joaquin River delta (California).[96] The farm, which already contributes to the support of wintering waterfowl and sandhill cranes, will be continued in production, and an attempt will be made to use farming practices that maximize wildlife benefit rather than profit. "We intend to show you can have both wildlife and a viable agricultural operation," a TNC spokesman said. "There simply isn't enough money to buy all the land you would need to accommodate migratory waterfowl, for example."

Of course, if TNC can identify areas that ought to be protected and persuade someone else to do the protecting, that's another way around the problem of insufficient money. Consequently, partnerships have assumed a greater importance than in earlier times. As a part of this general trend, TNC has paid greater attention to local land trusts serving any new focus areas. These can be productive partnerships when TNC's agenda—at any one time generally fully formed and basically immutable—corresponds with that of the local land trust. This won't automatically be the case.

One reason it won't is TNC's continuing emphasis on globally imperiled species and communities. Lip service is occasionally given to "conservation of all communities and ecosystems (not just the rare ones)," but the planning process almost inevitably leads to slighting ecosystems holding mostly species that seem secure at the global level.[97]

Suppose that one region has somehow retained a few sites of relatively undisturbed oak woods that lack any threatened or endangered species. It makes little conservation sense for a land conservation organization to adopt TNC's agenda if that means ignoring these intact ecosystems, with their contributions of scenery, ecosystem services, aesthetic experiences, and potential for teaching and research, in order to preserve small patches of another community type whose main distinction is the presence of an endangered butterfly. This is closer to philately than ecology.

One of the new wrinkles of Conservation by Design is that the framework for projects is the ecoregion. Ecoregions are regional landscape units that have been identified and mapped in several similar forestry-driven projects over the past twenty years. They are not based primarily on vegetation or plant-animal communities, but rather are supposed to be regions of some uniformity of landform and climate. The particular map adopted by TNC for the Conservation by Design efforts recognizes sixty-three ecoregions in the United States.[98] Some are named for the predominant vegetation—Central Tallgrass Prairie, Piney Woods—but most have geographic or landform names—North Central Tillplain, Edwards Plateau.

Ecoregions will be the framework for asking preservation questions. What and where in each ecoregion is the biodiversity that needs protecting? TNC says that the new approach "recognizes the value of comprehensive biodiversity planning on ecoregional rather than geopolitical lines."[99] Most states include portions of two or more ecoregions, and most ecoregions run across two or more states, hence, the chapter system that served TNC well for several decades is not ideally suited to the ecoregion approach. As a first step, more cooperative work among chapters has been called for.

A recurrent melody at TNC, at least since Richard Pough left, is that TNC can't raise enough money to buy all the land it needs to protect (and even if it could, can't raise enough money to take care of it). Almost anyone could agree that more land needs protecting than any private organization can afford to buy. Most of us would also agree that it would be better if society managed large segments of the land, not just preserves, in ways that preserved more of the native biota and kept the natural processes flowing. Preserves, even the biggest ones, will inevitably be affected by destructive human influences coming from elsewhere in the landscape: run-off, air pollution, alterations of hydrology, poaching, overpopulations of deer, the spread of alien organisms, rogue lumbering operations, dogs and cats running loose, disturbance or obliteration of adjacent habitat.

The question is whether TNC can contribute more to saving the Earth by the pluralistic approach of Last Great Places/Conservation by Design or by continuing to do what it is very good at: buying and accepting donations of land and turning it into preserves. In the long run, will doing all these other things—lining up conservation buyers, stewarding government lands, running farms and forests, helping the locals develop gourmet sweet-potato chips, promoting no-till agriculture—work well enough to preserve biodiversity? Or would the time and money be better used in buying land?

What Would Shelford Think about TNC in 2003?

No one can tell us what Shelford would think except Shelford, and he's unavailable. The Preservation Committee, the Ecologists Union, and The Nature Conservancy when Shelford left were advocacy organizations; the shift to a land trust had just begun. The answer to what Shelford would think may not have the same answer as the question of how successful TNC has been as a land trust.

Judging from Shelford's interests and efforts, we might suppose that he would welcome the renewed science emphasis of the 1970s to 1990s, the Natural Heritage Programs, preserve design based on conservation biology tenets. He would have been happy with TNC's prairie initiative. In 1938 to 1939, he and others formed the Grassland Research Foundation which turned out to be ineffectual, but he'd been advocating locating and protecting big blocks of prairie long before that.[100]

He'd probably find the cooperative efforts with government positive, in part. He'd probably not be dissatisfied with an international thrust. The *Naturalist's Guide to the Americas* included the best information available on Central America, South America down to the Amazon, several Caribbean islands, the Galápagos, and even the Philippines.

I'd guess that Shelford and also George Fell—both frugal men—would have disliked the dependence on vast sums of money raised from rich donors, business, foundations, and the government. The dominance of business-minded leaders rather than scientists that has sometimes accompanied this dependence would have troubled him.

Probably there would be other things that Shelford, cantankerous though kindly, would question.

I'd like to know what Shelford would think, but I don't. All I know is what I think: Whatever flaws TNC may have, we've been better off with it than without it. The "we" includes my family, the conservation community, the nation, and the Earth.

11 THE TRUST FOR PUBLIC LAND

Huey Johnson

The Trust for Public Land was founded in 1972, in San Francisco. It was a time when the mass movements for peace, civil rights, social justice, and the environment had already peaked, but didn't know it yet.

The Trust for Public Land was founded by Huey D. Johnson. He'd been western regional director of The Nature Conservancy (TNC) since January 1964 and briefly served as interim president in 1966.[1] However, Johnson's interests in the environment were broader than land conservation. He had, for example, spearheaded a 1969 UNESCO conference in San Francisco with the theme "Man and his Environment: A View toward Survival."

The participants—about sixty—included such heavy hitters as Arthur Godfrey and Margaret Mead along with professional environmentalists and ecologists such as Paul Sears, Barry Commoner, Paul Ehrlich, and Raymond Dasmann. There was a panel on the Activism of Youth, with fine, youthful activist sentiments:

We continue to commute, pollute, and salute in righteous arrogance the despoiled flag of our environment. This cannot and will not be tolerated any longer.[2]

In the library at Western Michigan University (WMU), there are still a dozen copies of the 1970 paperback edited by Huey Johnson that came out of the conference.[3] Called *No Deposit—No Return*, it had been ordered *en masse* for the reserve list of some large environmental studies class of the era. Fifteen years before, as it happens, Johnson had been finishing a biology degree at WMU. Afterwards, he held a variety of jobs, drifted around the world for a bit, took a few courses here and there in the western United States and did a master's in wildlife management at Utah State before landing with TNC.

Johnson's vision for the Trust for Public Land (TPL) combined his work with TNC and the spirit of the times. The preacquisition deals he was doing for TNC—buying land government agencies wanted and reselling it to them—made both business and environmental sense to him. Also, it seemed that, despite the great value of what TNC was doing, it was neglecting the cities and many of people who lived there. I surmise that "Power to the People" was a slogan that appealed to Johnson.

He assembled a group of like-minded individuals: lawyers and M.B.A.s, but also a San Francisco–style variety of others. The original, short-lived name for the enterprise was Project Lorax, which made perfect sense to small children and their parents but was thought too esoteric for the general population.

The centerpiece of the organization was to be exactly what the property rights people hate most about The Nature Conservancy. The twenty-five-year history of the TPL published in its magazine, *Land and People,* said the organization was designed to be "entrepreneurial, business-oriented, able to move quickly to protect land in the hurly-burly of the marketplace." Furthermore, "by offering landowners the tax advantages of selling to a non-profit, the organization could purchase land at a charitable discount—receiving in essence, a donation of land value from the owner. When TPL then transferred ownership of the land to a public agency, part of that donation of land value would pay TPL's transaction cost and forward its broader mission of acquiring land for public ownership."[4]

Oh, my! There could hardly be a clearer admission of exactly what the property rights activists have accused land trusts of doing: Buy low, sell high.

The original mission statement of TPL set forth four goals: (1) to acquire and preserve open space to serve human needs (2) to operate a self-sustaining conservation organization (3) to create a new profession of public-interest land specialists, and (4) to pioneer new techniques of land preservation and funding. The first three—the people, the self-sufficiency, and the training—are the features that distinguish TPL.

Johnson's experience with TNC enabled TPL to hit the ground running. With grants and other donations, it was able to start work with a $600,000 bankroll, a $10 million line of credit, and a staff of twelve. In its first two years, by 1974, TPL completed fourteen projects in four states and the staff had grown to nineteen.[5]

Its first land deal was acquiring 672 acres for a Los Angeles city park. Not long afterward, it was able to acquire the 1,300-acre Wilkins Ranch in western Marin County to help begin the National Park Service's Golden Gate National Recreation Area. (National Recreation Areas are, roughly, national parks close to population centers.)

Founder Johnson left in 1977 to become Governor Jerry Brown's Secretary for Resources in the California state government. In 1983, Johnson formed the nonprofit Resource Renewal Institute, which he continues to head. In 2001, he received the United Nations' premier environmental award, the Sasakawa Environment Prize.

Joel Kuperberg, who had been TPL's Southeast Regional Director, followed Johnson as TPL president, but was quickly succeeded by Martin J. Rosen, who kept the job eighteen years. Rosen, a San Francisco–area lawyer, had been on the TPL board since the beginning. TPL's fourth president, appointed January 1998, is William B. Rogers. A Harvard M.B.A., he was western regional director when selected as president.

A Self-sustaining Conservation Organization

The original idea of TPL was that the Huey Johnson approach to land deals would generate funds—the margin between the selling price and the cost—that would support the structure and operations of the organization.[6] TPL would find out what lands various government agencies needed for a project and buy or option them. Often, these were situations in which one of the agencies lacked funds to complete the deal soon enough to satisfy the owner.

TPL could step in and fashion a deal in which, for example, the owner sold the land at below-market value and claimed a charitable income tax deduction for the difference. When the agency's funding arrived, TPL would resell the land to the agency. The resale price might be fair-market value but was often lower. According to a 1982 article in the financial magazine *Barron's,* the organization as of that time had bought lands appraised at $79.1 million for $51.5 million and sold them to government agencies for $58.9 million.[7]

What an idea—a nonprofit that devoted all its attention to saving land, not one that spent half its time beating the bushes for money. No development staff lunching with wealthy donors. No need for circumspection to avoid offending corporations or the governing boards of foundations. No mass mailings of alarm-filled letters asking for donations.

It would be incorrect to say that the approach failed, but problems began to show up in 1981 when the Reagan administration tried to stop any new land acquisitions by the federal government. Besides trying to cut to zero the appropriation for the Land and Water Conservation Fund, it also refused to spend money already appropriated for buying land. Not only that, the Reagan Interior Department wanted to sell 35 million acres of national forest and other federal lands.[8]

TPL was able to continue to do deals with government agencies. Democrats and a few moderate Republicans in the Congress saved the Land and Water Conservation Fund from being zeroed out. The *Barron's* article on TPL mentioned with glee that in the first year and half, the Interior Department, despite its determination to quit buying land, had become the owner of a turn-of-the-century brothel added to the Cuyahoga Valley National Recreation Area, along with several thousand acres of natural lands in Georgia, West Virginia, California, and elsewhere.

Nevertheless, the great reduction of access to federal land money put a severe crimp in TPL's ability to function. At a board meeting in Santa Fe in 1981, the question of closing up shop, a year short of its tenth birthday, was raised. Martin Rosen, by then president, said no; they had an essential mission and would do it in bad times as well as good.[9]

TPL moved to a more diverse, perhaps more traditional, approach to raising money. Money is still made on transactions, sometimes in deals constructed with great ingenuity. For example, TPL has bought land wanted by public agencies, traded it for surplus public land, and sold the surplus land to finance the transaction. This avoids the expenditure of public money but hasn't escaped the wrath of elements that don't want any new land added to federal holdings.

TPL also does more deals involving partnerships with state and local government and provides a variety of services to local groups hoping to save land.[10] Such operations are structured to contribute to TPL's support. The board spends more of its time fund raising, and grants are aggressively sought. Today I received a letter from Will Rogers asking me to renew my annual support. This sounds quite a bit like a membership but is a more honest terminology. My contribution doesn't let me vote on anything at TPL. Many land trusts call me and the other people who give them money "members," even though our voice in the organization is limited to deciding whether to put the decal on the front or back window of our cars.

Urban Land Program

Part of TPL's conservation mission is making land available for people's use in the inner city, an effort that has sometimes been called the Urban Land Program. Improving life for the urban masses accords with Charles Eliot's original vision, but few land trusts have assigned high priority to urban initiatives.

TPL's urban efforts began in Oakland and later moved to many other cities. In Oakland, many of the vacant lots were owned by local savings-and-loan associations as the result of foreclosures. TPL persuaded some of the S&Ls to donate lots and bought others at tax sales. The lots ended up in the ownership of various local groups, which undertook to turn them into mini-parks and community gardens.[11]

TPL continues to work in the inner cities on parks, planning, and trails. One of its victories was to help save over a hundred community gardens on city-owned vacant lots in New York City. Over a period of twenty years, a cycle has developed in which neighborhood groups form to clean up the trash, grub out the brush, chase out the drug-dealers, and turn vacant lots into "sources of food, flowers, and neighborhood pride," in TPL's words. Only a few of the 800 or so gardens are secure, owned by small local land trusts as a result of earlier efforts by TPL.[12]

That's the first part of the cycle. The downslope is the city deciding to sell off the now-attractive real estate to developers to make some money, reward political contributors (as some critics claim), and, of course, get the land back on the tax rolls.

Rudolph Giuliani, then–New York City Mayor, was assiduous in his attempts to sell community gardens. In April 1998, he ordered cancellation of the short-term leases on about 750 of them. "This is a free-market economy," Giuliani was quoted as saying. "Welcome to the era after Communism."[13]

After a protracted period of law suits and protests from several quarters, 113 of the gardens were to come up for auction on 14 May 1999. On 13 May the gardens were saved by TPL buying sixty-three of them for $3 million. A private conservation group headed by actress Bette Midler, the New York Restoration Project, bought the other fifty for $1.2 million.[14]

The situation attracted media attention, generally sympathetic to the gardens and their contribution to the communities. Most of the later media accounts concentrated, of course, on Bette Midler's role. *The New York Times* opted for kitsch, devoting a third of their Op-Ed page to a six-panel cartoon showing Midler and Giuliani singing a duet of "Let's Call the Whole Thing Off."[15]

And so the gardens, with their contribution to the health, well-being, and community spirit of their neighborhoods, were saved. The outcome is satisfactory but not satisfying. As a TPL vice president admitted, the precedent is bad.[16] The New York City government was rewarded for ignoring the needs and efforts of people in some of its poorest neighborhoods. And it still has about 650 community gardens that it can cash in on.

Public Lands Program

TPL had also been doing non-urban land deals right along and in the late 1970s increased the percentage. "The hard reality was that government funds . . . far more often went to rural and suburban areas," according to TPL's twenty-five-year history. Its Public Lands Program was devoted to acquiring land for federal parks, forests, recreation areas, wildlife refuges, and similar state and local projects.

For example, TPL has worked on sixteen land projects for the Cuyahoga Valley National Recreation Area. This 33,000-acre park lies along the Cuyahoga River (generally pronounced by the natives as something like "Cuhhoga") between Akron and Cleveland. A large amount of relatively natural land remains in this scenic corridor, even though it's bisected by the Ohio Turnpike and dissected by several other expressways.

I visited Cuyahoga National Recreation Area in 1999 on a summer day when it seemed the insects were winning the war with the mammals. It was a seventeen-year-locust year, and the sound of thousands of stridulating cicadas was as loud as the noise from the turnpike. The birds didn't seem to mind the clamor, and on the rich forested slopes above a small creek, hooded warblers, rose-breasted grosbeaks, and Acadian flycatchers were busy feeding young.

Cuyahoga National Recreation Area has historic as well as natural features. A trail follows the route of the Ohio and Erie Canal, which opened in 1827 and was defunct forty years later, after the railroads came through. And, of course, the Cuyahoga River itself became an icon for water pollution in the late 1960s when a section a few miles downstream in Cleveland was so polluted with petroleum wastes that it caught fire.

The times have changed, but park brochures still warn us not to use the Cuyahoga for drinking, swimming, fishing, or canoeing.

A TPL project at Cuyahoga ought to be an inspiration to local governments everywhere. A large basketball coliseum was bought by TPL in the spring of 1999, turned over to the U.S. Park Service, and demolished. Restoration of native vegetation has begun on the land once under the concrete and asphalt of Richfield Coliseum and its parking lots.[17]

The deal became possible when the Cleveland National Basketball Association team, the Cavaliers, moved to a new sports complex in 1994. The family that owned the 327-acre site, which lies near the middle of the Recreation Area, sold it to TPL, preferring to see it become parkland instead of the mega-mall that was its probable destiny otherwise.

Would that there were a similar demolition and restoration project in every county in the United States.

Land Trust Program

TPL has had a strong connection with local land trusts since the late 1970s. Jennie Gerard, whose background was city and regional planning, was liaison with both existing and coalescing land trusts. She had come to TPL just after the switchover from Johnson to Kuperberg, both of whom were proponents of local land conservation organizations.

People would call TPL wanting information about protecting some piece of local land. If a group of concerned citizens existed or could be put together, TPL staff would visit them for a couple of days, eating potluck and sleeping in spare bedrooms. Gerard and the others thought of themselves as circuit riders, spreading the gospel on getting organized, nonprofit law, fund raising, and land deals.[18]

From the circuit riders and other help by TPL came several California land trusts including Sonoma, Napa County, Big Sur, and the Marin Agricultural Land Trust. TPL's supportive presence in California probably accounts more than any other single factor for the large number of land trusts in the state: 132 as of 2000, more than any other state except Massachusetts.

TPL's encouragement of local land trusts was felt more widely than just in California. The twenty-five-year history states that the organization helped found or provided training to one-third of the nation's land trusts. Among other initiatives were a National Land Counselor Program that taught land acquisition techniques to executive directors of local land trusts. A *Land Trust Handbook: Guide for Board Members* dated 1991 brought together relevant material generated over the preceding decade.[19]

In early February 1978, TPL's Land Trust Program held the first conference devoted to land trust issues outside New England. The meeting brought Robert Lemire, among others, to San Francisco. Lemire, a Harvard M.B.A., had become interested in land conservation while on the Lincoln, Massachusetts, Conservation Commission. He wrote an influential little book, *Creative Land Development: Bridge to the Future,* published in 1979.[20] Kingsbury Browne, the Boston tax attorney who instigated the 1981 National Consultation on Local Land Conservation, was supposed to speak but didn't make it because of the blizzard of '78 that closed much of New England for a week.

The 1970s were a time of great forward progress in environmental protection in California. Some of the progress involving land regulation and acquisition was provoking citizen resistance. One of the sore points was Trinidad, a city (population 300) in Humboldt County on the northern Pacific Coast a few miles north of Arcata.[21] The California Coastal Commission, enforcing the Coastal Act of 1976, was asking for planning that the townspeople did not feel up to dealing with. Also, the State Department of Parks and Recreation was planning to condemn about a third of the city land. Quite a bit of nearby land was already set aside in parks, and the townspeople feared that the private land base would be reduced below the threshold for a successful community.

A citizen's committee resisted the condemnation suits. They orchestrated petitions, newspaper articles, and call-ins to radio talk shows. Jennie Gerard heard one of these, in which a Trinidadian railed about the community being made subservient to the whims of a distant impersonal bureaucracy. She thought that it sounded like a case for a land trust and invited the caller to the February 1978 conference.[22]

The conference, along with other conversations with TPL, provided the impetus to start the Humboldt North Coast Land Trust. The state senator representing the Trinidad district sponsored a bill withdrawing the appropriation for the purchase, recognizing the new land trust as an "appropriate entity" to deal with the Coastal Commission, and granting $100,000 as seed money.

By 1983, the land trust—which chose the fun-with-fonts initials of HncLT—had accomplished much of what it and the state had desired. HncLT became the first land trust to have a certified coastal plan. It had acquired land and easements worth $2 million by leveraging the $100,000 seed money. For example, it bought an 18-acre parcel, sold with an easement an acre that was already developed, and permanently protected the other 17 acres. HncLT was also working on a trail system and other projects with the city and county.

"All of this is being accomplished," one of the HncLT founders wrote, "in an improved atmosphere of cooperation, as opposed to confrontation— all in a way that strengthens the social fabric of the community rather than threatening its ultimate decline."23

Eventually, most of TPL's land trust-training efforts were discontinued. In part, this came from a shift beginning in 1988 to a structure organized regionally rather than programmatically.24 Also, the Land Trust Alliance increasingly filled the need as it broadened its services and, after 1993, moved to an annual meeting schedule.25 TPL has maintained a special relationship with California land trusts, including a newsletter, *On Saving Land,* which has been published since 1991.

TPL worked at creating a new profession of public land specialists, just as its mission called for, during a long period when no other organization was involved. The importance of its role in land trust growth doesn't seem widely realized, even within the land trust community. The reason may be the low profile that TPL maintained for a good share of its history, combined with a general indifference to retrospection in the land trust movement.

TPL deserves full credit for its land trust work. Nevertheless, one may wonder if private land protection today might be different, and perhaps better, if such important training had come from a organization in which biological conservation played a more important role and where some lands were kept and stewarded, rather than passed through. To give TPL its due, its *Land Trust Handbook* contains a good section on stewardship, consisting of articles from *Exchange* and the book *Land-Saving Action.*

TPL Today

As far as land is concerned, TPL has always been a conduit. It obtains lands and passes them on to another organization or a government agency. TPL is not in the stewardship business. It's also true that basically all the land it saves has been brought to its attention by local groups or government agencies, rather than being targeted by studies or surveys of its own. Part of the reason for this set of traits is that few biologists, ecologists, or naturalists have served on the TPL board or staff—a curious situation for an organization founded by a biologist.

Except for a brief spurt at the end of the Clinton administration, federal land protection efforts have been slow since the early 1980s. In the mid-1990s, one of TPL's attempts to mitigate this blockage was to assist states and local units of government in providing open space funding. For example, it would help draft ballot proposals for bonds or millages to buy parkland. TPL discovered that despite the impediment in Washington, D.C., the citizens of many cities, counties, and states were willing to tax themselves to pay for open lands.

By 2000, TPL had formalized this approach in its Conservation Finance program and had also created a separate lobbying and campaign affiliate, the Conservation Campaign.[26] Among the services the two organizations combine to offer are everything from identifying the need to arranging the post-election victory party. In these efforts, as in most, TPL has partners that include local land trusts but also many other sorts of citizens' groups.

Local and state open-space initiatives, not all part of TPL's programs, have been highly successful. From 1998 to 2001, 529 referenda on taxes, bond issues, or related measures to preserve open space have passed, yielding $19 billion for land protection.[27]

A related TPL program, Greenprinting, is "TPL's comprehensive approach to helping communities identify land for conservation and strategies for protecting it." According to President Rogers, "We start by asking: 'What are your community's natural, cultural, and historic features that tell you who you are, where you are? What do you want to see here 50 years from now?' . . . The challenge then is to turn that vision into a protected system of parks, trails, watersheds, and working landscapes like farms and forests."[28]

It's the sort of planning process, harking back to Charles Eliot and Ian McHarg, that few regions do and every region ought to.

TPL willingly involves itself in small projects: urban gardens, a meadow forming the last 9 acres of open space in a New England town, a historic 32-acre cornfield that will be a park next to Chinatown in Los Angeles. But it saves big parcels too. One example is the 13,500-acre Pond of Safety Forest linking the northern and southern units of the White Mountain National Forest (New Hampshire).[29] Another, a collaboration with the Save-the-Redwoods League, with funding from the Packard Foundation, is the Coast Dairies property, up the California coast from Santa Cruz: 7,000 acres with seven miles of ocean shoreline.[30] TPL's cash flow is an order of magnitude below TNC's, but the approximately $70 million annual income allows it to save a lot of land. [31] The figures change constantly, of course, but in the twenty-five years from 1973 to 2000, it had done over 1,900 deals protecting about 1.2 million acres.

TPL has been an innovator in all the sorts of land protection with a strong human element. It was pushing farmland protection before the American Farmland Trust and greenways before the Rails-to-Trails Conservancy. Its 1999 book *The Economic Benefits of Parks and Open Space* is a useful contribution to the subject of why saving land often makes better economic sense than developing it.[32] At TPL's tenth anniversary (1982), Vice President Phil Wallin said that TPL was building the American commons—

A nationwide network of parks and forests and refuges and green spaces that belongs to the people. . . . where people can meet on equal terms, to work, to play, to talk, or just to be, and to share the precious experience of leaving something alone. . . . This is something America needs, and we are proud to dedicate ourselves to it.[33]

This human orientation has long been a core difference between TPL and TNC, but in current practice, the difference can be overemphasized. In San Diego County, where sprawl is overwhelming everything—90 percent or more of virtually every natural ecosystem is gone—TPL has been helping to save land for a new San Diego National Wildlife Refuge. When 950 acres of chaparral and sage scrub centrally located in the proposed refuge came on the market, no government agency was able to move fast enough to keep the land from another developer, but TPL did.[34]

It would have been no surprise if the initials had been TNC instead of TPL. And, on the other side of the coin, much of TNC's Last Great Places initiatives beginning in the late 1980s sounds suspiciously people oriented.

The Trust for Public Land gives Aldo Leopold a great deal of credit for its ideas. Huey Johnson would hand out copies of Leopold's *Sand County Almanac* to anybody who didn't already know it. He, himself, didn't become acquainted with the book until the summer of 1962, when he was a seasonal employee of the California State Fish and Wildlife Department. "When I read it, and especially his essay, 'The Land Ethic,' my life was changed. The land ethic became my theme of life," Huey said.[35]

In an interview in TPL's twenty-five-year history issue, Marty Rosen, near the end of his long term as president, stated that TPL was still animated by Leopold's land ethic. Asked by the interviewer to summarize it, Rosen said that, "human beings are part of nature and should be respectful of nature and not simply manipulate it for economic gain."

This is a pretty fair impromptu rendition of the tune, but it fails to include some of the harmonics. Leopold was making the point that people are not the captain of the biospheric galley-ship; we are there at the oars with all the rest of the creatures. Neither is the vessel's journey being made on our behalf. The galley sailed before we evolved to join the crew, and it will continue its voyage after we're gone.

Protected land unquestionably helps people in ways we've talked about before: psychologically, providing ecosystem services, and all the rest. It's true that connecting city dwellers with nature—weeds and bugs, birds migrating overhead, a reconstructed patch of prairie—may be the best way to bring them to love nature and, as citizens, to support its preservation.

It's true, too, that the message of saving land for the benefit of ourselves and future generations is an effective one in a land trust's campaigns for land and money. It's true, it's good tactics; but it's bad environmental philosophy.

The idea that land and its biota exist for us, that the reason land should be saved is for people, is narrow, humanistic, and anthropocentric. It's certainly un-Leopoldian. Leopold's reason is rather the opposite. We save land, we save endangered species, because we're all members of a community, but we're the only member of the community that has evolved the ability to recognize our mutual membership. "In this fact," wrote Leopold—not in our technological accomplishments, "lies objective evidence of our superiority over the beasts."[36]

Any land conservation organization saves land for people, but from the land ethic perspective, people aren't the reason to save land. Land is saved for the land, for the biodiversity, for the community. People benefit through the cascade of good things that saving land brings.

FARMLAND PROTECTION

Land trusts generally tend to be cool, in the jazz sense. They approach their work—their newsletters, their dealings with land owners, their discussions with the unconvinced—in a relaxed, even mellow way.

The supporters of farmland protection, on the other hand, are often as intense as a chorus of "Potato Head Blues" by Louis Armstrong and his Hot Seven. Part of the difference in attitude between preserving natural land and preserving farmland comes from the newness of farmland conservation. The natural lands conservators have been at it since the 1890s, when natural lands were already being rapidly lost—often by conversion to farmland. The decline in farmland began much later.

Another reason the urgency shows so clearly is that farmland advocates see themselves as defending not just land but a way of life. I say "farmland advocates." Both in manner and activities, most of the farmland protection groups are as much Sierra Club as Nature Conservancy. They're activists, defending a way of life that is vanishing or—perhaps they fear—already gone.

Almost no one would argue against the preservation of the family farms as advocated by Jefferson, Aldo Leopold, or Louis Bromfield. When novelist Bromfield came home from Europe just ahead of World War II and returned to the Ohio land of his ancestors, he re-created at Malabar Farm the approach to farming that most of us would like to keep in the American landscape. But Malabar Farm exists now only as a museum, and the kind of farming he promoted is as rare as a quilting bee.

There was a time when having a farm brought independence. The farmer had his cash crops that brought in enough money to buy seed for next year, clothes when the old ones wore out, a new car once in a great while, and some paint for the house (or the barn anyway) every couple of decades. Even when there was a drought or a depression and the cash crops didn't net any cash, he still had his garden, his woodlot, a place to live—the essentials of life. People that had pulled out and gone to the city might have been standing in breadlines during the Great Depression, but the farmer had his cow, some fruit trees, and a few chickens.

In the years following World War II, farm families increasingly wanted a standard middle-class life. Probably the single most important agent promoting the new materialism was television. The consumer goods people in the Soviet-led Eastern bloc saw on television killed Marxism in the late 1980s, but thirty years before that, starting in the 1950s, TV and the kind of life it promoted helped bring down traditional American farm culture.

To make money to pay for the TV set, clothes like the other kids wore, and all the other suburban middle-class trappings, farmers adopted the pesticides that the chemical companies began to push at them after 1945. Up to this time, most agriculture, except fruit-growing, was "organic"; it had never been any different. Probably the strongest current in agriculture in the late 1930s and early 1940s was an environmentally sound approach exemplified in the United States by Bromfield's Malabar Farm.

In an almost unbelievably short time, that current died. Nothing was left but the chemical tidal wave. The pesticides, herbicides, and synthetic fertilizers took over—produced by the chemical companies as substitutes for their wartime products, advertised heavily, and promoted by the ag colleges, then as now heavily dependent on the chemical companies for funding.

A long and deadly cascade had begun. The chemically dependent farmer could obtain higher yields. Farmers continuing to farm in the old way could still grow the crops, but they couldn't make a living, at least not a middle-class living, in competition with the chemically dependent farmers. They fell into line.

With less dependence on manpower, farmers could farm more land, and they needed to. They borrowed money to buy land. To farm that much land, they had to have a big tractor, so they borrowed more money. No need anymore for a tree in the middle of the field where a team of horses could rest in the shade while the farmer ate his lunch. The grasses, herbs, and shrubs in the fencerows—the fencerows themselves—were expendable; they took up room that could be in corn and were an obstacle to the big tractor and the big new corn picker.

There were costs to these things—interest to be paid to the bank, of course, but many others. Pest insects became more of a problem as their predators were poisoned and the habitats of the predators were demolished. Birds began to die from eating the animals that ate the plants coated with pesticides. Soils became less and less living systems and more and more just dirt that held the plants up while they absorbed the chemicals the farmer had to add every year.

The extension service told the farmer that it was inefficient to raise his own pigs or vegetables or to have a little orchard. He could use that land to plant more row crops. When you take your time into account, the experts told him, it's cheaper to buy chicken already cut up at the grocery store. Leave raising chickens to the specialists. There was no room anymore for a general-purpose farm. Ezra Taft Benson, Dwight Eisenhower's Secretary of Agriculture from 1953 to 1960, told the farmer the government's position: "Get big or get out."

So the 1950s brought TV, pesticides, and government policies that pushed a switch from agriculture as a way of life to agriculture as a specialized business. Nothing has improved since. "Adapt or die," Earl Butz, Nixon's and Ford's Secretary of Agriculture told the farmers, and they have adapted to many unnecessary and dangerous practices. Most recently, they've adapted to high-priced genetically engineered seeds developed by the chemical companies, which are also the seed companies now. The seeds don't grow better soy beans, but they're immune to the effects of the herbicide the company sells, so the farmer can soak his fields with it and not worry.

The farmer's independence has gone. He buys what he used to produce. He sells raw commodities from which others make the profits he once made. The bank owns the biggest part of his farm, the children have moved to the city. A crop failure is no longer a time for belt tightening; it's disaster, for him and also the American taxpayers, who pay ever higher subsidies.

But myths die hard. For many farmers and many farmland advocates, the old idea that owning land makes you a free man lives on. Saving the all-but-vanished farm culture is a powerful motivation for farmland conservationists. But there are also other reasons for thinking that we need to preserve farmland.

Why Preserve Farmland?

The reasons for thinking farmland ought to be preserved tend to differ between farmers and non-farmers. Farmers want to keep farmland so they can make a profit farming. Corporate farms have very little interest past the bottom line, but individual farmers usually also have interests related to a rural life style.

Non-farmers want to eat, of course, so they want the farms to grow crops that translate into food. More than most farmers, they also see farmland as important to the broader community. They see it as open space, scenic diversity, wildlife habitat (nongame as well as game), and as a living rather than museum expression of one feature of regional history.

As the farmland protection movement has developed, it has merged those two sets of big, relatively self-evident reasons and come up with a few others. Chapter 3 gave reasons for protecting natural lands. Following are reasons for saving farmlands. They are grouped, as in chapter 3, into practical, aesthetic, and ethical categories, but some of them as usually stated by farmland advocates have elements of two or even all three of the categories.

Aesthetic Reasons
  • Maintain scenic diversity.
  • Keep a living expression of regional history.

Practical Reasons
- Make it possible for farmers to make a living.
- Produce food and fiber we all need.
- Provide wildlife habitat for nongame and game animals.
- Retain open space.
- Provide for national security. The argument here is that if we had another major war, we wouldn't want to be in the position of having to import our wheat, corn, or soybeans. Even our biggest patriots would probably concede that we can't achieve coffee independence.
- Encourage agrotourism. Traditionally, people vacation in the mountains or at the seashore, drawn to the Earth's natural features. The vast stretches of Illinois and Iowa that consist of corn or soybeans growing up to the edge of narrow country roads, punctuated by an occasional interstate highway, are marvels of the photosynthetic conversion of sunlight to carbohydrate, but they aren't tourist draws. Some few agricultural settings do attract tourists: orchard country, vineyards, Amish farmland with its thriving unirrigated fields cultivated with teams of horses.
- Put a stop to imprudent land loss based on a malfunctioning market. Some types of political conservatives believe sprawl is good; it's just the free market at work. Farmland protection advocates point out that the playing field is tilted. The many government policies that subsidize road building and development and other incentives to sprawl produce a dysfunctional market in which prime agricultural land is worth more for condos than for growing crops.
- Save the local community money that would be spent in providing services to new residential development. This is the cost of community services (COCS) argument developed in chapter 3. Housing and, in the long run, commercial and industrial development, cost communities more in services and necessary infrastructure than they generate in taxes. Farmland that remains on the tax rolls pays more in taxes than it requires in services. Though most village, township, city, and county officials are ignorant of these facts, or at least act as if they were ignorant, dozens of studies have produced exactly the same results. Retaining farmland (or any open space) more than pays for itself. When we add farmland's contribution to community amenities and well being, a local government would have to be demented to favor the residential development of farmland.
- Keep agricultural jobs. Farms provide jobs for the farmer and his wife and perhaps a few hired hands, but the hired hands are dwindling. Any jobs that can be mechanized will be, for obvious reasons of saving money and avoiding hassles. But farms do provide jobs. They provide trucking jobs, wholesaler jobs, jobs in cereal factories, snack factories, sausage factories, and advertising agencies. They provide jobs at chemical companies and in farm equipment manufacturing and sales and at the loan office of the bank.

And they provide lots of jobs in ag colleges, extension services, and federal and state agriculture departments. So, farming does create jobs. It's just that most of them are hundreds or thousands of miles away.

• Be able to eat locally grown foods. This sensible idea visualizes saving local farmland to provide free-range chickens and fresh vegetables, grains, and fruits, organic if we wish. It makes sense all around. It supports the local economy and cuts down on energy wastage involved in shipping produce from California or Brazil.

Ethical and Mixed

• Retain a rural culture.

• Preserve features important to our sense of place. Some of us grew up in a diverse and pleasant patchwork of woodlots, orchards, wheat fields, lakes, and small towns. We feel at home in such a landscape and would like it perpetuated. Of course, our sense of this place is very different from what the place really is, based on the land. At the time European settlers arrived, the place was forest, savanna, wetlands, and prairies—or some other set of natural communities, such as desert, thornscrub, and riparian woodland, depending on where your place is.

• Thwart the forces of sprawl. A high percentage of the land area of the United States has been converted to farmland or ranchland. If what is left could be kept agricultural, sprawl would have almost nowhere to go. One land trust that seems to have taken this principle to heart is the Monterey County Agricultural and Historical Land Trust (MCAHLT), which operates in the Salinas Valley of California. Strung out along the Salinas River and Union Pacific railroad tracks are a few small towns among the vast fields of lettuce and artichokes. According to *Wall Street Journal*, MCAHLT "drew up plans to form a horseshoe of easements around each town to preserve valuable farmland."[1] Officials at one of the towns, King City, have expressed unhappiness. Able to sprawl in only one direction, the town faces a tarnished future, they fear: Children will have to be bused into the city for school; police and fire response to emergencies will take longer; new infrastructure will be expensive. But, of course, these are the consequences of sprawl everywhere, not just situations where the planning department can't sprawl in any direction it chooses.

One more (practical) argument for saving farmland is the retaining options argument. It goes like this: Granted we have a current surplus of farmland, we still should not let it be developed. If that happens, it's lost to other potential uses that may be more desirable in the future.

Note that this is not an argument for retaining farmland in production agriculture. Rather than growing surpluses of corn, soy beans, or watermelons, we could retain currently unneeded farmland in some type of a soil bank, in which someone (well, really, almost certainly the federal government) pays farmers to keep the land in, say, native grasses. We should also view it as an opportunity to gain back some of natural lands that were lost to agriculture during the past two hundred years.

Conservation Easements and PDRs

The 1981 National Agricultural Lands Study produced a 284-page guidebook, *The Protection of Farmland,* evaluating the ways in which farmland can be protected. Most writing on the subject since 1981 draws on or reinvents that discussion.[2] *The Protection of Farmland* listed ten separate types of programs at state through local levels. Of these, the most promising is the use of conservation easements.

What are PDRs? When the land-use experts come to town with their tray of slides to give their prescription for saving farmland, it's usually PDRs. PDR stands for Purchase of Development Rights. The American Farmland Trust prefers another name, Purchase of Agricultural Conservation Easements— PACE—but most such programs do little more than separate out development rights, rather than specifically identify and protect conservation values, as conservation easements are supposed to do. PDR is usually the more accurate abbreviation.

Agricultural conservation easements have the same basic features as other kinds of conservation easements, discussed more fully in chapters 7 and 8. The landowner transfers certain rights to a conservation organization or government agency. The big right removed from the landowner's bundle is the right to develop the parcel. As with other conservation easements, provision can be made for such things as another building site or adding onto the old house. Future owners have the same rights and are under the same restrictions as the owner who placed the conservation easement on the property.

The owners gain certain tax advantages. If the land is currently being assessed for its development value, then property taxes should go down. In any case, they shouldn't rise in the future, except as the value of the land for farming goes up. And the lower, post-easement value of the land will be the value included in the owner's estate. Consequently, it's less likely that a farmer's heirs will be forced to sell the farm to pay inheritance taxes. One tax benefit the landowners don't get is a charitable deduction, since they're selling their rights, not donating them.

Why Don't Farmers Like Conservation Easements? I attended a public meeting not long ago where the suits were out in abundance: public officials, university administrators, developers. The occasion was the presentation of a study on future land use in the county. The expert had basically sensible recommendations for a countywide plan to be based on an ecological survey and implemented by zoning. For saving farmland he favored PDRs. The academics and the city and county officials, by and large, liked the ideas. The township and village officials mostly didn't.

A supervisor from a rural township rose to speak about purchase of development rights. The gist of what he said was this: The farmers in his township—he didn't mention that he was one of the largest—liked the idea of PDRs, in part. The part they liked was the money. The part they didn't like was that when they got ready to sell their farm, they didn't have the development rights anymore.

One reason farmers shy away even from selling conservation easements (let alone donating them) is their worry that a farm without development rights won't find buyers. To them, farmland is working land. The time is coming, they fear, when most types of agriculture will become impractical on land within reach of our cities. What the average farmer cannot visualize is someone buying the land just for the sake of the land—someone who wants it for wildflowers in the woodlot and frogs in the marsh, someone who will let the cropfields return to young forest for the sake of eventually having old forest, who'll keep the hayfields not for hay but for nesting grassland birds. There are people like that ready to buy farm property, but they tend to be outside the ken of the average farmer.

I've heard other reasons why farmers don't like conservation easements. The reasons sound like the arguments put forth against rail-trails in farm country. Some are private property rights ideas, of a sort. The farmer doesn't like the idea that some outside party would have a say in the management of his land. If he wants his cows to climb down the river bank to drink, they'll damn well climb and drink. Plus, what's this about a bunch of strangers coming onto his land once a year to check up on him?

Other reasons are simply mistaken notions. The farmer has heard about other types of easements and worries that if there were one on his land, people from the city could wander around on his land and let the chickens out— if he still raised any chickens. Some of this misinformation can be corrected by well-designed educational campaigns.

Although some farmers won't have anything to do with PDR programs, enough others will that applicants far outpace funding. In the first two years of the Michigan PDR program, 1997 and 1998, there were 1,079 applications, of which 74—6.8 percent—were selected.[3]

The main reason farmers are rarely willing to *donate* conservation easements is that many of them see the farm as their retirement plan. They've always anticipated that they'd sell the land when they were ready to get out of farming—perhaps to one of their children if any wanted to farm or, if not, to a developer or an agribusiness corporation.

Some farmers don't have enough income to take good advantage of a large charitable donation. Suppose, for example, that a farmer could donate an easement worth $1 million on his spread. To take full tax advantage of such a deduction, he'd have to be able to deduct $160,000 per year. However, IRS regulations allow deductions only up to 30 percent of annual income. This means that he'd need an annual income of half a million dollars ($160,000 = 30 percent of $533,333) to take full advantage of the donation.

Not many farmers near where I live have an income of $500,000. Some have a cash flow of half a million, and a share of that cash flow (much of which can be written off as business expenses) contributes to the family's standard of living. But as to actual IRS-style income, it may be a few tens of thousands or less in a year of drought or low prices.

The upshot is that only big, successful farmers or ones who have income from other sources have a financial incentive to donate easements or land. Nevertheless, any farmer who wants to keep his land from being developed could work with a land trust to combine that aim with generating some cash. For example, a farmer might sell a conservation easement on some of his land to the government, thereby generating substantial income on which taxes would be due. If he gave other land to a land trust, the income tax generated by the sale would be partially offset by the donation. There are other possibilities. The American Farmland Trust has a Farm Legacy Program, consisting of an assortment of estate planning options such as charitable gift annuities based on donating the family farm to the organization.

PDR Programs. PDR programs started in the mid-1970s. Suffolk County, New York, the eastern part of Long Island, had the first, adopted in 1972 and making its first purchases in 1977.[4] Statewide programs were begun in Maryland, Massachusetts, Connecticut, and New Hampshire soon after. About twenty states and another fifty or more smaller units of government have PDR programs.

Programs differ, but a typical one begins with a farmland owner preparing an application to the appropriate agency.[5] Usually the local government must approve the application before it goes forward. In Michigan, the request of a fruit farmer for permission to apply to the Department of Natural Resources was turned down by the council of the village within which his 165-acre farm was located. One council member said he represented a silent constituency who didn't want to see the land's long-term future set in stone. He added that the village needed to expand its tax base.[6] And this is land in one of the twenty farm regions most in danger from sprawl nationally, according to the American Farmland Trust.

The farmer had written to *American Farmland,* the American Farmland Trust's magazine, a couple of years before.

My father's farm is losing its connection to other farmland. I envision it one day becoming an island surrounded by a sea of houses. Each year I pay the taxes that collectively provide for community improvements, attracting more people who buy the houses. I feel a certain resentment. . . .

Someday I'll be gone when the morning comes. Will anyone protect this land when I'm not here? What shall I tell my father became of his farm?[7]

The responsible agency ranks PDR applications based on development pressure and soil quality. Some programs include other considerations such as the presence of adjacent or nearby farms that seem secure: already under easement, applying, or protected in some other way. Some programs have requirements for geographical balance or favor farms that are producers of locally consumed food.

Since there are invariably more applicants than money, a committee ranks the applications. The high-ranking farms are appraised. The difference between the farm's fair market value without an easement and its value with the easement in place is the value of the development rights. Based on availability of funding, the government agency will make offers on the high-ranked properties, with the appraised value of development rights the upper limit. Negotiations may or may not end with a deal.

The fact that the farmer is getting paid for development rights and the voluntariness of the process—he has to apply and, if he doesn't like the deal, can turn it down—are the features that make PDR programs more or less palatable to many farmers.[8]

The Old Mission Peninsula. Saving the orchard lands of the Old Mission Peninsula of Michigan is a PDR success story.

Mission Peninsula is a 17-mile ridge that juts north into Lake Michigan's Grand Traverse Bay. The land was originally clothed with pine and northern hardwood forests, but these were mostly gone by the middle of the nineteenth century. The peninsula, very near the forty-fifth parallel of latitude, is pretty far north for most kinds of agriculture. The slopes, however, have a highly favorable microclimate for growing fruit because of the moderating influence of the bay along with cold air drainage taking the cold night air downslope to valleys and the shoreline. The peninsula has been famous for its tart cherry orchards since early in the twentieth century.[9]

The whole peninsula is one 17,000-acre township. In the 1950s and 1960s, its human population was growing at a rate of more than 3 percent per year. Hoping to slow the conversion of orchards to houses and condos, the township adopted a comprehensive plan in 1968 that established minimum lot sizes of 5 acres in a 10,000-acre agricultural zone. This restriction proved to be no brake at all on the loss of agricultural land. Between 1968 and 1989, the peninsula lost 1,100 acres of farmland. The population jumped from about 2,600 to 4,300, an increase of 65 percent.

People don't eat as much cherry pie as they used to, and in some cases, financial necessity forced farmers to sell their whole farm or individual building lots. However, land prices of $4,000 or more per acre tempted even successful farmers to sell. A casual reading of some farmland protection literature might lead one to believe that farmers faced with rising property taxes sell out when they can no longer make a living. It may come to that, but often the decision to sell is based on the same sort of economic analysis a corporation uses in deciding to sell off a division that's making money, just not as much as they'd like. A farmer making a profit of $60 an acre from agriculture doesn't need a financial analyst to tell him that if he sells it for $4,000 and invests the proceeds at 6 percent, he'll quadruple his return.

Anti-development feelings in Peninsula Township began to grow in 1974 when two farms with some of the best cherry-growing land were converted to subdivisions. Eventually, an advocacy group, Protect the Peninsula, was formed to lead the opposition to the continual business-as-usual rezonings. In 1988, three township board members were elected on a preservation platform. One of these, Rob Manigold, a fourth-generation farmer, became the president of a new land trust, the Old Mission Conservancy (OMC).

That same year, a bank foreclosed on a 500-acre farm at the very tip of the peninsula. Hoping to stave off residential development on this crucial site, Manigold called the American Farmland Trust (AFT). AFT bought the land for $2.1 million and eventually sold it to the state Department of Natural Resources, which has turned part of it into a new state park and kept some in agriculture. AFT also bought an adjacent farm, split off the orchard land, and sold it with an agricultural easement. The other, wooded parts of the farm were sold with covenants restricting residences to specified building envelopes.

These are things that land trusts do, but they were new to Peninsula Township and fueled interest in going on the offensive. With help from AFT and various other organizations and agencies, the Planning Commission began to design a PDR program. Peninsula Township cannot legally issue bonds, so the only way to raise money locally for a PDR program was a property tax increase. They decided on 1.25 mills (that is, .125 cent). Under Michigan's system at the time, this translated into $1.25 for every $2,000 of assessed value. In other words, a piece of property assessed at $160,000 would have its property taxes increased by $200 to pay for the PDR program. The increase would be in effect for fifteen years.

Among other features of the program were provisions to spend up to $1,000 per year for monitoring easement lands and to set aside a minimum of $40,000 as a defense fund. Easements would be held by the township and the Old Mission Conservancy. To administer the program, the OMC contracted with another area land trust, the Grand Traverse Regional Conservancy, with which it has since merged.

The vote on the millage was set for August 1994. A Concerned Citizens group, formed in 1993, began to campaign in May. In these months before the vote, the peninsula residents saw yet another conversion of farmland to residential development. This development was as environmentally sensitive as could be obtained under the existing zoning, but to many the sight of hundreds of blooming cherry and apple trees bulldozed into piles and burned was evidence that a new approach was needed.

The millage passed 1,208 to 1,081. Some citizens had doubted that farmers would be interested in selling their development rights, but by the spring of 1995, forty-five farmers owning 3,500 acres had applied. Although the original aim was to protect about 3,000 acres of farmland, the program has been so successful that 5,000 acres are already under easement.

Can We Afford to Save our Agricultural Landscapes? PDR programs have saved some farms and will save more in the future. They're an appealing idea because they cater to the farmer's desire to get money out of his land. But no careful analyst thinks that they'll save the nation's farmland in quantities sufficient to retain our rural landscapes.

A look at Michigan, which can serve as a kind of average farm state, will show the fundamental problem. The figures are for 1998, the last year for which I have complete statistics. In Michigan, 10.4 million acres of farmland remain.[10] This is a more than 40 percent drop since 1950; however, the decline has been slow but steady in the past decade at only about 0.5 percent per year.

The Michigan Department of Agriculture gives the total value of Michigan farms as $17.4 billion (about $1,700 per acre). However, we don't necessarily need to buy the development rights to all the farmland. Perhaps we could preserve the food supply and rural landscape by protecting half, or 5.2 million acres, worth about $8.7 billion.

How much it will cost to buy the development rights depends mostly on the value of the land for farming relative to its value for development. Let's say that, on the average, we'll have to pay 50 percent of the appraised value of the land for the development rights. Far from the path of development, this figure will be high; close to the cities, the interstates, the Great Lakes shores, and other desirable locations, it'll be low. At 50 percent, the bill to buy the development rights to half the state's farmland would be about $4.4 billion.

If we're content to buy the development rights to these 5.2 million acres over a period of 20 years, what will we need to come up with per year? Dividing $4.4 billion by 20 years (and ignoring inflation), we get $220 million per year.

This seems like a lot of money, but a dollar isn't what it used to be. The state of Michigan spent about $35 billion in 1998. So, really, we could do it. $220 million is a small, almost trivial fraction of $35 billion. It is, in fact, six-tenths of one percent. The problem is all the other, competing demands on the state dollar. Medicaid takes about one-quarter of the budget. Prisons take over a billion per year. And there are highways, education, welfare.[11]

The entire budget for Michigan state parks and recreation is $60 million, less than a third of what we'd be asking to buy development rights on farmland—not the land, just the development rights.

So saving the nation's farmland by buying development rights is financially possible. We've got the money. But it will difficult to convince the electorate that we should spend that much on PDR programs—as difficult as convincing them that we should spend what it would take to buy and preserve all the remaining natural areas.

A few states have several years' experience with PDR programs and give us a practical sample of what to expect. Maryland, with one of the oldest (1977) and most successful state programs, had as of 1997 spent $157 million. It had protected 968 farms totaling 140,000 acres. Total farm acreage (1996) is about 2 million. PDR expenditures have averaged about $8 million per year, but have increased in later years. So has farmland price. To protect another million acres at the same rate (7,000 acres per year) at the same level of expenditure would take over 140 years.[12]

In some states, local programs add to the total acreages protected. The Pennsylvania PDR program between 1988 and 1997 protected 110,000 acres. Lancaster County as of 1995 had saved over 20,000 acres through the actions of county government and the Lancaster Farmland Trust, combined.[13]

On the other hand, not every locality will be willing to start a PDR program. In 1998, the Potawatomi Land Trust was involved in an open-space preservation plan in Washtenaw County that the voters turned down. This is the home of the University of Michigan with its thousands of faculty, staff, and students and of many high-tech companies with their thousands of employees—just the sort of constituency that we think of as valuing such amenities as open space and local food production. In fact, the proposal passed in Ann Arbor township and city, but lost everywhere else in the county.[14]

The $5.5 million proposal would have been supported by a 0.4 mill (0.04 cent) property tax increase for ten years. This would have amounted to about a $400 increase in taxes for a $200,000 home. Included was farmland protection, mostly by PDR, and protection of other types of open space including natural lands, mostly by fee simple acquisition. Extensive polling during planning showed strong support for saving both farmland and other types of open space; however, support for a PDR program tended to run below 50 percent among most constituencies.

Supporters concluded that major reasons for the loss included the long period between announcement of the plan and the vote, giving well-heeled opponents plenty of time to organize; not enough demonstration that, no matter what farmers say, they will sell development rights; and too genteel a campaign that didn't do enough to rebut opposition claims.

Two years later, a $27 million open space–natural lands proposal without the farmland PDR passed with 64 percent of the vote.

The Problems of Monitoring and Duration. Most government PDR programs pay little attention to monitoring and enforcement. Well-run land trusts devote large amounts of time and energy to baseline documentation, monitoring, and building up funds for those activities and the eventual enforcement that will be required when a problem develops. Most government programs hardly address those issues. The Mission Township program with its $1,000 a year for monitoring and $40,000 defense fund is far ahead of the pack.

There's another potentially serious problem with government PDR programs. Although the enabling legislation usually contains language to the effect that the rights acquired shall be held in trust for the benefit of the citizens in perpetuity, there's something about governments that doesn't like perpetual arrangements. Nearly all PDR programs provide an out, by which development rights can be re-attached to the land.

Sometimes a minimum waiting period, often twenty-five years, is specified before a petition to buy back the development rights is allowed.[15] Other programs, including that of Peninsula Township, have no specified waiting period.

The Connecticut program, among others, allows the landowner to petition the town board to buy back the development rights. Approval would be by referendum. The Mission Township ordinance likewise gives the township board the power to decide whether the question of retaining the rights should be put to the township voters. The current owner is given right of first refusal if resale of rights is approved. In Maryland, resale can be administratively approved, but the county board, the state agency that administers the program, the state treasurer, and the secretary of agriculture all have to agree. Whether these four steps constitute separate, independent evaluations is unclear.

The stated justification for sinking agricultural easements is that the land can no longer reasonably or profitably be used for agriculture. Such language leaves room for debate. How profitable does it have to be? Does it have to be profitable for a farmer growing row crops and driving an air-conditioned tractor, or would profitability for a young couple willing to work hard in the community-supported agricultural business be good enough?

Most PDR programs are new enough that there are no answers to such questions. At the first level of testing, we'll find out how tough the townships and counties are going to be. Are they going to say, "This is still good farmland and if you can't make a living off of it, somebody else can"? Or will they say, "Aw, heck, Rollo, we share your pain. We'll put it on the ballot"? It's likely that there will be developers and farm owners pressing the view that the development rights belong back with the land.

It's still too early to decide whether PDR programs will actually preserve farmland or whether, like many other farmland protection devices, they'll just serve to put some cash in the owner's pockets while he waits for a more advantageous time to strike a deal with a developer.

Transfer of Development Rights

Transfer of development rights programs (TDRs) are another way of preserving farmland and potentially other types of open space by separating the development rights from it. TDRs can only exist in political units having a comprehensive plan and complex zoning. Authorized by specific legislation, they generally involve the transferal of development rights between two private individuals; however, the easement created on the farmland is usually held by a governmental agency.

Suppose that a county or township wants to preserve farmland in an agricultural district (called the "sending" area) and wants to encourage growth in a 80-acre tract of undeveloped land next to a city (called the "receiving" area). The receiving area, let's say, is currently zoned to allow one residence per 2 acres, or 40 houses. To shift development here, the county will allow density to go as high as two houses per acre, 160 houses, through the transfer of development rights from the agricultural district.[16]

Developments in the agricultural district have minimum lot sizes of, say, 20 acres. In the simplest case, a farmer owning 200 acres could sell development rights permitting the tract developer to add ten new houses, bringing the houses the developer could build in the Smart Growth area to fifty. The developer could negotiate with other landowners in the agricultural district and buy development rights for 110 more houses giving him his 160 total.

Farmland is thereby preserved, and the county planners have development where they want it and at the density they want.

TDR programs targeting farmland began in the 1970s. Recently, planners have become enthusiastic about TDRs as a way of attacking sprawl. Many new programs are being considered, but voters tend to reject TDR programs. They're hard to understand, and when people do understand, they don't necessarily like what they would be getting.

They may see the new developments as contributing to congestion. They may suspect that their own property taxes will go up to pay for services to their new neighbors in the receiving area. And they may also perceive that they're shouldering the costs of a program that allows large agricultural landowners to (1) sell their development rights at a good price (2) get a property tax break (3) continue to use the land as long as they wish, and then (4) sell out to rich buyers who want to live in the country, not in a congested receiving area.

A few places have programs related to TDRs, but slightly different. Davis, California, for example, enacted an ordinance in 1995 that provides that anyone developing farmland must acquire development rights on equivalent farmland in the area designated for permanent protection from development in the comprehensive plan.[17] The easements are co-held by the city and the Yolo Land Trust (Yolo is the county in which Davis lies).[18]

This process is the same as mitigation banking. Mitigation banking has been used in various localities to compel developers to save or construct wetlands somewhere else in order to gain permission to destroy them on the lands they wish to develop. Not all of these programs have worked well to save wetlands, though they've usually worked well to facilitate development. It seems possible that if a vigilant land trust is involved, the Davis-style programs could help save farmland.

In the overall picture, TDRs are currently a small, esoteric, but technically interesting approach to farmland protection.

The American Farmland Trust

Nearly all farmland was carved from a wilderness of forests, wetlands and prairie. Biodiversity has declined in the wake of the plow.

The greatest challenge facing us, then and today, is to create an agriculture that is in harmony with the environment. One that feeds us without harming other human and natural life support systems. One that is sustainable, both economically and ecologically.[19]

So wrote Patrick Noonan in a piece for the American Farmland Trust's (AFT) ten-year retrospective. Noonan, one of The Nature Conservancy's most successful presidents and a founder of AFT, was chairman of the AFT board at the time. They are brave and true words. They formed a context, perhaps, for AFT but not, apparently, a plan for action.

A group of farmers and conservationists concerned about the loss of prime farmland by development formed AFT in August 1980. The Marin Agricultural Land Trust (California) was an influential model.[20] The second president of AFT is Ralph Grossi, a dairy farmer who was one of the the the founders of the Marin group.

The first president (1980–1985) was Douglas Wheeler, a lawyer who has worked in the government and nonprofit worlds as deputy assistant secretary of the Interior and executive director of the Sierra Club, among other jobs.

AFT adopted a three-part mission. By conducting and publicizing research, it would educate the public to the reasons for saving farmland. Second, it would work directly with farm owners to demonstrate how farmland could be kept in production and out of the hands of developers. Thirdly, it would work with, and on, legislatures and government agencies to set policies that encourage farmland protection.

AFT is now past its twentieth anniversary. It has a membership of about 40,000, a staff of sixty plus, a yearly income around $11 million, and net assets of about $30 million. It has worked effectively in all three areas of its mission.

Research and Public Education. Perhaps AFT's most effective research has concerned sprawl and the cost of community services (COCS). The first such study, published in 1984, showed that all residential development costs more than it pays in taxes, but low density development costs the most.[21] A 1998 study of the land north of Chicago—one of the top ten threatened agricultural areas in the country by AFT's reckoning—found similar results but also documented safety issues. The low-density sprawl developments required much longer response times for emergency vehicles.

Work with Farmers: Cove Mountain Farm. AFT spends time and resources working with state and local farm groups and, to a degree, with individual farmers. As a part of its outreach, both to farm groups and state and local government, it has established field offices in several important agricultural regions. The first was in California in 1982.

In 1997, AFT began operation of Cove Mountain Farm in south-central Pennsylvania "to demonstrate farming techniques that lead to a healthy environment." Except for support of the federal Conservation Reserve Program, the healthy environment side of farmland conservation languished at AFT for a good many years. Cove Mountain Farm and increased attention to integrated pest management may be signs of renewed interest.

The 330 acres of Cove Mountain Farm came to AFT after the deaths of owners Anthony Smith (in 1992) and his wife, Anya (1994). It was their wish that the farm be used "as a center for ecological operations and studies . . ."[22] The Smiths' executor selected AFT as the organization that best matched those aims. With the property came a $500,000 farm improvement fund.

Anthony Smith was born in Pittsburgh in 1908 and had a law degree from Yale. For two years in the depth of the Depression, he was secretary to Gifford Pinchot, at that time governor of Pennsylvania. Smith was associated with the labor movement from 1937 to 1958, then from 1958 to 1980 served as president and general counsel of the National Parks and Conservation Association. Among Smith's conservation associates were William Vogt and Fairfield Osborn, noted proponents of the need for stabilizing world populations.

When Anthony was working for Governor Pinchot, Anya served as Mrs. Pinchot's secretary. Among later jobs, she edited *The Living Wilderness*, the magazine of the Wilderness Society, from 1953 to 1962.

AFT decided to use Cove Mountain Farm to demonstrate the economic and environmental soundness of grass-based dairy farming. Most dairy operations were grass-based not too many years ago. Now most are factory operations with confined cows receiving recombinant bovine growth hormone and eating genetically modified grains.

The small herd of cows, about 120 of them, at Cove Mountain spend most of their time outside, coming inside only for milking. They graze on the grass-legume pastures, rotating among 2- to 3-acre paddocks on a schedule to keep the forage in good condition. The farm is 200 acres pasture and 130 wooded. The cows are fenced out of the woods and streams.[23]

AFT doesn't claim that the milk factories, the confined animal feeding operations, don't work. In some sense they do; the cows give milk, the milk is sold, and the operators make money. The main lesson from Cove Mountain is that a farmer can make a profit off a small milk operation that, if the land is available, costs about a quarter of a million dollars to set up versus $1 million or more for a confinement operation. The only building needed for the grass-based operation is a milking center that can handle about 100 cows per hour.

More important from the standpoint of the Smiths' desires are the environmental advantages. The operation uses only a small amount of corn, which is bought. Consequently, little or no pesticide, herbicide, or fertilizer is used on site. This obviously yields a healthier environment at Cove Mountain but is better globally also, contributing to lower use of fossil fuel energy, hence lower CO_2 emissions. Energy requirements for heating and lighting are low. No recombinant bovine growth hormone is used.

By eliminating row crops, the soil erosion that accompanies this style of agriculture is eliminated. Lowering fertilizer usage cuts nitrate and phosphate in groundwater. Soils are improved by the continual fertilization by the grazing cows. The noxious smells that tend to accompany confinement operations are reduced.

Some corn is fed, which has to be grown somewhere, so to this degree the environmental damage is merely shifted off-site. Financially, outsourcing corn production is a major saving, keeping land for pasture and avoiding high-priced equipment as well as the expenses of herbicides, pesticides, and fertilizers. Currently, no attempt is made to use organically grown corn.

AFT owns Cove Mountain Farm and holds easements on several thousand acres in various states, but this aspect of being a land trust—acquiring and holding land—has not been its main concern.

Local Agricultural Land Trusts

Just because you do a conservation easement doesn't mean you're a damn environmentalist.[24]
—*Marvin Schmid, 2001*

The Marin Agricultural Land Trust (MALT), formed in California in 1980, is often credited with being the earliest farmland trust. Clearly it served as an important stimulus for the formation of other agricultural trusts, but the idea was in the air. The Land Conservation Trust, which had been spun off by the Trustees of Reservations in 1972 with the purpose of protecting open space, was transformed in 1980 into the Massachusetts Farm and Conservation Lands Trust.[25] In this incarnation, it focused on protecting farmland using a variety of devices including limited development. By the 1990s, the agricultural aspect of the organization's mission had declined and it was renamed simply Massachusetts Land Conservation Trust.[26]

Definitely earlier was the Michigan Land Trustees of America, incorporated in 1976 (federal nonprofit status, 1977).[27] The organization was begun with several agricultural aims, including that of serving as a community land trust for aspiring farmers who lacked land. The trust would acquire farmland to be made available to those who would apply environmentally sound farming practices. As it turned out, only one farm was acquired. It was used for a School of Homesteading, run for many years by Maynard Kaufman of Western Michigan University. The School provided theory and practical experience to students interested in organic agriculture.

Marin Agricultural Land Trust. Marin County lies across the bay from San Francisco. Its original vegetation was diverse, based on diversity in topography, geology, and climate. Plant communities ranged from Douglas fir and coastal redwood forests through Bishop pine forest, oak woodland and savanna, grasslands, chaparral, and coastal scrub, to salt marshes and duneland.[28]

Logging had removed almost all the old-growth forest by the 1920s. Beginning before 1850, cattle for beef, hides, and tallow were grazed on the natural grasslands. A little later, dairy cattle were added. Overgrazing has led to replacement of the native bunch grasses with alien annuals such as wild oats, annual brome grasses, and filaree.

Some areas of near-pristine vegetation survived the 180-odd years of European occupation, but these are not the focus of the land trust that developed here. It aims to protect ranchlands. Though degraded, they're still relatively productive, highly scenic, and a stronghold of family-style farming.

Opening of the Golden Gate Bridge in 1937 set off explosive growth in Marin County's population. By the 1970s, the eastern part had become a bedroom suburb of San Francisco. Although the western part of the county was still largely agricultural, it was tottering. Two hundred dairies in the county in 1950 had dwindled to fewer than one hundred by 1972. Zoning that required minimum lot sizes of 60 acres in agricultural areas was adopted in 1973; however, 60-acre ranchettes proved quite attractive to many seeking a rural home.[29]

When the dairy farm of Ellen and Bill Straus was threatened by a scenic parkway that would run from the eastern part of the county to Point Reyes, on the coast, they battled the proposal but also began to look around for a pro-active way to protect farmland. "We were told we couldn't stop progress," Ellen Straus remembered.[30]

If turning farmland into subdivisions and highways is progress, they have stopped it, or at least slowed it from sprawl to crawl in western Marin County. In 1978, Ellen Straus and environmental activist Phyllis Faber found their way to the Trust for Public Land and, two years later, started the Marin Agricultural Land Trust (MALT).[31] By that time, they'd been joined by Ralph Grossi, a third-generation Marin County rancher and head of the local Farm Bureau's land-use committee.

MALT protects farmland by acquiring easements, mostly by purchase. Its first easement didn't come until 1983, when it bought one on an 840-acre dairy farm near Petaluma with money from the Marin County Open Space District. The second easement, in 1984, 1,500 acres, was a gift from the San Francisco Foundation.

By the spring of 2002, MALT held forty-five easements on 30,000 acres. Most properties are dairy farms. Over two-thirds of the easement purchases were funded by Proposition 70, the California Wildlife, Coastal, and Park Land Conservation Bond Act adopted in 1988. A $1 million grant in 1984 from the California State Coastal Conservancy was an important early boost.[32]

The Straus Farm, easement protected in 1992, became the first organic dairy operation west of the Mississippi. Ellen Straus died at age seventy-five in November 2002.

MALT has a staff of nine. In fiscal 1999, income for purchasing easements totaled about $1.1 million, mostly from grants. Operating income was nearly $600,000, 60 percent from dues, contributions, and bequests. Membership is currently about 3,500.

One of MALT's successful fund-raising events is its "Ranches and Rolling Hills" landscape art show held in May. About three dozen invited artists enter paintings and drawings of west Marin County scenes, mostly easement-protected ranches. The 2002 show brought in more than $160,000. Artists donate half the proceeds to MALT. Fifty percent is a sizable commission, but it's a charitable donation and a worthy cause.[33]

MALT has played around with its acronym a bit. It offers its T-shirts, greeting cards, baseball caps, and limited edition prints through The MALT Shop. As far as I know, it hasn't yet made use of the A. E. Housman line,

And MALT does more than Milton can
To justify God's ways to man.

Colorado Cattlemen's Agricultural Land Trust. Probably more printer's ink has been spread over the Colorado Cattlemen's Agricultural Land Trust (CCALT) than any other agricultural trust. The media are intrigued because they see conservation as a liberal issue and cattle ranching as conservative. "Rare allies," the *New York Times* said of cattlemen and environmentalists. But it's not such an odd match. Land trusts as a whole form the most conservative element of the environmental movement; after all, much of what land trusts want is to maintain the status quo, and this is especially true of farmland trusts.

CCALT was formed in 1995. Among the statistics generating concern were that more than half of all Colorado land is owned by farmers and ranchers and that agricultural land was declining by 90,000 acres per year. By the late 1990s, the rate of loss had jumped to 270,000 acres per year, or 0.8 percent.

Jay Fetcher, a rancher who launched the idea of such a trust, realized that

. . . a land trust put together by a commodity group would bridge the suspicion between landowners and the typical land trust, which grows out of the environmental community. Another thing that added a level of comfort is that the board of the land trust is controlled by the Colorado Cattlemen's Association.[34]

The eastern two-fifths of Colorado was originally grassland, and the western three-fifths was all the vegetation zones associated with mountains and valleys. CCALT sells its mission by talking about sprawl and the loss of rangelands by development. Its motto is "Protecting open space by preserving agriculture." Most of the impetus for the formation of CCALT came, however, not from the vast agricultural stretches of the eastern plains, but from the rapidly populating, vegetationally diverse areas of the Rockies. The CCALT office is in Arvada, a suburb of Denver.

In this western region of foothills, mountains, and mountain valleys, natural vegetation and open space in general are threatened by rapid development, both residential and recreational, and also by mining, logging, and air pollution.

In the heavily agricultural eastern part of the state in what was once mostly short-grass plains, conversion to non-agricultural use is not proceeding very rapidly. Most of the relatively small amount of cropland in Colorado is in the northeast corner, mostly corn, wheat, and alfalfa, and mostly irrigated. The rangelands of the eastern part of the state, though overgrazed, tend to approximate natural vegetation more closely than do many locations in the United States—more so than where I live in southern Michigan where the forests, savannas, and prairies exist only as fragments, or memories. In eastern Colorado, cattle feed on the grama and buffalo grass much as did the bison.

The greatest threat to the grasslands and associated birds, mammals, and butterflies in eastern Colorado is the replacement of ranching by farming or, to use the term from the old Western movies, sodbusting.[35] CCALT's easements, in general, prevent development but not conversion to farming. In this, CCALT follows the same line as most of the strictly agricultural trusts. They're out to keep agricultural land in agriculture, and any kind of agriculture will do. Lynne Sherrod, Executive Director of CCALT, put it this way: "We hesitate to preclude any type of agricultural activity that might very well be the one thing that becomes the only feasible economic activity at some point in the future."[36]

The dry grazing areas of the valleys and foothills of western Colorado supported few or no large native grazers. They have been much more damaged than the eastern grasslands. The idea that cattle grazing is compatible with retention of a reasonably natural ecosystem probably doesn't apply to arid and semi-arid regions of 12 inches or less annual precipitation.[37]

Invasive exotics such as cheatgrass have been a serious problem in this region for more than half a century. In "Cheat Takes Over," written around 1940, Aldo Leopold talked about the replacement of the native grasses by this alien annual: "The cause of the substitution is overgrazing. When the too-great herds and flocks chewed and trampled the hide off the foothills, something had to cover the raw eroding earth. Cheat did."[38]

By March 1996, CCALT had accepted its first easement, 392 acres in the Telluride area. The donor had already protected (through another land trust) a companion ranch, the Last Dollar Ranch, best known as the site of many of the Marlboro man cigarette ads. As of 2001, after only seven years, CCALT had the impressive total of 116,000 acres under easement. Donations and bargain sale purchases were both well represented. Money for easement purchases has come from a variety of private and public sources, including Great Outdoors Colorado funded from the state lottery.

CCALT revenues in 1998 were $135,000. It has a staff of three. CCALT is not a membership organization, but has a database of about 1,000 consisting of everyone who has made a donation or asked for information.

Protecting Farmland in Context

Farmland trusts see their mission narrowly. They're protecting farmland as farmland. In this, they'll succeed, to a degree. And they'll fail, because under current circumstances there's more farmland than is needed.

Conservationists need to look at farmland protection as one facet of land protection. It's an important facet because agricultural land still occupies vast amounts of America. In fact, cropland, pastureland, and rangeland combined account for 65 percent of the non-federal land in the United States. Those of us interested in land protection need to try to make sure that when this land is converted from agriculture as much of it as possible is put to some sensible use.

We'll hope that a fair amount of land is retained in agriculture. Increasingly, thoughtful farmland advocates have pulled back from a focus on the mechanics of protection to make the case that the best way to retain farmland is to ensure the profitability of farming.

This is a difficult prescription and one in which land trusts can have only a minor role. There are three main reasons why farms are unprofitable. The first is that the federal government wants cheap food. The second is that there's too much farmland. The third is that farmers have allowed the profit they once made to be stolen away by other sectors of agribusiness.

The Cheapness of Food. Eighty percent of the income of the average farm household comes from off-farm sources.[39] The low profitability of farm operations is the result of many government programs. The federal government wants cheap food, just as it wants cheap gasoline. When food or gas prices rise, the voters become restless. The U.S. government has been more successful than most in keeping its subjects fat, happy, and on four wheels.

Many programs have favored pricing farm products below the real cost of producing them. For example, fuel in the United States is cheap, because prices don't include replacement or environmental costs. A great deal of the cost of any farm crop is the fossil energy embedded in its production and distribution, and this price is grossly understated.

The damage done to the soils, the water, the biota, the neighbors, and the neighborhood by American agriculture is not included in the costs of food. The right-to-farm laws of most states provide protection for many sorts of damages that would be settled in court if caused by any other industry or individual. The factory farms, the concentrated animal feeding operations (CAFOs), are the worst offenders.

Even other farmers mostly don't want CAFOs in their neighborhood, but most won't speak out against them. The government for its own reasons considers the CAFOs agriculture rather than industry. This being so, farmers worry that if the CAFOs can be sued or regulated, their own farms will be next. A spokesman for the Michigan Farm Bureau fed this fear: "They're regulating the livestock people today, but tomorrow it could be the fruit and vegetable industry. It's scary."[40]

Consider why factory farms exist at all. There was no shortage of pork, chicken, or milk, no clamor to increase production. But this kind of operation, despite its damage to community and environment, can—if these costs are paid by others—produce these products cheaper than traditional farm practices.

Another way in which farm commodity prices have been kept artificially low for many years is by governmental toleration of large numbers of immigrant workers, often illegal aliens, who work for low wages and tolerate unsatisfactory, sometimes dangerous working conditions. The apologists for this kind of labor give the same excuse in the fields or in the slaughterhouse: "They're the only ones that'll do this kind of work." Left unsaid is the rest of the sentence, "at this wage, with the rest rooms locked and the safety equipment turned off."

Too Much Farmland. Do we really need 65 percent of our non-federal lands to be in agriculture? Obviously not, based on oversupplies of many crops and the inability of many farmers to make a living without heavy subsidies from the taxpayers. The reason we have so much farmland is historical. Farming is the way the country was settled. Farming was a way people could make a living. As late as the census of 1900, over 40 percent of the population lived on farms. In the census of 1990, it was less than 2 percent. As a way of making a living, farming is now nearly insignificant.

The other reason farmland is in surplus is the increase in productivity that American agriculture has achieved. To be sure, part of this increase is illusory, based on large inputs of herbicides, fertilizers, and fossil fuel energy. More and more land is irrigated.[41] In the long run, the petroleum required to run farm equipment, to power irrigation, and to produce the chemicals on which farmers have become dependent will become scarce and expensive. In some irrigated regions, the water table is dropping. Groundwater in some places is contaminated with fertilizer chemicals.

For these and other reasons, the current level of per-acre productivity may not be sustainable. But for the foreseeable future, there's too much farmland and this oversupply is a major reason that it has been easy to keep food prices perversely low.

The Shrinking Role of Farming in Agriculture. One analysis of American farming was titled, "Is there Farming in Agriculture's Future?"[42] Agricultural economists sometimes divide agribusiness into three sectors: farming, marketing, and inputs. Farming is production agriculture, what the farmer does on the farm. Marketing includes everything after the farmer sells the food until the consumer eats it: handling, preparation, processing, transporting, advertising. Inputs are what the farmer needs to buy in order to farm: machinery, fuel, seeds, pesticides, fertilizers, electricity.

The analysis showed that agribusiness was a $300 billion enterprise in 1990, up from $75 billion in 1910.[43] In those eighty years, the marketing sector had grown 470 percent, the input sector had grown 580 percent, and the farming sector hadn't grown at all. The upshot is that currently only 7 percent of the money spent on agriculture goes to the farmer; 30 percent goes to the input sector, and 63 percent goes to marketing.[44]

Why has the farming part of agribusiness shrunk to such an absurdly small fraction? Richard Cartwright Austin, a minister and farmer in southern Appalachia, explained:

Farmers have become accustomed to purchasing more and more inputs to replace their own labor and ingenuity. Rather than raising work horses and mules, modern farmers buy tractors. Rather than growing feed, they buy fuel. Rather than using cover crops and manure to generate fertility, farmers buy fertilizer.[45]

At the other end of the process, the modern farmer now sells most of what he grows as bulk commodities. No more does he sell to neighbors and townspeople, no more does he barter wheat for sausage or pickles. Austin writes:

The farmer who worked my farm two generations before me delivered eggs to families and traded chickens to the local grocery for other supplies. He also ground his neighbors' corn for their animal feed and their kitchen cornmeal. . . . The families of wheat farmers [now] eat Wonder Bread. They have no grinding mill, and they are too busy to bake.

The farming profits of past generations are siphoned off at both ends, for inputs and marketing. Large, vertically integrated agribusiness corporations can make money at one or both ends even if their on-the-farm operations make little money. They do even better in the situation where they can contract the chicken raising or other farming operations out to individual farmers who take the risks but reap no benefits beyond those set by the corporations.

That farmer who sold chickens to his neighbors while his wife sold coffee cakes and apple butter is gone. The farmland conservationists trying to save the farming way of life had better look to organic farming, community-supported agriculture, a few young farmers with small farms and big ideas, and the Amish. That's where, if anyplace, it still exists. That's also where farmers may continue to make a living, responsibly rather than destructively.

A Mixed Strategy

Despite the best efforts of the farmland advocates, large-scale conversion of farmland to something else will occur in the next few decades. There are cogent arguments for saving as much of this as possible, though not necessarily all of it as farmland.

Some of it shouldn't be saved. Most of the irrigated farmland of the arid West should be allowed to return to creosote bush or bunch grasses as quickly as possible. Ditto the sugar cane of Florida, which should have stayed marsh. The tobacco farms should be shrunk to whatever level the free market will support. The same is true for peanut farms, though for national defense purposes we would, of course, want to be able to ramp up our peanut butter production in a national emergency.

We have still-excellent, though deteriorating cropland producing more corn, soy beans, and wheat than we need. We should be much more careful than we have been that this prime land, such as the black soil prairies of the northern Midwest, does not end up under asphalt, concrete, and lawn. However, there's no reason why it shouldn't end up back in big bluestem, Indian grass, and prairie dock. If it were ever returned to agriculture, the soil would be the better for it.

Any land that's marginal for crops could be allowed or encouraged to return to natural vegetation as small preserves and wildlife corridors. A news article in the *Farm Journal* for January 2000 noted that researchers for the University of Minnesota Rural Community Landscapes were suggesting that any land that had historically produced less than 124 bushels of corn per acre could be treated in this way.[46]

If you skim down the list of reasons for protecting farmland, many of them are equally good reasons for turning farmland back into natural preserves. Among these are the open space, wildlife habitat, sense of place, tourism, cost of community services, and thwarting sprawl arguments. To these, we could add the reasons for preserving natural lands set forth in chapter 3. All are valid, but the higher quality of ecosystem services provided by natural lands compared with croplands is especially compelling. And any opportunity should be taken for decreasing the amount of acreage exposed to agricultural chemicals.

The chance to turn some of this 65 percent of our lands back to forests, wetlands, prairies, and deserts that would once again be home to our native biota must not be lost. Agricultural land trusts should join with other land trusts in seizing the opportunity.

We need a mixed strategy. Let's (1) save a great deal of farmland as farmland, (2) help the federal government soil bank some current farmland, and (3) restore large quantities of farmland to the native vegetation that was obliterated a century or two ago.

For the first, we can count on the farmland trusts to keep doing what they've been doing, which is primarily participating in PDR programs, taking an occasional gift easement, and proselytizing.

General conservation trusts should also save farmland as a part of their mission but should approach it differently. If an owner wants to donate farmland to a land trust, the trust should be willing to accept it, but not feel constrained to maintain it as farmland. Its best conservation use, tempered by the land trust's resource limitations, should guide how the land is used. The trust might choose to keep part of the farm open—as hayfields, for example—to retain some landscape diversity while providing habitat for a grassland biota.

As for conservation easements on lands possessing active agriculture, the land trust should design them carefully. Easements based primarily on the land's use for agriculture will be ripe for extinguishment if a later owner's lawyer can convince a judge that agriculture is no longer feasible. If the land has no conservation value other than for agriculture, extinguishment would make sense.

For most conservation easements, the fact that certain areas are designated agricultural doesn't mean that a new owner, or even the original donor, has to farm them, but a recent wrinkle in a few PDR programs around the country has been language imposing an affirmative obligation: owners of the property must farm it, or at least keep fields open.

Considering farmland advocates' devotion to preserving farmland as farmland, this development is understandable, but it's unwise. It reduces the number of potential buyers for the land. For this reason and others, appraisers will have difficulty in determining the restricted value. In a situation where farming is not longer practicable, the restricted value may be zero for buyers who believe that a court would uphold the affirmative requirement. But few courts are likely to uphold it; including the requirement will facilitate extinguishment as soon as a case can be made that farming is impractical.

For conservation trusts, the opposite direction is the one to take. Their best prospects for easements are farms like the old-time version, with crop-fields but also wetlands, a pond, a woodlot, and other relatively natural lands. The easement should set aside as much of the land as possible as natural areas. Timber cutting should be eliminated or limited by a conservative management plan. The aim shouldn't be land use according to generally accepted agricultural management practices but land use that's environmentally responsible.

Depending on what the land trust sees as the best future use of the land, it could suggest one of two additional provisions in the easement. One option would be to set up a private land bank arrangement in which any land taken out of active agriculture would be planted in a hayfield mixture, either native grasses and forbs or something like brome grass–alfalfa. The latter would be attractive to some grassland birds and mammals and would be slowly invaded by native grasses and goldenrods.

Or, the land trust could ratchet the land toward natural vegetation by including a provision that any land out of active agriculture for some period of time—say, five years—would be allowed thereafter to undergo natural succession. With additional conservation values identified and protected, a conservation easement might well be sustained even when conventional agriculture became impractical.

13 TRAILS AND GREENWAYS

People—like deer, foxes, and other mammals—make trails. In North America, Indians made trails. Explorers, traders, and pioneers made trails when they needed to go where the Indian trails didn't. Where I live, in the Midwest, most roads today conform to the land survey grid; the occasional road that slants across the grid often is built on an old Indian trail. It may go from one prairie to another (both long disappeared now), follow the ridge above a river valley, or follow or connect other present or former features.

In England, with its long history of foot travel, many thousands of miles of trails still exist—2 miles of trail for every square mile of land.[1] There are some conflicts with landowners wanting to extinguish the ancient right to travel along these trails, but for the most part the right of walkers to use the old footpaths isn't seriously disputed.[2]

In the United States, where the concept of private real property has become increasingly extreme, the battle was lost long ago. The old trails have almost totally disappeared except where transformed into public highways. We have trails, but they're mostly contained within a single parcel of land. We can go to the nature center or a park and satisfy our urge to hike, but the trails don't go anyplace. Trails that we can use to go from one place to another, in the way that humans have traveled since humans evolved, are scarce.

There are, however, more such trails now than thirty years ago because of a widespread, though still rather thin trails and greenways movement. The most visible manifestation of this is the conversion of abandoned rail-lines to trails.

In my high-school days in southern Illinois, few of us had regular access to an automobile. After school, when we wanted to bird watch or botanize south of town, we'd head out along the Gulf, Mobile & Ohio track. It ran past a little marsh where we sometimes found wintering common snipe (Wilson's snipe, then), through fields, to and over the Big Muddy River.

Only a narrow strip of woods still fringed the river, but in it in the summer were blue-gray gnatcatchers, parula, prothonotary, and—in the tall sycamores—yellow-throated warblers. The tracks crossed the river on a high trestle. If you walked briskly, you couldn't see the river between the ties.

Beyond the river a spur line ran east, and the main line continued south along Lewis Creek. A mile or so farther out was a swimming hole. It was below a cliff a little higher than the rest, called High Rock. Nearby, under the rock overhangs on the other side of the track was a hobo jungle, still occasionally used in the 1940s and early 1950s. Prairie warblers nested in the old fields running back from the bluff above the creek.

The GM&O *Rebel* no longer runs from Cairo, Illinois, to St. Louis. The tracks are gone, removed after the line was abandoned in 1977. The trestle—where a friend once got caught by a train, had to climb down to one of the supporting columns, fell off, and got a dousing—has been demolished.

This account isn't a rails-to-trails success story. The line was part of the 270,000 miles of track that formed the U.S. rail system at its peak around 1920 and part of the 150,000 miles lost permanently between then and 1983.[3]

Rails-to-Trails Conservancy

The Rails-to-Trails Conservancy (RTC) was founded by David Burwell, who became its long-time president, and Peter Harnik. Burwell, a lawyer, was working for the National Wildlife Federation (NWF) when the idea of such an organization was hatched. Incorporated in 1985, RTC began operations in February 1986 using small grants from Laurance Rockefeller and NWF.[4] Burwell stepped down early in 2001 and was replaced by Keith Laughlin, whose background has been as a proponent of sustainable development and livable communities.

Headquartered in Washington, D.C., with offices in six other locations, RTC has been involved in many of the rail conversions that have occurred. RTC approaches its mission of "creating a nationwide network of public trails from former rail lines and connecting corridors" mostly by advocacy to the public and to decision makers in Washington and state capitols and by advice to local trails organizations. The organization doesn't itself develop or own trails.

Membership of RTC is about 100,000. Revenue in 1998 was over $6 million, half from contributions. Assets at the end of the year amounted to about $2.5 million, of which $1.3 million was in cash, cash equivalents, and securities.

Railbanking

Major impetus was given the rails-to-trails movement in 1983 when Congress amended the National Trails Systems Act to provide for a process called railbanking. One aim of the legislation was to preserve the rail corridors so that they could eventually be put back into service if needed. If a right-of-

way were dissipated by allowing it to be taken over by adjacent landowners—which happened with many of the lines abandoned in the years prior to
1983—putting it back together again would be nearly impossible. In the
meantime, the rail company is permitted to sell, give, or lease the right-of-
way to a state agency or a private trail association, which assumes the costs
and liabilities of ownership.

The other aim of the legislation was, of course, the trails themselves. In
fact, railbanking came out of the Public Commission on the American Outdoors (PCAO), which recommended that the United States begin to establish
a system of greenways. Oddly enough, the PCAO was appointed by Ronald
Reagan, who also signed the rails-to-trails act (Public Law 98–11) into law.
"In the President's defense," wrote an opponent of rails-to-trails conversions, "I am sure he didn't have the foggiest idea what was in PL 98–11."[5]

The rails-to-trails opposition sometimes claims that reconversion back to
operating rail lines is unlikely, but, in fact, railbanked corridors have been
put back into service in Ohio, Missouri, and Iowa.[6]

The first application for a railbanked trail was for the Katy Trail in Missouri. The Katy line—the Missouri Kansas and Texas (MKT)—ran west of
St. Louis, from St. Charles to Sedalia. A local rails-to-trails enthusiast
bought the 200-mile line from Union Pacific and gave it to the state of Missouri along with $2 million to develop it.[7] The first part opened in 1992,
and the whole length is now complete. A long section along the limestone
bluffs flanking the Missouri River includes campsites of the Lewis and Clark
expedition.

The RTC did not invent rails-to-trails conversions, but only ninety-three
rail trails were in existence when RTC began. By October 1998, after twelve
years of RTC advocacy, there were 1,000, totaling 10,000 miles. As of 2002,
the mileage was close to 12,000. These miles are all part of rail-trail conversions, but most were acquired through processes that didn't involve railbanking. Only about 4,000 miles have been railbanked. Of these miles,
about three-fourths represent current or future trails, and the rest are in corridors acquired by local governments for future light rail or other transportation projects.[8]

The RTC credits the Cathedral Aisle Trail, established in 1939, with
being the first rail trail. This 1-mile trail in Aiken, South Carolina, on a segment of the first route designed for steam locomotion, is of interest as an
item of historical trivia. However, if one trail is to be assigned credit for
starting the rails-to-trails movement, it's probably the Illinois Prairie Path.

When the Chicago, Aurora & Elgin Railway (called by its many friends,
"The Third Rail") ceased operations, May Theilgaard Watts wrote a letter
to the *Chicago Tribune* recommending that it be turned into a trail.[9] Seventy
years old at the time, Watts was a highly regarded naturalist and long-time
teacher of ecology and botany at the Morton Arboretum in the southwest
suburban fringe of Chicago.

In her letter of 30 September 1963, Mrs. Watts wrote, "We are human beings. We are able to walk upright on two feet. We need a footpath. Right now, there is a chance for Chicago and its suburbs to have a footpath—a long one. . . . If we have courage and foresight . . . we can create from this strip a proud resource."

The public responded enthusiastically. A group, mostly women and mostly Mrs. Watts's former students, set to work to make a trail out of the vision. Help came also from the just-founded Openlands Project. In 1966, after two and half years and a great deal of negotiating with local governments, utility companies, and other landowners, the trail was in operation.

Committees around the country wanting to set up similar trails wrote asking for information. By the early 1970s, the Illinois Prairie Path had been the subject of articles in several national magazines. William H. Whyte described its formation and operation in his 1968 book *The Last Landscape*. Insightful as usual, he wrote, "It is a rare right-of-way which does not have an incredibly complicated legal and political history behind it, and unsnarling questions of title and jurisdiction is difficult under the best of circumstances. It takes a hard core of screwballs to see this kind of project through."[10]

The Illinois Prairie Path now extends 61 miles. It's still operated by a hard core of volunteers, perhaps including some screwballs.

ISTEA and TEA-21

Many recent trails, including more than six hundred rail-trails, have been made possible with money from the Intermodal Surface Transportation Efficiency Act, passed in 1991. This act, called ISTEA, was the work of Senators Patrick Moynihan and John Chafee. Little federal encouragement for alternatives to the automobile had been provided during the whole time the federal government had been in the highway business. This act was revolutionary in mandating that states spend 10 percent of their federal surface transportation funds on "transportation enhancement," including rail-trail conversions and other types of trails and greenways. This 10 percent amounted to $2.6 billion nationwide for the period 1992 to 1997. Results were slow at first because of the reluctance of state highway departments to spend money on anything except building roads. In some states, the disdain continues for trails, mass transit, and anything else that isn't concrete and at least four lanes wide. None of Louisiana, Massachusetts, Missouri, Texas, Virginia, or Wisconsin has obligated as much as half of the money potentially available to it.[11]

At the other end of the scale, the American Association of Highway and State Transportation Officials honored four states for excellence in implementing Transportation Enhancement programs. They were Kansas,

Nebraska, Vermont, and New Jersey. Twenty states didn't bother to nominate their programs.[12]

At a meeting I attended, the state Department of Transportation representative responsible for the Enhancement projects spent most of his time trying to get his Powerpoint presentation to work. His oral comments were not much more enlightening. One part of TEA-21 is "Environmental mitigation to . . . reduce vehicle-caused wildlife mortality while maintaining habitat connectivity." The idea trapped in this unfortunate jargon is a good one: reducing the destruction by automobiles of animals while still allowing their necessary movements for breeding or dispersal.

Included are salamander tunnels and cougar underpasses, as well as more ambitious solutions. For example: the construction of I-75 split the Cross Florida Greenway. The break was remedied by an unusual overpass, 52 feet wide with 18-foot sand strips of native vegetation along each side and a 16-foot crushed shell trail down the middle. It reconnects the greenway for people and also for possums, foxes, and coyotes.[13]

The DOT representative didn't tell us about any of these projects but did mention, "We call this the 'roadkill program.'"

Nevertheless, with RTC as the watchdog, several thousand trail projects have been undertaken. The Enhancement program's success led to increasing opposition in the mid-1990s, as the time approached for reauthorization. The anti-trail groups and the highway lobbies were hopeful, and the trail, greenway, and mass transit advocates were fearful that the Transportation Enhancement money would be removed. In the end, it stayed in the Transportation Equity Act of the 21st Century (TEA-21), passed in June 1998. It was, in fact, increased by about 40 percent making as much as $3.6 billion available during the next six years. As of 2001, $4.2 billion had been made available in ISTEA and TEA-21 combined.[14]

Rail Trails

Last December, I walked a couple of miles on a rail-trail that begins not far from where I live. The trail surface is about 10 feet wide, of a limestone-slag mixture that is permeable and, though not as fast as asphalt, still satisfactory for either mountain or touring bikes. The total width of the right-of-way is about 100 feet. Like most rail-conversions, the trail is nearly flat. The railroad companies cut through the hills and filled in the valleys to keep the grades low, preferring to spend money on the original construction rather than each time the trains ran.

As I walked, I saw birds—cardinals, juncos, tree sparrows—in the strips of relatively natural vegetation that lie between the roadbed and the private property on each side of the right-of-way. One of the interesting features of this trail is a large flat area of muckland, originally tamarack forest, where peppermint was grown from the 1890s into the 1940s. This year, the large fields had been planted to corn. In the top of a small tree at the edge of the trail I saw a northern shrike, a masked raptorial songbird, down from its summer home in the taiga.

The railroad had been a spur line that ran about 30 miles westward from Kalamazoo to South Haven on the Lake Michigan shore. It has a history typical of many rail lines. Built in 1870, it ceased passenger service in 1937. Freight trains ran with diminishing frequency into the early 1970s. The road was abandoned in 1973, the tracks removed in 1977.

I attended a few of the planning sessions of the Friends of the Trail group that sprang up, and a few of the public meetings. Both followed well-worn grooves. The friends gathered supporters from as many environmental and civic groups, local governments, and trail users as possible. The hikers, bikers, and skiers would have preferred to exclude the snowmobilers, but the snowmobiling leader gave a presentation in which he said that if they were in, they'd work hard for the trail and if they were out, they'd work hard against it.

In the end, only a small section of the trail was zoned against snowmobiling, but global warming has solved the problem. Although the last three winters of the 1970s were cold and snowy, the years since have had few days with the 4-inch snow base specified for snowmobiling.

At the public meetings, adjacent property owners raised the usual objections. The hikers and bikers would trespass. They'd steal the trailside owners' garden truck and fruit and burglarize the houses. The trail would be populated by hippies, who might commit rape and mayhem. The lands had been conveyed to the railway company with reverter clauses, so, by rights, they should come back to the adjoining owners.

It's a familiar list, partly because some of the objections are real fears of people who live in the country and visualize a stream of strangers filing past their backyards—or as they come to think of it, *in* their backyards. But it's also familiar because many local opposition groups take their lead from a small but active anti-trail movement that publishes directions on how to oppose rail-trails.

The Friends, the state of Michigan (which had taken title to the land), and the local governments were unpersuaded by the opposition to this trail, and it was built. No one has been raped or murdered, but, of course, either could occur.

Crime on Trails. A detailed study by RTC addressed the crime issue. It gathered crime reports for 1995 and 1996 from the managers of 36 rural, 81 suburban, and 255 urban trails.[15] Direct comparison with standard crime statistics is difficult, but clearly crime on trails occurs at very low rates. For example, the 255 rural trails (5,282 miles), with an estimated 26 million users per year, had three assaults in each of the two years. There were two forcible rapes in 1995 and one in 1996. None of the trails reported any murders during the two years.

One statistical comparison, admittedly imperfect, is to compare rates for 100,000 trail users to FBI Uniform Crime figures (for 1995), which are stated as crimes per 100,000 population. Doing this, we find an FBI rural assault rate of 203 assaults per 100,000 population versus 0.02 assaults per 100,000 rural trail users. The FBI rural rate for forcible rape is 26; the rural trail rate is 0.01. For murder, the FBI rate is 5, the trail rate is 0.00.

Suburban trails have low crime rates, comparable to the rural trails. Most urban trails also have low rates; however, one urban trail (in South Boston) had several assaults, raising the overall assault rate for 100,000 trail users to 0.6. This is unacceptably high, but the comparable FBI statistic for urban areas is 531 assaults per 100,000 population.

Burglary of adjacent buildings was similarly low. For all 372 trails (rural, suburban, and urban) combined for both years, there were only seven reported instances, mostly on rural trails.

Trespass is usually brought up as a concern by owners of property adjacent to a proposed trail. Even people who don't see murder, rape, or burglary as high-probability fears don't like the idea of hikers climbing a fence and eating lunch at their picnic table. But most trail users seem extremely mannerly. Fewer than 4 percent of the trails overall reported any cases of trespass.

RTC also solicited comments from law enforcement agencies whose jurisdiction included rail-trails. Most stated that trails were among the most crime-free parts of the city or county because of the regular presence of citizens using the trail for its legitimate purposes. The Police Chief of South Burlington, Vermont, said it well: "Crimes and the fear of crime do not flourish in an environment of high energy and healthy interaction among law abiding community members."

A 2001 study of hikers along the Appalachian Trail found that about 98 percent felt reasonably or very secure from threat or attack while on the trail. They felt less secure (though only slightly so) when they left the trail—to go to a nearby town, for example. Nevertheless, about 4 percent of the hikers reported some sort of security problem along the trail in the preceding year. The majority of these were vandalism or theft from automobiles at parking lots; the rest were mostly coming across people acting "strangely" or drunk on the trail or in camp.[16]

Reactions of Adjacent Landowners to Trails. The National Park Service's Rivers, Trails and Conservation Assistance Program (RTCA) has been an important partner with RTC, though RTCA's mission is broader than just rails-to-trails conversions. One of their joint ventures is an early warning system whereby community activists and local agencies are notified of impending railroad abandonments.[17]

An RTCA study surveyed trail users and adjacent property owners to find out, among other things, what they thought of the rail-trail. Three trails were studied: The Heritage Trail, 26 miles through the farmland of eastern Iowa; the St. Marks Trail, a 16-mile trail that runs south from Tallahassee, Florida, through small towns and pinelands to St. Mark's National Wildlife Refuge; and the Lafayette/Moraga Trail, 7.6 miles in the suburbs east of Oakland, California. When the study was conducted in 1990 and 1991, the trails had been open for eight, two, and fourteen years, respectively.[18]

The differences in levels of support by adjacent landowners when the trail was first proposed were expectable but worth documenting. At the St. Marks trail, 47 percent were very supportive and 7 percent very opposed; at Lafayette/Moraga, the percentages were 37 percent and 7 percent. In the agricultural land of Iowa, the percentages were flip-flopped, 17 percent very supportive and 39 percent very opposed.

Perhaps the one most telling landowner statistic was "attitude about living near trail now compared to initial reaction." At the three sites, from 27 to 33 percent said they felt much better now and only 1 to 5 percent said they felt much worse. Asked their opinion about the effect of the trail on the resale value of their property, 87 percent of the Iowa landowners thought that the value was increased or unaffected. The increased/unaffected figure was still higher for the other trails: 90 percent in Florida and 97 percent in San Francisco.

Most of the hikers and bikers were found to come from the vicinity of the trail. Even for the Iowa trail with its relatively low population density, 69 percent of the users lived within 20 miles; the corresponding figures were 82 percent for Florida and 96 percent for the suburban California trail. The percentage of trail users in another study, in suburban Baltimore, Maryland, was even more concentrated near the trail. Sixty percent lived within 3 miles of the Northern Central Rail Trail. Nevertheless, most of the trail users (71 percent) in this study got to the trail by car. The streets and highways nearby, many trail users mentioned, were so exclusively dedicated to the automobile that walking or biking to the trail was too dangerous.[19]

The three-trail study calculated that the annual expenditures in connection with trail use—meals, lodging, equipment—were from $1.2 to $1.9 million, figures to gladden the hearts of local businessmen and politicians. "New money," money spent in the county by non-resident trail users, was a substantial percentage for the Iowa trail—just over 50 percent—but smaller percentages for Florida and California.

The economic benefits of trails were also demonstrated at a Michigan trail where two special bike events brought in 2,900 participants and generated local spending of $467,000 (for the two events combined).[20]

What Good Are Trails? Trail opponents have a long list of things they don't like about trails. I mentioned the most common ones earlier, but there are others. A list by one anti-trail group includes "unsanitary behavior by trail users" and "stress caused by lack of control of ones' destiny." Adjacent landowners—though not all of them—see problems. Potential users—and some other people—see benefits.

The same RTCA three-trail study asked hikers and bikers what they saw as the highest benefits of the trails. The top choices were the same at all three trails. Number one was health and fitness, two was aesthetic beauty, and three was preserving open space. In fourth place was either community pride or recreational opportunities. Recreational opportunities include hiking and biking, of course, possibly skiing and horseback riding, but also bird-watching, flower watching, photography, sketching, and probably several others.

Someone with a strong environmental bent might also see energy conservation and reduction of the impulse toward urban sprawl as important benefits.

The best trails take you from where you are to where you want to be: from your home to school or work or to a park or nature center. A 1995 Chicago Area Transportation Study reported that two-thirds of the people using trails used them to get to places to which they would otherwise need to drive.[21] According to a Harris poll of 1991, 52 percent of the Americans polled said they'd ride a bike to work, at least occasionally, if they could do it on a separate, safe, designated bicycle path.[22]

Besides access to the trail, another potential benefit to adjacent property owners is the opportunity to make money. Most trails attract businesses such as bike shops, bed-and-breakfasts, and stores that sell food and drink, regional books, and tourist items. But most people with their residence next to the trail have no plans to become shopkeepers. If they were to gain a financial advantage from the trail, it would probably come from an increase in the value of their property.

It is well established that property with a park nearby appreciates faster than comparable property with no park.[23] Studies have shown that nearby trails have similar effects; however, probably none of the trail studies would satisfy the dedicated trail opponent. Some of the data can be interpreted as showing that immediate trail-side property appreciates more slowly than property close but not adjacent to the trail. Needed is a well-designed study taking statistical account of pre-trail value, type and condition of house, topography, distance from trail, type of publicity during trail development, and other potentially important factors.

My own experience is that people seek out land near trails, but then the people I know value open space and the things that come with it. Not everyone does. *USA Today* quoted one of the leaders of the rail-trail opposition as saying of rail-trails, "We do not want them, do not like them and do not care about a city's open space."[24]

The Opposition. When the railroads came through an area, they acquired the rights-of-way by various means. Usually, they bought the land in a voluntary sale, though the willingness to sell was facilitated by the fact that railway companies usually were given condemnation power by states.

Often, the deeds included reversionary provisions whereby the land was to be returned to the sellers if it ceased to be used by the railroad. However, the common law has never liked long-running restraints on salability of land, and most states have provided for the extinguishment of such reverters after a certain term. In Michigan, the marketable title act of 1968 limits the former property owner's right to exercise a reverter interest to thirty years.[25]

The land agents sometimes acquired use of the land by easement. Recent legal scholarship has concluded that (1) unless the federal Surface Transportation Board has granted a certificate of abandonment, a right-of-way acquired by easement remains in the national transportation system, even if it is now to be used as trail, and (2) rails-to-trails conversion does not represent a governmental taking because, among other reasons, perpetuation of an already existing easement would not be expected to diminish the value of the land.[26]

Litigation in which adjoining property owners sue various parties has clarified some matters but muddied others. The litigation is usually funded by advocacy groups for private property rights; however, the motivation of adjoining property owners is rarely ideological. They want the land. After all, a hundred-foot right-of-way a quarter of a mile long amounts to more than 3 acres. Or they want the money they can make off the land, either from such things as leases to telecommunication companies or as compensation for what someone has told them is a "taking." And, of course, they want to keep outsiders from traipsing around.

Opposition to rail-trails is not confined to the heavily agricultural states, but that's where it's strongest. Often state agencies, such as Natural Resources and Parks Departments, are strong proponents of the conversions, though they usually work behind the scenes if they can. Individual farm owners are often opposed. The American Farm Bureau and some, though not all, state farm bureaus, are opposed. The Indiana Farm Bureau has been a notable opponent, keeping up a drum-beat of anti-rail-trail press releases and bankrolling several suits. Trail mileage in Indiana as of 2001 was 55 miles. Michigan, the next state to the north, has 1,122 miles open.[27]

The ten states with the most miles of trails are (in descending order) Minnesota, Michigan, Pennsylvania, Iowa, New York, Washington, Maine, Illinois, West Virginia, and Ohio.

Local governments vary. In September 1999, a proposal to renovate a bridge across the Platte River in Sarpy County, Nebraska, came to the county commission. The bridge was to connect abandoned portions of the Rock Island Railroad in a hiking-biking trail from Omaha to Lincoln. Although the state, the appropriate natural resources district, and the Sarpy County planning and building director, among others, favored the bridge renovation, the county commission turned it down.

One commissioner said, "We've done everything but stand on our head for federal dollars for roads, and we can't get it for several years. And then a bike trail comes along, and it gets money in no time." Another said, "We've got enough trails in Sarpy County. . . . How far do they want to go, California?"[28]

Well, yes, California is one place they want to go. The American Discovery Trail is designed to start in Delaware, split into northern and southern routes in Ohio, and reconverge in Denver on the way to Point Reyes National Seashore. The northern route is the one that goes through Nebraska. Part of the American Discovery Trail uses rail-trails, including the KATY trail in Missouri, but elsewhere old canal tow-paths and river levees, as well as long stretches of road shoulders, are being pressed into service.[29]

Besides agricultural land, another situation in which initial resistance is often heavy is where rail-trails bisect lots in affluent residential districts. One example is in an eastern suburb of Seattle. The Seattle area has an admirable network of trails; however, a new one that came to public attention in 1996 ran into opposition.

The Burlington Northern–Santa Fe ceased service in August 1996 on a spur line from Redmond to Issaquah. King County officials had long been thinking of this corridor as a route to connect the Burke-Gilman/Sammamish River Trail and the Mountains to Sound Greenway. It had been included in open-space plans and other public documents since 1971.

Part of the line runs along the east shore of Lake Sammamish (pronounced with the accent on the "mam"). This is where resistance developed.[30] As it happened, the executive director of the National Association of Reversionary Property Owners (NARPO), an anti-rail-trail organization, lived along the route. NARPO, in fact, had its origin as a local group opposing an earlier King County trail.[31]

Although many residents of the lake shore favored the proposed trail, others did not. These were mostly people who lived where the railroad ran between their houses and the lake, rather than on the other side, between the houses and the East Lake Sammamish Parkway. "Most of us are pro-trail, but not this trail," one of them said.[32]

A good deal of tugging and hauling has gone on since 1996. One approach considered by the opposition was to assess themselves $25 per foot of frontage and buy out Burlington Northern. They would then own the railroad and, when Burlington Northern decided to abandon it, would turn down the idea of rail-banking.[33] This didn't happen. Instead, a local land trust bought it. Near the beginning of May 1997, The Land Conservancy of Seattle and King County paid $1.5 million for the 11-mile right-of-way.[34]

Funding for the purchase came from a variety of philanthropic sources including Recreational Equipment, Inc.(REI), the Paul Allen Foundation, and the Bullitt Foundation. The Conservancy (now the Cascade Land Conservancy after merger with two adjacent land trusts) quickly secured loans totaling about $2.25 million. The ease with which the money was raised reflected the donors' knowledge, according to Gene Duvernoy, executive director of the Conservancy, that this was the most important open space corridor that had become available in decades.[35]

The Conservancy sold the right-of-way to King County for $2.9 million, and the Parks Department proceeded with plans to construct the trail.[36] However, the process has not been smooth. Some adjoining property owners built fences across the trail. Trail opponents have lobbied, litigated, and appealed. In what could be taken as partial acquiescence, the County Council took the unusual decision in the fall of 1998 not to open the trail while planning was going on.[37]

At mid-2000, the Environmental Impact Statement was done, and the County Executive had sent legislation forward to the Council asking that the trail be opened on an interim basis.[38] Not until December did the Council approve interim use—to begin in 2002. A few politicians and the same property owners with houses on the wrong side of the trail remained in dogged opposition.[39] A permanent, paved trail may still be years away.

Reading about Sarpy County or East Lake Sammamish, a person with no other knowledge of the rails-to-trails movement might get the idea that it's a losing cause, facing determined, well-financed opposition on every front. This isn't true at all. Nationally, of 125 trails opened between January 1994 and August 1996, 107 (85 percent) opened with, at most, routine expressions of concerns that were addressed and allayed by the trail supporters.[40] Of fourteen trails that faced court challenge, trail supporters won twelve cases outright. The other two trails had to give up certain sections of the right-of-way but opened using alternate routes around the disputed sections.

The U.S. Supreme Court upheld the validity of railbanking in 1990, ending most kinds of anti-rail-trail litigation. A residue remains, mostly not challenging railbanking or the trails themselves but asking for compensation based on the idea that the railbanking process constitutes a taking of private property. Legal scholars have concluded that this will only rarely be true, but courts have decided a few cases otherwise. For example, a December 2002 decision of the U.S. Court of Federal Claims in Missouri awarded thirteen landowners along the Katy Trail $410,000 in compensation for the strip of land railbanked in 1986. Compensation will come from the federal government if the decision is upheld.

Few owners of land adjacent to railbanked corridors are likely to end up with any compensation. Most have no property rights in the corridor; even if they do, most railbanking doesn't constitute a taking. But litigation will probably continue in certain states. Individual awards will usually be small, but attorneys' fees will be large. In one case, a compensation award of

$10,000 was accompanied by a request for attorneys' fees of $778,500—
also to be paid by the federal government. In the end the amount of money
that the government will have to spend defending railbanked corridors is not
likely to amount to a lot. "Perhaps the most significant effect of this litigation," according to Danaya Wright, an authority on railbanking, "is the
chilling effect it has had on communities seeking to prevent rail corridor destruction. Threats of multi-million-dollar lawsuits and recall elections have
stifled many city and county commissioners from taking advantage of the
opportunity to railbank. . . ." The biggest cost to America of the anti-rail-
trail movement will be the lost environmental and societal benefits the missing railbanked corridors would have brought.[41]

Greenways

Greenways may include trails but are usually broader, geographically and
conceptually. Two definitions from *Greenways for America,* the standard
book on the subject, are:

A linear open space established along either a natural corridor, such as a riverfront,
stream valley, or ridgeline, or overland along a railroad right-of-way converted to
recreational use, a canal, a scenic road, or other route.
    An open-space connector linking parks, nature reserves, cultural features, or his-
toric sites with each other and with populated areas.[42]

Perhaps the two definitions need to be merged to justify the name "green-
way."
    Greenway supporters list many potential individual and community ben-
efits, including the following:
- Promote sustainable economic growth by helping attract and keep de-
  sirable industry;
- Preserve community character;
- Provide habitat for wildlife in otherwise developed areas;
- Serve as a possible dispersal corridor for native biota where the green-
  way connects sizable natural areas;
- Reduce flooding, if the greenbelt is along the floodplain of a stream;
- Help aquifer recharge by cutting runoff and providing a permeable sur-
  face for absorption of rain water;
- Provide safe places to walk and bike to school, work, and stores;
- Serve as a focus for community recreation and tourism.[43]

Putting together a greenway typically requires a lot of money and the involvement of many organizations, including government agencies at every
level. A poster for Southeast Michigan Greenways lists twenty-two partners
along with the Michigan Chapter of the Rails-to-Trails Conservancy.

Almost always, greenways must be created in areas where property ownership is fragmented. A first step usually consists of mapping all the public and quasi-public land, such as parks, state game and recreation areas, preserves, and nature centers, and then trying to connect them with one another and with towns and cities. The process usually involves a complicated combination of devices, including land purchases, purchases and gifts of easements, and alteration of roads and highways to include bike paths,

Well-thought-out greenways are assets to their region. Unfortunately, they are usually achieved only after a long period of planning, grant-writing, consultations, committee meetings, workshops, and public meetings. Only people with a high tolerance for sitting in meetings and drinking bad coffee are likely to be enduring participants in the process.

Local Land Trusts

Something more than two dozen local land trusts have trails or greenways as one of the main items of their mission. Few actually own trails, and when they're involved in land acquisition the land is generally passed on, usually to a government body. Land trusts can be effective participants in trail deals through their ability to move more swiftly than their government partners— and perhaps also more swiftly than a loose confederation of opponents who might see their own purchase of a right-of-way as a good defense.

The Allegheny Valley Trails Association (AVTA), operating in the northwest corner of Pennsylvania, is a slightly unusual example of a trail land trust in that it owns the railroad rights-of-way on which its trails lie. As a result, opposition to its trails has been light.

AVTA began in 1991 when a salvage company offered to donate 19 miles of abandoned right-of-way along the Allegheny River. To accept it, a small group of bicycle enthusiasts met at Clarion University that fall and began a local trails organization. Not long afterward, David Howes and James Holden, two Clarion University faculty members who were spearheading the effort, convinced another company to donate another 15 miles of abandoned right-of-way.[44]

By 1992, the group had incorporated, obtained federal nonprofit status, and received start-up money from the Rivers, Trails, and Conservation Assistance program of the National Park Service and a local charitable trust. The first 5 miles of trail, utilizing the existing ballast of the roadbed, opened in 1993.

As of 1999, 10 miles of asphalt-surfaced trail were open, with 8 more miles in the works. The completed trail runs both directions from Franklin, a small town that was the first center of the oil industry in the United States. Most of us don't think of northwestern Pennsylvania as oil country, but it is, or at least was. The first oil well anyplace was drilled by Colonel Drake near

Titusville in 1859, and in the 1870s, Pennsylvania was the world's leading oil-producer.

One section of the AVTA trail runs to near the beginning of a state-owned trail, the Oil Creek State Park Bicycle Trail. More than a century ago, in June 1892, Oil Creek flooded and wrecked oil tanks in the bottomlands. Oil spread over the floodwater and caught fire. About sixty persons were killed and a quarter of Titusville was destroyed.[45] But for today's hikers and canoeists, these events of the petroleum past are hardly evident.

Like most local trails group, AVTA is all-volunteer. Income is modest, but AVTA has been successful in obtaining several grants, including an ISTEA grant for over $600,000.

"Chary" is a mild term to describe the attitude of most general land trusts to issues that might generate even a whiff of controversy. Consequently, only a few have shown any enthusiasm for trails, with their built-in set of potential adversaries in the adjacent landowners.

When Gene Duvernoy was asked about community reaction to his land trust's involvement in the East Lake Sammamish Trail, he indicated that opposition had been deep but narrow. After the Conservancy's purchase became widely known, a significant number of people joined the organization, citing its willingness to take on a civically beneficial, though somewhat controversial, project. But he wanted to warn other land trusts that might contemplate such action: "Make sure the corridor is vital to life in the region. Never take on such a project cavalierly!"[46]

Non-rail trails are put together across privately owned land by some combination of purchase, easement, lease, or simple permission. There are local examples, but best known are the long-distance trails such as the Appalachian, Pacific Crest, and North Country trails. Such trails do not have the same automatic adversaries as rail-trails but do encounter the same fears of intrusion and crime.

Assembling either sort of trail and most greenways often involves dealing with people who are indifferent, unwilling, or hostile. The process, with its lengthy negotiations, meetings, hearings, and frequent contentiousness, can be more akin to environmental advocacy than to most types of land trust deals.

Even land trusts that don't have or want trails or greenways as a part of their mission can, nevertheless, contribute to a trail's good effects by targeting natural lands next to or near trails. It would be advisable to do this as soon as possible after plans for the trail are known, because land prices are likely to rise. Such preserves benefit trail users by maintaining scenic vistas and habitats for wildlife and, if the land trust chooses, by providing off-trail places to walk. To the degree that the trail functions as a wildlife corridor, the trail may help maintain biodiversity on the land trust's preserve.

Even easement-protected property next to a trail may have desirable effects by restricting development and retaining vegetation and views that enhance the trail users' enjoyment, from a distance.

14 A DIVERSITY OF LOCAL LAND TRUSTS

Man tends to produce a forest edge condition. . . . The sharp natural differences between regions are thus reduced and "forest edge" species with wide climatic tolerance are encouraged to spread. Thus, lists of roadside and farmland birds which we compiled on a 6,000 mile trip through western North America were monotonously the same regardless of the [original vegetation], whereas birds of natural communities were excitingly different. . .—Eugene P. Odum, 1945

The same flattening of diversity Odum describes has occurred in many aspects of human life.[1] Along the same interstate where you see red-winged blackbirds and mourning doves at every rest area, you can eat the same breakfast sandwiches, pizza, and burgers every meal for 3,000 miles. You could spend every night in what looks like the same motel room where you woke up twelve hours earlier and 500 miles back.

Local land trusts, by contrast, are still diverse. The land trusts around Portland, Oregon, approach saving land differently than those in Massachusetts, Colorado, or Michigan. The diversity is based on what the natural vegetation is like, how much is left, what happened and is still happening to the rest of it. Differences also stem from state and local laws and human culture. Cultural differences show themselves in how much of a land ethic exists, how philanthropic people are, and how open they are to new ideas.

Like the local populations of a species of plant or animal, local land trusts are adapted to their environment. New ideas can pop up in any land trust where creativity resides. After being communicated through *Exchange*, at the Land Trust Alliance national meetings, or over the land trust e-mail list, such ideas can spread—or not. The main limitation is the fact that not every good idea is good for every land trust everywhere.

This Darwinian arrangement is ideal for adaptation to the continental needs of land protection.

Table 3 summarizes some features of land trusts by region.[2] "Dominant mode of protection" compares acreage protected in fee relative to conservation easement; "balanced" means both modes are well represented.

Table 3. Features of Local Land Trusts

Region (number of land trusts)	States	Dominant mode of land protection	State(s) with most land trusts	State(s) with most acres protected
West (188)	AK, CA, HI, NV, OR, WA	Easement, except CA, NV	CA 132	CA 1,252,000
Southwest (41)	AZ, NM, OK, TX	Fee, except TX	TX 22	NM 496,000
Rocky Mountains (59)	CO, ID, MT, UT, WY	Easement	CO 35	MT 506,000
Plains (25)	IA, KS, MN, MO, ND, NE, SD	Balanced	MO 10	IA 65,000
Great Lakes (162)	IL, IN, MI, OH, WI	Fee	WI 46 MI 38	MI 79,000
New England (425)	CT, MA, ME, NH, RI, VT	Balanced	MA 143 CT 112 ME 176	VT 444,000 NH 288,000 MA 210,000
Mid-Atlantic (222)	DE, DC, MD, NJ, NY, PA	Easement, except DE	PA 75 NY 72 MD 42	NY 552,000 PA 341,000 NJ 138,000
South (141)	AL, AR, FL, GA, KY, LA, MS, NC, SC, TN, VA, WV	Mostly easements	NC 26 FL 23	VA 236,000 NC 112,000

The West. Each state in this diverse region has its own character, reflected in the nature of its land trusts; however, the location of many of the trusts of California, Washington, and Oregon in the mountains and valleys next to the Pacific is a mild unifying influence. Also, most of the states have large amounts of federally owned land (four have 30 percent or more). Residents in such states may see less urgency for private land protection.

Water law based on the doctrine of prior appropriation ("first in time, first in right") is another peculiarity of many states in this region, along with the Rockies and the Southwest. It has frequently given rise to the situation in which all of the water of a stream becomes committed elsewhere (to irrigation, mining, watering lawns), so there's none to support a stream biota. This in turn led, at the end of the 1990s, to "water trusts" that buy water rights—water rights can be bought and sold, unconnected to land—and return the water to the stream. The Oregon Water Trust was the first.[3]

The mail survey I conducted in 1996 was designed to represent states in proportion to the number of land trusts operating in them. The response from this region was unusually low, only 15 percent were returned, a return rate less than half that of the rest of the country.[4] Doubtless, each land trust had its own individually valid justification for not filling out yet one more survey, but there may be a general reason.[5] My guess is that many of the land trusts of the West have not felt a strong connection with the land trust movement as a whole. They are separated from the numerous land trusts of the East and Midwest by the large expanse of land trust–poor plains and deserts and the only slightly more populated Rockies. Also, many of the region's trusts have a shared history in which midwife activities of the San Francisco–based Trust for Public Land was important. The generous financial support available to California trusts from state government and the Packard Foundation may have had a unifying, but isolating influence.

The Southwest. Only the Plains states have fewer land trusts than the Southwest, and only the Rocky Mountain region has shown faster recent growth. Arizona and New Mexico have large amounts of federal land; Texas has almost none, so if land protection is to occur in Texas, land trusts will probably play an important role in it. The scale of protection needed in this arid country is large, perhaps larger than anywhere else. There are, nevertheless, opportunities for ecologically valuable small- and medium-scale projects. Migratory bird stopover sites, areas of occurrence of plant and animal species of limited range, and any riparian sites with semi-intact or restorable vegetation are examples.

Rocky Mountain Region. Certain traits are widespread: a high percentage of public land (the federal government owns 30 percent or more of the land in every state), an economy dependent on federal subsidies, a disdain for the rule of law similar to many Third World countries, and a recent slight dilution of the older sagebrush mentality through immigration from other regions of the United States. But each state has its own attributes, and these play out in land trusts as in other aspects of life.

In the latest LTA census (2000), Colorado is credited with thirty-five land trusts, Utah with four. John B. Wright, a geographer at the University of New Mexico and one of the relatively few serious students of the land trust movement, suggested that the difference between the two states has been the pervasive influence of the Mormon Church in Utah. The two states are similar in many ways—economics, ethnicity, growth rates. They have the two large cities of the Rocky Mountain states, Denver and Salt Lake City. But at the time of Wright's study, Colorado land trusts had saved 42,000 acres and the single Utah trust had saved 220 acres. The explanation for the differences lies, Wright suggested, "in cultural attitudes about the role of human beings in changing the face of the earth."

These cultural attitudes in Utah come from the Brigham Young model of Mormonism. Development is seen "as a way to prove that the people are living righteously. . . . Belief in the inherent ethical goodness of large families and in unlimited economic expansion and a millennial mandate to build a radiant city for God have combined to produce the most challenging setting for conservationists in the American West. In Utah, to speak of limits is tantamount to apostasy."[6]

Untangling cultural influences on conservation in this region and elsewhere would be worthwhile theoretically, and also practically. With a little ingenuity, cultural biases could be fulcrums rather than roadblocks. Wright suggested, for example, that a land trust that set itself the mission of protecting the trace of the Mormon trail might be favorably viewed in Utah.

The Plains. The seven states of this region are largely agricultural. In many sections, attitudes are similar to those of the Rocky Mountain region as regards the federal government, private property rights, and environmental protection. There are not many land trusts and not many new ones are being formed. Between 1988 and 1998, only two new trusts were formed in the whole region.

Great Lakes Region. Large stretches of relatively natural forest and wetlands remain in the northern reaches of this region; elsewhere the natural lands tend to be fragmented by cities, suburbs, and farmland. The five states all have a substantial number of good land trusts doing a serious job of protecting land.

New England. One might think that the high number of land trusts here is the result of a long accumulation that began in 1891 with the formation of the Trustees of Reservations. Curiously, this isn't true; the pattern of land trust establishment in New England is similar to the rest of the country;

more than two-thirds have come along since 1970. Although most states have substantial amounts of land in both owned and easement categories, the balance is shifting as land trusts in Maine, New Hampshire, and Vermont have begun to protect large acreages of timber company lands by easement. The region includes large state or regional organizations with staff size in double digits—the Trustees of Reservations and the Maine Coast Heritage Trust, for example—but most of the trusts are small all-volunteer groups, some of them serving only a single village or town.

Mid-Atlantic Region. Away from the several large urbanized areas of this region are surprising amounts of natural land and farmland. Maryland has a unique state agency, the Maryland Environmental Trust (MET), that provides assistance to local land trusts and buys and accepts donations of easements, especially on agricultural lands. Mainly as a result of MET, the ratio in Maryland of acres protected by easement to acres protected by ownership is high, 16 to 1. Agricultural protection is also prominent in Pennsylvania, where the Lancaster Farmland Trust has been successful in obtaining easements on farms of Old Order Amish and Mennonites.

The South. Much of the land area is in the Coastal Plain, and much of it was originally swamp or Southeastern Evergreen Forest. Florida, especially, has a large number of endemic species. In a region this size, variability in outlook is present; by and large, though, the land ethic does not run strong. "It is difficult," wrote the executive director of a Georgia land trust, "to have a land ethic . . . where land is is seen primarily as a commodity."[7] Nevertheless, both land trust formation and land protection proceeded at a good clip in the decade 1990 to 2000.

Seven local conservation land trusts chosen for diversity in size, age, approach, and geography are described in the following pages. A good many other local land trusts have been given a paragraph or a page elsewhere in earlier chapters, and two local farmland trusts and a local trails trust have been treated separately (chapters 12 and 13).

Kestrel and Other Amherst Area Land Trusts

June 7. In Pelham woods today I found the pink azalea blooming, filling all the air with spicy fragrance. On little knolls, or where the woods were deep, it lighted up the landscape like a flame. It comes before the hardy laurel ventures out, while the wild apples yet retain their bloom. By old stone walls the blackberry brier spreads a mist of white, and once I saw a locust tree that hummed with many bees.—David Grayson, The Countryman's Year

Amherst, Massachusetts, is a pleasant village east of the tobacco fields along the Connecticut River and in sight of hills and small mountains mostly clothed with oak or northern hardwood forest. Although the woods are second-growth, many of the trees are old, because the hills were cutover long ago. This is, for America, a long-settled land.

Emily Dickinson lived out her life here, writing frequently of bumblebees, daisies, and bobolinks of the meadows near the Dickinson house. Perhaps a better feeling for what Amherst is like comes from the writings of David Grayson.[8] Though they're from the first half of the twentieth century, they still ring true—at least to a visitor like me.

Three land trusts serve the Amherst region. The Kestrel Trust was begun in 1970 as the land acquisition arm of the Amherst Conservation Commission.[9] Most Massachusetts towns and cities have a conservation commission to protect and preserve natural resources and acquire land for conservation and recreation. The original legislation was adopted in 1963; the reach and power of the commissions were increased in 1972 when they were given the job of enforcing a new wetlands protection act.

Considerable portions of the lands up and down the Connecticut River valley can't be developed because of Massachusetts' strong environmental regulations protecting wetlands and groundwater. Much of the ridge lands remain wild because the thin soil over bedrock won't pass a perk test—that is, won't allow percolation of water at a rate sufficient for operation of a septic system. Massachusetts, unlike certain other states, has generally held the line on these standards.

Over the years, the Kestrel Trust has expanded its service area to include the eight towns around Amherst. Its board consists of representatives from each of the nine conservation commissions plus five at-large members. It's not a membership organization but numbers its member-like supporters at around 300.

The Kestrel Trust notes that it preserves natural resources "both for their intrinsic value and for the benefit of the general public."[10] The connection between a healthy environment and the well-being of people is captured in the Trust's motto, "*Salus naturae, salus populi.*"[11]

In its thirty years, Kestrel has been involved in the protection of more than fifty properties totaling about 4,000 acres. These figures include purchases, gifts, and conservation easements. When the trust acquires ownership of a property, it tries to pass it on as conservation land to the conservation commission of the appropriate town.

Kestrel preserves both conservation and agricultural lands. There is, for example, the 44-acre Amethyst Brook site just east of Amherst.[12] It has a small parking area, but is also accessible along the Robert Frost Trail. The 1.5-acre Hawley Swamp Conservation Area is a breeding site for spotted salamanders, which come from wooded areas east of Henry Road and cross through tunnels installed for their use.

An early cooperative venture led to protection of a 276-acre farm that also includes forest, the headwaters of Adams Brook, and sections of two trails. The Trust, two towns, and two state departments cooperated to purchase a conservation easement (called in Massachusetts an agricultural preservation restriction). On the death of the farm owner, the restricted land was left in a trust to be farmed, but finding someone who was willing to work this hill farm took two years. Finding farmers for the better agricultural land near the Connecticut River has proved easier.[13]

One of Kestrel's first projects was to help establish a nature center, the Hitchcock Center for Environmental Education.[14] Kestrel contributes to the Center's educational programs as well as helping maintain and improve the building and grounds.

For the 1998 fiscal year, Kestrel had revenue mostly from contributions and government grants of about $80,000. An annual appeal letter is the major funding device. It also places collection jars for public contributions at community events.

A part-time administrator is paid an hourly wage. Help with many tasks is provided by the conservation commissions; the trust also makes use of legal and other professionals, pro bono if possible, paid if necessary.[15]

Both Rattlesnake Gutter Trust and Valley Land Fund are newer than Kestrel. Rattlesnake Gutter's main objective is the protection of a remarkable large rocky ravine that originated as a glacial spillway. The vegetation of the gutter is rich hemlock–northern hardwood forest.[16] Kestrel Trust helped with the first land deal, a key 40-acre parcel in the Gutter purchased by the town of Leverett in 1990.

One of Rattlesnake Gutter's clever fund-raising ideas is collecting returnable bottles and cans at the Leverett Transfer Station, or Dump, and taking them to the nearest redemption center. This may seem a paltry source of money, but Massachusetts does not have an arrangement whereby bottles can be turned in at every grocery and convenience store. The Trust receives $2,000 to $3,000 per year from bottle deposits. To celebrate the Dump's importance, the 1996 annual meeting was held there. The two volunteers who had borne the brunt of the work were crowned Redemption Kings.[17] Rattlesnake Gutter's income for fiscal 1998 was less than $22,000. It has no staff.

Valley Land Fund was set up to be able to do deals where a broader focus was needed. Its purview is the whole Massachusetts section of the Connecticut River Valley.[18] Much of the early direction of the Valley Land Fund came from Terry Blunt, currently with the Massachusetts Department of Environmental Management. In the late 1960s, Blunt worked at the western office of The Nature Conservancy with Huey Johnson, later founder of the Trust for Public Land. Blunt admired Johnson's skills in buying land needed by public agencies and reselling it to them for more money. Valley tries to emulate this method of facilitating the acquisition of publicly desirable land. Kestrel and various other land trusts in Massachusetts and elsewhere do the same, but there are still states and local governments not yet enlightened enough to have funds dedicated to purchasing land for protection.

Valley Land Trust is relatively uninterested in owning and stewarding land. With some misgivings, it has begun to take conservation easements, realizing that monitoring and eventually defending the easements represents an escalating commitment. Valley believes that facilitating deals by others is as important as saving land on its own. Through 1999, it had been involved in about ninety land-saving deals, totaling well over 4,000 acres. Most deals involved between one and four partners.

Revenue in fiscal 1998 was about $250,000, mostly from contributions. In other recent years, income had never approached $100,000.

Valley is low-key. It doesn't publish a newsletter or much else. Its one-page brochure gives its philosophy and its pitch: "As we are an all-volunteer organization, with no office rent or glossy mailings to cover, your tax-deductible contribution will go directly towards land preservation."

Terry Blunt said, "I personally think if you have a dedicated bunch of directors, you don't need staff."[19] Many of Valley's directors are professionals with expertise related to land conservation. The whole board does title searches, and they divide up other jobs. Tasks outside their expertise, they contract for. "With staff and a non-active board, you begin to get board members who just want their names on the letterhead," Blunt said. "We cut to the chase and say we're in the land trust business, not the bake sale business."

The Western Pennsylvania Conservancy

The Western Pennsylvania Conservancy (WPC) is a large and successful land trust, but it is best known as the organization entrusted with the Frank Lloyd Wright house called "Fallingwater."

Fallingwater is a remarkable structure cantilevered over a waterfall on Bear Run, 60 miles southeast of Pittsburgh. A 1991 poll of the members of the American Institute of Architects voted it the best all-time work of American architecture. Built in the late 1930s, it was used by the Edgar J. Kaufmann family as a weekend retreat. The Kaufmanns were a prominent Pittsburgh family, philanthropists, patrons of the arts, and owners of the city's premier department store.

When Edgar Kaufmann, Sr., died in 1955, Fallingwater came to the family's only child, a son whose name the WPC always renders as "Edgar Kaufmann, jr. (sic)." Nevertheless, most news accounts steadfastly refer to him as Edgar Kaufmann, Jr. He continued to use the house until 1963. Then, following his father's wishes, he offered it, the surrounding grounds, and a half-million dollar endowment to the WPC. The conditions were that the building and grounds be maintained and operated as a cultural center open to public visitation.[20]

I can imagine the soul-searching at any land trust faced with such an offer. There was land associated with Fallingwater, 1,300 acres of oak forest on the ridges and mesic forest in the ravines, that any land trust ought to be happy to own. But with the land and the stream came a house that would require continuous maintenance—many times more than any ordinary house—and, further, that had to be open to the public. And things would need to be done right, because Pittsburgh and every Frank Lloyd Wright fan would be watching.

WPC did what it probably had to do. It accepted the gift. Over 20,000 visitors came the first year, instead of the few hundred that were expected.[21] Current attendance is 150,000 per year. As the decades went by, visitor facilities were upgraded, including the construction of a new visitors' pavilion. Building maintenance and restoration were constant companions.

In the mid-1990s, concern over the continuing deterioration of the house caused WPC to hire an engineering firm to analyze and prescribe for the house's problems. The worst problem was the continuing droop of the concrete main deck, which amounted to seven inches at one corner. This made the national news, generating stories with headlines on the order of "Fallingwater is Falling Down."

Temporary scaffolding was installed as a stopgap, but the remedy for stabilizing the cantilevers is an expensive process using high strength steel cables installed along the major concrete beams. Adding in other needed restorative procedures brought the bill to $7 million.[22]

Even compared with other large, successful land trusts, WPC is a wealthy organization. Edgar Kaufmann, jr., had added to the Fallingwater endowment over the years. This endowment and others, plus other capital funds, amount to around $40 million. In fiscal 1998, WPC's revenues from these investments was about $1.5 million. But WPC had already spent large amounts of money on the house in the two preceding years, and the $7 million was needed quickly. A capital campaign was launched in 1999 specifically to fix Fallingwater. The original $7 million goal was eventually raised to $11.5 million, as additional needs became evident.[23]

WPC might bridle at a characterization of Fallingwater as the tail that wags the dog, but it's clear that a large part of the organizational effort goes to this single project. Clear it is, too, that the organizational mission has metamorphosed as a result of Fallingwater. The fifty-year history of WPC in 1982 characterized the mission in straightforward land trust fashion: "The conservancy has one essential purpose: to conserve water, land, and wildlife."[24] Current characterizations, four decades later, are different. On its Web site, the following is attributed to Larry Schweiger, president and CEO: "Fallingwater is the flagship of Western Pennsylvania Conservancy because it represents a metaphor of WPC's vision and work—protecting outstanding elements of creation while protecting and enhancing the built environment. . . ."[25]

The Western Pennsylvania Conservancy began in 1932 as the Greater Pittsburgh Parks Association (GPPA), which consisted of about a dozen wealthy Republicans with civic interests. Its most noteworthy achievement was the acquisition of McConnells Mill northwest of Pittsburgh in 1945, the first and, except for adjacent properties along Slippery Rock Creek, only land project.[26] McConnells Mill was a traditional Sunday outing site—swimming in the old mill pond, hikes on the trails in the hemlock gorge. It was one of those privately owned scenic sites once found throughout the United States but now mostly gone, either through development or by becoming parks. This one eventually became McConnells Mill State Park.

In the mid-1940s, several local conservationists were persuaded by Frank W. Preston that land in the watershed of Muddy Creek—a little east of McConnells Mill—ought to be protected. Preston was a British immigrant who operated a glass research company.[27] He had broad science and technology interests and contributed some slight but original insights in community ecology.

A nonprofit organization was needed to hold the Muddy Creek land. The group selected the GPPA, but when they began to try to raise money they found that people in the surrounding counties wouldn't donate to a "Greater Pittsburgh" organization.[28] Actually, the GPPA might have come to that same realization earlier; in its original fund raising for McConnells Mill in the 1940s, it was unsuccessful in raising any money from the closest city, New Castle.[29]

Preston proposed that the name of the organization be changed to Western Pennsylvania Conservancy (after the British Nature Conservancy). This was at a meeting on 18 October 1950, about a month after the Ecologists Union voted to become The Nature Conservancy.[30] Preston had briefly been a board member of TNC. The name change for the western Pennsylvania group became official in March 1951.

The aim of the Western Pennsylvania Conservancy (WPC) was quite different from that of the GPPA. The newly named organization was imbued with a sense of the need to find and protect remaining natural areas. It had a strong scientific orientation coming from Preston and several others, including herpetologist Graham Netting and botanist O. E. Jennings, both connected with the Carnegie Museum of Natural History.

Netting, a Pennsylvania native with a Ph.D. from the University of Michigan, served as secretary of the GPPA and then the WPC for several decades. His history of WPC, *Fifty Years of the Western Pennsylvania Conservancy*, is probably the best and most attractive history of a land trust so far.[31] The only close rival, or perhaps equal, is the hundred-year history of the Trustees of Reservations done by Gordon Abbott, Jr.[32]

WPC continues to save land, some of which it holds but most of which is now, as in the past, sold to public agencies. In the old days, prior to 1981, most funding for such purchases was from the federal Land and Water Conservation Fund.[33] In all, WPC has protected more than 200,000 acres. Current holdings—land that is owned as well as land on which conservation easements are held—total about 43,000 acres.[34]

Unusual among land trusts is WPC's large Community Conservation program, which supports gardens in the Pittsburgh area: beautification projects along roads, school gardens tended as "outdoor laboratories," and various types of community gardens. One-fourth of WPC's program service budget goes to these various types of gardens and plantings.

Nearly 40 percent of WPC's program service money, about $2.1 million, goes to Fallingwater. Admissions to Fallingwater bring in about $1.2 million annually.

WPC, though not a membership organization, has about 25,000 supporters. The Board is selected in a process that involves the executive staff and the current board members. Although large, the board has little or no representation from outside the city of Pittsburgh. The staff includes more than 160 members, including Fallingwater as well as the Pittsburgh office.

Green Horizon Land Trust

The survey I sent to a couple of hundred land trusts in 1996 included the question, "Does your conservancy have any special feature or emphasis that you see as different from the average conservancy?" The executive director of the Green Horizon Land Trust (GHLT), an honest man, answered, "No." This is probably the correct answer for many land trusts, and an honorable one. Saving land is one of the most important things anyone can do and needs no embellishments.

Nevertheless, GHLT is not without distinctive features. In its central Florida service area, it specializes in lands of the Lake Wales Ridge, a north-south band of highlands made up of ancient beach sands with old dunes up to 300 feet above current sea level. The ridge is a striking feature in a basically flat state. More importantly, the droughty, sterile sand supports a rich biota with a high percentage of endemic species.[35]

The natural ecosystems, with their threatened and endangered organisms, have already been destroyed on 85 percent of the uplands. These ridgelands are still being converted to citrus plantations, pasture, or development, or even just cleared and left idle to avoid government regulations that might apply if someone found one of the threatened or endangered species on the land.[36]

The uplands were originally clothed with two main vegetation types: sand pine scrub and sandhill vegetation. In the latter, longleaf pine grew in open stands with an understory of wiregrass. Such longleaf pine forests and savannas once dominated much of the coastal plain from southeastern Virginia to eastern Texas, but they've been nearly obliterated by grazing, fire suppression, and lumbering.

Sand pine scrub is the most distinctive community of the Lake Wales Ridge. Nearly restricted to Florida, scrub occurs mostly on this ridge system and others of similar origin. The two communities, longleaf and scrub, are both fire dependent, but the longleaf areas were visited by frequent, even annual, low-intensity fires that kept the community much the same from one five-year period to the next.

Scrub, on the other hand, was burned under natural conditions only once every several decades. Forty, fifty, or eighty years after a fire, scrub is generally dominated by sand pines 25 feet tall, and with a lower story of dwarf evergreen oaks. But scrub exists in a cyclically varying structure based on time since the last fire. The intense fires, when they come, kill pretty much all the above-ground vegetation. The oaks, saw palmetto, and most other shrubs and herbs resprout from roots, but the sand pines must grow from seeds. The result is that scrub in the years following a fire has a low, open, broad-leaved structure. Just as the ocean beach is still the ocean beach whether the tide is in or out, this open vegetation with its groundcover of gopher apples and lichens is as much scrub as the dense thickets of pine and oak that eventually develop.

Sand pine scrub is a minor ecoregion in geographical extent but major in its contribution to biodiversity. It also has a major writer, Marjorie Kinnan Rawlings, author of *The Yearling* and other books set in the Big Scrub of northern Florida. There, Ocala National Forest captures some parts of the natural landscape not yet lost to Disney World and other commercial interests. In the best of her books, *Cross Creek,* Rawlings wrote of why she and others chose to live in this wild landscape. "We need above all, I think, a certain remoteness from urban confusion."[37] But remoteness, of course, is exactly what is being lost.

Several organizations are cooperating to try to save the Lake Wales landscape. Among them are government agencies and nonprofits such as Audubon societies, The Nature Conservancy, and Archbold Biological Station. Archbold's research programs focus on organisms and interactions of the local ecosystems on and around its 5,100 acres. Particularly intensive studies have been done on the Florida scrub jay, an endangered species of the more open phases of sand pine scrub.[38]

Most of these organizations concentrate on large blocks of habitat, some already preserved in the sense that the land is owned by a public agency or nonprofit organization. A group of citizens concluded that smaller, but still ecologically significant parcels were being neglected. This was the origin of GHLT, founded in 1991.

GHLT is not a membership organization; it has a board of about a dozen trustees, who elect the next board. Its regular supporters number about 120 families and individuals. The executive director, Luther Parrott, has been the only staff member, but grant support has been sought to add positions, including a development person.[39]

Like many of the current generation of land trust executive directors, Parrott's background is not in land conservation; he was a banker. After he retired, he agreed to take the job with the new land trust, thinking it sounded like fun. It is, but it has also turned into hard work. "When I'm able to get out in the field these days, I'm negotiating deals," he said.

The deals most often involve locating land that deserves protection, taking an option on it, arranging with an appropriate government agency to buy it, and then having a simultaneous closing, so that GHLT owns the land only momentarily. Some land is donated, and this is also generally transferred to a government agency. In Florida, protection of environmentally important land has had a high priority at several levels of government. GHLT has passed through land to both the Polk County land protection program and the South Florida Water Management District.

GHLT has shied away from retaining ownership of land. This is partly because of its need to recoup purchase costs, but also because it fears what it sees as the never-ending need for stewardship.

GHLT does not neglect altruistic motives for land protection, but it's also frank about the financial benefits. "Green Horizon Land Trust can turn your problem real estate into tax savings!" says one brochure, which goes on to define trade lands and concludes, "Your gift of a trade land will make the magic work!" The approach is successful. A local attorney gave the land trust a $150,000 office building in the Lake Wales historic district in 1998. Though most of it was leased to The Nature Conservancy as a field office, GHLT opened a small office of their own there—with a large Green Horizon sign in front.

One of GHLT's most aesthetically pleasing fund-raising ventures were two collector's prints, the Florida scrub jay and sandhill crane, made available as gifts to new supporters. Diane Pierce, a wildlife artist and Lake Wales resident, painted the watercolors and donated the signed, numbered prints to GHLT.

Big Sur Land Trust

Big Sur is 3,000 miles west of the Amherst, Massachusetts, land trusts and a long way from them in other dimensions as well. Its annual fund-raising dinner in June 1999 was "An Evening with Ted Turner." Among the 250 attendees were Ted Turner and Jane Fonda, Clint and Dina Eastwood, Jean-Michel Cousteau, and Leon Panetta, President Bill Clinton's first Chief of Staff.[40] The weekly *Carmel Pine Cone* called it "a glittering event."[41]

Big Sur Land Trust (BSLT) was founded to preserve the scenic, rocky coast in Monterey County, California, where the Santa Lucia range rises steeply from the Pacific. Later, the Trust extended its service area south to include the north edge of Monterey Bay. In so doing, the trust connected the spectacular mountainous coast of Robinson Jeffers with the sandy beaches, mudflats, and Cannery Row of John Steinbeck.

In the 1970s, few places in the United States were as obviously deserving of protection as the lands along Highway 1 from Carmel south to San Simeon. Many other large landscapes with the same power to move the human mind and spirit had already been lost or sadly compromised, but much of the Big Sur region was intact.

The idea that a land trust was needed came out of a coastal planning process encouraged by state government. After the interested parties acquainted themselves with how Eastern land trusts operated, a process facilitated by the Trust for Public Land (TPL), they filed incorporation papers in 1978. Six families, including long-time general counsel Zad Leavy, were the leaders.[42]

The first land deal was half interest in a 26-acre parcel at the north border of Esalen Institute at Big Sur. Esalen is a retreat founded in 1962 with the aim of exploring unrealized human capacities. The gift was by one of the Esalen founders. TPL held the half interest until BSLT's federal tax-exempt status came through.

This was also true for the second land deal, the 3,000-acre Gamboa Ranch. The trust bought the land for about half the appraised value from nineteen New York lawyers, who had foreclosed on a mortgage. The lawyers were credited with a $900,000 charitable donation. After putting a highly restrictive conservation easement on the property, BSLT sold it to David and Lucille Packard for the price it had paid to the lawyers.

BSLT has claimed this deal as the first use of the conservation buyer strategy.[43] "We were on the cutting edge," Zad Leavy said.

BSLT's 1,100-acre Mitteldorf Preserve was bought in 1990 from a lumber company. Several sessions of a nature center day camp are held there each summer. The program is unusual in being free. Another education initiative is "Nature's Journal," a trademarked name for a program in which elementary and junior high students in Monterey County classrooms prepare illustrated journals.

Although BSLT has been a successful land trust for many years, its success took a leap forward in the late 1990s. Income in fiscal 1997 was more than $8 million and $3 million in 1998, but as recently as 1994 it was closer to $1 million. Expenses for 1998 were more than $9 million. Almost $8 million of this was for the purchase of conservation easements.

BSLT's 1998 balance sheet showed, among other assets, about $4 million dollars in investments, mostly U.S. Treasury notes in a ladder reaching out five years and mutual funds. Membership is about 2,000.

Corey Brown, formerly with TPL, succeeded Zad Leavy as executive director in October 2000.

By 2001, BSLT had completed about one hundred transactions that protected about 20,000 acres of increasingly high-priced real estate. Approximately 3,000 acres are held by BSLT, 10,000 are easements, and 7,000 were passed on to various agencies. Then, in May 2002, the amount of land protected jumped 50 percent with one deal.

BSLT and the California chapter of The Nature Conservancy bought the 9,898-acre Palo Corona Ranch for $37 million, a bargain price since the owner, Craig McCaw, had put it on the market for $65 million. The property runs as an elongated, crooked "L" from the edge of Carmel southward 10 miles to Los Padres National Forest. On the way, it connects the preserved habitats of Point Lobos State Preserve, Garrapata State Park, Joshua Creek Canyon Ecological Preserve, the Ventana Wilderness, and nine other protected areas. To pay off their loans, the two land trusts will receive $32 million from California's Proposition 40 (an environmental bond issue passed in March 2002) and $5 million from the Monterey Regional Park District. They will also do some fund raising for a stewardship endowment, though it's likely that most of the land will be conveyed to the California Department of Parks and Recreation.[44]

Iowa Natural Heritage Foundation

In 1833, at the time of the first permanent white settlement in what would become Iowa, most of the land was tall-grass prairie of big bluestem, Indian grass, and many forbs. There were bison and elk and wolves. Almost the only woods were the strips of oaks and other trees that outlined the floodplains and bluffs of the streams.

That was then.

Today, nearly 90 percent of the state's acreage consists of cropfields, pastures, and feedlots. Corn, hogs, and soybeans are the big three. This percentage was achieved by obliterating the prairie—in 1980 only 3,000 out of the original 30,000,000 acres remained—by cutting much of the originally treed land, and by draining the shallow lakes and sloughs. The original 7,000,000 acres of wetlands had been reduced to 60,000 by 1980.[45]

This was the landscape in which the Iowa Natural Heritage Foundation (INHF) was established in the summer of 1979 with the aim of facilitating the acquisition of natural lands. There was less left to save than in many states, but, on the other hand, the list of high priority sites was easy to compile.

The organization opened an office in Des Moines, the state's capitol and largest city, current population about 200,000. There were a dozen original board members, but thirty-three more were added within the first year. A

Des Moines advertising group produced an evocative motto, "For those who follow."[46]

By 1980, the INHF had received its first land, 130 acres they named Whitham Woods. This mixed area with planted conifers, some oaks and hickories, and a small pond would probably not have appeared on a priority list of state natural areas, but it was 130 acres, a donation, and what Iowa organization would not be glad to have as its first preserve a gift from a supporter whose name was Daisy Iowa Whitham?

Setting what has become its usual pattern, the organization passed the land on—by lease, in this case—to a government agency for management.

Mark Ackelson, currently president of the INHF, joined the organization in 1980 to negotiate and find funding for a $3.5 million, 1,400-acre purchase of the Mines of Spain. The parcel has 3½ miles of Mississippi River frontage just south of the city of Dubuque. It's in the Driftless Area, a region of spectacular terrain unlike the rest of Iowa, with deep-cut gorges and bluffs at the edge of the Mississippi floodplain. The odd name, Mines of Spain, came from the Governor of Spain in New Orleans, who in 1788 granted Julien Dubuque the right to operate lead mines on the site.

Most of the forest on the parcel was cut for steamboat fuel in a twenty-five-year period from 1865 to 1890; however, some trees were spared, including large bur oaks that date back to the time of settlement.

This northeast corner of Iowa, along with the adjacent corners of Wisconsin and Illinois, forms a pocket that many geologists believe was never covered with glacial ice. The gorges and cliff-faces hold a substantial number of plants with limited geographic ranges in or centered on the Driftless area. The most interesting group, having implications for movements of the biota during glaciation, consists of a few species that occur on shaded cliffs here and occur elsewhere only in similar habitats south of the glacial border, in southern Ohio, Indiana, and Kentucky.[47]

Over the years, the INHF has accepted about fifty gifts of land and fifty conservation easements. It has also helped protect other land in partnership with state or local government. Its Web site claims 50,000 acres "protected or restored." Outright land protection is, however, only a part of what INHF does. It is heavily involved in cooperative ventures with government, sportmen's groups, private industry, and individual farmers.

As an example of such activities, the organization helped out the Natural Resources Conservation Service (NRCS) with its Wetland Preserve Program. The backlog of applications in Iowa for this U.S. Department of Agriculture program had grown so large that Washington refused to pay for any more easements until the backlog was fixed. The Wetlands Preserve Program is a purchase-of-development-rights program in which the government gives farmers money and they give up the right to continue farming the wetlands and also give up development rights.

According to INHF, "Limited by a national hiring freeze, the NRCS state wetlands office turned to INHF for help." INHF recruited two law students willing to process easements as interns and raised $7,500 from the NRCS's usual partners, such as Pheasants Forever, to pay them. The interns broke the back of the backlog and federal PDR money flowed again to the farmers of Iowa.[48]

Following the floods of 1993, INHF made creative use of a related program, the Emergency Wetland Reserve Program. The program is similar to the ordinary Wetlands Reserve Program but is basically flood relief, triggered by disasters. INHF helped farmers who were farming floodplains enroll in the program. Once the federal government had paid the farmers for the easements, INHF either bought the land—now less expensive with development and farming rights gone—or accepted it as gifts. For the farmers, such gifts would help offset the income from the easement sales.

Most such land, with its requirement for wetland restoration, is passed on to government agencies, often to county parks. In an article on restoration by land trusts, these sites are mentioned with the comment that, "available restoration resources vary according to each county's financial resources and environmental policies." This may be a diplomatic way of saying that little wetland restoration gets done on a substantial number of the sites.[49]

Some might argue that the narrow and repetitive work of processing easements doesn't provide the professional growth and insights into land conservation that students should be able to expect from an internship. Aside from such ad hoc efforts, however, INHF has an evidently thriving internship program through which pass ten to twelve students a year. The design is one that other land trusts might emulate.

The stated aims are that interns will complete significant projects, such as developing site management plans, reconstructing prairies, and researching grant opportunities. Also, they will receive regular training that covers job duties, nonprofit operations, and Iowa's natural features. Applicants are college students, undergraduate or graduate, in a variety of curricula including environmental studies, communications, and landscape architecture. They must be Iowa residents or enrolled at an Iowa college. Hourly pay for interns in 2000 was substantially above minimum wage. Funding is from earmarked trust money.[50]

More than most land trusts, INHF has been involved in trail and greenway establishment. Its initial involvement with two early rail-trails, in the early 1980s, "galvanized those who promoted or opposed trails," according to the organization's twenty-year history.[51] Nevertheless, INHF persisted and has been involved in about twenty of the state's forty-five trails.[52] An advocacy group, the Iowa Trails Council, has also been an important force. In most of the state today, opposition tends to be light and short-lived, except in pockets of property rights activism.[53]

A 1998 cooperative project produced the longest trail in the state, the 63-mile Wabash Trace Nature Trail along the former Wabash Railroad. It slants across the southwest corner of Iowa in the Loess Hills region, a strip along the Missouri River with hills and bluffs formed of deep deposits of fine silt. The loess is wind-deposited outwash blown from the broad bed of the river when it was a drainageway carrying water from the glacial front.

"The Foundation will be funded from the generosity of private citizens concerned with Iowa's future," said the original mission statement of INHF, and that's true, to a degree. Of the revenue for fiscal 1998, about $4.7 million, almost half was from contributions and memberships. There are about 4,500 members. Much of the rest of the $4.7 million was from "program services," mostly contractual payments for assistance to other organizations.

Expenditures totaled about $3.2 million, mostly going to "program services." Program services in this case are broader than program services in the revenue sense. The category includes staff salaries for those providing the contracted services, but also most other expenditures other than fund raising and support services.

The balance sheet at the end of 1998 showed assets of nearly $8 million, of which about $6.5 million was in investments. This was a 36 percent increase during the fiscal year.

Michigan Nature Association

The Michigan Nature Association is not well known outside of Michigan but ought to be. A case can be made that it is the purest land trust of them all. As of 2000, the MNA had about 160 preserves owned in fee simple. A few were gifts, but most were bought. No government money has ever been used. The MNA holds only a few easements and has passed no parcel through to any government agency.

In 1981, when about two dozen land trusts were invited to meet in Cambridge as the National Consultation on Local Land Conservation, the MNA was not among them, nor was it at a similar, smaller meeting in San Francisco later that same year. Nevertheless, in 1981, when leaders of these groups, with their five, ten, or twenty properties protected, were congratulating themselves on being pioneers, the MNA had already bought and paid for sixty-five preserves.

The MNA has had many people in nominal leadership roles and has managed to attract hundreds of dedicated volunteers, including many competent naturalists. However, the direction, tone, and projects of the organization have mainly been set by one of the founders, long-time Executive Secretary-Treasurer Bertha Antonie Daubendiek.

Daubendiek (by her pronunciation, Dobbindick) grew up on farms in Montana, where she was born in 1916, and Iowa. After a B.A. from Grinnell College, she moved to Michigan and soon became a court reporter. She stayed in this profession until 1971, when she retired to devote full time to the MNA.

Daubendiek has never taken a salary, and much of the work of the organization is done by volunteers. However, the organization does employ paid staff, who are only occasionally identified in the organization's publications. For fiscal 1998, salaries and wages were a little over $85,000, just under 40 percent of the organization's total functional expenses. Its office has for many years been the upstairs of Daubendiek's house near the village of Avoca.

In the home town of my youth, the J. C. Penney store had a system of cables that ran from each sales counter to a central point in a balcony above the sales floor. When you bought something, the clerk put your money and the sales slip in a cup, pulled a handle, and the cup ran along the cable to someone in the balcony who handled all the cash. The structure of the MNA reminds me of that J. C. Penney store. All lines run to Avoca, and details of land deals and finances are known to few.

The MNA began in 1952 as the St. Clair Metropolitan Beach Sanctuary Association, a local group formed to protect a common tern nesting site. This problem solved, the organization changed its name in 1954 to Macomb Nature Association and spent five years trying to educate the people of the northern Detroit metropolitan region about the destructive effects of urban sprawl on nature. Association leaders gave talks, published leaflets, and sponsored a Junior Nature Patrol.[54]

In a chronology of the organization, the laconic entry for 1958 reads, "Realized educational efforts were not saving a single acre of wild land, that natural areas in southeastern Michigan were rapidly disappearing, and that there was a need for outright purchase of some natural areas. . . ." A white paper sent to leading conservation organizations in the state urging such a program brought no action, so the Macomb Nature Association decided it would have to do it itself. This has been the organization's method, and its creed, ever since.[55]

The organization assembled a list of ninety-five prospective purchases and found five willing landowners. It borrowed $15,000 for down payments and by the end of 1960 owned its first preserve, Red Wing Acres.

A final name change, to Michigan Nature Association, occurred in 1970 about the time the organization began a project at the far northern tip of the Upper Peninsula of the state, 650 miles from the Detroit suburb where it was born. The project was Estivant Pines, a stand of virgin white pines, one of only two sizable tracts that survived Michigan's Timber Era. The MNA preserve that resulted includes about 400 acres of large pine groves and buffer areas.

The MNA has followed a consistent approach. Its aim is to set aside preserves that include every species of plant or animal known to occur in Michigan. It's no trick to find land that will save cardinals and chickadees, so the tactic has been to search out the rare species and buy the land where they live.

The founders were not scientists; in the early days, the best guide they had to what they should be trying to protect was a Michigan Conservation Department bulletin, *Living Beauty, Michigan's Rare Wild-flowers,* listing thirty-three species. In 1968, a skilled amateur botanist with taxonomic interests, Robert Kilgore, began helping direct the search. He compiled a "want list" of less-common native plant species not yet represented on MNA preserves, and the search intensified. Even though the first preserve was named for a bird, the early emphasis was heavily on plants. More attention was paid to animals after state lists of endangered and threatened species became available in 1975. Also increasingly sought were examples of natural community types and natural features such as waterfalls and heron colonies.[56]

The MNA's approach has been similar to that followed for a time by The Nature Conservancy. In effect, the MNA has had its own Heritage program or Natural Features Inventory going for forty years. It hunts down the rare, threatened, and endangered species and communities. Then it buys the land that holds them.

Since the organization is continually buying land, it is also continually fund raising. Some of the money comes from individual donors, often in modest amounts; what fraction of the total comes in this way is hard to determine. Wherever it comes from, the total of gifts, grants, and contributions for the five-year period from 1994 to 1998 was about $3.1 million. Through most of the MNA's history, its emphasis was on fundraising for individual land purchases rather than an endowed land fund, but it has accumulated capital of about $1 million.

The MNA's approach to preserving biodiversity has been successful. An assessment in 1988 found that the organization's preserves at that time included 82 percent of the state's native plant species. Most of the other 18 percent are known only from already protected lands or else are probably extirpated. MNA preserves included half of all the state's species listed as threatened, endangered, or of special concern.[57] Perhaps no other local or state land trust could make similar claims—or would have the data to back them up if it did.

This is not to say that the MNA's methods have been without fault. A serious early problem was the tendency to protect areas too small to sustain the target species over the long term. Often, only a few acres or less—the small area actually occupied by a rare species—were purchased, even though a larger area was available that would have provided a buffer and included a bigger sample of the biotic community to which the species belonged. This defect has been moderated, and, in fact, the organization now often adds to the size of its preserves by later purchases.

Another problem has been insufficient attention to stewardship. The tendency has been to concentrate resources on acquiring preserves and then letting them take care of themselves. Although the criterion for choosing lands has been science based, the attitude toward management has not. Suspicion of active management, especially the use of fire, has allowed some of its preserves to deteriorate.

One way in which the MNA has differed from the conventional land trust is its willingness to engage in advocacy. It started as an activist organization and has not flinched from advocacy since. Among other battles, the MNA proposed the Michigan Natural Beauty Roads Act and led the fight to get it adopted. It protested oil drilling in a state forest and refused to join in the compromise agreed to by other environmental groups that eventually allowed the oil wells in.

The organization has shown the temperament of a pit bull in meeting threats to its own property, a trait valuable to any land trust no matter how much it avoids general advocacy. In 1973, MNA intervened in U.S. Atomic Energy Commission hearings to license two new nuclear power plants for Detroit Edison. The transmission lines would have occupied much of Red Wing Acres. The MNA won the concession that the lines would go around instead of through the preserve, but in the end, with the collapse of the nuclear power industry, Detroit Edison cancelled plans for the new plants.

With MNA's emphasis on owning land instead of holding easements, on keeping land instead of passing it on to government, on saving organisms and communities rather than open space or working landscapes, on going it alone rather than seeking partnerships, on volunteers rather than paid staff—in all these ways, MNA seems old fashioned. Maybe it's a relict, like the places it most likes to save—the patches that remain of the landscapes that the Indians and first settlers saw. But perhaps relict isn't quite the right word. Maybe we ought to think of both the organization's mission and the fragments of the natural landscape as irreplaceable models of how things could be.

A CLEANER, GREENER LAND

"Without a positive vision of the future, conservationists are doomed to fight, and probably lose, a series of rearguard actions," cautioned a 1997 book on the ecological basis of conservation.[1] Most of us have heard people say—perhaps said it ourselves—that the trouble with environmentalists is that they're prophets of gloom and doom. Even if they're right, we don't want to hear it anymore.

One reason land trusts are effective is that the land trust approach *is* positive. Land trusts say, Land needs to be saved because of all the good things that come from preserved land. They don't spend time threatening people with the dire consequences of not saving land (though dire they are, I'd say—but in parentheses). Another aspect of the positive approach is that land trusts are proactive. Land needs saving, they say; we'll save it. If other types of organizations and the government also save land, that's great, but we're not going to wait for them.

Land trusts are positive and proactive and effective and efficient. They're doing a lot of things right. But they're not perfect; here are some ways they could do things better.

What Lands to Save. Land trusts should give priority to lands that serve the functions for which land ought to be saved: maintaining biodiversity and ecosystem services. This implies trying to save all the natural and nearly natural land that is left. Land trusts may also wish to save land that yields ecosystem goods, such as food and fiber. If so, they should emphasize those working lands that keep the soil intact and export nothing harmful beyond their borders—no pesticide, herbicide, fertilizer, silt, noise, or stench. If farmland or other working land becomes surplus to its practical or commercial function, every effort should be made to return it to the region's natural successional pathways.

Bringing Back Science. Most early land trusts (as well as land advocacy organizations) were begun by people with strong science or natural history backgrounds: Charles Eliot, William Brewster, John Muir, William Dudley, John Merriam, Henry Fairfield Osborn, Victor Shelford, George Fell. For recent land trusts, post-1960, this has been much less true. We all owe a debt of gratitude to the lawyers, urban planners, environmentalists, M.B.A.s, and the rest who took up the slack. But the time has come for the scientists who study the Earth and its inhabitants to return to practical conservation. Too many land trusts don't have the expertise to choose the land that is most important or to take care of it. Land trusts need to recruit more scientists for their boards and other volunteer positions as well as more young people trained in science for their staffs. For their part, biologists, geologists, and scientifically inclined geographers need to take the service component of their professional commitment seriously and get involved in land trust operations.

Educating Public Interest Land Specialists. The workshops and other training sessions put on by the Trust for Public Land and later by the Land Trust Alliance (recently joined by The Conservation Fund) have done a good, even essential job, but usually a narrow, nuts-and-bolts one. What we really need to produce "a new profession of public-interest land specialists," as Huey Johnson hoped, are academic programs. One model might be a master's program that used a supplementation approach. Students from a variety of backgrounds could enroll; their graduate coursework would be chosen to fill gaps. For example, a biology major whose undergraduate work had included ecology and systematics might spend most of his or her time taking courses in geography, geology, agriculture, law, marketing, and business. An internship at a land trust and a research project could be included. Departments at one or several universities, using the LTA as a resource, need to get to work.

Nothing Beats Data. The activities and effects of land trusts need to be seen as subjects for research. Useful studies have been on done on the costs of community services (COCS), effects of preserved land on adjacent property values, motivations of land donors, costs of monitoring easements, local cultural effects on land conservation, and a few other topics. But the surface has barely been scratched. More needs to be known about almost everything concerning land trust operations and their conservation consequences. It is desirable to have more and better data on the frequency of easement violations and the costs of correcting them. Equally important is information on infringements on preserves. We probably are not going to learn anything fundamental by doing more COCS studies, but more sophisticated studies of the fiscal impacts of development versus preservation would have things to tell us. What is the comparison of land protected (types and amounts) per dollar expended for unstaffed land trusts and those with various levels of staffing? The shape of the resulting curve might suggest optimal land trust staff size: 1, 10, as many as possible, or 0. On these topics and many others, testimony and anecdote are interesting, but nothing beats data.

Taking Easements Seriously. Conservation easements are a revolutionary tool for protecting land but are still nearly untested. The Land Trust Alliance has always been on the right side in recommending that they be done correctly, which involves careful drafting, immediate and thorough baseline surveys, at least yearly monitoring, prompt attention to violations, and an unmistakably adequate enforcement fund. But only recently has the urgency for implementing these measures been well conveyed. For the sake of land trusts holding easements—in other words, almost every land trust nowadays—and for the sake of the land, these obligations need to be taken seriously.

A Return to Fee. Because of the unproven stability of conservation easements, land trusts ought to pay more attention to acquiring lands in fee. That's one reason for land trusts to own land. They also ought to do this for all the other advantages that land ownership brings—the ability to steward the land to best advantage and to provide public access where appropriate, for example. For close to twenty years, the land trust community has been putting most of its eggs in the easement basket. Maybe that will turn out to be a big winner. But when you can't know the future, it's a mistake to bet against diversity. Having diverse ways of protecting land may turn out to be as important as the biological diversity on the chosen parcels.

Sound Stewardship. Land protection doesn't mean just acquiring land or rights to it; it also means taking care of the land. A responsible land trust with a dedicated and knowledgeable crew of staff and volunteers will always do the best job of stewardship. More land trusts need to take on stewardship responsibilities. In situations where this is impossible, land trusts need to devote serious effort to assuring that a good stewardship job is done by the government agencies to which property is transferred and by the owners of easement-protected lands.

The Second Essential. Protecting land is one of two essential tasks for a land trust. The second is a corollary: maintaining a viable organization. This involves several jobs, many of which are easy or fun. Probably the hardest and least enjoyable for most people is raising money to assure financial viability. Staff and volunteers needn't have raising money uppermost in their minds, but every situation they encounter ought to trigger an assessment of its fund-raising potential as automatic as looking both ways for traffic. For the board, fund raising should be a prime concern—on a par with organizational ethics and effectiveness.

Education, Education, Education. No land trust can do everything. Each is unique, a product of its place and its people. Some land trusts will choose to help with community gardens or land-use planning; others won't. But one activity that more land trusts need to take on is education. The audience is the public at large. Two obvious mandatory subjects are the ways of protecting land and the values that flow from protected land. Every newsletter, press release, and talk should routinely promote such knowledge, but special initiatives are also needed, particularly ones aimed at families and children. A third obligatory topic for education is a sense of place. Land trusts need to learn the history, the natural history, the literature, and the art that deals with the lands and waters of home. Expressing what makes this place special—words and pictures that catch the landforms, the vistas, the flora and fauna, the sights and smells—will connect with people who love their home habitat and, perhaps, also with those who so far have lived oblivious of place.

Some members of the land trust community aim to protect land, others to protect the Earth. A group was writing the case statement for a land trust. (A case statement is the message about why an organization exists and is worthy of support. Inspirational is better than plodding.) A sentence had been included to the effect that the land trust would make the region a cleaner, greener land. Someone on the committee said, "That's good. Yes. . . . When we make statements like that, I always have to add to myself, 'cleaner and greener than it would be without us.'"

In the long run, we hope that land trusts, together with other people and other organizations, will make the world a better place, better than it is now. That worthy effort may fail, and the trends of overexploitation and degradation may continue or worsen. If so, we will have done our best, in a way that was constructive, hopeful, and full of love for the land and the people here today and yet to come. Even if land trusts fail to save the Earth, they will at least have made the Earth a better place than it would have been without them.

NOTES

Preface (pages ix–xi)

1. The 1996 Survey: In July 1996, I sent out questionnaires to 216 land trusts, about 20 percent of the approximately 1,095 in the Land Trust Alliance's 1995 *National Directory of Land Trusts*. A stratified random sampling method was used to select land trusts in numbers proportional to the numbers operating in each state. A postcard reminder was sent to land trusts that had not responded by September.

The questionnaire was long, twelve pages, and covered many aspects of land trust operations. Included were questions on several topics for which little information was currently available, such as land management techniques in use, easement violations, easement endowments, characteristics of board members, and educational initiatives.

Seventy usable questionnaires (32 percent) were returned. The only evident biases were a high rate of return from Michigan and a low rate of return from California, or perhaps the whole Pacific Coast region. A higher rate of return from staffed trusts, where someone is being paid to spend time filling out forms, might be a potential source of bias. Fifty-four percent of the trusts responding had at least part-time staff. Of the trusts listed in the 1995 directory (1994 data), 46 percent had at least part-time staff; by 1998, the percentage had grown to about 50 percent. It's possible, then, that staffed land trusts—hence possibly larger and more affluent—were slightly over-represented in the 1996 sample.

Introduction (pages 1–12)

1. Joy Williams, "One Acre," *Harper's Magazine* 302 (February 2001): 59–65.
2. Not every land trust would necessarily be interested in protecting a property as small as this one.
3. See chapter 10 for more about the Illinois Natural Areas Commission.
4. John William Hardy, "Records of Swainson's Warbler in Southern Illinois," *Wilson Bulletin* 67, no. 1 (1955): 60.
5. Rasa Gustaitis, "The Wonders of Joel Hedgpeth," *California Coast & Ocean* 15, no. 1 (1999): 20–23.
6. Joel W. Hedgpeth, "Progress—The Flower of the Poppy," *American Scientist* 35, no. 3 (1947): 395–400.
7. J. Ronald Engel, *Sacred Sands* (Middletown, Conn.: Wesleyan University Press, 1983).
8. Rachel Carson, *Silent Spring* (Boston: Houghton Mifflin, 1962).

9. William J. Darby, "Silence, Miss Carson!" *Chemical and Engineering News* (1 October 1962): 60–63.

10. Tom Knudson, "Fat of the Land," *Sacramento Bee,* 5-part series, 22–26 April 2001.

11. Stephen Fox, *The American Conservation Movement* (Madison: University of Wisconsin Press, 1985).

12. John T. Curtis, *The Vegetation of Wisconsin* (Madison: University of Wisconsin Press, 1956).

13. Richard Brewer, "Characteristics of Land Trust Boards," *Exchange* 16, no. 3 (1997): 8–11.

14. Pamela K. Stone, *National Directory of Local and Regional Land Conservation Organizations* (Bar Harbor, Maine: Land Trust Exchange, 1986); Rob Aldrich, personal communication, 1 March 2002.

15. Martha Nudel, "Conserved Acreage, Numbers of Trusts Soared in the 1990s," *Exchange* 20, no. 4 (2002): 5–7.

16. Institute for Community Economics, *The Community Land Trust Handbook* (Emmaus, Pa.: Rodale Press, 1982).

17. Charles C. Geisler, "In Land We Trust," *Cornell Journal of Social Relations* 15, no. 1 (1980): 98–115.

18. Michael L. Fischer, "The Land Trust Community: The Strongest Arm of the Conservation Movement," delivered to Napa County Land Trust, 5 October 1996.

Chapter 1. History (pages 13–40)

1. Henry David Thoreau, *The Maine Woods* (1862; reprint, New York: Thomas Y. Crowell, 1961).

2. Otherwise unattributed facts, dates, and Charles Eliot quotations are from Charles W. Eliot, *Charles Elliot: Landscape Architect* (Boston: Houghton Mifflin, 1902).

3. Judith B. Tankard, *Charles Eliot: The Education of a Landscape Architect* (Cambridge: Mass.: Harvard University Frances Loeb Library Graduate School of Design, 1987).

4. Keith N. Morgan, "Held in Trust: Charles Eliot's Vision for the New England Landscape," *National Association for Olmsted Parks Workbook* series 1 (1991): 1–98.

5. Thomas Jefferson, "Notes on the State of Virginia," in *The Life and Selected Writings* (1782; reprint, New York: Modern Library, 1944).

6. Jacob A. Riis, *How the Other Half Lives* (1890; reprint, New York: Hill and Wang, 1957).

7. Ibid.

8. Tankard, *Charles Eliot.*

9. Gordon Abbott, Jr., *Saving Special Places* (Ipswich, Mass.: The Ipswich Press, 1993).

10. Edward L. Rand and John H. Redfield, *Flora of Mount Desert Island, Maine, with a Geological Introduction by William Morris Davis* (Cambridge, Mass.: John Wilson and Son University Press, 1894).

11. Ian L. McHarg, *A Quest for Life* (New York: John Wiley & Sons, 1996).

12. The first survey typically included in the formal ecology canon is the exploration of Isle Royale led by Charles C. Adams between 1903 and 1906. This work, by Adams and H. A. Gleason, both pioneers of the science of ecology, and two other experienced biologists understandably shows a level of ecological sophistication well beyond the Mount Desert Island group.

13. Richard Brewer, "A Brief History of Ecology, Part 1—Pre-nineteenth Century to 1919," *Occasional Papers of the Charles C. Adams Center for Ecological Studies* 1 (1960): 1–18.

14. Ian L. McHarg, *A Quest for Life.*

15. My calculations; a 1900 population base of 560,000 gives a ratio of 58.8.

16. Abbott, *Saving Special Places.*

17. Frank Graham, Jr., *The Audubon Ark* (New York: Alfred A. Knopf, 1990); Oliver H. Orr, Jr., *Saving American Birds* (Gainesville: University Press of Florida, 1992).

18. Graham, *The Audubon Ark.*

19. Thoreau, *The Maine Woods.*

20. Samuel H. Scudder, "The Alpine Club of Williamstown, Mass.," *Appalachia* 4 (1884): 45–54.

21. John Ritchie, "Fifty Years of Progress," *Bulletin of the Appalachian Mountain Club* 19, no. 7 (1926): 323–46; Charles W. Blood, "The Club Reservations," *Appalachia* 31 (1956–1957): 210–15.

22. Holway R. Jones, *John Muir and the Sierra Club* (San Francisco: Sierra Club, 1965).

23. Michael P. Cohen, *The History of the Sierra Club 1892–1970* (San Francisco: Sierra Club, 1988).

24. Jones, *John Muir.*

25. Charles Richard Van Hise, *The Conservation of Natural Resources in the United States* (New York: Macmillan, 1910).

26. Stephen Fox, *The American Conservation Movement* (Madison: University of Wisconsin Press, 1985).

27. Jones, *John Muir.*

28. Reprinted in *Sierra* (October 1993): 58.

29. Fox, *The American Conservation Movement.*

30. Based on data provided by the Land Trust Alliance.

31. Sylvester Baxter, "A Trust to Protect Nature's Beauty," *American Monthly Review of Reviews* 23, no. 1 (1901): 42–48.

32. Abbott, *Saving Special Places;* Eliot, *Charles Eliot.*

33. Joseph H. Engbeck, Jr., *State Parks of California* (Portland, Ore.: C. H. Belding, 1980); Susan Rita Schrepfer, *A Conservative Reform: Saving the Redwoods 1917–1940,* Ph.D. diss., History, University of California, Riverside, 1971.

34. Willie Yaryan, Denzil Verardo, and Jennie Verardo, *The Sempervirens Story* (Los Altos, Calif.: The Sempervirens Fund, 2000).

35. Ibid.

36. Ibid.

37. Schrepfer, *A Conservation Reform.*

38. Madison Grant, "Saving the Redwoods," *Zoological Society Bulletin* 22, no. 5 (1919): 91–118.

39. John B. Dewitt, *California Redwood Parks and Preserves* (San Francisco: Save-the-Redwoods League, 1993).

40. The Web site is <www.savetheredwoods.org>.

41. Save-the-Redwoods League, "Save-the-Redwoods League Purchases Key Forest Habitat for Wildlife Corridor from the Redwoods to the Sea," press release at <www.savetheredwoods.org>, 4 October 1999; Idem., "Ancient Redwoods Protected," press release at <www.savetheredwoods.org>, 13 June 2001.

42. Peter Farquhar, *A Brief Summary of the Save-the-Redwoods League August 1917 to February 1921* (San Francisco: Save-the-Redwoods League, 1964).

43. John van der Zee, *The Greatest Men's Party on Earth* (New York: Harcourt Brace Jovanovich, 1974); Suzanne Bohan, "Movers, Shakers from Politics, Business

Go Bohemian: Annual Sonoma Fête Draws Bushes, Kissinger, Powell, Gingrich," *Sacramento Bee,* 2 August 1999: 11.

44. Schrepfer, *A Conservation Reform;* Susan R. Schrepfer, *The Fight to Save the Redwoods* (Madison: University of Wisconsin Press, 1983).

45. George E. Street, *Mount Desert Island: A History* (Boston: Houghton Mifflin, 1926).

46. Judith S. Goldstein, *Tragedies and Triumphs: Charles W. Eliot, George B. Dorr, John D. Rockefeller, Jr.: The Founding of Acadia National Park* (Somesville, Maine: Port in a Storm Bookstore, 1992).

47. Ibid.; Samuel A. Eliot [published as S. A. E.], *The Hancock County Trustees of Public Reservations: An Historical Sketch and a Record of the Holdings of the Trustees* (Bar Harbor, Maine: Trustees of Hancock County Trustees of Public Reservations, 1939).

48. Goldstein, *Tragedies and Triumphs.*

49. Fox, *The American Conservation Movement.*

50. R. Shaffner, *Brief History of the Highlands Improvement Society* (Highlands, N.C.: Highlands Land Trust, 1997).

51. M. Graham Netting, *Fifty Years of the Western Pennsylvania Conservancy* (Pittsburgh: Western Pennsylvania Conservancy, 1982).

52. "Special Report: The 1994 National Land Trust Survey," *Exchange* 13, no. 4 (1994): 2.

53. A. F. Gustafson et al., *Conservation in the United States* (Ithaca, N.Y.: Comstock Publishing Co., 1947); James M. McEflish, Jr., Philip Warburg, and John Pendergrass, "Property: Past, Present, Future," *Environmental Forum* 13 (1996): 20–35.

54. Aldo Leopold, *A Sand County Almanac* (1949; reprint, London: Oxford University Press, 1968).

55. Based on dates of formation of existing land trusts in data supplied by the Land Trust Alliance.

56. From the Web site, <www.lta.org>, 17 September 2001.

57. Jack D. Gunther, "How to Preserve Small Natural Areas," *Catalyst for Environmental Quality* 3, no. 3 (1973): 19–22.

58. Frederick John Pratson, "Yankee Heritage is Secured without Government Aid," *Smithsonian* 8 (June 1977): 92–99; Hal Rubin, "Reserves, Preserves, and Land Trusts," *Sierra* (November–December, 1979): 27–32.

59. William H. Whyte, Jr., *Securing Open Space for Urban America: Conservation Easements,* Urban Land Institute Technical Bulletin no. 36 (1959): 1–67.

60. Russell L. Brenneman, *Private Approaches to the Preservation of Open Land* (New London, Conn.: Conservation and Research Foundation, 1967).

61. Ian McHarg, *Design with Nature* (Garden City, N.Y.: The Natural History Press, 1969).

62. Jennie Gerard, personal communication, 31 August 1999.

63. Joan Vilms, personal communication, 1 April 1999.

64. Jennie Gerard, personal communication, 31 August 1999.

65. Kingsbury Browne, ed., *Case Studies in Land Conservation,* numbers 1–6. (Boston: New England Natural Resources Center, 1976–1977).

66. Comments by Kingsbury Browne at 18 October 1996 Land Trust Alliance Rally.

67. "A Perspective on the Land Trust Movement: An Interview with Kingsbury Browne," *California Waterfront Age* 3, no. 4 (1987): 38–40.

68. Alan D. Spader, Leonard Wilson, and Terry Bremer, "National Consultation on Local Land Conservation: A Review," in *Private Options: Tools and Concepts for Land Conservation,* ed. Barbara Rusmore, Alexandra Swaney, and Alan D. Spader (Covelo, Calif.: Island Press, 1982), 14–132.

69. Richard D. Cochran, personal communication, 21 September 2001.

70. Jeanie McIntyre, personal communication, 21 September 2001.

71. William H. Dunham, "Call to Action," in *Private Options,* 9–11.

72. Figures are from Kirkpatrick Sale, *The Green Revolution* (New York: Hill and Wang, 1993).

73. Sierra Club, *Defend Our Resources: Replace Interior Secretary Watt* (San Francisco: Sierra Club, undated [1981]).

74. David Hess, "It's Watt vs. Udall for Control of the Country's Riches," *Detroit Free Press,* 6 September 1981: 4B.

75. Jean Hocker, "Cutbacks in Public Land Acquisition: Opportunities for Innovation," in *Private Options,* 226–28.

76. "1964 and All That—A Quick History of the Land and Water Conservation Fund Program" at <www.ncrc.nps.gov/lwcf/history>, 2001.

77. Phyllis Myers, "Financing Open Space and Landscape Protection: A Sampler of State and Local Techniques," in *Land Conservation through Public/Private Partnerships,* ed. Eve Endicott (Washington, D.C., 1993) 223–57.

78. Martin J. Rosen, *Trust for Public Land Founding Member and President, 1972-1997: The Ethics and Practice of Land Conservation* (Berkeley: Regional Oral History Office, the Bancroft Library, University of California, 2000).

79. Hocker, "Cutbacks."

80. Terry Bremer, "A Review of the 1981 National Survey of Local Land Conservation Organizations," in *Private Options,* 177–81.

81. From Land Trust Alliance Web site, <www.lta.org>.

82. Bremer, "A Review of the 1981 National Survey."

83. Land Trust Alliance, *1994 National Land Trust Survey* (Washington, D.C.: Land Trust Alliance, 1995).

84. Data for the graph for 1950 to 2000 are from the 2000 National Census summary on LTA Web site. For 1910 to 1940, numbers are based on founding dates as given in LTA directories with a few corrections, such as correction of Block Island Land Trust founding date from 1896 to 1986 and inclusion of the Hancock County Trustees for 1910 to 1930.

Chapter 2. Sprawl (pages 41–56)

1. James Howard Kunstler, *The Geography of Nowhere* (New York: Simon & Schuster, 1993).

2. Rick Bragg, "It's the Traffic, Not the Heat, that Makes Miami Torpid," *New York Times,* 4 August 1999: Y12.

3. Sam Bass Warner, Jr., *The Urban Wilderness* (New York: Harper & Row, 1972).

4. Kenneth T. Jackson, *Crabgrass Frontier: The Suburbanization of the United States* (New York: Oxford University Press, 1985).

5. Data on new housing starts is from *Historical Statistics of the United States,* pt. 2, Chapter N., U.S. Department of Commerce Bureau of the Census, 1975.

6. Buzz Bissinger, *A Prayer for the City* (New York: Random House, 1997).

7. Ibid.; Jackson, *Crabgrass Frontier.*

8. Charles Schmidt, "The Specter of Sprawl," *Environmental Health Perspectives* 106, no. 6 (1998) at <www.plannersweb.com/sprawl/focus.html>; Andrew Guy, "Fuel for Thought," *The Paper,* 6–12 July 2000: 9.

9. Charles W. Eliot, *Charles Eliot: Landscape Architect* (Boston: Houghton Mifflin, 1902).

10. Robert E. Coughlin and John C. Keene, *The Protection of Farmland: A Reference Guidebook for State and Local Governments* (Washington, D.C.: U.S. Government Printing Office, no date [1981]).

11. James Howard Kunstler, *Home from Nowhere* (New York: Simon & Schuster, 1996).

12. Warner, *The Urban Wilderness.*

13. Kunstler, *Home from Nowhere.*

14. John D. Warbach and Mark A. Wyckoff, *Local Tools & Techniques to Achieve Smart Growth* (Lansing, Mich.: Planning and Zoning Center and Land Information Access Association, 1999); Schmidt, "The Specter of Sprawl."

15. Ken Zapinski, "The Debate over Urban Sprawl," *Cleveland Plain Dealer,* 22 October 1996: B1, B10.

18. David Poulson, "Small Wetlands Get Little Protection from Regulators," *Kalamazoo Gazette,* 26 July 1999: A5.

17. "The Most Dangerous Intersections in USA," *USA Today,* 27 June 2001: 1A.

18. David Schrank and Tim Lomax, *2001 Urban Mobility Study* (College Station: Texas Transportation Institute, 2001).

19. Robert D. Putnam, "Bowling Alone: America's Declining Social Capital," *Current* (June 1995): 3–9.

20. Robert D. Putnam, "Tuning In, Tuning Out: The Strange Disappearance of Social Capital in America," *PS: Political Science and Politics* (December 1995): 664–83.

21. Robert D. Putnam, *Bowling Alone: The Collapse and Revival of American Community* (New York: Simon and Schuster, 2000); Lance Freeman, "The Effects of Sprawl on Neighborhood Social Ties," *Journal of the American Planning Association,* 67 (no. 1): 69–77.

22. Cat Lazaroff, "Suburban Sprawl Contributes to Poor Health," *Environmental News Service* Web site <ens.lycos.com/ens/nov2001/2001L-11-06-07.html>, 2001.

23. One critical review is Randal O'Toole, "Fake CDC Study Full of Holes," *Environment and Climate News* <www.heartland.org/environment/jan02/cdc.htm>, January 2002.

24. Larry Fish, "N. M. Official Links Land Use to Fatal Heroin Overdoses," *Philadelphia Inquirer,* 9 December 2001.

25. Ibid.

26. Morton White and Lucia White, *The Intellectual Versus the City* (New York: Mentor, 1964).

27. Warbach and Wyckoff, *Local Tools.*

28. Joseph Perkins, 1999, "Gore's Growth Policy Not Smart," *Kalamazoo Gazette,* 3 March 1999: A8.

29. Robert Costanza, "Social Traps and Environmental Policy," *BioScience* 37, no. 6 (1987): 407–12.

30. Russell Shay, *Voters Invest in Open Space: 1998 Referenda Results* (Washington, D.C.: Land Trust Alliance, 1999).

31. Timothy Beatley, *Green Urbanism* (Washington D.C.: Island Press, 2000).

32. Victoria Ranney and George Ranney, Jr., personal communication, 24 November 2000.

33. Diane Mastrull, "The Woodmont Proposal," *Philadelphia Inquirer,* 6, 7, and 8 May 2001.

34. Natural Lands Trust, *Growing Greener* (Philadelphia: Natural Lands Trust, 1997).

Chapter 3. Why Save Land? (pages 57–77)

1. Much of this chapter expands on chapter 19 in Richard Brewer, *The Science of Ecology,* 2nd ed. (Philadelphia: Saunders College Publishing, 1994); the Ingalls quotation is from Walter M. Kollmorgen, "On the Inferiority of Prairie Grass and Other Pioneer Doctrines," *Prairie Plains Journal* 13 (1998): 26–29.

2. Victor E. Shelford, ed., *The Naturalist's Guide to the Americas* (Baltimore: Williams and Wilkins, 1926).

3. As in Fred Waage, "The Dump Chronicles," *Interdisciplinary Studies in Literature and Environment* 6, no. 1 (Winter 1999): 95–103.

4. Albert Fein, *Frederick Law Olmsted and the American Environmental Tradition* (New York: George Braziller, 1972).

5. Cathy Jean Maloney, *The Prairie Club of Chicago* (Chicago: Arcadia Publishing, 2001).

6. J. Ronald Engel, *Sacred Sands* (Middletown, Conn.: Wesleyan University Press, 1983); Robert E. Grese, *Jens Jensen: Maker of Natural Parks and Gardens* (Baltimore: Johns Hopkins University Press, 1992).

7. Ian McHarg, *Design with Nature* (Garden City, N.Y.: The Natural History Press, 1969).

8. Stanley White, "The Value of Natural Preserves to the Landscape Architect," in *The Naturalist's Guide,* 8–9.

9. Hugh H. Iltis, "A Requiem for the Prairie," *Prairie Naturalist* 1 (1969): 51–57.

10. Franz X. Bogner and Michael Wiseman, "Environmental Perception of Rural and Urban Pupils," *Journal of Environmental Psychology* 17 (1997): 111–22.

11. Roger S. Ulrich et al., "Stress Recovery During Exposure to Natural and Urban Environments," *Journal of Environmental Psychology* 11 (1991): 201–30.

12. Carolyn Tennessen and Bernadine Cimprich, "View to Nature: Effects on Attention," *Journal of Environmental Psychology* 15 (1995): 77–85.

13. Ernest O. Moore, "A Prison Environment's Effect on Health Care Service Demands," *Journal of Environmental Systems* 11, no. 1 (1982): 19–34.

14. Roger S. Ulrich, "View through a Window May Influence Recovery from Surgery," *Science* 224 (1984): 420–21.

15. Hugh H. Iltis, "Biological Diversity, and the Social Responsibility of the Systematic Biologist," Presented at a symposium, *The Role of the Systematist in the Population and Environmental Crisis,* American Institute of Biological Sciences, August 1970, Bloomington, Indiana.

16. Gretchen C. Daily, ed., *Nature's Services* (Washington, D.C.: Island Press, 1997).

17. Norman Myers, "Biodiversity's Genetic Library," in *Nature's Services,* 255–73.

18. Kirsten Ferguson, "Upstream New York," *American Farmland* 19 (Fall, 1998): 14–17.

19. Robert Costanza et al., "The Value of the World's Ecosystem Services and Natural Capital," *Nature* 387 (15 May 1997): 253–60.

20. Robert Costanza et al., "The Value of Ecosystem Services: Putting the Issues in Perspective," *Ecological Economics* 25 (1998): 67–73.

21. David Pilz et al., "Mushrooms and Timber," *Journal of Forestry* 97, no. 3 (1999): 4–11.

22. Bill Krasean, "Key to Stent's Success Lies in Exotic Fungus," *Kalamazoo Gazette,* 13 May 2002: C2.

23. "Fungal Formulas: Industry, Academics, and Conservationists Team Up to Hunt for New Drugs in a New York Preserve," Cornell University Press release at <www.news.cornell.edu/releases/Feb98/bioprospect2.hrs.html>, 27 February 1998.

24. William Moir, "Natural Areas," *Science* 177 (1972): 396–400.

25. May Theilgaard Watts, *Reading the Landscape of America* (New York: Collier Books, 1975).

26. Robert B. Smythe, with Charles D. Laidlaw and Carol Fesco, *Density-related Public Costs* (Washington, D.C.: American Farmland Trust, 1986).

27. Data for Massachusetts is from Leah J. Smith and Philip Henderson, *Cost of Community Services Study for Truro, Massachusetts*, Association for the Preservation of Cape Cod, 2001; data for Georgia is from Nanette Nelson and Jeffrey Dorfman, *Cost of Community Service Studies for Habersham and Oconee Counties, Georgia*, University of Georgia Center for Agribusiness and Economic Development Special Report no. 5 (2000); data for Michigan is from Laura Friedeman Crane, Michelle M. Manion, and Karl F. Spiecker, *A Cost of Community Services Study of Scio Township*, Washtenaw-Potawatomi Land Trust, 1996; data for Texas is from Margaret Allie Bowden, *The Cost of Community Services in Hays County, Texas*, M.S. Report Department of Community and Regional Planning, 2000; data for Washington is from Town of Dunn, at <userpages.churs.net/towndunn/cos/htm>, 1994.

28. Crane, Manion, and Spieker, *A Cost of Community Services Study of Scio Township*.

29. Deb Brighton, *Open Land, Development, Land Conservation and Property Taxes in Maine's Organized Municipalities* (Brunswick, Maine: Maine Coast Heritage Trust, 1997).

30. Smythe, *Density-related Public Costs*.

31. Gene Bunnell, "Fiscal Impact Studies as Advocacy and Story Telling," *Journal of Planning Literature* 12, no. 2 (1997): 136–51.

32. Fred Bayles, "Nightmare of Buildings that Stand Empty Haunts Cities," *USA Today*, 20 March 2000, A21–22.

33. Deb Brighton, *Property Taxes in Vinalhaven, Maine* (New Brunswick, Maine: Maine Coast Heritage Trust, 1996).

34. Brighton, *Open Land*.

35. Steve Lerner and William Poole, *The Economic Benefits of Parks and Open Space* (San Francisco: The Trust for Public Land, 1999).

36. Thomas R. Hammer, Robert E. Coughlin, and Edward T. Horn, "The Effect of a Large Urban Park on Real Estate Value," *AIP Journal* 40 (July, 1974): 274–77; Mark R. Correll, Jane H. Lillydahl, and Larry D. Singell, "The Effects of Greenbelts on Residential Property Values," *Land Economics* 54, no. 2 (1978): 207–17.

37. Spencer Phillips, "Windfalls for Wilderness: Land Protection and Land Values in the Green Mountains," in *Wilderness Science in a Time of Change Conference*, volume 2, ed. Stephen F. McCool (Ogden Utah: USDA Forest Service Rocky Mountain Research Station, 2000), 258–67.

38. Lerner and Poole, *Economic Benefits*.

39. Phillips, *Windfalls for Wilderness*.

40. Aldo Leopold, *Game Management* (1933; reprint, New York: Charles Scribner's Sons, 1948).

41. J. Baird Callicott, ed., *Companion to "A Sand County Almanac"* (Madison: University of Wisconsin Press, 1987).

42. Aldo Leopold, *A Sand County Almanac* (1949; reprint, London: Oxford University Press, 1968).

43. John Muir, *A Thousand-mile Walk to the Gulf* (1916), reprinted in *John Muir: The Eight Wilderness-Discovery Books* (London: Diadem Books, 1992).

44. Clara Barrus, *The Heart of Burrough's Journals* (Boston: Houghton Mifflin, 1928).

45. James Oliver Curwood, *God's Country, The Trail to Happiness* (New York: Cosmopolitan Book Corporation, 1921).

46. Daniel Quinn, *Ishmael* (New York: Bantam Books, 1992); idem, *The Story of B* (New York: Bantam Books, 1996).

47. Loren Wilkinson, ed., *Earthkeeping* (Grand Rapids, Michigan: Eerdmans Publishing Company, 1980).

48. C. N. Catrevas, Jonathan Edwards, and Ralph Emerson Browns, *The New Dictionary of Thoughts* (Standard Book Company, 1960).

Chapter 4. Who Will Save the Land? (pages 78–96)

1. Alexander B. Ruthven, "The Edward K. Warren Foundation and Two Wild Life Reservations in Michigan," *Science* 49 (1919): 17–18.

2. Mike Phillips, "Conserving Biodiversity on and Beyond the Turner Lands," *Wild Earth* 10, no. 1 (2000): 91–94; Bill Lickert, "Ted Turner's Deep Pockets," at <www.green-watch.com/top20/deep_pockets.asp>, 2002.

3. John T. Carter, *Louis Bromfield and the Malabar Farm Experience* (Mattituck, N.Y.: Amereon House, 1995).

4. John L. Pulley, "Iowa State's Handling of a Bequest Leaves Critics Questioning its Values," *Chronicle for Higher Education* 48, no. 2 (2001): A38.

5. Class findings were substantiated by research by Christy Stewart. The 278-year-old oak was by Stewart's careful count.

6. W. J. Gillbert, "The Harvey N. Ott Biological Preserve of Albion College," *Michigan History* 38 (1954): 157–67.

7. "County Completes Purchase of Ott Biological Preserve," *Battle Creek Enquirer*, 20 July 1977.

8. Robert H. Levin, "When Forever Proves Fleeting: The Condemnation and Conversion of Conservation Land," *New York University Environmental Law Journal* 9 (2001): 591–637.

9. Calhoun County Parks and Recreation Commission, Harvey N. Ott Biological Preserve Application to Land and Water Conservation Fund (1975).

10. Karen Emerson, "Kindest Cut of All for Forest," *Battle Creek Enquirer*, 14 January 1994.

11. C. G. Smith, "Not 'Kindest Cut'," *Battle Creek Enquirer*, 28 January 1994: 6A.

12. Manuscript copy of Daniel Skean, "Talk to [Calhoun] County Commission," 1994.

13. Karen Emerson, "County Board Halts Logging on Delicate Nature Preserve," *Battle Creek Enquirer*, 4 March 1994.

14. George W. S. Trow, "The Harvard Black Rock Forest," *New Yorker* (11 June 1984): 44–89.

15. David Ehrenfeld, *Beginning Again* (New York: Oxford University Press, 1993).

16. Trow, "The Harvard Black Rock Forest."

17. Tom Horton, "Of Tall Trees, Thrushes, and a Sacred Trust," *Land and People* 9, no. 1 (1997): 7–13.

18. Robert E. Stewart and Chandler S. Robbins, *Birds of Maryland and the District of Columbia* (Washington, D.C.: U.S. Fish and Wildlife Service North American Fauna No. 62, 1958).

19. Horton, *Of Tall Trees.*

20. Pamela Cooper, personal communication, 25 April, 17 July 2000.

21. Most of the specifics in this section are from Jim Northup, "Joseph Battell, Once and Future Wildlands Philanthropist," *Wild Earth* 9, no. 2 (1999): 15–22.

22. Robert Braile, "Despite Wish, Vt. Parcel 'Primeval' No More," *Boston Globe,* 15 July 1999: A1.

23. Jim Northup, personal communication, 16 June 2000.

24. Joan Dranginis, "A Day at Pepperwood," *Madrone Audubon Society Leaves Newsletter* 30, no. 8 (1997).

25. George Lauer, "Pepperwood Preserve North of Santa Rosa Is Lively Example of Nature's Classroom," *Santa Rosa Press Democrat,* 25 April 2002.

26. Thomas B. Allen, *Guardian of the Wild* (Bloomington: Indiana University Press, 1987).

27. Much of the specifics and otherwise unattributed quotations are from Alston Chase, "The Betrayal of Claude Moore." *Outside* 12 (November, 1987): 41–42, 44.

28. Allen, *Guardian of the Wild.*

29. Chase, "The Betrayal of Claude Wood."

30. Ibid.

31. Allen, *Guardian of the Wild.*

32. Levin, "When Forever Proves Fleeting."

33. Jon Binhammer, personal communication, 22 August 2000.

34. *National Audubon v. Hoffman,* U.S. Second Circuit Court of Appeals, docket nos. 96-6037, 96-6049.

35. Wilderness Society, "Lamb Brook Survives Yet Another Attempt at Logging and Road Building," Conservation Coast to Coast at <www.wilderness.org/ccc/northeast/lambrook.htm>, 1998.

36. Evan Hill, *A Greener Earth* (Concord, N.H.: Society for the Protection of New Hampshire Forests, 1998).

37. Howard Mansfield, *The Same Ax, Twice* (Hanover, N.H.: University Press of New England, 2000).

38. Hill, *A Greener Earth.*

39. Rosemary Conroy, "The People Behind the Society," *Forest Notes* (229, 2001): 10–11.

40. Charles Niebling, personal communication, 20 June 2000.

41. Karen W. Arenson, "Making Those Good Causes Do What the Donor Intended," *New York Times,* 24 August 1997, 10.

42. Robert H. Levin, "When Eminent Domain Comes Knocking," *Exchange* 20, no. 2 (2001): 389–93.

Chapter 5. Choosing Land to Save (pages 97–114)

1. Aldo Leopold, *A Sand County Almanac* (1949; reprint, London: Oxford University Press, 1968).

2. Richard Brewer, *The Science of Ecology,* 2nd ed. (Philadelphia: Saunders College Publishing, 1994).

3. Michael Soulé, *Conservation Biology* (Sunderland Mass.: Sinauer Associates, 1986).

4. The quotation from the bird-finding guide is Olin Sewall Pettingill, *A Guide to Bird Finding East of the Mississippi* (New York: Oxford University Press, 1951); William B. Robertson, Jr. and Glen E. Woolfenden, *Florida Bird Species* (Gainesville: Florida Ornithological Society, 1992).

5. Reed F. Noss and Allen Y. Cooperrider, *Saving Nature's Legacy* (Washington, D.C.: Island Press, 1994).

6. Robert S. Rogers, "Early Spring Herb Communities in Mesophytic Forests of the Great Lakes Region," *Ecology* 63, no. 4 (1982): 1050–63.

7. Andrew J. Hansen et al., "Global Change in Forests: Responses of Species, Communities, and Biomes," *BioScience* 51, no. 9 (2001): 765–773; Linda A. Joyce and Richard Birdsey, eds., "The Impact of Climatic Change on America's Forests," USDA Forest Service Gen. Tech. Rep. RMRS-GTR59 1–133, 2000; and Louis R. Iverson et al., "Atlas of Current and Potential Future Distributions of Common Trees of the Eastern United States," USDA Forest Service Gen. Tech. Rep. NE-265 1–245, 1999.

8. Iverson et al., "Atlas of Current and Potential Future Distributions."

9. Robert L. Peters, "Conserving Biological Diversity in the Face of Climate Change," in *Biodiversity and Landscapes,* ed. Ke Chung Kim and Robert D. Weaver (Cambridge: Cambridge University Press, 1994), 105–32.

10. J. M. Scott et al., "Gap Analysis: A Geographic Approach to Protection of Biological Diversity," *Wildlife Monographs* 123 (1993): 1–41.

11. L. Hannah et al., "Conservation of Biodiversity in a Changing Climate," *Conservation Biology* 16, no. 1 (2002): 264–68.

12. James C. Woodruff, "LaSalle's Walk on the Wild Side," *Michigan History* 83, no. 2 (1999): 6–15.

13. Anna D. Chalfoun, Frank R. Thompson III, and Mary J. Ratnaswamy, "Nest Predators and Fragmentation: A Review and Meta-analysis," *Conservation Biology* 16, no. 2 (2002): 306–18.

14. Rosie Woodroffe and Joshua R. Ginsberg, "Edge Effects and the Extinction of Populations Inside Protected Areas," *Science* 280 (1998): 2126–28.

15. Francis C. Golet et al., "Relationship between Habitat and Landscape Features and the Avian Community of Red Maple Swamps in Southern Rhode Island," *Wilson Bulletin* 2 (2001): 217–27.

16. R. W. Howe, G. J. Davis, and V. Mosca, "The Demographic Significance of 'Sink' Populations," *Biological Conservation* 57 (1991): 239–55.

17. No case like this is known, but an island population of the black-footed rock-wallaby came close, having only 10 percent of its genes with more than one alternative form (allele). Mainland populations average three or four alleles per gene; Mark D. B. Eldridge et al., "Unprecedented Low Levels of Genetic Variation and Inbreeding Depression in an Island Population of the Black-Footed Rock-Wallaby," *Conservation Biology* 13, no. 3 (1999): 531–41.

18. R. Lande and G. F. Barrowclough, "Effective Population Size, Genetic Variation, and Their Use in Population Management," in *Viable Populations for Conservation,* ed. M. E. Soulé (Cambridge: Cambridge University Press, 1987), 87–124.

19. Paul Beier and Reed F. Noss, "Do Habitat Corridors Provide Connectivity?" *Biological Conservation* 12, no. 6 (1998): 1241–52.

20. In my 1996 survey, 54 percent of the responding land trusts said their acquisition approach was wholly opportunistic, 38 percent said ecological factors were at least partly considered, and 7 percent indicated a planned approach based on nonecological considerations.

21. David E. Morine, "Preserving the Pascagoula," *TNC News* 26, no. 4 (1976): 12–16.

Chapter 6. Stewardship (pages 115–38)

1. Alice S. Lumpkin, "Protecting Land through Ownership," *Exchange* 8, no. 4 (1989): 14.

2. N. Linda Goldstein et al., "Recreational Use Statutes: Why They Don't Work," *Exchange* 9, no. 2 (1990): 10–12, 18; John C. Becker, "Landowner or Occupier Liability for Personal Injuries and Recreational Use Statutes: How Effective is the Protection?" *Indiana Law Review* 24 (1991): 1587–1613.

3. Such as in Stephen J. Small, *Preserving Family Lands: Essential Tax Strategies for the Landowner,* 2nd ed. (Boston: Landowner Planning Center, 1992).

4. Pete Holloran, "Deliberate Amateurs," *Fremontia* 26, no. 4 (1998): 73–75.

5. F. E. Clements and V. E. Shelford, *Bio-ecology* (New York: John Wiley & Sons, 1939).

6. Mary F. Willson, Scott M. Gerde, and Brian H. Marston, "Fishes and the Forest," *BioScience* 48, no. 6 (1998): 455–62.

7. Richard Brewer, "Original Avifauna And Postsettlement Conditions," in *The Atlas of Breeding Birds of Michigan,* ed. Richard Brewer, Gail McPeek, and Raymond J. Adams, Jr. (East Lansing, MI: Michigan State University Press, 1991), 33–58.

8. U.S. Department of the Interior Fish and Wildlife Service, "Proposed Rule to Remove *Potentilla Robbinsiana* (Robbins' Cinquefoil) from the Endangered and Threatened Plant List," *Federal Register* 66 no. 111 (2001): 1–12.

9. Bruce A. Stein and Frank W. Davis, "Discovering Life in America," in *Precious Heritage,* ed. Bruce Stein, Lynn S. Kutner, and Jonathan S. Adams (Oxford: Oxford University Press, 2000), 19–53.

10. Jim Aldrich, personal communication, 5 April 2002.

11. *The Flora of Ashland: Wooded Pastures and Wilderness Remnants* at <www.henryclay.org/flora.htm>; Marjorie S. Becus and John B. Klein, "Mowing Schedule Improves Reproduction and Growth of Endangered Running Buffalo Clover (Ohio)," *Ecological Restoration* 20, no. 4 (2002): 295.

12. Richard Brewer, *The Science of Ecology,* 2nd ed. (Philadelphia: Saunders College Publishing, 1994).

13. Richard Brewer, "A Half-Century of Changes in the Herb Layer of a Climax Deciduous Forest in Michigan," *Journal of Ecology* 68 (1980): 823–32.

14. M. L. Fernald, "Must All Rare Plants Suffer the Fate of Franklinia?" *Journal of the Franklin Institute* 226, no. 3 (1938): 383–97.

15. George W. Cox, *Alien Species in North America and Hawaii* (Washington, D.C.: Island Press, 1999).

16. John D. Madsen, "Methods for Management of Nonindigenous Aquatic Plants," in *Assessment and Management of Plant Invasions,* ed, James O. Luken and John W. Thieret (New York: Springer-Verlag, 1997), 143–71.

17. Brian C. McCarthy, "Response of a Forest Understory Community to Experimental Removal of an Invasive Nonindigenous Plant (*Alliaria petiolata,* Brassicaceae)," in *Assessment and Management of Plant Invasions,* 117–30.

18. George W. Cox, *Alien Species.*

19. D. Q. Thompson, R. L. Stuckey, and E. B. Thompson, *Spread, Impact, and Control of Purple Loosestrife* (Lythrum salicaria) *in North Amrican Wetlands* (U.S. Department of Interior Fish and Wildlife Service, 1987).

20. The name Warren G. Kenfield is said to be a pseudonym of Frank Egler—in real life a mildly contrarian plant ecologist—formed as an anagram, not of "Frank Egler," of course, but of "Frank Edwin Egler." Fewer Kingel Rand is another anagram, but if Egler ever used that as a pseudonym, I haven't come across it.

21. Warren G. Kenfield, *The Wild Gardener in the Wild Landscape* (New York: Hafner, 1966).

22. Lewis Regenstein, *America the Poisoned* (Washington, D.C.: Acropolis Books, 1982).

23. Beverly J. Brown and Randall J. Mitchell, "The Impact of an Invasive Species *(Lythrum salicaria)* on Seed Set and Pollinator Visitation Rate in a Native *Lythrum (L. alatum)*," at <www.ou.edu/cas/botany-micro/bas-abst/section3/abstracts/25.shtml>.

24. K. D. Woods, "Effects of Invasion by *Lonicera tatarica* L. on Herbs and Tree Seedlings in Four New England Forests," *American Midland Naturalist* 130 (1993): 62–74.

25. Kenneth A. Schmidt and Christopher J. Whelan, "Effects of Exotic *Lonicera* and *Rhamnus* on Songbird Nest Predation," *Conservation Biology* 13, no. 6 (1999): 1502–06.

26. Robert J. Pleznac, "Management and Native Species Enrichment as an Alternative to Prairie Reconstruction," in *Proceedings of the Eighth North American Prairie Conference*, ed. Richard Brewer (Kalamazoo: Western Michigan University, 1983), 132–33.

27. Roger S. Sheley, James S. Jacobs, and Michael F. Carpinelli, "Distribution, Biology, and Management of Diffuse Knapweed *(Centaurea diffusa)* and Spotted Knapweed *(Centaurea maculosa)*," Weed Technology 12 (1998): 353–62.

28. Stephen J. Small, *The Federal Tax Law of Conservation Easements: Second Supplement (1988-1995)* (Washington, D.C.: Land Trust Alliance, 1996).

29. Sylvester Baxter, "A Trust to Protect Nature's Beauty," *American Monthly Review of Reviews* 23, no. 1 (1901): 42–48.

30. Gordon Abbott, Jr., *Saving Special Places* (Ipswich, Mass.: The Ipswich Press, 1993).

31. Kenneth Kirton, personal communication, 12 December 2002.

32. Of course, the annual return on investment will also vary. Keeping withdrawals to 4 percent of principal is not too conservative; John Ameriks, Robert Veres, and Mark J. Warshawsky, "Making Retirement Income Last a Lifetime," *Journal of Financial Planning* (December 2001): 60–76.

33. Darla Guenzler, *Ensuring the Promise of Conservation Easements* (San Francisco: Bay Area Open Space Council, 1999).

34. Ibid.; Leslie Ratley-Beach, "Vermont Land Trust Reevaluates the Costs of Easement Stewardship and How to Cover Them," *Exchange* 21, no. 4 (2002): 14–17.

35. Ibid., based on reading numbers from the graph on date of easement formation, figure 2.

36. Melissa Danskin, "Conservation Easement Violations: Results from a Study of Land Trusts," *Exchange* 19, no. 1 (2000): 5–19.

Chapter 7. How to Save Land (pages 139–62)

1. Russell L. Brenneman, *Private Approaches to the Preservation of Open Land* (New London, Conn.: Conservation and Research Foundation, 1967).

2. David M. Walker, *The Oxford Companion to Law* (Oxford: Clarendon Press, 1980).

3. This is the result of the common law doctrine of merger recognizing the fact that an organization can't sue itself to force compliance; Bill Silberstein, 1999, "The Doctrine of Merger as Applied to Conservation Easements," *Exchange* 18, no. 1 (1999): 17–18.

4. Stephen J. Small, *Preserving Family Lands: Essential Tax Strategies for the Landowner,* 2nd ed. (Boston: Landowner Planning Center, 1992); idem, *Preserving Family Lands: Book II* (Boston: Landowner Planning Center, 1997); idem, *Preserving Family Lands: Book III* (Boston: Landowner Planning Center, 2002).

5. Stephen Small, "Leveraging Acquisition Dollars," in *National Land Trust Rally '98 Workbook* (Washington, D.C.: Land Trust Alliance, 1998), 499–520.

6. The legalese definition in the Uniform Conservation Easement Act, reprinted in Appendix A, Julie Ann Gustanski and Roderick H. Squires, *Protecting the Land: Conservation Easements Past, Present, and Future* (Washington, D.C.: Island Press, 2000), is as follows:

> "Conservation easement" means a nonpossessory interest . . . in real property imposing limitations or affirmative obligations the purposes of which include retaining or protecting natural, scenic, or open-space values of real property, assuring its availability for agricultural, forest, recreational, or open-space use, protecting natural resources, maintaining or enhancing air or water quality, or preserving the historical, architectural, archeological, or cultural aspects of real property.

7. Stephen J. Small, *Preserving Family Lands: Book II.*

8. Nick Williams and John Bernstein, "The Maryland Experience: Private Local Land Trusts Co-Holding Conservation Easements with a Public Agency," *Exchange* 18, no. 4 (1999): 16–21.

9. Gathering Waters Conservancy, *The Impacts of Conservation Easements on Property Taxes in Wisconsin* (Madison: Gathering Waters Conservancy, n.d.).

10. Ibid.; Daniel C. Stockford, "Property Tax Assessment of Conservation Easements," *Environmental Affairs* 17 (1990): 822–53.

11. Michigan Tax Tribunal docket 157543, no. 205036, *Indian Garden Group v. Resort Township,* entered 17 February 1995.

12. Warren Illi, "Appraising Conservation Easements," in *Landsaving Action,* ed. Russell L. Brenneman and Sarah M. Bates (Covelo, Calif.: Island Press, 1984) 205–209; James L. Catterton, "Appraising Conservation Easement Gifts: A Primer for Landowners," Exchange 9, no. 3 (1990): 4–7.

13. William H. Whyte, Jr., *Securing Open Space for Urban America,* Urban Land Institute Technical Bulletin no. 36 (1959): 1–67.

14. Land Trust Alliance, "National Land Trust Census," at <www.lta.org>, 12 September 2001.

15. Ross D. Netherton, "Environmental Conservation and Historic Preservation through Recorded Land-Use Agreements," *Real Property, Probate, and Trust Journal* 14 (1979): 540–80.

16. Melissa Waller Baldwin, "Conservation Easements: A Viable Tool for Land Preservation," *Land and Water Review* 32, no. 1 (1997): 89–123.

17. Netherton, "Environmental Conservation."

18. Ibid.; Jeffrey A. Blackie, "Conservation Easements and the Doctrine of Changed Conditions," *Hastings Law Journal* 40 (August 1989): 1187–1222.

19. Stewart Udall, *The Quiet Crisis* (1963; reprint, New York: Avon Books, 1964).

20. Netherton, "Environmental Conservation."

21. Blackie, "Conservation Elements."

22. Whyte, *Saving Open Space.*

23. Russell L. Brenneman, *Private Approaches to the Preservation of Open Land* (New London, Conn.: Conservation and Research Foundation, 1967).

24. Roderick H. Squires, "Introduction to Legal Analysis," in *Protecting the Land,* 69–77.

25. Baldwin, "Conservation Easements."

26. Dennis G. Collins, "Enforcement Problems with Successor Grantors," in *Protecting the Land,* 157–65.

27. Baldwin, "Conservation Easements."

28. Todd D. Mayo, "A Holistic Examination of the Law of Conservation Easements," in *Protecting the Land,* 26–54.

29. Ibid.

30. John F. Rohe, Appendix 17A, in *Protecting the Land,* 275–86.

31. Hank Goetz, "A Cooperative Approach to River Management: The Blackfoot Experience," in *Land-saving Action,* 3–7.

32. Annie M. Byers, "25 Deals that Led the Way," *Nature Conservancy* 51, no. 1 (2001): 18–19.

33. Environmental News Network, "Maine Celebrates Largest U. S. Conservation Easement," at <www.enn.com:80/news/enn-stories/2001/04/04022001/maine_42776.asp>, 2001.

34. John B. Wright, "Conservation Easements: An Analysis of Donated Development Rights," *Journal of the American Planning Association* 59, no. 4 (1993): 487–92.

35. Darla Guenzler, *Ensuring the Promise of Conservation Easements* (San Francisco: Bay Area Open Space Council, 1999).

36. "Vineyard Loophole," *Wall Street Journal,* 24 August 1999, A18.

37. Lynn Asinof, "Conservation Easements Lighten Taxes," *Wall Street Journal,* 9 August 1999, C1, C15.

38. James A. Ochterski, *Why Is Land Protected? Summary Report of the 1995–1996 Michigan Land Conservancy Research Project* (Ann Arbor: University of Michigan School of Natural Resources and Environment, 1996).

39. Paul Elconin and Valerie A. Luzadis, *Evaluating Landowner Satisfaction with Conservation Restrictions* (Syracuse: SUNY College of Environmental Science and Forestry, 1997).

40. My study was a survey sent in August 1999 to the first sixteen donors of preserves and conservation easements to the Southwest Michigan Land Conservancy. The questionnaire consisted of five questions, one multiple choice, the others open-ended.

41. Louise Chawla, "Life Paths into Effective Environmental Action," *Journal of Environmental Education* 31, no. 1 (1999): 15–26.

42. Whyte, *Securing Open Spaces.*

43. A study of a state PDR program also found that more participants gave farmland preservation than financial reasons as their goal; Leigh J. Maynard *et al.,* "Early Experience with Pennsylvania's Agricultural Conservation Program," *Journal of Soil and Water Conservation* 53, no. 2 (1998): 106–12.

Chapter 8. Defending Conservation Easements (pages 163–75)

1. Darla Guenzler, *Ensuring the Promise of Conservation Easements* (San Francisco: Bay Area Open Spaces Council, 1999).

2. Ann Schwing, personal communication, July 2002.

3. Tammara van Ryn and Brenda Lind, "How Strong Are Our Defenses: LTA's Northern New England Conservation Easement Quality Research Project," *Exchange* 19, no. 3 (2000): 14–16.

4. Bob van Blaricom, personal communication circa 1965; Peter Thompson Web site, "How much did the Liberty Shipbuilders Learn?" at <www. andrew.cmu.edu/~pt/liberty/photos/liberty_summary.html>.

5. Dan Burke, personal communication, 27 February 2002; <www.geocities. com/dcit_html/Archives_link3.htm>.

6. H. William Sellers, "Lessons from a Long Easement Battle," *Exchange* 18, no. 2 (1999): 19–21; FPCCT flyer, "Family Told: Move It or Lose It," 1996; Opinion of Judge Stephen Raslavich, United States Bankruptcy Court, Eastern District of Pennsylvania, in re: chapter 13 at <www.paeb.uscourts.gov/Pubopinons/natalew. htm>; oral report by Robert J. Sugarman, Esq. at 18 October session, 1996 LTA Rally.

7. Robert J. Sugarman, personal communication, 2 February 2002.

8. William T. Hutton et al., "Conservation Easements in the Ninth Federal Circuit Court," in *Protecting the Land: Conservation Easements Past, Present, and Future,* by Julie Ann Gustanski and Roderick H. Squires (Washington, D.C.: Island Press, 2001).

9. Brenda Biondo, "Dealing with Conservation Easement Violations," *Exchange* 16, no. 1 (1997): 5–8; oral report by Robert Harbour at 18 October session, 1996 LTA Rally.

10. Steven H. Gifts, *Law Dictionary,* 2nd ed. (Woodbury, N.Y.: Barron's Educational Series, Inc., 1984).

11. Biondo, "Dealing with Conservation Easement Violations."

12. Melissa Danskin, "Conservation Easement Violations: Results from a Study of Land Trusts," *Exchange* 19, no. 1 (2000): 5–9.

13. "Little Traverse Conservancy Survey and Results," Report to 10th Annual Michigan Land Conservancies Conference, 2000.

14. Federico Cheever, "Public Goods and Private Magic in the Law of Land Trusts and Conservation Easements: A Happy Present and a Troubled Future," *Denver University Law Review* 73, 4 (1996): 1077–1102.

15. Ann Schwing, personal communication, July 2002.

16. Karin Marchetti, "Dealing with Requests for Amendments," in *Land Trust Alliance Rally 2000 Workbook* (Washington, D.C.: Land Trust Alliance, 2000), 639–48.

17. Land Trust Alliance, "National Land Trust Census," at <www.lta.org>, 12 September 2001.

18. Jon Roush, "What's Wrong with Conservation Easements?" in *Private Options: Tools and Concepts for Land Conservation,* ed. Barbara Rusmore, Alexander Swaney, and Allan D. Spader (Covelo, Calif.: Island Press, 1982), 71–72.

19. Dale Bonar, "Growing Pains and Stewardship Funds: The Northwest Experience," *Exchange* 16, no. 4 (1997): 8–11.

20. Biondo, "Dealing with Conservation Easements."

21. Danskin, "Conservation Easement Violations."

22. Cheever, "Public Goods and Private Magic."

23. Ibid.

24. Stephen J. Small, *The Federal Tax Law of Conservation Easements,* 3rd ed. (Washington, D.C.: Land Trust Alliance, 1994), chapter 16, Reg. Sec, 1.170A-14(g)(6).

25. Unless state law provides otherwise.

26. Melissa K. Thompson and Jessica E. Jay, "An Examination of Court Opinions on The Enforcement and Defense of Conservation Easements and Other Conservation and Protection Tools: Themes and Approaches to Date," *Denver University Law Review* 78, no. 3 (2001): 373–412.

27. Ibid.

28. Karin Marchetti and Jerry Cosgrove, "Conservation Easements in the First and Second Federal Circuits," in *Conservation Easements,* 78–101.

29. Darla Guenzler, "Exploring Options for Collective Easement Defense," *Exchange* 21, no. 4 (2002): 10–13.

30. Alexander Arpad, "Interpreting Conservation Easements as Charitable Trusts under the Uniform Conservation Act," *Real Property, Probate, and Trust Journal,* in press.

31. Ibid.; "National Preservation Group Faces Conservation Easement Court Challenge," *Exchange* 17, no. 2 (1998): 15.

32. LTA Staff, "Myrtle Grove Case Settled," *Exchange* 18, no. 1 (1999): 17.

33. Richard B. Collins, "Environmental Law: Alienation of Conservation Easements," *Denver Law Review* 73 (1996): 1103–06.

34. Cheever, "Public Goods and Private Magic."

Chapter 9. The Land Trust Alliance (pages 176–84)

1. Alan D. Spader, Leonard Wilson, and Terry Bremer, "National Consultation on Local Land Conservation: A Review," in *Private Options: Tools and Concepts for Land Conservation,* ed. Barbara Rusmore, Alexander Swaney, and Allan D. Spader (Covelo, Calif.: Island Press, 1982), 124–32.

2. "Land Trust Exchange," *Exchange* 1, no. 1 (March 1982): 1.

3. Most information on the early years of LTE/LTA came from *A History of the Land Trust Alliance* (Washington, D.C.: Land Trust Alliance, 1992); "The First Five Years," *Exchange* 5 no. 3–4 (1987): 11–16; Caroline Pryor, personal communication, 25 June 2002; Joan Vilms, personal communication, 30 May 2002; Jennie Gerard, personal communication, 30 July 2002.

4. Caroline Pryor, personal communication, 25 June 2002.

5. Pamela K. Stone, *1985-86 National Directory of Local and Regional Land Conservation Organizations* (Bar Harbor, Maine: Land Trust Exchange, 1986).

6. "Overview: Rally 85," *Exchange* 4, no. 4 (1986): 4, 23.

7. Kendall Slee, "Jean Hocker's Legacy," *Exchange* 20, no. 4 (2001): 8–13.

8. Reported in "Mt. Conservation Trust Launches $5 Million Preservation Campaign" at <www.pickensprogress.com>.

9. Land Trust Alliance, *The Standards and Practices Guidebook,* 2nd ed. (Washington, D.C.: Land Trust Alliance, 1997).

10. "Land Trust Exchange."

11. Martha Nudel, "Conservation Easements Emerge as the Decade's Top Land Protection Tool," *Exchange* 18, no. 1 (1999): 5–6.

12. Kendall Slee, personal communication, 10 July 2001.

13. Land Trust Alliance, *National Land Trust Survey Summary, May 1995* (rev.) (Washington, D.C.: Land Trust Alliance, 1994).

14. Land Trust Alliance, *1998 National Directory of Conservation Land Trusts* (Washington, D.C.: 1998).

15. Kendall Slee, "United We Stand: Land Trusts Find New Strengths through Mergers," *Exchange* 18, no. 1 (1999): 11–14, 18.

16. Jean Hocker, "Thinking Regionally," *Exchange* 19, no. 2 (2000): 3.

17. Jean Hocker, "Message from the President," *Landscape* (Spring–Summer 2000): 2.

18. Jean Hocker and Jay Espy, *Strategic Directions* (Washington, D.C.: Land Trust Alliance, 1998).

19. Jean Hocker, "Stepping Up to Urgent Challenges," *Exchange* 19, no. 4 (2000): 3.

20. Hocker and Espy, *Strategic Directions.*

21. JWH [Jean Hocker], *Critical Issues Facing the Land Trust Movement* (Washington, D.C.: Land Trust Alliance, 1998).

Chapter 10. The Nature Conservancy (pages 185–215)

1. John C. Sawhill, "The Nature Conservancy," *Environment* 38, no. 5 (1996): 43–44.
2. Ed Goldstein and Evan Johnson, "Nature by the Numbers," *Nature Conservancy* 51, no. 1 (2001): 30–31.
3. Richard Brewer, "A Brief History of Ecology, Part 1—Pre-Nineteenth Century to 1919," *Occasional Papers of the Charles C. Adams Center for Ecological Studies* 1 (1960): 1–18.
4. Very helpful for this section was S. Charles Kendeigh, *Memoirs of a 20th Century Avian Ecologist,* vol. 5, *The Fight to Preserve Natural Areas* (Urbana: Box 35 Kendeigh Papers University of Illinois Archives, unpublished).
5. An example can be seen in "Extracts from the Proceedings of the Ecological Society of America," *Ecology* 19, no. 2 (2000): 3–5.
6. Victor E. Shelford, ed., *The Naturalist's Guide to the Americas* (Baltimore: Williams and Wilkins, 1926).
7. V. E. Shelford, "Twenty-Five-Year Effort at Saving Nature for Scientific Purposes," *Science* 98 (1943) 280–81.
8. Kendeigh, *Memoirs.*
9. Shelford, "Twenty-five-year Effort."
10. "Referendum," *Ecological Society of America Bulletin* 26, nos. 1&2 (1945): 4–5.
11. Kendeigh, *Memoirs.*
12. Robert A. Croker, *Pioneer Ecologist: The Life and Work of Victor Ernest Shelford 1877-1968* (Washington, D.C.: Smithsonian Institution Press, 1991).
13. Kendeigh, *Memoirs.*
14. Ibid.
15. *Ecologists Union Circular* no. 6, April 1950.
16. Kendeigh, *Memoirs; Rock River Valley Natural Areas Notes* 12 (Spring 1994).
17. Frank M. Graham, Jr., "Dick Pough: Conservation's Ultimate Entrepreneur," *Audubon Magazine* 86 (November 1984): 102–11.
18. *Ecologists Union Circular* no. 6.
19. Graham, "Dick Pough."
20. Ibid.
21. Dorothy Behlen, "Thirtieth Anniversary Issue: A History," *Nature Conservancy News* 31, no. 4 (1981): 4–18.
22. *Newsletter from Ecologists Union,* 8 Aug 1950; *Ecologists Union Circular* no. 6.
23. George Fell letter to Ecologists Union Board of Governors, 20 May 1950 (Urbana: Box 15, Kendeigh Papers University of Illinois Archives).
24. H. Sheail, "War and the Development of Nature Conservation in Britain," *Journal of Environmental Management* 44, no. 3 (1995): 267–84.
25. Richard Pough, Curtis Newcombe, and Frank W. Preston have also claimed, or had claimed for them, credit for suggesting the name "Nature Conservancy." Possibly all four men were aware of the new British organization and did suggest the name on some occasion to someone.
26. Behlen, "Thirtieth Anniversary Issue."

27. As shown in *Ecological Society of America Bulletin* 18, no. 4 (1937): 60–68.

28. Behlen, "Thirtieth Anniversary Issue."

29. S. Charles Kendeigh et al., "Nature Sanctuaries in the United States and Canada," *Living Wilderness* 15, no. 35 (1950–1951): 1–45.

30. George Fell letter to Ecologists Union Board of Governors, 20 May 1950 (Urbana: Box 15, Kendeigh Papers University of Illinois Archives).

31. "The Nature Conservancy," *Ecological Society of America Bulletin* 33, no. 4 (1952): 85.

32. Behlen, "Thirtieth Anniversary Issue."

33. Alexander B. Adams, *Eleventh Hour* (New York: G. P. Putnam's Sons, 1970).

34. Richard H. Goodwin, "Nature Preserves Recently Established by The Nature Conservancy," *AIBS Bulletin* (June 1958): 20–21.

35. Stephen Fox, *The American Conservation Movement* (Madison: University of Wisconsin Press, 1985).

36. Rosalie Edge, *The Ducks and the Democracy* (New York: Emergency Conservation Committee, Publication no. 87, 1942); a useful capsule biography of Edge is in Fox, *The American Conservation Movement*.

37. William D. Blair, Jr., *Katharine Ordway: The Lady Who Saved the Prairies* (Arlington, Va.: The Nature Conservancy, 1989).

38. Graham, "Dick Pough."

39. Blair, *Katharine Ordway*.

40. Adams, *Eleventh Hour*.

41. Ibid.

42. Eve Endicott, ed., *Land Conservation through Public/Private Partnerships* (Washington, D.C.: Island Press, 1993).

43. David E. Morine, *Good Dirt: Confessions of a Conservationist* (1990; reprint, New York: Ballantine Books, 1993).

44. Tom Holt, "Are Nonprofit Land Trusts Taking Advantage of the Public's Trust?" *Insight on the News* (Washington Times Corporation) 12, no. 5 (1996): 22–25.

45. This is not a current TNC practice according to W. William Weeks, *Beyond the Ark* (Washington, D.C.: Island Press, 1997), though it would seem entirely ethical.

46. Hans A. Suter, *A Voice of Reason* (Corpus Christi Texas: Audubon Outdoor Club, 1986).

47. Anne M. Byers, "A Light in Someone's Eye," *TNC News* 26, no. 3 (1976): 14–15.

48. Suter, *The Voice of Reason*.

49. David E. Morine, "Preserving the Pascagoula," *TNC News* 26, no. 4 (1976): 12–16.

50. Ibid.

51. Weeks, *Beyond the Ark*.

52. Morine, *Good Dirt*.

53. Ibid.

54. To be fair, Aldo Leopold's paleobotanist daughter, Estella, and herpetologist Graham Netting were on the board.

55. Robert E. Jenkins, "Heritage Programs: Inventory Progress Report," *TNC News* 25, no. 2 (1975): 26–27.

56. Richard Brewer, *The Science of Ecology*, 2nd ed. (Philadelphia: Saunders College Publishing, 1994).

57. Phillip M. Hoose, *Building an Ark* (Covelo, Calif.: Island Press, 1981).

58. Morine, *Good Dirt*.

59. Alton A. Lindsey, Damian V. Schmelz, and Stanley A. Nichols, *Natural Areas in Indiana and their Preservation* (Lafayette: Indiana Natural Areas Survey, Purdue University, 1969).

60. Cloyce Hedge, "The Indiana Natural Heritage Data Center 20 Year Anniversary," *Indiana DNR Natural Area News* 2, no. 3 (1998): 6–7.

61. Bruce Stein, Lynn S. Kutner, and Jonathan S. Adams, *Precious Heritage* (Oxford: Oxford University Press, 2000).

62. Morine, *Good Dirt*.

63. Brenda Bionda, "In Defense of the Longleaf Pine," *Nature Conservancy* 47, no. 4 (1997): 10–17.

64. Ben Thomas, "The Hills Have Eyes," *Nature Conservancy* 48, no. 2 (1998): 18–23.

65. John C. Sawhill, "The Nature Conservancy," *Environment* 38, no. 5 (1996): 43–44.

66. Walt Mattia, "Preserve Stewardship—Coping with Success." *TNC News* 31, no. 5(1981): 23–24.

67. Fayette Krause, "Respecting Our Natural Areas," *TNC News* 31, no. 5 (1981): 4–7.

68. Russell Van Herik, "Financial and Legal Aspects of Land Management," *Exchange* 8, no. 4 (1989): 4–5.

69. Blair, *Katharine Ordway*.

70. Mattia, "Preserve Stewardship."

71. "News for Members," *The Nature Conservancy of California* (Summer 1999): 6.

72. Alexander B. Adams, banker, FBI agent, author, and president from 1960 to 1962 (on the board 1960 to 1972) and Patrick Noonan, president from 1973 to 1980, have been credited with bringing business discipline to the organization.

73. Weeks, *Beyond the Ark*.

74. Morine, *Good Dirt*.

75. This section depends heavily on John Terborgh, *Requiem for Nature* (Washington, D.C.: Island Press, 1999).

76. Ibid.

77. Carel P. van Schaik, John Terborgh, and Barbara Dugelby, "The Silent Crisis: The State of Rain Forest Nature Preserves," in *Last Stand,* ed. Randall Kramer, Carel P. van Schaik, and Julie Johnson (New York: Oxford University Press, 1997), 64–89.

78. Kent H. Redford, Jane A. Mansour, and Monica Ostria, "An Overview of the Parks in Peril Program," in *Neotropical Biodiversity and Conservation,* ed. Arthur C. Gibson (Los Angeles: Mildred E. Mathias Botanical Garden, University of California, 1996), 185–95.

79. Shelford had proposed the same approach in 1933. All but the smaller reserves should be subdivided into "(1) sanctuary (2) buffer area of partial protection, and (3) area of development for human use where this is one of the aims of the reserve." The three subdivisions were to be arranged so as to give the best conditions for roaming animals within the buffer area and the sanctuary; Victor E. Shelford, "The Preservation of Natural Biotic Communities," *Ecology* 14, no. 2 (1933): 240–45.

80. Katrina Brandon, "Policy and Practical Considerations in Land-use Strategies for Biodiversity Conservation," in *Last Stand,* 90–114.

81. Terborgh, *Requiem for Nature;* Douglas Southgate, *Tropical Forest Conservation* (New York: Oxford University Press, 1998).

82. P. V. Ostervee, "Ecotourism and Biodiversity Conservation—Two-Way Track," *Pacific Conservation Biology* 6 (2000): 89–93.

83. Andrew C. Revkin, "Biologists Sought a Treaty; Now They Fault It," *New York Times,* 7 May 2002, D1–2.

84. John Vandermeer and Ivette Perfecto, *Breakfast of Biodiversity* (Oakland, Calif.: Institute for Food and Development Policy, 1995).

85. Terborgh, *Requiem for Nature.*

86. Behlen, "Thirtieth Anniversary Issue."

87. L. Gregory Low, "The 1982 Program: A Plan for Preserving Biological Diversity," *TNC News* 27, no. 1 (1977): 13.

88. Annie M. Byers, "25 Deals that Led the Way," *Nature Conservancy* 51, no. 1 (2001): 18–19.

89. Appendix D in Committee on Scientific and Technical Criteria for Federal Acquisition of Lands for Conservation, *Setting Priorities for Land Conservation* (Washington, D.C.: National Research Council, 1993).

90. John C. Sawhill, "The Good-Neighbor Policy," *Nature Conservancy* 48, no. 1 (1998): 5–11.

91. John C. Sawhill, "Last Great Places," *Nature Conservancy* 41, no. 3 (1991): 6–15.

92. Malcolm G. Scully, "On Virginia's Eastern Shore Striving for Community Based Conservation," *Chronicle of Higher Education* (8 October 1999): B10–11.

93. Ibid.

94. Steven J. McCormick, *The President's Report—2001 Year in Review* (Arlington, Va.: The Nature Conservancy, 2002).

95. Andy Mead, "Couple Buys Rural Land to Keep It Undeveloped," *Kentucky News* (Winter 2001): 6–7, 15.

96. Glen Martin, "Greens Buy a Farm," *San Francisco Chronicle,* 4 December 2001, A19–20.

97. TNC Conservation Process at <www.consci.org/scp/consproc.htm>.

98. William Stolzenburg, "The United States of Nature," *Nature Conservancy* 48, no. 3 (1998): 8–9; Stein, Kutner, and Adams, *Precious Heritage.*

99. TNC Conservation Process at <www.consci.org/scp/consproc.htm>.

100. Croker, *Pioneer Ecologist.*

Chapter 11. The Trust for Public Land (pages 216–26)

1. "Appointment of Western Regional Director," *TNC News* 14, no. 1 (1964): 7.

2. Pennfield Jensen, "The Young Generalist and Political Action," in *No Deposit—No Return,* ed. Huey Johnson (Reading, Mass.: Addison-Wesley, 1970).

3. Huey D. Johnson, ed., *No Deposit—No Return.*

4. Trust for Public Land, "Building the American Commons," *Land & People* 9, no. 1 supplement (1997): 1–20.

5. Ibid.

6. Martin J. Rosen, *Trust for Public Land Founding Member and President, 1972-1997: The Ethics and Practice of Land Conservation* (Berkeley: Regional Oral History Office, The Bancroft Library, University of California, 2000).

7. Michael Brody, "Watt's Line," *Barron's* 6 (September 2000): 24, 26, 54.

8. Ibid.

9. Rosen, *Trust for Public Land Founding Member.*

10. Trust for Public Land, "Building the American Commons."

11. Rosen, *Trust for Public Land Founding Member.*

12. "Save the Gardens!" *Land & People* 10, no. 2 (1998): 37.

13. Ralph Nader, "Socialism for the Rich," *New York Times* 15 May 1999: A27.

14. TPL Mid-Atlantic Press Release, "The Trust for Public Land Buys 63 Community Gardens from City for $3 Million," 14 May 1999.

15. Ward Sutton, "Bette and Rudy: The Duet," *New York Times:* 15 May 1999: A27.

16. TPL Mid-Atlantic Press Release, "The Trust for Public Land."

17. Sarrah Clark, "From Sports Complex to Open Space," *On the Land* (Summer/Fall 1999): 3.

18. Jennie Gerard, personal communication, 31 August 1999.

19. Trust for Public Land, *Land Trust Handbook: A Guide for Board Members* (San Francisco: Trust for Public Land, 1991).

20. Robert A. Lemire, *Creative Land Development: Bridge to the Future* (Boston: Houghton Mifflin, 1979).

21. Steele Wotkyns, "Trinidad and the Humboldt North Coast Land Trust: A Solution for Land-use Conflict," in *Land-saving Action,* ed. Russell L. Brenneman and Sarah M. Bates (Covelo, Calif.: Island Press, 1984): 8–11.

22. Jennie Gerard, personal communication, 31 August 1999.

23. Steele Wotkyns, "Trinidad."

24. Rosen, *Trust for Public Land Founding Member.*

25. Jennie Gerard, personal communication, 31 August 1999.

26. Richard M. Stapleton, "Conservation Financing Comes of Age," *Land & People* 13, no. 1 (2001): 27–31.

27. "Voters Commit Nearly $1.7 Billion to Open Space," at <www.lta.org/publicpolicy/landvote2001.htm>.

28. Dan Whipple, "Greenprinting for Success," *Land & People* 13, no. 2 (2001): 25–30.

29. Richard M. Stapleton, "A Small Town Thinks Big," *Land & People* 13, no. 2 (2001): 10–15.

30. Peter Steinhart, "The Once and Future Coast," *Land & People* 10, no. 2 (1998): 14–19.

31. "TPL Annual Report 2001," *Land & People* 13, no. 2 (2001): 39–64.

32. Steve Lerner and William Poole, *The Economic Benefits of Parks and Open Space* (San Francisco: The Trust for Public Land, 1999).

33. Trust for Public Land, "Building the American Commons."

34. Peter Steinhart, "Sprawl or Species," *Land & People* 11, no. 1 (1999): 14–19.

35. Robert Cahn, *Footprints on the Planet* (New York: Universe Books, 1978).

36. Aldo Leopold, "On a Monument to a Pigeon," in *A Sand County Almanac* (1949; reprint, London: Oxford University Press, 1968).

Chapter 12. Farmland Protection (pages 227–52)

1. Queena Sook Kim, "A Farmland Trust Checkmates Developers," *Wall Street Journal,* 13 November 2002: B1, B6.

2. Robert E. Coughlin and John C. Keene, *The Protection of Farmland: A Reference Guidebook for State and Local Governments* (Washington, D.C.: National Agricultural Lands Study, no date [1981]).

3. Associated Press, "Farm Preservation Program Saves Few Farms," *Kalamazoo Gazette,* 24 August 1999.

4. Henry E. Rodegerdts, "Land Trusts and Agricultural Conservation Easements," *Natural Resources & Environment* 13, no. 1 (1998): 336–40, 370.

5. Thomas L. Daniels, "The Purchase of Development Rights," *APA Journal* 57, no. 4 (1991): 421–31; American Farmland Trust Information Center, Fact Sheet,

The Farmland Protection Toolbox (Washington, D.C.: American Farmland Trust, no date).

6. Chris Knape, "Farmer's Effort to Thwart Development Fails Again," *Kalamazoo Gazette*, 19 May 1998: C3.

7. Francis Ryan, "AFT Member Letter," *American Farmland* (Summer 1996): 22.

8. Daniels, "The Purchase of Development Rights."

9. This section is mostly based on Dennis P. Bidwell et al., *Forging New Protections: Purchasing Development Rights to Save Farmland* (Washington, D.C.: American Farmland Trust, 1996).

10. U.S. Department of Agriculture statistics.

11. Statistical Abstract of the United States.

12. Michigan Land Use Institute, "Innovative Farmland Protection Programs," *Great Lakes Bulletin* 3, no. 1 (1998): 9.

13. "Lancaster County Reaches Milestone with 20,000 Acres Preserved," *Lancaster Farmland Trust News* 9, no. 1 (1996): 1.

14. Barry Lonik, personal communication, April 2000; "Washtenaw County Agricultural Lands and Open Space Preservation Plan" at <www.co.washtenaw.mi.us>, December 1997.

15. Coughlin and Keene, *The Protection of Farmland*; Thomas Daniels, personal communication, 20 November 1997.

16. *Fact Sheet #5: Transfer of Development Rights* (Minneapolis: Green Corridor Project [1997]); Coughlin and Keene, *The Protection of Farmland*.

17. Rodegerdts, "Land Trusts and Agricultural Conservation Easements."

18. Eric Vink, "Land Trusts Conserve California Farmland," *California Agriculture* 52, no. 3 (1998): 27-31.

19. Patrick F. Noonan, "Conservation for a Sustainable Agriculture" in *AFT: The First 10 Years* (Washington, D.C.: American Farmland Trust, 1991), part two.

20. "American Farmland Trust: The First 10 Years," in *AFT*, 4-5.

21. Robert B. Smythe, with Charles D. Laidlaw and Carol Fesco, *Density-related Public Costs* (Washington, D.C.: American Farmland Trust, 1986).

22. AFT News Release, *Prominent Washington Conservationist Leaves 330-acre Rural Pennsylvania Farm to American Farmland Trust*, 7 June 1996; American Farmland Trust, *Anthony Wayne and Anya Freedel Smith* (Washington, D.C.: American Farmland Trust, no date).

23. Information on Cove Mountain Farm from American Farmland Trust, *Cove Mountain Farm Agricultural Plan* (Washington, D.C.: American Farmland Trust, no date); Brian Petrucci, personal communication, 25 March 2000.

24. Mark Obmascik, "Land Deal Saves View, Aids Owner," *Denver Post*, 11 February 2001, at <www.denverpost.com:80/news/news0211.htm>.

25. Gordon Abbott, Jr., *Saving Special Places* (Ipswich, Mass.: The Ipswich Press, 1993).

26. Wesley T. Ward, personal communication, 11 November 2001.

27. Sally Kaufman and Maynard Kaufman, "How It All Began: Memoirs of Surviving Founders," *Michigan Land Trustees Newsletter* (September 1997).

28. W. David Shuford, *The Marin County Breeding Bird Atlas* (Bolinas, Calif.: Bushtit Books, 1993).

29. Marin Agricultural Land Trust, *Tenth Anniversary Report* (Pt. Reyes Station: Marin Agricultural Land Trust, [1990]).

30. "Twenty Years Preserving Marin County Farmlands," *Marin Agricultural Land Trust News*, 16, no. 1 (2000): 1, 7.

31. Jennie Gerard, "The Growing Importance of Private Local Activity in Farmland Preservation," in *Private Options: Tools and Concepts for Land Conservation*,

ed. Barbara Rusmore, Alexandra Swaney, and Allan D. Spader (Covelo, Calif.: 1982): 191–92.

32. Marin Agricultural Land Trust, *Land Preservation Report,* Autumn 1999 (Pt. Reyes Station: Marin Agricultural Land Trust, 1999).

33. Jennifer Andes, "Fund-raising Events: Community Outreach that Builds Your Coffers," *Exchange* 21, no. 3 (2002): 16–19.

34. Michelle Nijhuis, "'Our First Focus Is the Landowner,'" *High Country News* 32, no. 4 (2000).

35. Taylor H. Ricketts et al., *Terrestrial Ecoregions of North America* (Washington, D.C.: Island Press, 1999).

36. Lynne Sherrod, personal communication, 28 April 2000.

37. Debra Donahue, "The West 'Ain't No Cow Country,'" *High Country News* 32, no. 4 (2000); idem, "Livestock Spoil the Native Diversity on America's Public Lands," *Watersheds Messenger* 8, no. 3 (2001) at <www.westernwatersheds.org/archives/watmess/watmess_2001/2001html_fall/>; Jayne Belnap, "Cryptobiotic Soils: Holding the Place in Place," <http//geochange.er.usgs.gov/sw/impacts/biology/crypto/>.

38. Aldo Leopold, *A Sand County Almanac* (1949; reprint, London: Oxford University Press, 1968).

39. David Blandford, "Forces for Change in Pennsylvania Agriculture," in *Agricultural Law Forum: Environmental Law & the Agricultural Industry* (Mechanicsburg, Penn.: Pennsylvania Bar Association, 1999), 1–3.

40. John Flesher, "Farmers Want Statewide Standards for Expansion," Associated Press story in *Kalamazoo Gazette,* 10 Dec. 1998, C5.

41. "1998 Farm and Ranch Irrigation Survey Released," *Michigan Agricultural Statistics Service,* 9 November 1999.

42. Stuart Smith, "Is there Farming in Agriculture's Future?" Cited by Richard Cartwright Austin, "The Spiritual Crisis of Modern Agriculture," *Environmental Review* 3, no. 7 (1996): 9–15.

43. In constant (1984) dollars.

44. Blandford, "Forces for Change."

45. Austin, *The Spiritual Crisis.*

46. Deb Hyk, "Small Scenic Preserves May Have Public Relations Benefits," *Farm Journal* (January 2000).

Chapter 13. Trails and Greenways (pages 253–68)

1. Automobile Association, *Book of the British Countryside* (Basingstoke, England: Drive Publications Ltd, 1974).

2. Paul Lewis, "Footpaths: Access v Privacy," *Country Life* (13 January 1994): 34–36.

3. Rita Sutter, "Banking on the Rails," *Rails to Trails* 1 (Spring 1999): 16–19.

4. Harry Jaffe, "David Burwell on the Move," *Rails to Trails* (Spring 2001): 14–15.

5. Richard Welch, "Federal Rails to Trails Act: Ten Years of Hell for 62,000 Property Owners," National Association of Reversionary Property Owners Web site at <www.halcyon.com/dick/>, 1 July 1997.

6. Sutter, "Banking on the Rails."

7. Colleen Kelly Warren, "Pat Jones Vision and Verve," *Rails to Trails* (Winter 1999): 14–15.

8. John Greenya, "1,000 trails, 10,000 miles," *Rails to Trails* (Winter 1999): 19; Andrea Ferster, Prepared Statement, Litigation and its Effect on the Rails-to-Trails

Program, Hearing before the Subcommittee on Commercial and Administrative Law of the Committee on the Judiciary, House of Representatives, 20 June 2002, at <commdocs.house.gov/committees/judiciary/hju80320.000/hju80320_0.HTM>.

9. Samual S. Holmes and Elizabeth R. Holmes, "Illinois Prairie Path Trials and Triumphs," delivered at Illinois Prairie Path meeting, 12 April 1979, at Mill Race Inn, Geneva, Illinois.

10. William H. Whyte, *The Last Landscape* (1968; reprint, Garden City, N.Y.: Anchor Books, Doubleday and Co., 1970).

11. Susan Kellam, "Tea Time," *Rails to Trails* (Fall 1998): 16–19; Megan Betts Russell, "National TE Obligation Rate Improves," *Connections* 4, no. 3 (2001): 1–3, 6.

12. Kate Valentine, "TEA Challenge Salutes State Excellence," *Connections* 4, no. 2 (2001): 1–2.

13. Federal Highway Administration Office of Natural Environment, *Critter Crossings* (Washington, D.C.: Federal Highway Administration Publication No. FHWA-EP—00-004 HEPN-30-2-00 (20M) EW 31, 2000); Land Bridge Offers Wildlife Connectivity," *Connections* 5, no. 4 (2002): 3.

14. Russell, "National TE Obligation Rate Improves."

15. Tammy Tracy and Hugh Morris, *Rail-trails and Safe Communities* (Washington, D.C.: Rails-to-Trails Conservancy in cooperation with National Park Service Rivers, Trails, and Conservation Assistance Program, 1998).

16. James J. Bacon et al., "Security Along the Appalachian Trail," in *Proceedings of the 2001 Northeastern Recreation Research Symposium*, Sharon Todd, comp. (Newtown Square, Penna.: USDA Forest Service Northeastern Research Station, 2002), 326–32.

17. "A Decade Of Public/Private Partnering," *Trailblazer* 13, no. 1 (1998): 10.

18. Roger L. Moore, et al., *The Impacts of Rail-trails: A Study of the Users and Property Owners from Three Trails* (Washington, D.C.: Rivers, Trails, and Conservation Assistance Program, National Park Service, 1992).

19. PFK Consulting, *Analysis of Economic Impacts of the Northern Central Rail Trail* (Annapolis, Md.: Maryland Greenways Commission, 1994).

20. Charles Nelson, "Rail-trails and Special Events: Community and Economic Benefits," in *Proceedings of the 2001 Northeastern Recreation Research Symposium*, 220–24.

21. Rogers Worthington, "Future of Prairie Paths May Prove Expandable," *Chicago Tribune*, 23 April 1997.

22. Ed McMahon, "Socio-economic Benefits of Greenways and Trails," Keynote address, Michigan Statewide Trails and Greenways Conference, Battle Creek, Michigan, 28 September 1998.

23. Steve Lerner and William Poole, *The Economic Benefits of Parks and Open Space* (San Francisco: The Trust for Public Land, 1999).

24. Patrick McMahon, "Residents Push to Derail Trails," *USA Today* (7 October 1999): 3A.

25. Michigan Public Acts 1968 No. 13.

26. Danaya C. Wright, "Private Rights and Public Ways: Property Disputes and Rails-to-Trails in Indiana," *Indiana Law Review* 30 (1997): 723–61; Marc A. Sennewald, "The Nexus of Federal and State Law in Railroad Abandonments," *Vanderbilt Law Review* 51 (1998): 1399–1425.

27. *Check Inside to See the Most Recent Rail-trail Information on Your State* (Washington, D.C.: Rails-to-Trails Conservancy, 2001).

28. Todd Cooper, "Sarpy Board Blocks Bike Trail by Denying Permit," *Omaha World Herald*, 22 September 1999.

29. Christopher Hall, "A Nice Possibility for a Very Long Stroll," *New York Times*, 27 August 2000, TR3.

30. Karl Kunkel, "Opposite Sides of the Trail," *Issaquah Press*, 2 October 1996.

31. Tom Exton, personal communication, 28 August 2000.

32. Patrick McMahon, "Residents Push to Derail Trails," *USA Today*, 7 October 1999: 3A.

33. Stacy Goodman, "Rails-to-Trails Opponents Face a Difficult Battle," *Issaquah Press*, 9 October 1996.

34. "Group Buys Rail Line to Make Hiking Trail," *The Spokesman-Review*, 2 May 1997.

35. Eugene Duvernoy, personal communication, 14 August 2000.

36. "East Lake Sammamish's Rocky Rail-to-Trail Ride," *Seattle Times*, 24 September 1998.

37. Brier Dudley, "East Lake Sammamish Trail May Open in Summer, But Fight's Not Over," *Seattle Times*, 24 November 1998.

38. Robin Cole, personal communication, 28 August 2000.

39. Friends of the East Lake Sammamish Trail, "Congratulations—County Council Approves Interim Use," *Newsletter of the Friends of the East Lake Sammamish Trail*, February 2001.

40. Susan Doherty, *Rail-trails and Community Sentiment* (Washington, D.C.: Rails-to-Trails Conservancy, 1998).

41. Danaya C. Wright, Andrea Ferster, Prepared Statements, Litigation and its Effect on the Rails-to-Trails Program, Hearing before the Subcommittee on Commercial and Administrative Law of the Committee on the Judiciary, House of Representatives, 20 June 2002, at <commdocs.house.gov/committees/judiciary/hju80320. 000/hju80320_0.HTM>; "Landowners Along Hiking Trail Win $410,000," *Washington Post*, 15 December 2002.

42. Charles E. Little, *Greenways for America* (Baltimore: Johns Hopkins University Press, 1990).

43. Southeast Michigan Greenways, *A Vision for Southeast Michigan Greenways* (Ann Arbor: Southeast Michigan Greenways, 1998).

44. Allegheny Valley Trails Association, *Bicycle Trails of Venango County* (Franklin, Pa.: Allegheny Valley Trails Association and Venango County Planning Commission); Jim Holden, "The Trails of Venango County: A Brief History," *Newsletter of the Allegheny Valley Trails Association* (Spring 1999): 1–2; Jim Holden, personal communication, 12 March 2000.

45. *Encyclopedia Brittanica*, 11th ed., S.V. Titusville.

46. Eugene Duvernoy, personal communication, 14 August 2000.

Chapter 14. A Diversity of Local Land Trusts (pages 269–89)

1. Eugene P. Odum, "The Concept of the Biome as Applied to the Distribution of North American Birds," *Wilson Bulletin* 57, no. 3 (1945): 191–201.

2. Regions follow Land Trust Alliance, *1988 National Directory of Conservation Land Trusts* (Washington, D.C.: Land Trust Alliance, 1998).

3. Janet C. Neuman and Cheyenne Chapman, "Wading into the Water Market: The First Five Years of the Oregon Water Trust," *Journal of Environmental Law and Litigation* 14 (1999): 135–84.

4. The California, Washington, and Oregon trusts that did respond—my thanks—were Sempervirens Fund, Pacific Forest Trust, Back Country Trust, Yolo Land Trust, and Skagit Land Trust. Also, the Kachmemac Heritage Land Trust of Alaska responded.

5. A few of the California land trusts sent letters explaining why they weren't filling out the questionnaire, though these tended to be somewhat cryptic. One was Bartlebyesque: "We are very reluctant to supply information at this time."

6. John B. Wright, "Cultural Geography and Land Trusts in Colorado and Utah," *Geographical Review* 83, no. 3 (1993): 269–79.

7. Mary A. Elfner, "Conservation Easements Can Help to Protect Land," *Savannah Morning News,* 16 May 2001: letters.

8. David Grayson, *The Countryman's Year* (Garden City, N.Y.: Doubleday Doran & Co., 1936).

9. Jim Scott, personal communication, 25 May 1998.

10. *Guide to Amherst Conservation Areas and Trails,* 5th ed. (Amherst: Kestrel Trust, 1994).

11. *The Kestrel Trust 20th Anniversary 1970–1990* (Amherst: Kestrel Trust, 1990).

12. *Guide to Amherst Conservation Areas and Trails.*

13. Jim Scott, personal communication, 25 May 1998.

14. *The Kestrel Trust.*

15. Jim Scott, personal communication, 25 May 1998.

16. *1998 Data Sheet* (Leverett, Mass.: Rattlesnake Gutter Trust, 1998); Friends of Rattlesnake Gutter Trust, *1989 Fund Drive* (Leverett, Mass.: Rattlesnake Gutter Trust, 1989).

17. "1996 Annual Meeting," *Rattlesnake Gutter Trust Annual Meeting* (May 1996): 3.

18. Terry Blunt, personal communication, 22 May 1998.

19. Ibid.

20. M. Graham Netting, *Fifty Years of the Western Pennsylvania Conservancy* (Pittsburgh: Western Pennsylvania Conservancy, 1982).

21. Ibid.

22. Wray Herbert, Wright's Fallingwater is Slowly Falling Down," at <www.usnews.com/usnews/issue/990503/falling.htm>, 1999.

23. Matthew L. Wald, "Rescuing a World-Famous But Fragile House," *New York Times* 150, 2 September 2001: 1, 21.

24. Netting, *Fifty Years.*

25. Western Pennsylvania Conservancy, "2000 Season Opens at Fallingwater," at <www.wpconline.org/aboutwpc/news/press/FW_opening2000.htm>.

26. Netting, *Fifty Years.*

27. Ibid.

28. Frank W. Preston, letter to Patrick F. Noonan, 4 June 1980 (Urbana, Ill.: Box 15, Kendeigh Papers University of Illinois Archives).

29. Netting, *Fifty Years.*

30. Preston, letter to Noonan.

31. Netting, *Fifty Years.*

32. Gordon Abbott, Jr., *Saving Special Places* (Ipswich, Mass.: The Ipswich Press, 1993).

33. John Oliver, "The Next 50 Years," in *Fifty Years,* 195–97, 1982.

34. Brian Gallagher, personal communication, 26 December 2000.

35. Ronald L. Myers and John J. Ewel, *Ecosystems of Florida* (Orlando: University of Central Florida Press, 1990).

36. H. W. Kale, II, "Who Is Your Neighbor?" *Florida Naturalist* 60 (Winter 1987): 14.

37. Marjorie Kinnan Rawlings, *Cross Creek* (New York: Charles Scribner's Sons, 1942).

38. Tricia Martin, *Florida's Ancient Islands* (Lake Wales, Fla.: Lake Wales Ridge Ecosystem Working Group, 1998).

39. Information on Green Horizon Land Trust is from 1995 to 2000 newsletters; Lou Parrott, personal communication, 11 October 2000.

40. "An Evening with Ted Turner," *Big Sur Land Trust News* (Summer, 1999): 1–4.

41. Tamara Grippi, "Celebrated Donors Helped Green Dreams Come True," *Carmel Pine Cone,* 25 June–1 July 1999: 1A, 5A.

42. Information from Big Sur newsletters; Zad Leavy, personal communication, 26 Jan 2001.

43. Grippi, "Celebrated Donors."

44. Michael McCabe, "10,000-Acre Deal Links Big Sur, Carmel Parklands," *San Francisco Chronicle,* 10 May 2002: A1, A4.

45. Mark C. Ackelson, "Conservation Issues in the Midwest," in *Private Options: Tools and Concepts for Land Conservation,* ed. Barbara Rusmore, Alexandra Swaney, and Allan D. Spader (Covelo, Calif.: Island Press, 1982), 156–57.

46. Cathy Engstrom and Anita O'Gara, *Iowa Natural Heritage,* 20th Anniversary Edition (Des Moines: Iowa Natural Heritage Foundation, 1999).

47. John T. Curtis, *The Vegetation of Wisconsin* (Madison: University of Wisconsin Press, 1956).

48. Anita O'Gara and Cathy Engstrom, *Iowa Natural Heritage 1998 Annual Report* (Des Moines: Iowa Natural Heritage Foundation, 1999).

49. David Tenenbaum, "Land Trusts: A Restoration Frontier?" *Ecological Restoration* 18, no. 3 (2000): 167–72.

50. INHF Internship Programs at <www.inhf.org/intern00.HTM>.

51. O'Gara and Engstrom, *Iowa Natural Heritage 1998 Annual Report.*

52. *Iowa's Multiple-use Conservation and Recreation Trails* (Des Moines: Iowa Natural Heritage Foundation, no date).

53. Anita O'Gara, personal communication, 15 November 2000.

54. Bertha A. Daubendiek and Edna S. Newnan, eds., *In Retrospect* (Avoca, Mich.: Michigan Nature Association, 1988).

55. Richard A. Holzman et al., *Nature Sanctuary Guidebook,* 7th edition (Avoca, Mich.: Michigan Nature Association, 1994).

56. Harvey E. Ballard, Jr., "The Scientific Significance of the Michigan Nature Association Program," in *In Retrospect,* 86–87.

57. Ibid.

Chapter 15. A Cleaner, Greener Land (pages 290–93)

1. Joel E. Cohen, "A Vision of the Future," in *The Ecological Basis of Conservation,* ed. S. T. A. Pickett et al. (New York: Chapman & Hall, 1997), 400–403.

GLOSSARY

Included here are brief definitions of a few terms, mostly ecological or legal, that are not defined each time they occur in the text. Definitions of many other terms can be located by use of the Index.

Abiotic. Non-living.

Bargain sale. A purchase by a nonprofit at less than fair market value.

Biomass. Quantity or weight of living material.

Biosphere. The layer of the globe containing living organisms, also the Earth as an ecosystem.

Biota. The species of plants, animals, and other organisms of an area.

Build out. The situation in which development has occurred on all property where legally permissible. Said of a governmental unit.

Building envelope. A designated portion of easement-protected property on which construction of a structure is permitted.

Community. The organisms of a particular area, linked by interactions such as competition and mutualism.

Conservation easement. A contract between a landowner and a conservation organization or agency by which the land's conservation values are protected.

Development. The conversion of open space to residential, commercial, or industrial use.

Ecoregion. A large area of land or water showing some unity of landform, climate, and landscapes.

Ecosystem. The organisms and physical features of an area considered as an integrated unit.

Ecosystem services. Natural processes (of ecosystems) that benefit humans.

Endemic. Occurring in a particular area and nowhere else.

Exotic. Non-native; in the United States, said of an organism introduced since the beginning of European exploration.

Fair market value. The price at which a willing buyer and a willing seller will do business.

Fee simple. The type of land ownership in which the owner is entitled to enjoy the property for life and pass it without limitation to his heirs.

Hydrology. The study of water on and below the surface of the Earth.

In fee. Equivalent to "in fee simple."

Land trust. A nonprofit organization that as its primary or sole mission conserves land by direct land transactions.

Land Trust Alliance (LTA). The national umbrella organization for land trusts.

Landscape. In ecological terminology, a substantial piece of terrain, usually a few to thousands of square miles and comprising a mosaic of ecosystems.

Mesic. Said of habitats of medium moisture relations, neither wet (hydric) nor dry (xeric).

Mesophytic. Pertaining to situations where plants of medium moisture requirements occur.

Neotropical. Occurring in or pertaining to the New World Tropics.

New Urbanism. Planning that emphasizes walkable communities containing a mix of residential and commercial land uses.

Nonprofit. An organization not seeking a profit and generally dedicated to good works; also used as an adjective.

Preacquisition. Referring to land deals in which a land trust buys land with the expectation of reselling to a government agency.

Preserve. Land owned by an organization or agency and maintained in a natural state protected from development.

Private benefit. Action (prohibited for nonprofits) that transfers assets at less than fair market value to an individual or for-profit corporation.

Real property. Land, including the surface, buildings, soil, vegetation, minerals, etc.

Riparian. Pertaining to the banks of rivers.

Smart Growth. Development that discourages sprawl by shifting public incentives to urban redevelopment and alternative transportation.

Standing. The right of an individual or group to challenge in court the conduct of another person, group, or government agency.

Succession. The natural process of replacement of one community by another.

Taking. Government appropriation of private property without just compensation.

Title. Ownership (usually of real property).

BIBLIOGRAPHY

This section consists of books and articles cited in two or more parts of the book.

Abbott, Gordon, Jr. *Saving Special Places.* Ipswich, Mass.: The Ipswich Press, 1993.

Austin, Richard Cartwright. "The Spiritual Crisis of Modern Agriculture." *Environmental Review* 3, no. 7 (1996): 9–15.

Baxter, Sylvester. "A Trust to Protect Nature's Beauty." *American Monthly Review of Reviews* 23, no. 1 (1901): 42–48.

Behlen, Dorothy. "Thirtieth Anniversary Issue: A History." *Nature Conservancy News* 31, no. 4 (1981): 4–18.

Blair, William D., Jr. *Katharine Ordway: The Lady Who Saved the Prairies.* Arlington, Va.: The Nature Conservancy, 1989.

Brenneman, Russell L. *Private Approaches to the Preservation of Open Land.* New London, Conn.: Conservation and Research Foundation, 1967.

Brenneman, Russell L., and Sarah M. Bates, eds. *Land-saving Action.* Covelo, Calif.: Island Press, 1984.

Brewer, Richard. *The Science of Ecology,* 2nd ed. Philadelphia: Saunders College Publishing, 1994.

Carson, Rachel. *Silent Spring.* Boston: Houghton-Mifflin, 1962.

Croker, Robert A. *Pioneer Ecologist: The Life and Work of Victor Ernest Shelford 1877–1968.* Washington, D.C.: Smithsonian Institution Press, 1991.

Coughlin, Robert E., and John C. Keene. eds. *The Protection of Farmland: A Reference Guidebook for State and Local Governments.* Washington, D.C.: U.S. Government Printing Office, [1981].

Danskin, Melissa. "Conservation Easement Violations: Results from a Study of Land Trusts." *Exchange* 19, no. 1 (2000): 5–9.

Eliot, Charles W. *Charles Eliot: Landscape Architect.* Boston: Houghton Mifflin, 1902.

Endicott, Eve, ed. *Land Conservation Through Public/Private Partnerships.* Washington, D.C.: Island Press, 1993.

Engel, J. Ronald. *Sacred Sands.* Middletown, Conn.: Wesleyan University Press, 1983.

Fox, Stephen. *The American Conservation Movement.* Madison: University of Wisconsin Press, 1985.

Guenzler, Darla. *Ensuring the Promise of Conservation Easements.* San Francisco: Bay Area Open Space Council, 1999.

Gustanski, Julie Ann, and Roderick H. Squires. *Protecting the Land: Conservation Easements Past, Present, and Future.* Washington, D.C.: Island Press, 2000.

Land Trust Alliance. *1998 National Directory of Conservation Land Trusts.* Washington, D.C.: Land Trust Alliance, 1998.

Leopold, Aldo. *A Sand County Almanac.* 1949. Reprint. London: Oxford University Press, 1968.

Lerner, Steve, and William Poole. *The Economic Benefits of Parks and Open Space.* San Francisco: The Trust for Public Land, 1999.

McHarg, Ian. *Design with Nature.* Garden City, N.Y.: The Natural History Press, 1969.

Morine, David E. *Good Dirt: Confessions of a Conservationist.* 1990. Reprint. New York: Ballantine Books, 1993.

Netting, M. Graham. *Fifty Years of the Western Pennsylvania Conservancy.* Pittsburgh: Western Pennsylvania Conservancy, 1982.

Ricketts, Taylor H., et al. *Terrestrial Ecoregions of North America.* Washington, D. C.: Island Press, 1999.

Rosen, Martin J. *Trust for Public Land Founding Member and President, 1972–1997: The Ethics and Practice of Land Conservation.* Carl Wilmsen, interviewer. Berkeley, Calif.: Regional Oral History Office, The Bancroft Library, University of California, 2000.

Rusmore, Barbara, Alexandra Swaney, and Allan D. Spader, eds. *Private Options: Tools and Concepts for Land Conservation.* Covelo, Calif.: Island Press, 1982.

Sale, Kirkpatrick. *The Green Revolution.* New York: Hill and Wang, 1993.

Shelford, Victor E., ed. *The Naturalist's Guide to the Americas.* Baltimore: Williams & Wilkins, 1926.

Small, Stephen J. *Preserving Family Lands: Essential Tax Strategies for the Landowner,* 2nd ed. Boston: Landowner Planning Center, 1992.

Smythe, Robert B., with Charles D. Laidlaw and Carol Fesco. *Density-related Public Costs.* Washington, D.C.: American Farmland Trust, 1986.

Stein, Bruce, Lynn S. Kutner, and Jonathan S. Adams. *Precious Heritage.* Oxford: Oxford University Press, 2000.

Van Herik, Russell. "Financial and Legal Aspects of Land Management." *Exchange* 8, no. 4 (1989): 4–5.

Weeks, W. William. *Beyond the Ark.* Washington, D.C.: Island Press, 1997.

Whyte, William H., Jr. "Securing Open Space for Urban America." Urban Land Institute Technical Bulletin no. 36 (1959): 1–67.

INDEX

Note: Page numbers in **boldface** indicate **definitions;** those in *italics* followed by the letter *f* or *t* indicate *figures* or *tables*.